THE UNIVERSITY OF ILLINOIS · 1867-1894

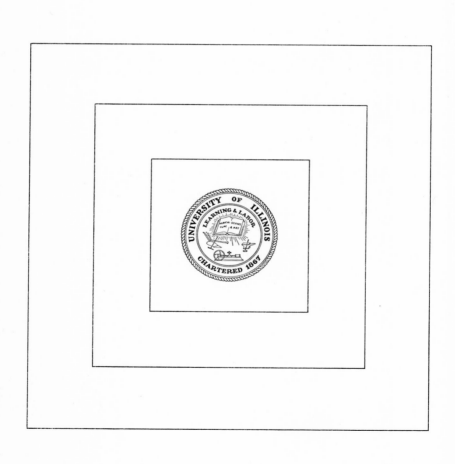

The University of Illinois 1867-1894

An Intellectual and Cultural History

BY WINTON U. SOLBERG

UNIVERSITY OF ILLINOIS PRESS · 1968

Urbana Chicago London

THIS BOOK IS FOR GAIL

Preface

This book is the outgrowth of a conviction, an opportunity, and considerable adjustment to the practical realities of scholarship.

First came the conviction — in this case a belief that academic annals provide a key to intellectual and cultural history and are a vital part of general history. For the period since the late nineteenth century the university has been the dominant form of higher education in the United States, but until very recently the number of good critical accounts of the whole university scene or of individual institutions has been disappointingly small.

Second came the opportunity. Shortly after I had begun to acquaint myself in some detail with the available literature on the emergence of the American university, Professor Norman A. Graebner, then the chairman of an advisory committee on a centennial history, invited me to write a history of the University of Illinois. The initial impulse for this project came from President David D. Henry, who envisioned the publication of such a book as part of the observance of the University's centennial in 1967-68. I accepted the offer and agreed to write a one-volume history that would be critical and interpretive down to the recent past (1955) and descriptive thereafter. In addition, I received written assurances that I would be granted free access to all the materials in the University Archives, and that my manuscript would be published without any institutional censorship.

Third came the adjustment to the practical realities of scholarship, which has engaged my constant attention throughout the writing of this book. Several factors gradually forced me to conclude that it was inadvisable to treat so broad a span in a single volume to be published in 1968. By far the most important of these was what I learned as the University Archives became a reality. President Henry had provided for their effective establishment when he arranged for the production of a new history. At the time, however, no one had a good idea as to the extent or value of whatever documents had survived nearly a century of neglect. Mr. Maynard J. Brichford assumed his duties as University Archivist when I began my research, and by persistent effort assembled an enormous quantity and variety of papers.

These remarkably rich sources, which are even better after than before 1894, provided a splendid opportunity to write a broad-scaled history of the University. I thought that Illinois, a major American university, deserved such treatment, and apparently nothing stood in the way. The existing literature on the school was surprisingly thin in bulk, and in addition it was dated, narrow in perspective, and often untrustworthy in factual matters. By the time I had completed the basic research on the whole century of the University's history, I had concluded that it would be shortsighted to let the transient if legitimate needs of observing the Centennial dictate the terms of scholarship. I suggested a change in the original plans, and other interested parties agreed that it was desirable. This Centennial history is the result. Since man proposes and God disposes, it is best not to make promises about succeeding volumes.

This book takes a longer and different perspective than earlier accounts, and differs from them frequently in factual details and interpretations. My conclusions rest on much fresh material and are carefully documented. The first three chapters describe the forces which conditioned and gave rise to the University of Illinois before it opened. I consider them essential and not mere background, because both the old-time college and the land-grant movement exerted a continuing influence on higher education after the Civil War. These three chapters show the options available as the University emerged in the late nineteenth century, and provide a basis for evaluating as well as understanding events at Champaign-Urbana. The next six chapters analyze the critical formative years when the character of the institution received its molding. In dealing specifically with Illinois in this period I have tried to illuminate general problems which confronted the American people at the time.

I have accumulated debts of gratitude in preparing this volume and in research on the years after 1894 which cannot readily be discharged. The University Research Board under the direction of Dean Frederick T. Wall, Acting Dean Herbert E. Carter, and Dean Daniel Alpert has been unfailingly generous with support. The research assistants without whom extensive investigations could not have been made include Anne d'Alquen, Harry Cahalan, David Gentry, William Glidden, Judy Hancock, David Hoeveler, David Huehner, Henry Johnson, Jon McKenna, Lewis Robinson, and Duane Rose. As Chairman of the Department of History and of the advisory committeee on a centennial history during the writing of this book, Professor Robert W. Johannsen made my departmental duties as light as possible — (to the colleagues who assumed an extra load I am also grateful) — and freed me psychologically to concentrate on research and writing. Librarians at Urbana, especially Robert W. Oram, Helen Welch, and Thomas E. Ratcliffe mobilized the superb resources of their respective departments to help me, as did Mrs. Marguerite Pease and Professor Robert M. Sutton of the Illinois Historical Survey. James R. Payne facilitated my use of the student records in his charge. Maynard J. Brichford has been a critical and creative co-partner in the enterprise. Professor Elmer Roberts freely and good-humoredly shared his wide knowledge about the College of Agriculture. Both of the latter gave me the benefit of their reading of several chapters of my manuscript. Henry Johnson and David Hoeveler read nearly all of it, and were as rewarding as they were critical. On some matters we still do not agree, but I am nevertheless deeply grateful for their unstinting aid. David Huehner bore the brunt of making the index and gathered loose ends as the book went through the press while I was abroad. I could not have asked for a better editor than Mrs. Elizabeth Dulany. Above all I thank my wife, Connie, and my children, Gail, Andrew, and Kristin, for the special contributions each has made in this collaborative undertaking. Needless to say, I alone assume full responsibility for any shortcomings the volume may possess.

Bologna, Italy   Winton U. Solberg

Contents

CHAPTER ONE

The Granite of the Past

THE UNIVERSITY OF ILLINOIS was the product of a revolution in American life. It arose in the late nineteenth century when new forces were laying the foundations of the modern United States. In the years between Appomattox and the Spanish-American War the nation accelerated its flight from farms to cities and from agricultural to industrial pursuits. The frontier officially closed and the country directed its expansion onto the world stage. At the same time Darwinism destroyed old verities and necessitated a reconstruction of thought. The emergence of the American university, which both reflected and stimulated the maturing of the nation's intellectual life, was part of this swift and fundamental transformation.

[1]

The dramatic changes which overtook higher education after the Civil War make it tempting to focus on the new university at the expense of the old-time college. Yet the college had long been the characteristic form of America's advanced learning when President Lincoln signed the Morrill Act in 1862. Illinois at the time was one of seven commonwealths which had founded no state university, but this legislation induced her to open such a center six years later on the bleak prairie at Champaign-Urbana. Its builders were nevertheless not free to fashion the school along totally original lines. The University of Illinois, like other institutions, initially took shape from influences which antedate its founding.

The classical-sectarian college was the dominant form of the nation's advanced learning until well after passage of the Morrill Act. It had taken root in the colonial period and gained new vitality early in the nineteenth century. In important ways, moreover, it continued to mold higher education after the university era began. For this reason the search for the origins of the American university properly begins with an inquiry into its legacy from the old-time college, and that is where the history of the University of Illinois commences. Certain structural features as well as the religious, curricular, and disciplinary ideals and patterns of the older education exerted a decisive influence on the Urbana institution. To look to the past only for origins of the state university idea prejudges critical issues about the "new education" that developed between 1862 and 1900. This period witnessed a great conflict between competing modes of how to shape the nation's mind, and thus it carried deep meaning for the future of the United States and the world.

The negative influence of the pre–Civil War college also materially shaped the modern university. The alleged inadequacies of the system imported at an early day created during the American Revolution a demand that education be adapted to the conditions of American life. This feeling produced an abortive wave of protest in the 1820's, and it spurred later treatises on university reform and industrial education. The ideological and material forces which reconstructed American society during the Jacksonian era intensified the rebellion against the old-time college which gathered

strength after 1840. That movement led directly to the establishment of Illinois Industrial University 27 years later.

The first American settlers laid foundations for later educational development when they tried to reproduce in their new land
the English and Scottish universities with which they were familiar.
The college became the basic structure of higher education because
circumstances enabled the colonists to erect only single colleges
rather than a collection of colleges such as formed a university in
Britain. Massachusetts Puritans, for example, modeled Harvard
after Emmanuel College of the English Cambridge. The eight other
colleges founded before the American Revolution (six of which date
from between 1746 and 1769) imitated both Harvard and the colleges of Cambridge, Oxford, or Aberdeen. The Americans added
to their institutions some university attributes, such as the power to
confer degrees. But they avoided the pattern of the continental university, which offered professional training to individuals who had
completed preparatory instruction and assumed no responsibility for
the discipline and morals of students. Furthermore, they insisted
on perpetuating the English "collegiate way," which aimed at
educating the whole man rather than training merely the intellect.
For this purpose a society of scholars and students lived together as
a family under the common discipline of a body of rules which
minutely governed undergraduate conduct. The colleges offered
close parental supervision, and thus they could admit very youthful
students.

The colonial college was the child of religion. Protestant settlers
regarded ignorance as the mother of heresy rather than of devotion.
They wanted youth to acquire knowledge less for its own sake than
in order to comprehend God's nature through his works. In addition, the colonies considered it vital to educate clergymen, and down
to the mid-eighteenth century half of their graduates became ministers. Although filled with the spirit of religion, the colleges drew on
the Renaissance as well as the Reformation heritage. They existed
to fit young men for civil employments as well as the church.

Although the religiously oriented college reigned supreme until
the American Revolution, its prescribed and narrow curriculum
underwent liberalization beginning about 1730. The Enlightenment

encouraged greater emphasis on science, which in America found its main institutional support in the colleges. The rise of religious diversity, a drift toward secularism, the increasing importance of politics, a growing urbanism, and an emphasis on utilitarianism also affected formal institutions of learning as the eighteenth century advanced. Two colleges founded in the 1750's illustrated these trends. King's College in New York gave an impetus to the ideal of a liberal nonsectarian college stressing practical subjects. The College of Philadelphia (later the University of Pennsylvania) was the one advanced school not explicitly founded for religious purposes.

The college designed for the few whose way of life required education met its first challenge during and after the American Revolution. France now replaced Britain as the chief foreign influence on American thought, and the *philosophes* stimulated a growing native demand for an educational system adapted to the needs of the Republic. A spirit of nationalism whetted the desire for distinctively American schools which would widen the dissemination of knowledge and promote the social and cultural integration which true nationhood required. Educational theories based on the ideas of Bacon, Locke, and Rousseau led to insistence that the curriculum prepare men for practical pursuits and civic usefulness. An influential body of thinkers charged the state with the duty of expanding educational opportunity so as to insure the success of republican government and of freeing it from religious controls and commitments.

The principle that the state was responsible for higher education was not widely held before the Revolution. To be sure, the colleges had enjoyed support from provincial assemblies. Legislatures had granted subsidies and enacted laws to aid institutions within their borders. Harvard, for example, got the revenues of the Boston-Charlestown ferry; William and Mary, the export duties on skins, furs, and tobacco and an import duty on liquor. But colonial assemblies refused to accept the principle that they were responsible for fully nourishing and sustaining schools of higher learning. Hence the governing boards of these institutions ingeniously sought funds from a variety of sources. Repeated solicitation of their communities for financial aid rather than assistance from the state gave the colleges a quasi-public character. Collegiate education therefore remained tied to religion as long as orthodoxy prevailed in various colonies. But rising secularism and the separation of church and state freed the state to support education, which became regarded as the surest foundation of liberty, virtue, and equal rights.[1]

Numerous spokemen now suggested that the federal government actively foster learning. However, the proposal of a national university as the apex of the educational pyramid, which every president through John Quincy Adams supported in varying degree, foundered on fears of centralized government. Hence the Northwest Ordinance, which reserved two townships in each state to be formed in the Northwest Territory for support of an institution of higher learning, remained the primary expression of federal responsibility for advanced learning from 1787 until the Morrill Act.

The main achievement in realizing the principle of the state's responsibility for higher education in the first years of the Republic therefore came from the state university movement. Jefferson, the foremost educational statesman of the Revolutionary generation, was its main inspiration. He keenly appreciated the relation between a system of free public education and the creation of a society that would improve the condition of mankind. His "Bill for the More General Diffusion of Knowledge" submitted to the Virginia legislature in 1779 was the first attempt to erect a graduated system of education adapted to all ages and capacities. Jefferson envisioned the state university as the crown of the public system of education, and his continued agitation for educational reform culminated a half-century later in the opening of the University of Virginia.

The state university idea achieved its greatest success in the late eighteenth and early nineteenth centuries in the Southeast, where

[1] Much has been made of the notion that the colonial colleges were incipient state universities because of the aid given them by colonial governments ever since Charles Kendall Adams (who became President of the University of Wisconsin in 1892) asserted this opinion in his review of Andrew Ten Brook's *American State Universities, Their Origin and Progress,* in *North American Review,* CXXI (Oct., 1875), 365-408. But see Bernard Bailyn, *Education in the Forming of American Society: Needs and Opportunities for Study* (Chapel Hill, 1960), 41-45. See also Rush Welter, *Popular Education and Democratic Thought in America* (New York, 1962), 23-41; and Allen Oscar Hansen, *Liberalism and American Education in the Eighteenth Century* (New York, 1926), *passim.*

there had been no colonial college and where organized religion was not strong enough to oppose public education effectively. In the Northeast, where colonial colleges were well entrenched and often allied with vigorous religious interests, the attempt to make higher education a phase of civil policy failed. New western states usually wasted little time in enlisting themselves in the progressive ranks. A total of 21 publicly supported institutions arose by 1860 and more were on the verge of opening. Seven commonwealths founded no state university before the Civil War. Of these, Illinois was the oldest and most economically developed. The fact that her neighbors had all erected state universities before midcentury — Indiana in 1828, Michigan and Kentucky in 1837, Missouri in 1839, Iowa in 1847, and Wisconsin in 1848 — highlighted the unique educational backwardness of Illinois.[2]

However, none of these universities fully realized the state university ideal. They were for all practical purposes like their denominational counterparts. Local legislatures reflected the attitudes of the electorate, which insisted that public higher education impart religious and moral training. Before 1860, more than nine out of ten college presidents, including the heads of state universities, were ordained clergymen.[3] The United States did not provide a favorable environment for state universities until a century after the founding in 1769 of Dartmouth, the last colonial college.

Meanwhile, the conditions of American culture nourished the small denominational college with a prescribed curriculum that emphasized the ancient languages, mathematics, and moral philosophy. At the opening of the nineteenth century organized Christianity recovered ground previously lost, partly as a result of the Enlightenment. The churches now forged a new alliance with the colleges for possession of higher education. Each separate religious group used its own schools to strengthen and enlarge denominational ranks and as a training ground for its clergymen. As voluntary

[2] Donald G. Tewksbury, *The Founding of American Colleges and Universities Before the Civil War,* Teachers College, Columbia University, Contributions to Education No. 543 (New York, 1932), *passim.* Arkansas, Florida, Kansas, Maine, Oregon, and Texas also founded no state university before the Civil War. It should be noted, however, that the General Assembly founded Illinois State Normal University in 1857. On this development and its relation to the movement for a state university, see below, ch. ii.
[3] George Paul Schmidt, *The Old Time College President* (New York, 1930), 184.

unions of believers the denominations were superbly equipped to make the colleges responsive to the public will and to the added responsibilities imposed upon higher education by the civic spirit liberated during the Revolution. Individual states were often less well prepared to sponsor schools than was organized religion. The churches therefore appropriated the demands for democratic equality and patriotic sentiments which had accumulated since 1776 and "wove them into one seamless garment of responsible Christian democracy."[4] Major impetus for the profusion of colleges came from the Presbyterians, Methodists, Baptists, and Congregationalists in that order. Perhaps as many as 700 colleges were started before the Civil War, although the high mortality rate justifies the statement that settlement of the United States was carried out intellectually "over the bones of dead colleges."[5]

The colleges and state universities together constituted one system of higher education. Its decentralization reflected the voluntaristic principle which characterized American life. The absence of central controls and accrediting agencies permitted the widest variation in standards, mostly from bad to worse. Nevertheless, the countless hilltop colleges set their institutional compasses by the same ideals as venerable Harvard, Yale, and Princeton.

Religious purposes remained paramount during the heyday of the ante-bellum college. Public opinion insisted that education was genuine only when it included moral and religious training. The colleges therefore required attendance at daily morning and evening chapel and everywhere made the Sabbath a day of worship, not of study. The Church of Christ in Yale College existed to receive students into the household of faith. Ideally, Yale was the Church of Christ at prayer, and Yale along with Princeton perfected the collegiate model.[6] Campus revivals periodically nourished special out-

[4] George Paul Schmidt, *The Liberal Arts College: A Chapter in American Cultural History* (New Brunswick, 1957), 29.
[5] Richard Hofstadter and Walter P. Metzger, *The Development of Academic Freedom in the United States* (New York, 1955), 212. On the denominational sources and mortality rate, see Tewksbury, *The Founding of American Colleges and Universities, passim;* and Frederick Rudolph, *The American College and University: A History* (New York, 1962), 44-67.
[6] Ralph Henry Gabriel, *Religion and Learning at Yale: The Church of Christ in the College and University, 1757-1957* (New Haven, 1958), excellently illustrates the religious ideal of the colleges.

pourings of Christian piety. The alliance with religion made the higher learning a bastion of the status quo.

The college curriculum had changed little since it was borrowed from England in the colonial period. A compound of Renaissance and Reformation ideals, the prescribed four-year course sought to discipline the mind while transmitting a traditional body of knowledge. Its foundation was the ancient classics and mathematics, on top of which came a thin layer of science and a thick topping of philosophy and ethics. Most college youths between the Revolution and the Civil War pursued a program similar to the one taken in the 1840's at Union College by John M. Gregory, the first Regent (President) of the University of Illinois. He read Livy, Horace, Cicero, Tacitus, Juvenal, and Terence in Latin, and in Greek, Xenophon, Herodotus, Thucydides, Lysias, Isocrates, Demosthenes, Homer's *Iliad*, Hesiod, and Sophocles. Gregory studied algebra, plane and solid geometry, trigonometry, and conic sections. In science his courses included geology, botany, technology, chemistry, natural philosophy, and astronomy, which was no doubt more than most colleges offered.[7] All but the best ante-bellum colleges feared science as a threat to religious faith.

Philosophy crowned the curriculum and sealed the union of church and college. Clergymen presidents traditionally taught the senior class moral and mental philosophy and probably Christian evidences or Butler's *Analogy*. Moral philosophy treated ethics, the principles of duty and obligation, as well as other subjects into which the omnibus course later developed, especially economics and political science. Mental philosophy took as its province the mind's fitness or capacity for its various operations. The foundation of this study was the psychology of mental faculties, the science of a Platonic soul endowed with Aristotelian faculties which had been Christianized and enmeshed in various philosophical disciplines. Mental philosophy assumed a threefold division of the faculties into the understanding, the will, and the affections (sometimes called taste). These beliefs had been reformulated in the Common Sense philosophy or Scottish Realism, which John Wither-

[7] These subjects were in the Union College classical curriculum during Gregory's student days. See U.S. Bureau of Education, *Historical Sketch of Union College* (Washington, 1876), 26, 28.

spoon imported to Princeton in 1768. They became widespread by
the early nineteenth century and henceforth dominated American
higher education until after the Civil War. Scottish Realism emphasized feelings and the original moral truths in the mind. By
teaching that the will was free and accountable and that the mind
did in fact perceive reality, this body of thought enabled colleges
to safeguard students from philosophical materialism and skepticism on the one hand and from philosophical idealism and Transcendentalism on the other. The mind's perceptions were regarded
as the dictates of common sense and the foundation of all reasoning. Since the truths of religion were given through the senses, man
could validate his faith in the biblical account of miracles and in
other supernatural manifestations. Countless seniors studied Arch-
deacon William Paley's *View of the Evidences of Christianity*
(1794) in courses which gave college presidents a last chance to
brand youths for lives of permanent usefulness.[8]

The "collegiate way" remained a leading feature of pre–Civil
War higher education. Strict discipline was an inherent part of the
authoritarian mold in which the colleges were cast. Even though
older students were mature men, often twice the age of their younger
fellows, the assumption was that students were immature and per-
verse and that wise and virtuous teachers could reproduce their own
kind by proper supervision. Hence faculties required residence in
college buildings and strictly governed conduct by detailed rules.
They employed many devices in order to furnish the complete security to "youthful" manners and morals which society demanded
of them. Authorities asked pupils to pledge loyalty and obedience
upon entering college, and maintained a vigilant espionage to ferret
out evils on the campus and in the dormitories, called by one observer "the secret nurseries of every vice and the cages of unclean
birds."[9] Whole faculties sat as courts to try offenders, imposing

[8] Schmidt, *The Old Time College President*, 108-45; Sydney E. Ahlstrom, "The
Scottish Philosophy and American Theology," *Church History*, XXIV (Sept.,
1955), 257-72; Jay Wharton Fay, *American Psychology Before William James*
(New Brunswick, 1939), 50-128. Joseph Butler, *The Analogy of Religion, Natural and Revealed* (London, 1736), was widely used during the early nineteenth
century.
[9] John S. Brubacher and S. Willis Rudy, *Higher Education in Transition* (New
York, 1958), 41.

demerits, monetary fines, suspension, or expulsion according to the gravity of the offense.

These controls embittered student-faculty relations to the detriment of learning. They also tempted students to regard as legitimate those wrongs which they could commit without being caught. The belief that informing on one's fellows was dishonorable permitted a small minority, often seasoned men, to dissipate and to do evil with relative impunity. Students gained revenge on the authoritarianism of the colleges by resistance and insubordination. They defied faculty judgments, underscored their dissent by gunpowder explosions and physical assaults, and even whipped, shot, and stabbed professors and presidents. Princeton had serious riots in 1807 and 1817, and Julian M. Sturtevant found Yale's government and internal discipline bordering on anarchy in the late 1820's. At some time in their history most institutions experienced similar unrest.[10]

The government of American higher education aggravated these disciplinary disorders and caused other problems as well. The first Americans had tried to imitate English administrative practice, which made resident scholars responsible for ruling their colleges under charters from the crown. But during the colonial period laymen who did not reside within the colleges had gained supreme authority over institutions of higher learning. These boards of trustees delegated executive power to a president, who served at the pleasure of the governing body. College faculties possessed little authority, no more than their presidents gave them. The American college president, responsible only to a group of nonresident laymen, tended to become authoritarian.[11] Students, however, did not need to tread warily for fear of their jobs, and those convicted of disciplinary offenses saw no reason to accept as final the adverse judgments of the internal management. They therefore appealed over the heads of the faculty and the president to the trustees, who had

[10] Thomas Jefferson Wertenbaker, *Princeton, 1746-1896* (Princeton, 1946), 138-43, 167-69; Julian M. Sturtevant, *An Autobiography*, ed. J. M. Sturtevant, Jr. (New York, 1896), 94-98.
[11] John E. Kirkpatrick, *Academic Organization and Control* (Yellow Springs, Ohio, 1931), *passim;* Hofstadter and Metzger, *The Development of Academic Freedom in the United States*, 114-51 and *passim*.

not yet learned that interference worsened rather than improved student government.

A revolt against the old-time college arose in the 1820's, even before the mania for planting these institutions gained full force. The crux of the dissatisfaction was with the curriculum. Critics arraigned it for superficiality and for failure to produce learned men. These charges grew out of the deterioration which commenced after the American Revolution, when both the severing of ties with Britain and the moving frontier lowered educational standards. Moreover, uncontrolled proliferation created far more colleges than the country could support. The poverty resulting from a shortage of students and thus of revenues forced most colleges into academic weakness.[12] In addition, the authorities began to add new subjects without either eliminating old ones or extending the time spent in school. Students therefore raced lightly over a prescribed four-year course, memorizing and reciting daily upon portions of textbooks. The authoritarian approach to a body of knowledge which was regarded as fixed made instructors stern drillmasters. Beginning tutors knew more than they could ever teach, and they had no incentive to increase their stock of knowledge. Awareness of these defects became acute when Americans began learning about the German universities in 1815. After returning from Göttingen to Harvard, George Ticknor asked, "who has been taught anything at our colleges with the thoroughness that will enable him to go safely and directly onward to distinction in the department he has thus entered without returning to lay anew the foundations for his success?"[13] Three decades later Louis Agassiz, recently arrived from Europe, said that Harvard was "only a respectable high school, where they taught the dregs of learning."[14]

In addition, critics blasted the curriculum for its unsuitability

[12] In 1829 Yale had 359 students and was the largest in the country. Dartmouth with 131 students was fifth in size. George Paul Schmidt, "Intellectual Crosscurrents in American Colleges, 1825-1855," *American Historical Review*, XLII (Oct., 1936), 53n.

[13] George Ticknor, *Remarks on Changes Lately Proposed or Adopted, in Harvard University* (n.p., 1825), 45. See also David B. Tyack, *George Ticknor and the Boston Brahmins* (Cambridge, Mass., 1967), 85-128.

[14] As quoted in David Starr Jordan, *The Trend of the American University* (Stanford, 1929), 18; see also Edward Lurie, *Louis Agassiz, a Life in Science* (Chicago, 1960), 218, 327-28.

to nineteenth-century America. They held that a course of study designed to train monks had changed little since the colonials imported it. The curriculum, a relic of the past, lacked relevance for an aggressively democratic nation whose genius was practical. The emphasis on utility was not new in the 1820's, but it gained strength in that decade. The internal discipline and government of the colleges also came under attack.

The demand for reform was not inspired by the frontier, which perpetuated the type of college being condemned, but by Eastern innovators who were familiar with European thought and practice. The most important critics of higher education in the 1820's were Professor George Ticknor of Harvard, President James Marsh of the University of Vermont, Professor Jacob Abbott of Amherst College, President Eliphalet Nott of Union College, Philip Lindsley, a former Princeton professor who initiated significant changes upon becoming President of the University of Nashville in 1825, and Thomas Jefferson.

These spokesmen shared many common goals, one of which was the elective principle. Freedom of choice permitted individuals to choose programs adapted to their abilities and interests and it aimed at elevating academic standards and overcoming America's educational backwardness. The result divided colleges into many subjects rather than four classes and gave rise to the academic department. Election also enabled students to concentrate and to study as long as necessary to demonstrate the proficiency required for a degree. Second, the reformers devised the parallel course as an alternative to the classical curriculum. This new departure permitted students to pursue subjects which both interested them and prepared them for contemporary usefulness — modern languages, English literature, history and political economy, physics and chemistry. Nott was particularly instrumental in securing for the "side-fixings" such prestige as they commanded. Third, they stressed scientific and professional studies, as indicated by the Scientific Course at Union College. Jefferson gave scientific and professional pursuits importance among the eight schools which he organized into the University of Virginia, and Lindsley insisted that "The farmer, the mechanic, the manufacturer, the merchant, the sailor, the soldier . . . must be educated."[15]

In addition, these leaders tried to improve student-faculty relations and relations among students by improving discipline. Ticknor, Nott, Marsh, and Jefferson made this reform their particular concern. "The article of discipline is the most difficult in American education," wrote Jefferson, adding that it was the rock on which many colleges had foundered.[16] He joined with the others in substituting an appeal to the students' honor and self-respect for the old punitive system based on the theory of youthful depravity. Experience soon taught Jefferson that strict regulations were necessary to preserve order, and that coercion and fear had value. Nott relied largely on his immense personal influence along with a vigilant espionage, but he proved remarkably effective in governing students by teaching them to govern themselves.[17]

Another innovation was the manual-labor school movement, first introduced in 1825 and popular for several reasons. Many believed that manual labor was more effective in improving health than were gymnastics or ordinary games and sports. Also, manual labor enabled students to earn their way by working, and thus met the need of economy. Finally there was the influence emanating from Fellenberg's schools at Hofywl near Berne. Here the pedagogy took its inspiration from Pestalozzi, the chief contemporary spokesman of the doctrine that children should be educated according to nature and that handwork should promote learning.[18]

Americans borrowed the manual-labor system primarily for reasons of health and economy, with Maine Wesleyan Seminary

[15] *The Works of Philip Lindsley, D.D.,* ed. LeRoy J. Halsey (3 vols., Philadelphia, 1866), I, 81.
[16] Roy J. Honeywell, *The Educational Work of Thomas Jefferson* (Cambridge, Mass., 1931), 134.
[17] Andrew V. Raymond, *Union University: Its History, Influence, Characteristics and Equipment* (3 vols., New York, 1907), I, 155-56, 216; C. Van Santvoord and Tayler Lewis, *Memoirs of Eliphalet Nott, D.D., LL.D.* (New York, 1876), *passim;* Schmidt, *The Old Time College President,* 154-55.
[18] L. F. Anderson, "The Manual Labor School Movement," *Educational Review,* XLVI (Nov., 1913), 370-74; Charles Alpheus Bennett, *History of Manual and Industrial Education up to 1870* (Peoria, 1926), 132-40. See also Earle D. Ross, "The Manual Labor Experiment in the Land Grant College," *Mississippi Valley Historical Review,* XXI (March, 1935), 513-28.

initiating the movement in 1825. Thereafter, some institutions oriented their entire program around manual labor and required it of all students; others made the work requirement optional. But the imported pedagogical theory which stressed the unique value of uniting learning and labor found few adherents in America. Even the Society for Promoting Manual Labor in Literary Institutions, established in 1831, disregarded the doctrine. "We would have the cultivation of the mind the leading object in literary institutions," the Society asserted, "and labor used only as a healthful auxiliary."[19] It proved impossible to combine labor with study so as to obtain maximum benefit from either, however, and the system failed to serve pecuniary needs. Colleges spent more in equipment and supervision than they realized from the sale of products made or grown by students. Consequently the experiment with the exotic Fellenberg system began to lose momentum in the 1830's and declined rapidly in the following decade.

Both the assault of the collegiate reformers and the manual-labor movement were abortive, but they laid foundations that others built on in later years. Meanwhile, the challenge to the existing order met rebuttal. As the largest American college and a pillar of things as they were, Yale formulated the answer to the curricular protest. In response to the Trustees' request for the Faculty's opinion about eliminating the "dead languages," President Jeremiah Day and Professor James L. Kingsley wrote a statement which the Corporation endorsed and published. The Yale Report of 1828, a landmark in American intellectual history, gave the classic defense of the ante-bellum college.[20]

It argued that the fundamental purpose of a college was to lay the foundation of a superior education rather than to train with special reference to future professional pursuits. "The two great points to be gained in intellectual culture are the *discipline* and *furniture* of the mind," said Day, who gave mental discipline priority because he unquestioningly accepted the faculty psychology and regarded the mind as an organ which could perform any intel-

[19] As quoted in Anderson, "The Manual Labor School Movement," 385.
[20] "Original Papers in Relation to a Course of Liberal Education," *American Journal of Science and Arts,* XV (Jan., 1829), 297-351.

lectual exercise after proper training.[21] The ancient languages and mathematics were best suited to discipline the faculties, and since nothing could be subtracted from the fixed curriculum without loss, the elective principle was inadmissable until a student had mastered basic subjects. The recitation system was particularly valuable because it forced a student to exercise his intellectual powers, and study therefore sought to focus on textbooks rather than subjects. The diversities in different authors would only confound the learner. Academic needs required that college government be paternal. Students should constitute one family under constant and close supervision of their instructors. Hence the German university was no fit model for American colleges, whose province was not to include professional studies or to prepare youths for mercantile, manufacturing, or agricultural pursuits, which were best learned on the job.

The Report elaborated on the merits of the traditional curriculum. "The learned world long ago settled this matter" of the classics, it peremptorily declared, "and subsequent events and experience have confirmed their decision."[22] Classical learning was interwoven through all literature, and Greek and Roman writers, apart from the mental discipline they afforded, were superior in forming the taste and preparing one for professional study. The study of mathematics was especially adapted to strengthening the faculty of reason and a good prerequisite for understanding many sciences.

The Yale Report insisted that liberal and humanistic learning was most suited to America's requirements. A bustling democracy had an especial need to make certain that its impulse to action was guided by sound intelligence. To heed the public clamor and adapt higher education to the special demands of merchants, manufacturers, or agriculturists would lower the professional character of the country. This route would weaken public confidence in the colleges and imperil the Republic. "Let the value of a collegiate education be reduced and the diffusion of intelligence among the people would be checked; the general standard of intellectual and moral worth lowered; and our civil and religious liberty jeoparded

[21] *Ibid.*, 300.
[22] *Ibid.*, 344.

[*sic*] by ultimately disqualifying our citizens for the exercise of the right and privilege of self-government."[23]

The Yale Report effectively summarized an inherited pattern of thought, and it provided the rationale for American higher education until the late nineteenth century. The timing of this portentous pronouncement facilitated the supremacy of the classical liberal arts college, for these institutions proliferated wildly after 1830. Of the 182 "permanent" colleges established between 1636 and 1861, 49 were erected before 1829 and 133 after that year.[24]

The higher education that developed in Illinois prior to the Civil War was cast in the mold of the Yale Report. Religion was the leading intellectual influence on the frontier, and denominations regarded education as vital to civilization and the church. They established institutions of advanced learning before there were lower schools. The denominations pre-empted the field because Illinois was especially laggard in erecting a publicly supported system of education crowned by a university.

One reason for this situation was the character of the early population which settled along the Mississippi and Wabash rivers in southern Illinois. At the time of statehood in 1818 75 per cent of the residents were Southern in origin and only 3 per cent were from New England. A high degree of illiteracy, poverty, and a tradition that education was a private matter prompted most of these people to oppose tax-supported schools. The inhabitants destroyed the excellent free common-school law of 1825 and rebuffed proposals for a public seat of higher learning. These conditions provided an excellent opportunity for denominational leaders. By the 1830's, when New Englanders began emigrating via the Erie Canal to northern Illinois, religious groups had laid foundations for the first colleges. In 1827 John Mason Peck, a Baptist missionary who advocated a common-school system, began the seminary that became Shurtleff College at Alton. The following year Methodists initiated McKendree College at Lebanon, the earliest school of their denomination west of the Appalachians. In 1829 seven divinity students at Yale

---

[23] *Ibid.,* 346.
[24] Tewksbury, *The Founding of American Colleges and Universities,* 16. The "permanent" colleges were those which survived down to the time Tewksbury wrote in 1932, but some have since perished.

united for the purpose of preaching and establishing a college at Jacksonville. The Yale Band received encouragement from the Reverend Absalom Peters of the Home Missionary Society and from Yale officials, and Illinois College opened in 1830.

A second reason for delay was the state's refusal to pay for public higher education by taxation. Illinois had squandered the aid furnished by the federal government, which was contained in two separate accounts. The Seminary Fund consisted of the money derived from the sale of two townships, one given under an 1804 act of Congress when the Territory of Illinois was organized and the other awarded in the act granting statehood. In 1829 the General Assembly authorized sale of these lands at public auction at a minimum of $1.25 an acre; 67.5 of the 72 sections were soon sold, mostly below the minimum price. The state borrowed the derived proceeds of about $60,000 to defray general expenses and to avoid raising taxes. Interest at 6 per cent was added on the books to the principal rather than paid as due. The Seminary Fund "is fairly entitled to the distinction of having been the worst-abused educational trust fund in the Northwest Territory."[25]

The College Fund originated in a provision of the congressional act admitting Illinois to the Union which was especially favorable to higher education. Instead of granting 5 per cent of the revenue from the sale of public lands in Illinois for building roads as was customary, the act allowed 2 per cent for that purpose and 3 per cent for education. A sixth of the latter sum was to be used to support a college or university, the remainder for common schools. In 1829, however, the prodigal state borrowed the proceeds of the College Fund on the same terms as it borrowed the Seminary Fund.

In February, 1833, legislators introduced a bill into the General Assembly to establish Illinois University and endow it with the College and Seminary funds. A number of factors combined to defeat the measure. Senator George Forquer excited jealousies by trying to locate the institution in Springfield. No doubt Peter Cartwright raised suspicions when he sponsored the bill in the House, for he was a leading Methodist and boasted that he had not wasted time

[25] George W. Knight, *History and Management of Land Grants for Education in the Northwest Territory,* Papers of the American Historical Association, I, No. 3 (New York, 1885), 135.

rubbing his back against the walls of a college. More important was the fear of the existing unincorporated colleges that a state university would overshadow them, and the fact that the College and Seminary funds, worth about $109,000, had been despoiled.[26]

The state therefore confined its aid to granting charters to private colleges, and even that the General Assembly did reluctantly. Legislators feared that schoolmen were land speculators, they sympathized with their member who boasted in 1835 that he was "born in a briar thicket, rocked in a hog trough and had never had his genius cramped by the pestilential air of a college,"[27] and they allowed their anticlericalism to bring about restrictions against the teaching of theology and the maintenance of theological departments. After two colleges rejected charters for the latter reason in 1833, a compromise allowed the operation of an attached seminary. An omnibus bill of February 9, 1835, finally chartered Shurtleff, McKendree, Illinois, and Jonesborough colleges, the latter a school of the Christian denomination which was never organized. Two years later the General Assembly awarded George W. Gale and New School Presbyterians a charter for Knox Manual Labor College. In 1841 lawmakers repealed the religious restriction and in 1842 they passed a general law for incorporating colleges. At least a score of denominational colleges were founded by 1861.[28] The religious groups behind this effort, especially the friends of Illinois College, were responsible for the people abandoning the idea of a state university.[29]

This situation explains why Constantine Samuel Rafinesque's

---

[26] *Illinois Senate Journal* (1833), 426, 430, 537-38; *Illinois House Journal* (1833), 533; *Autobiography of Peter Cartwright,* ed. Charles L. Wallis (New York, 1956), 8; Sturtevant, *Autobiography,* 162.

[27] Charles Henry Rammelkamp, *Illinois College: A Centennial History, 1829-1929* ([New Haven], 1928), 65.

[28] Tewksbury, *The Founding of American Colleges and Universities,* 31, lists 12 permanent colleges in Illinois before the Civil War, a number exceeded only by Ohio (17), Pennsylvania (16), and New York (15). But the number is likely to have been appreciably higher. Although all 13 of the new collegiate institutions chartered by the General Assembly in 1855 were not actually established, one writer reports 26 chartered colleges and similar institutions in existence in 1868. See William L. Pillsbury, "The Influence of Government Land Grants for Educational Purposes upon the Educational System of the State," Illinois State Historical Society, *Transactions for 1901,* Illinois State Historical Library Pub. No. 6 (Springfield, 1901), 36.

[29] Society for the Promotion of Collegiate and Theological Education at the West, *Twentieth Annual Report* (New York, 1863), 42.

plan to establish a University of Illinois was premature. A brilliant but eccentric natural scientist who took up residence in the United States in 1815, Rafinesque taught at Transylvania for eight years, traveled widely, wrote and published prolifically, and was friendly with prominent scientists. He settled in Philadelphia in 1826, and having visited Illinois published in 1838 a curious book entitled *Celestial Wonders and Philosophy, or The Structure of the Visible Heavens with Hints on Their Celestial Religion, and Theory of Futurity.* One of his purposes was to celebrate the sublimity of Nature revealed in recent astronomical discoveries, which Rafinesque avowedly popularized for his own use "and that of our students in the great University, Colleges and Institutions which are going to be established in Illinois, chiefly through my exertions and care." A second motive was to announce his plans for "a great Central University in the fine and flourishing State of Illinois, wherein in the course of time all the branches of Human Knowledge shall be made free and gratuitous to all human beings." He dedicated his book to those who had helped — he had already obtained land endowments from residents of Illinois and had in hand books and apparatus valued at $3,000 — or would join in founding "a perpetual Beneficial Institution under-taking to unite Knowledge with Agriculture." Rafinesque hoped to form gradually a university consisting of normal colleges in agriculture and labor, arts and sciences, teachers and languages, as well as a college of medicine and medical sciences, and an eleutherium, or college of knowledge and philosophy.[30] His death in 1840 ended these grandiose visions and spared the author obloquy in a state which was just completing the frontier phase of its development and was not receptive to educational innovation.

The old-time college continued to dominate both Illinois and the nation until after the Civil War. In these years the Yale Report emboldened numerous college authorities to spurn curricular innovation and stand firmly on the granite of the past. "The introduction of studies on the ground of their practical utility is, pro tanto, subversive of the college," said one such statement in 1854. "It is not the office of the college to make planters, mechanics, lawyers,

[30] Constantine Samuel Rafinesque, *Celestial Wonders and Philosophy* (Philadelphia, 1838), 2, 4, 135.

physicians or divines. It has nothing directly to do with the uses of knowledge. Its business is with minds, and it employs science only as an instrument for the improvement and perfection of the mind. With it, the habit of sound thinking is more than a thousand thoughts."[31] In genteel circles under the college elms these principles were too well established to permit controversy, as President John Maclean announced in his 1854 inaugural address at Princeton: "We shall not aim at innovation. No chimerical experiments in education have ever had the least countenance here."[32]

However, Jackson entered the White House in the year that the Yale Report provided the classic defense of the ante-bellum curriculum. His presidency marks the advent of forces which profoundly altered society and thought. In subsequent decades the nation changed but the college remained fixed in traditional ways. As Charles Francis Adams, Jr., wrote, "there is no conservatism . . . so unreasoning, so impenetrable, as the conservatism of professional educators about their methods."[33] Rather than change, the college accepted the fact of its isolation from the mainstream of American life.

The price of that aloofness was high. About 1830 the number of students seeking a college education began a decline which reflected public lack of confidence. Enrollments lagged for the next half-century, during which time they failed to keep pace with population growth. A total of 351 students were attending private Illinois colleges in 1860, at which time some 20,000 men and a few young women constituted the collegiate population of the entire United States. Since advanced education was clearly not essential to worldly success, the prestige of college graduates and of the colleges themselves touched bottom.[34]

[31] This statement from the University of Alabama was co-authored by Frederick A. P. Barnard and is quoted in William G. Roelker, "Francis Wayland: A Neglected Pioneer of Higher Education," American Antiquarian Society, *Proceedings,* LIII (April, 1944), 50.
[32] As quoted in Schmidt, "Intellectual Crosscurrents in American Colleges," 66.
[33] Charles Francis Adams, Jr., *A College Fetich: An Address Delivered Before the Harvard Chapter of the Fraternity of the Phi Beta Kappa . . . June 28, 1883* (Boston, 1883), 9.
[34] Charles Kendall Adams, review of Ten Brook's *American State Universities,* 389-92; Arthur M. Comey, "Growth of the Colleges of the United States," *Educational Review,* III (Feb., 1892), 126; George Paul Schmidt, "Colleges in Ferment," *American Historical Review,* LIX (Oct., 1953), 19.

The bitter reminiscences of the men who attended these institutions also testified to the heavy costs. In defiance of his father Andrew D. White fled a small church college which boasted of its direct Christian influence upon every student but was in fact a center of carousing and wild dissipation because the impoverished authorities dared not offend any student. At Yale, however, White found rote recitation and "gerund grinding" prevalent, and he formed an abiding contempt for these practices.[35] Charles Francis Adams, Jr., condemned the Harvard that graduated him in 1856 for a superstitious reverence for the dead languages and for the superficiality of the classical learning it imparted. He regarded French and German and the ability to follow out a line of exact, sustained thought to a given result as essential to modern life. "In these days of repeating-rifles," he charged, Harvard "sent me and my classmates out into the strife equipped with shields and swords and javelins. . . . It seems to me I have heard, somewhere else, of a child's cry for bread being answered with a stone." Adams found the experience "too bitter, too humiliating" to relate fully, and he believed that he would never overcome some disadvantages Harvard had inflicted upon him.[36]

Despite defects which enabled White to criticize the antebellum colleges for being "as stagnant as a Spanish convent, and as self-satisfied as a Bourbon duchy,"[37] these institutions had considerable merit. Their devotion to ideas and values which transcended the national needs of the Republic constituted the essence of their worth. They existed to develop character and to train Christian gentlemen for leadership and usefulness. However traditional and narrow, the prescribed curriculum was capable of educating men well. The ethical and didactic view in Greek and Roman writers, purged of paganism when necessary, and the religious and moral purposes of the colleges instilled a high sense of purpose and self-esteem. But the educational revolution that gathered momentum shortly after publication of the Yale Report swept aside these strengths along with the many weaknesses of the old-time higher learning.

[35] Andrew D. White, *Autobiography* (2 vols., New York, 1907), I, 18-19, 26-33.
[36] Adams, *A College Fetich*, 5, 28-29.
[37] As quoted in Walter P. Rogers, *Andrew D. White and the Modern University* (Ithaca, 1942), 6.

CHAPTER TWO

The Leaven of the Future

THE MODERN AMERICAN UNIVERSITY was woven of many strands, and the most significant was the land-grant college movement. The question as to who "fathered" the College Land Grant Act has been much disputed, with partisans advancing the rival claims of two different men. Writers associated with the University of Illinois have labored for nearly a century to establish and defend the proposition that the "definite movement for a Federal land grant for the support of agricultural and mechanical institutes in every State originated not with Vermont . . . but with Illinois, and was headed not by Justin Morrill but by Jonathan B. Turner."[1] The assertion

[1] Allan Nevins, *Illinois* (New York, 1917), 12. Nevins' statement may be viewed as the capstone of an edifice which Turner himself and President John M.

[22]

exaggerates Turner's contribution, and likewise advocates have magnified Morrill's role. At most both men figured prominently in a development to which a complex of persons and forces gave the creative impulse. In any event, determining the paternity of the Morrill Act is less important than understanding that measure in relation to other influences which reconstructed national life and thereby affected higher education.

There were five factors of great relevance in effecting collegiate reform, and they had been gathering momentum for some time when an 1851 address by Turner initiated the crusade for industrial education in Illinois. But Illinois' effort was only part of a concerted national campaign to improve intellectual and cultural conditions, and that endeavor aimed at much more than agricultural and mechanical schools. An evaluation of Turner's role and that of Illinois must be made in the light of the total struggle. A com-

Gregory began constructing soon after passage of the Morrill Act. Later, after spokesmen had emphasized Morrill's role, Dean Eugene Davenport of the College of Agriculture sought to rehabilitate Turner. See his "History of Collegiate Education in Agriculture," Society for the Promotion of Agricultural Science, *Proceedings,* XXVIII (Lansing, 1907), 43-53. After he became President of the University in 1904, Edmund J. James zealously sought to establish Turner's contribution. He wrote that "the credit for having first devised and formulated the original plan [of a land grant to each state for the promotion of education in agriculture and the mechanic arts] and of having worked up the public interest in the measure so that it could be passed belongs clearly to Professor Turner and should be accorded him." *The Origin of the Land Grant Act of 1862 (the So-Called Morrill Act) and Some Account of Its Author, Jonathan B. Turner,* University of Illinois Studies, IV, No. 1 (Urbana, 1910), 8. James stressed the same conclusion in other articles and inspired the writing of three books which featured this interpretation: Mary Turner Carriel (the daughter of Turner), *The Life of Jonathan Baldwin Turner* (n.p., 1911); Burt E. Powell, *Semi-Centennial History of the University of Illinois, I: The Movement for Industrial Education and the Establishment of the University, 1840-1870* (Urbana, 1918); and Nevins' book. Unfortunately, the centennial of the Land Grant Act stimulated a new round of similar statements, as exemplified in the Introduction to a second edition of Mary Turner Carriel, *The Life of Jonathan Baldwin Turner* (Urbana, 1961). Morrill also was self-vaunting, and apart from himself, George W. Atherton, an original member of the University of Illinois faculty, from which he was the first man to resign, early argued for Morrill's contribution in "The Legislative Career of Justin S. Morrill," *Proceedings of the Fourteenth Annual Convention of the Association of American Agricultural Colleges and Experiment Stations, 1900,* U.S. Department of Agriculture, Office of Experiment Stations, Bulletin No. 99 (Washington, 1901), 60-72. Earle D. Ross, "The 'Father' of the Land-Grant College," *Agricultural History,* XII (April, 1938), 151-86, is a model of historical analysis which shows how enthusiasts erected a mountain of conjecture about Turner's role on a molehill of fact.

prehensive approach both illuminates the conflicting aims of the reformers and brings to light the tensions between this group and
the public. In addition, it shows how the battle conditioned the
University of Illinois before that institution even opened.

The democratic ferment which permeated the United States
as well as Europe starting in the late 1820's was basic among the
influences which transformed the higher as well as the lower learning in America. Andrew Jackson was elected to the presidency in
the year which produced the Yale Report, and "Old Hickory's"
triumph symbolized a new democratic era. The rise of the common
man gave a mighty impulse to the Jeffersonian belief that education
should be freely available to all ages and capacities of men. In no
sphere of activity was the demand for equality of opportunity more
intense than in education, for in a mobile and open society education was the most powerful weapon in the struggle for individual
betterment. During Jackson's first term spokesmen for the mechanics' and "workingmen's" groups in Pennsylvania, New York, and
New England began to denounce educational privilege as a fount
of political privilege. They insisted on the establishment of an effective system of public schools which would guarantee equal educational privilege for all. The belief that universal public schooling
was absolutely indispensable in a democracy gradually became a
leading characteristic of the social thought of the age, and by 1850
most northern states were making provision for a permanent system
of tax-supported common schools.

The ferment of change exerted a similar influence on higher
education. During the 1840's powerful voices began to insist on
realizing the promise contained in the earlier state university movement. They urged the democratization of educational opportunity
so that the producing as well as the professional classes could receive
advanced training, and equality of status between scientific and
utilitarian subjects on the one hand and those of the traditional curriculum on the other. Some educational reformers, notably the
Lazzaroni, a group discussed below, proposed a more elitist reconstruction of the higher learning in America. But it was the spokesmen for democratization of the nation's colleges who were the
strongest. They gained force in the land-grant movement and

realized the fruit of some two decades of effort in the Morrill Act of 1862.[2]

A second influence for a new kind of education was the revolt against the sectarian-classical college, a lingering remnant of the old aristocratic order, which the steady advance of democracy stimulated. The rising pressure evoked particularly noteworthy proposals from Francis Wayland and Henry P. Tappan, and the public response to their radically different solutions for the improvement of higher education showed the democratic leaven at work. A protégé of Eliphalet Nott and a prominent Baptist minister, Wayland built upon the abortive collegiate reforms of the 1820's when he began agitating for reconstruction of Brown University in 1842. Both a financial crisis brought on by declining enrollments and a tour of Europe convinced him that it was imperative to adapt higher education to contemporary American realities. In addition to repeating charges that the colleges encouraged superficiality and failed to produce classical scholars and mathematicians despite their emphasis on Greek, Latin, and mathematics, he declared that the colleges lost students and influence because they failed to furnish the education demanded by the people. "We have produced an article for which the demand is diminishing," he lamented. "We sell it at less than cost, and the deficiency is made up by charity. We give it away, and still the demand diminishes."[3] In Wayland's opinion, the main defect was the colleges' continued practice of training a small number for the learned professions at a time when steam, machinery, and commerce made the productive professions of primary importance. "What," he asked, "could Virgil and Horace and Homer and Demosthenes, with a little mathematics and natural philosophy, do towards developing the untold resources of this continent?"[4] The nation needed knowledge of all the emerging sciences in order to

[2] Rush Welter, *Popular Education and Democratic Thought in America* (New York, 1962), 45-73, 103-23; Allan Nevins, *The State Universities and Democracy* (Urbana, 1962), 16-22.

[3] Francis Wayland, *Report to the Corporation of Brown University, on Changes in the System of Collegiate Education, Read March 28, 1850* (Providence, 1850), 34. See also his *Thoughts on the Present Collegiate System in the United States* (Boston, 1842); and *The Education Demanded by the People of the United States* (Boston, 1855).

[4] Wayland, *Report to the Corporation of Brown*, 12-13.

survey its lands, construct its roads, build and navigate its ships, cultivate its soils, and establish its manufactures.

Wayland's solution lay in making education democratic, popular, and utilitarian. He praised the productive class — merchants, mechanics, manufacturers, and farmers — as the choicest part of the community and urged the colleges to supply these groups knowledge as they had supplied the learned professions. This new education would vastly increase national wealth. In 1850 Wayland asked his Corporation to make Brown serve the whole community and material welfare by initiating certain reforms. One was the elective system, which would permit every student to study "what he chose, all that he chose, and nothing but what he chose."[5] Another was the partial course. Students could take a few courses without working for a degree and obtain a certificate showing the proficiency attained in each. A third was enlargement of the curriculum by adding modern languages, policical economy, history, pedagogy, agriculture, law, and courses in applied chemistry and science. The ancient classics would merely have parity with other studies. These proposals, though unoriginal, voiced a growing popular demand. Although the Trustees adopted reforms designed to make Brown a national leader and solve its financial problem, the productive classes were not ready for Wayland's New System. Brown reverted to the old ways by the early 1860's.

Meanwhile, Tappan, another remarkable product of Eliphalet Nott's Union College, had published *University Education* (1851) after studying the advanced learning in Europe. He agreed with much of Wayland's analysis of the defects of the existing collegiate system, but disagreed with the solution offered by the President of Brown. Popularity was no criteria for higher education, especially since Americans could achieve material success without ever attending college. An appeal to the commercial spirit would cheapen the colleges and create distaste for study. Moreover, American youth lacked the preparation to use the elective system wisely. Tappan opposed Wayland's idea of uniting a university, a college, and commercial, manufacturing, and agricultural schools in one institution. In addition, he doubted the value of agricultural and commercial colleges, however they might be developed.

[5] *Ibid.*, 51.

Tappan's main contribution was neither in criticizing the ante-bellum college nor in exposing as meretricious many collegiate re-forms that became popular. It was rather in insisting that the true question was what the people needed, not what they wanted, and in describing that need. In Tappan's view, the overhauling of the entire system of American education depended upon the establish-ment of universities which embraced a philosophic conception of education such as that which animated the German educational sys-tem. This architectonic idea aimed at developing the capacities of the mind without regard for the mere utilities of life. Ideally, edu-cation should cultivate all the faculties, preparing individuals for the responsibilities and duties of men rather than merely training them for a trade or profession. When education took the lower ground of professional preparation it failed to develop full strength of mind and to communicate the highest principles of action. When it took the higher ground and developed active intellectual power relating to any possible course of life, it aimed directly at both. Therefore true education was practical, as the country would see when genuine universities became operative and cast "dignity, grace, and a resist-less charm about scholarship and the scholar."[6] Not everyone could obtain such a thorough education, but universities did more for mankind by sending forth a few men of learning rather than a multitude of superficial graduates. In this way they could raise a counter influence against the prevalent commercial spirit and demagogism.

Wayland and Tappan presented the nation with sharply de-fined alternatives, and the reception accorded their proposals was significant for the future. Called to head the University of Michigan in 1852, Tappan tried to erect a Prussian-style school and to inte-grate it with the entire educational system of the state. His ideas and aristocratic manners offended the raw democracy of the Mid-west, which drove him from office. "Tappan was the largest figure of a man that ever appeared on the Michigan campus," said one of his successors. "And he was stung to death by gnats!"[7] Wayland, despite his temporary eclipse at Brown, gave new vitality to ideas

[6] Henry P. Tappan, *University Education* (New York, 1851), 69.
[7] Charles M. Perry, *Henry Philip Tappan: Philosopher and University President* (Ann Arbor, 1933), 274.

that inspired the land-grant colleges. John M. Gregory, Illinois' first President, carefully assimilated the ideas of his fellow Baptist, although he also observed Tappan at close range in Michigan in the 1850's. Gregory imitated Wayland when he devised the first curriculum for the University of Illinois, and his act symbolized the preference of most Americans.

Demand for industrial education was a third ingredient of the land-grant movement. It rested both on a revolution in pedagogical theories and on material tranformations taking place in the country. The older ideas associated with Bacon, Comenius, Locke, and Rousseau were one source of the intellectual change. To shift mankind's interest from abstract speculation to observation of nature, Bacon had emphasized familiarity between the mind and things and sought a union between the experimental and rational faculty. Locke built on these foundations by holding that sense perceptions furnished the mind, and Rousseau contributed by insisting that "education comes to us from nature, from men, or from things." These doctrines strongly affected educational practice by the early nineteenth century. Pestalozzi was one leading exemplar in Europe, and the American disciples were numerous. Although the manual-labor school movement in the United States did not attempt to unite learning with labor for pedagogical reasons, the early agricultural and mechanical trades schools actually combined them.[8]

Another ideological source of industrial education was the romantic revolt against eighteenth-century empiricism and sensationalism. Emerson's *Nature* (1836) sounded the manifesto for those who sought liberation from older beliefs. Transcendentalists valued the truths about the visible world which the understanding apprehended, but they held that the senses did not reach the higher laws governing the spirit, of which Nature was the outward symbol. Reason or intuition rather than the ordinary understanding grasped this truth. This a priori school of thought regarded book-learning and inductive science as suspect. Emerson's declaration in "The American Scholar" that books were for a scholar's idle times implied

[8] Robert R. Rusk, *The Doctrines of the Great Educators* (rev. ed., London, 1955), chs. v-ix; Basil Willey, *The Seventeenth Century Background: Studies in the Thought of the Age in Relation to Poetry and Religion* (London, 1934), 24-25.

that scholarship was at war with Nature, and some leaders of the land-grant movement gave fuller vent to the anti-intellectual strain in romanticism.

Nevertheless, Transcendentalist ideas stimulated industrial education. Thoreau illustrated the connection with his assertion, "We reason from our hands to our head."[9] But Emerson more than anyone else inspired the significant shift in American culture from a neo-classical emphasis on the sublime and the beautiful to a stress on "the near, the low, the common," and this shift lay at the heart of the transition from the old-time college with its classical curriculum to the land-grant college with its practical orientation. "What," Emerson asked, "would we really know the meaning of?" His reply justified the preoccupation with familiar everyday things which early characterized schools founded on the Morrill Act:

The meal in the firkin; the milk in the pan; the ballad in the street; the news of the boat; the glance of the eye; the form and the gait of the body; — show me the ultimate reason of these matters; show me the sublime presence of the highest spiritual cause lurking, as always it does lurk, in these suburbs and extremities of nature . . . and the shop, the plough, and the ledger referred to the like cause by which light undulates and poets sing; — and the world lies no longer a dull miscellany and lumber-room, but has form and order; there is no trifle, there is no puzzle, but one design unites and animates the farthest pinnacle and the lowest trench.[10]

The clamor for industrial education also arose from deep-seated economic forces at work. Even though the vast majority of people still lived on the land, the agricultural era of American history began drawing to a close about the time Turner's 1851 address galvanized a few Illinois farmers. Perceptive agrarians had realized even earlier that husbandmen had to abandon ancestral ways in which superstition still figured prominently for an education that would enable them to offset Nature's niggardliness. Moreover, steam, iron, railroads, factories, and national labor unions adumbrated the shape

[9] As quoted in F. O. Matthiessen, *American Renaissance: Art and Expression in the Age of Emerson and Whitman* (New York, 1941), 87.
[10] *The Complete Works of Ralph Waldo Emerson* (12 vols., New York, 1883-1906), I, 110-11. The quotation is from "The American Scholar." See also the Introduction to *Emerson on Education: Selections,* ed. Howard Mumford Jones (New York, 1966).

of the future. The system of training apprentices was no longer adequate to national needs. The productive classes required an education that would fit them for novel tasks. These developments must be seen in relation to a fourth factor which profoundly affected higher education.

This was the new role of science and technology in American culture which emerged about 1830. American science was maturing rapidly at this time. Increasing specialization and greater vocational opportunity fostered the growth of a small class of professionals, men like Benjamin Silliman, Joseph Henry, James Dwight Dana, and Alexander Dallas Bache. Their achievements widened the gap between pure and applied science. These men sought to discover the laws by which Nature operated. The public, however, merely wanted practical benefits from science. Businessmen, industrialists, and most agriculturists failed to see the value of basic research and refused to support pure science. The country's insistence on realizing the benefits promised by mastery over Nature resulted from a fundamental shift in modes of thought which occurred about the time Jackson entered the White House. Earlier, the scientific rationalism of the Enlightenment had held that the unity and coherence of the physical universe registered on man's senses and demonstrated Nature's perfections. According to this doctrine, Mind could aesthetically appreciate the sublimity of Nature and enjoy its utilities without trying to subdue a universe considered benevolent and moral. Now, however, the conviction that Mind would actively conquer Nature replaced the older belief that Mind was primarily the passive spectator of Nature's simple plan.[11]

As a people, Americans preferred to borrow their basic science from Europe while enjoying the fruits of technology. That word was still unknown in 1829 when Jacob Bigelow, a Harvard professor, used it in *Elements of Technology*. Perry Miller concluded that Bigelow's book describing the application of the sciences to the useful arts declared the independence of the materialistic and utilitarian nineteenth century from the ideological and benevolent eigh-

[11] Richard H. Shryock, "American Indifference to Basic Science During the Nineteenth Century," *Archives Internationales d'Histoire des Sciences*, V (1948), 50-65; Perry Miller, *The Life of the Mind in America: From the Revolution to the Civil War* (New York, 1965), 269-87.

teenth century. The rise in the number of patents awarded, from 437 in 1837 to 4,778 in 1860, underscored that point. The public praised major technological triumphs which promised mastery over Nature. They accorded the telegraph unreserved enthusiasm, and Rufus Clark's 1848 address on the *Agency of Steam Power in Promoting Civilization and Christianity* demonstrated reverent confidence in the beneficial capacity of applied science. Moreover, the spread of Jacksonian democracy facilitated the belief that pure science was elegant and snobbish, applied science practical and homespun. This anti-intellectual strain was the property of no single area or class. In the year of Jackson's first inauguration, Joseph Story of the Harvard Law School told the Boston Mechanics' Institute that "the superior attachment to practical science over merely speculative science was the outstanding characteristic of the age."[12] The future Supreme Court Justice promised that factory laborers would henceforth instruct the scientists rather than vice versa.

The increased importance of science and technology and the advent of a new economy based on productivity and industrialization spurred the establishment of schools where applied science was paramount. It led also to the introduction of science into collegiate curricula. The U.S. Military Academy, reorganized after the War of 1812, remained exemplary as a seat of scientific and technical training until midcentury. It was the nation's only source of trained engineers until after 1824, when Stephen van Rensselaer founded at Troy, New York, the school that became Rensselaer Polytechnic Institute. The aristocratic patron anticipated the land-grant college in his wish to help the lower classes improve their material condition by teaching them "the application of science to the common purposes of life," and by preparing teachers who could instruct "the sons and daughters of farmers and mechanics . . . in the application of experimental chemistry, philosophy, and natural history, to agriculture, domestic economy, the arts, and manufactures."[13] Until his death in 1842, the gifted Amos Eaton made Rensselaer famous

[12] Miller, *Life of the Mind,* 289, 291-92, 310; A. Hunter Dupree, *Science in the Federal Government: A History of Policies and Activities to 1940* (Cambridge, Mass., 1957), 47.
[13] Palmer C. Ricketts, *History of Rensselaer Polytechnic Institute, 1824-1914* (3rd ed., New York, 1914), 9.

for educational innovation. The school introduced the first civil engineering curriculum and led students by a variety of methods from the study of practical applications and systematic field work to knowledge of basic principles.

The pluralistic system of American higher education permitted an advance in science, although religious suspicions made most sectarian colleges reluctant to admit it into the curriculum. The largest and most reputable Eastern institutions were the friendliest to science, and yet the careers of Benjamin Silliman and Louis Agassiz show that they were also religious. Yale initiated a program in applied agricultural science in 1846 which developed into the Sheffield Scientific School. Harvard used a gift intended for training engineers to found the Lawrence Scientific School, which opened in 1847 with an undergraduate curriculum leading to a B.S. degree. Agassiz joined the Harvard faculty in that year and made the School a center for geological and zoological study. The precedents at Rensselaer, Sheffield, and Lawrence stimulated at least nine other institutions to introduce some type of separate scientific department in the 1850's, and at least 25 more in the following decade.[14]

Prominent scientists attempted in these same years to create central scientific institutions, and their efforts had far-reaching implications for the land-grant movement. The growing maturity of science created a need for effective national institutions to integrate and foster the work of practitioners scattered throughout the country in colleges and federal or state government positions. The older voluntary associations by which private sponsors tried to fill this role were no longer adequate to the task. Even in earlier days the American Philosophical Society, which Franklin had been instrumental in founding at Philadelphia in 1743, and the American Academy of Arts and Sciences, established at Boston in 1780, had fallen short of the national role to which they consciously aspired. New learned organizations therefore arose, the most important being

[14] Russell H. Chittenden, *History of the Sheffield Scientific School of Yale University, 1846-1922* (2 vols., New Haven, 1928), I, 21-74; Samuel Eliot Morison, *Three Centuries of Harvard, 1636-1936* (Cambridge, Mass., 1936), 279-80; Frederick Rudolph, *The American College and University: A History* (New York, 1962), 232-33, 246.

the American Association for the Advancement of Science, organized at Philadelphia in 1848 by broadening an assembly of geologists and naturalists. More democratic than the older groups, the
AAAS sought to unite and to give stronger impetus to all interested
practitioners of science and to give more systematic direction to
scientific research.

However, the best minds realized that private patronage of
science could not reach the problem. Only the government could
foster and coordinate certain sciences upon which public welfare
depended. The government was in fact the leading sponsor of science by the 1840's. Fifteen states had appropriated public funds
for geological surveys by the middle of that decade, and others were
on the verge of doing so for the agricultural, commercial, and industrial rewards these explorations promised. Moreover, a federal scientific establishment had arisen by 1840, its most important component being the U.S. Coast Survey. But in theory the national
scientific establishment comprised only temporary agencies. The
federal government acknowledged no more responsibility for fostering science than for maintaining a national university.[15]

The problem of a burgeoning science as well as competing
proposals for improving the country's intellectual and cultural institutions explain why James Smithson's bequest precipitated a ten-
year debate in Congress. An English devotee of science who had
been snubbed in his native land because of illegitimacy, Smithson
willed a legacy of more than $500,000 to the United States to found
at Washington "an Establishment for the increase and diffusion of
knowledge among men."[16] Congress overrode opponents of centralized government to accept the bequest, but the ensuing conflict over
use of this money reflected wide differences as to what knowledge
was of most worth. Various objectives briefly held the stage in early
years of debate: a national university featuring postgraduate instruction; a national observatory, which John Quincy Adams single-
mindedly urged; and an agricultural experiment station. Proponents of a big museum dominated discussion for a few years after

[15] Ralph S. Bates, *Scientific Societies in the United States* (New York, 1945),
73-77 and *passim;* Dupree, *Science in the Federal Government,* 46-65.
[16] George Brown Goode, ed., *The Smithsonian Institution, 1846-1896: The
History of Its First Half Century* (Washington, 1897), 20.

1840. Led by Secretary of the Navy Joel R. Poinsett, they wanted the Smithsonian Institution to receive collections from government exploring expeditions and to operate under the National Institution for the Promotion of Science. This amateur scientific organization had pretensions of being a national society. But it was essentially a private group of prominent Washington residents and thus not responsible to public control. When Poinsett's circle did not capture the prize, powerful advocates of a noble national library tried to do so, as did proponents of a national normal school.

The act of 1846 chartering the Smithsonian Institution compromised conflicting interests, and postponed resolution of the dispute to the future. The choice of Joseph Henry as Secretary by the Board of Regents, which included officials from the three branches of the federal government, determined the outcome. A Princeton physicist whose discoveries in electricity and electromagnetism vied for honors with those of Faraday, Henry insisted that the Smithsonian serve all mankind rather than only Americans, and he regarded the increase and diffusion of new knowledge resulting from original research as the best means of doing so. Henry made the Smithsonian a great center of science. The presence of the Institution and the debate over it were preconditions for the land-grant colleges.[17]

Turner, out in Illinois, looked to the Smithsonian as a great beacon of national light. But Eastern leaders of the scientific community were not satisfied that it met the need for a central agency. The clique known as the Lazzaroni (a name borrowed from Neapolitan beggars) formulated a program that looked toward creation of a national academy of science and a true national university. The Lazzaroni were mainly government and academic scientists who lived in several cities, especially Washington and Cambridge, Massachusetts. Their leader was Benjamin Franklin's great-grandson, Alexander Dallas Bache. Since 1843 Bache had been Director of the U.S. Coast Survey, the most important activity in the federal scientific establishment. He made the Survey a genuinely national agency by enlisting the aid of leading American scientists, and as a regent he was instrumental in securing Henry's appointment to

[17] *Ibid.*, 25-62; Dupree, *Science in the Federal Government*, 79-90.

direct the Smithsonian. Bache's position, his talents, and his personality made him strategically situated to direct the politics of science.[18]

In his presidential address before the American Association for the Advancement of Science in 1851, Bache enunciated the Lazzaroni's goal of a national academy of science. After tracing the history of national science organizations he observed that an institution of science supplementary to existing ones was needed to guide public opinion in scientific matters. The legislative and executive branches of government were increasingly being invoked to decide questions which belonged to scientific rather than to political tribunals. Recommendations from a scientific council would both relieve the government of embarrassment and insure the progress of science.[19]

In addition to such an academy, political spokesmen of the scientific community wanted the federal government to aid in establishing a national university. They desired an institution patterned after the University of Berlin with a series of graduate faculties. Although they looked to Germany, the Lazzaroni were strong nationalists who yearned for an *American* center of learning. They hoped to raise the level of democracy by creating a university which would foster intellectual and moral rather than material and physical excellence. They envisioned a research-oriented university which would bring together all the powerful minds of the country. Apart from Bache, vocal proponents of the idea were Louis Agassiz, Benjamin Apthorp Gould, and Benjamin Peirce of Harvard.[20] These men hoped to convert the country's oldest college into its first national university. To accomplish their end, they were ready to remove colleagues who stood in their way and to secure appointments to the Cambridge center for themselves and other prominent

[18] Merle M. Odgers, *Alexander Dallas Bache: Scientist and Educator, 1806-1867* (Philadelphia, 1947); Dupree, *Science in the Federal Government*, 115-48; Dupree, "The Morrill Act and Science," unpublished MS. furnished to me by the author.
[19] American Association for the Advancement of Science, *Proceedings*, VI (Washington, 1852), xli-lx.
[20] Bache, "A National University," *American Journal of Education*, I (May, 1856), 477-79; Gould, "An American University," *American Journal of Education*, II (Sept., 1856), 265-93; Peirce, *Working Plan for the Foundation of a University* (Cambridge, Mass., 1856).

scientists. Thus the Lazzaroni ardently supported a federal grant for higher education. They labored for subsidy from the national government at the same time that others sought land-grant colleges, but their reasons differed substantially from those which inspired the industrial education movement. The Congress which passed the Morrill Act also created the National Academy of Sciences in 1863.

The agricultural community provided the main impetus for the Morrill Act, and was a fifth force behind the reconstruction of higher education. Agriculture, which had long been regarded more as the natural state of mankind than as a mere means of livelihood, dominated American industry before the Civil War. But despite persistence of the pastoral ideal and Jefferson's exaltation of rural virtue, it became apparent in the early years of the Republic that God's chosen people confronted serious new problems. Criminally wasteful husbandry created the fear that population would outrun productivity. "Our country is nearly ruined. We certainly have drawn out of the earth three fourths of the vegetable matter it contained," warned one writer about 1812. "Forbear, oh forbear matricide, not for futurity, not for God's sake, but for your own sake."[21] These apprehensions, which no doubt went deeper in older eastern areas than on the western frontier, permitted nineteenth-century science to make its most effective appeal in agriculture.

A few perceptive persons concluded that the land would not part with its treasure until intellect percolated the soil. Hence leaders of the agricultural societies formed at the turn of the century began to promote theoretical science as a means of making reluctant Nature more bountiful. They prodded the rural masses to follow their lead, but the average dirt farmer was mired in tradition and refused to do so. He had much to justify his hostility, for agricultural science was just beginning to divorce itself from speculative philosophy. Many theories enunciated on the subject were unsound, and science did not demonstrate its capacity to improve husbandry until the 1840's. Europeans paved the way, and Justus von Liebig was the great experimenter who applied the laws of organic chemistry to practical farm problems. His *Organic*

[21] As quoted in Albert Lowther Demaree, *The American Agricultural Press, 1819-1860*, Columbia University Studies in the History of Agriculture, No. 8 (New York, 1941), 5-6; see also Miller, *Life of the Mind*, 314-15.

Chemistry in Its Applications to Agriculture and Physiology (1840) was a landmark. A translation of that book and later volumes by the German met a ready reception in the United States. In 1841 the U.S. Patent Office called for application of chemistry to agriculture. Decades passed, however, before most rural people realized that science could in fact improve their condition.[22]

Meanwhile, both agricultural science and education failed to make headway. Agricultural journalism came into existence in 1819, and editors of farm papers were prominent in advocating the application of science to the improvement of husbandry. Since science columns long remained unpopular with rural readers, the farm press joined others in urging formal education as the path to betterment. Robert Gardiner established the first exclusively agricultural school at Gardiner, Maine, in 1821. The Gardiner Lyceum and similar academies combined farm labor with a general education biased toward the natural sciences. This venture at the secondary-school level proved premature, and a few private colleges — the pathmakers were Rensselaer and Washington (later Trinity) College in Connecticut in 1824 — introduced agricultural studies alongside their other programs. Failure of this collegiate undertaking lay behind agriculturists' attempts to capture the Smithsonian legacy in the next decade. More promising for the future was the idea of a separate state agricultural college which appeared early in the nineteenth century. Simeon DeWitt of New York publicly enunciated such a plan in 1819, and Jesse Buel labored for it in the New York legislature and in his farm journals for years.[23]

The agricultural community became well organized to pursue its objectives in the 1840's. The agricultural societies became the

[22] Professor John W. Webster of Harvard brought out the first American edition of the 1840 work at Cambridge, Mass., the following year. Another American edition with the word "organic" omitted from the title was published in New York in 1849. Meanwhile, three American publishers almost simultaneously reprinted the London edition of Liebig's *Animal Chemistry, or Organic Chemistry in Its Applications to Physiology and Pathology* (1842). American editions of other books by Liebig appeared in 1848, 1855, 1856, and 1863. See Forest Ray Moulton, ed., *Liebig and After Liebig: A Century of Progress in Agricultural Chemistry* (Washington, 1942), 1-2. See also Dupree, *Science in the Federal Government*, 111.

[23] Demaree, *The American Agricultural Press*, 51-54; Alfred Charles True, *A History of Agricultural Education in the United States, 1785-1925*, U.S. Department of Agriculture, Misc. Pub. No. 36 (Washington, 1929), 35-43, 46-48.

source of a demand for federal agriculture about the time the U.S. Patent Office program for farmers proved inadequate. In contrast to the societies founded earlier along literary and learned lines, the new ones copied the plan of Elkanah Watson. They featured an annual fair and strongly appealed to most farmers. Hundreds of such societies arose at the state and local level in the 1840's, sometimes with state aid and alongside state boards of agriculture. Their burgeoning growth inevitably revived the old idea of a national agricultural society. A group that met in 1841 failed to realize this purpose, but a decade later Marshall P. Wilder of Massachusetts initiated a call for a national agricultural convention. Delegates met in the Smithsonian Institution in 1852 and organized the U.S. Agricultural Society. At the time there were about 300 state and county societies, a number that rose to more than 900 before the decade ended. These organizations became the mainspring behind unrelenting pressure to secure a system of agricultural schools, experiment stations, and a separate federal agricultural bureau.[24]

Men who traveled to Scotland, England, France, or Germany for advanced training returned to commanding roles in the struggle for improvement. Such persons were Evan Pugh, who took a doctorate at Göttingen and then studied at Rothamsted in England, and John P. Norton, John Addison Porter, and Samuel W. Johnson, the last three of Yale's Sheffield Scientific School. The Yale trio especially influenced the institutionalization of agricultural research. In Scotland, Norton observed that the Agricultural Chemistry Society's research laboratory found it impossible to rely on data furnished by farmers who conducted home trials. The ordinary husbandman lacked the training or interest to make him a reliable investigator. Although Scottish chemists concluded by the mid-1840's that an agricultural laboratory should devote itself solely to research without connection with a farmers' organization or a university, Norton tirelessly urged the establishment of agricultural colleges which pos-

[24] Bates, *Scientific Societies in the United States,* 58-60; Demaree, *The American Agricultural Press,* 198-201; Lyman Carrier, "The United States Agricultural Society, 1852-1860: Its Relation to the Origin of the United States Department of Agriculture and the Land Grant Colleges," *Agricultural History,* XI (Oct., 1937), 278-88; Dupree, *Science in the Federal Government,* 112-13.

sessed experimental farms and conducted research — in effect, college-connected experiment stations. He inaugurated at Yale in 1848 a two-month course for practical farmers which tried to unite theory with practice. Porter, his successor, arranged a short winter course of lectures on agricultural science in 1860 which attracted 500 farmers to New Haven. Meanwhile, Johnson had observed on a visit to Saxony in 1854 what some Germans had done in the light of Scottish experience. At Moeckern they had developed a state-chartered, tax-supported research station which combined a laboratory directed by a chemist with a farm superintended by an experienced agriculturist. Johnson became a leading exponent of government-sponsored agricultural research stations without collegiate affiliation. However, these men and other advanced thinkers were far ahead of the rank and file in the agricultural community. The gap between the two groups vitally affected the land-grant college struggle and thus the early schools themselves.[25]

These advances intensified interest in agricultural education in the 1850's, when the apparent limitations of private and state colleges spurred a demand for federal subsidy for the purpose. The Farmers' College organized by Freeman Grant Cary near Cincinnati in 1846 ran into financial trouble in the 1850's. Cary, a prominent advocate of industrial universities, turned to Washington for relief. In New York, Harrison Howard's plan to combine manual labor with education in agriculture and other subjects attracted the enthusiastic support of Horace Greeley, left-wing reformers, and businessmen. Although the People's College secured a charter in 1853, it later met reverses which required the aid of a millionaire philanthropist before the promoters could lay the cornerstone in 1858. In these same years Edmund Ruffin and Philip St. George Cocke of Virginia outlined plans for agricultural education which essentially anticipated the land-grant college. The New York legislature chartered a state agricultural college in 1853; Pennsylvania, Michigan, and Maryland did likewise in 1854, 1855, and 1856 respectively. Institutions in the latter three states began operating

[25] H. C. Knoblauch, E. M. Law, W. P. Meyer, *et al.*, *State Agricultural Experiment Stations: A History of Research Policy and Procedure*, U.S. Department of Agriculture, Misc. Pub. No. 904 (Washington, 1962), 5-17, 19-21; Chittenden, *Sheffield Scientific School*, 42, 43-45, 64, 89-90.

shortly thereafter, but the agricultural colleges incorporated in Macoupin and Putnam counties by the Illinois General Assembly in 1851 and 1853 never advanced beyond the paper stages. All these schools failed to flourish because rural folk could not appreciate their value. Farm leaders realized that private and state aid were insufficient to bring about the improvement they deemed imperative, and so they turned to the federal government for aid.[26]

By the early 1850's, then, multiple forces were transforming the country's intellectual and cultural life. The movement for industrial education was only part of the attempt to adapt American higher learning to new ideas and material conditions, and that effort was in turn but one aspect of a larger social reconstruction. Illinois was a latecomer to the national struggle for betterment, for the rural frontier was less a source of ideological innovation than the Atlantic seaboard, which was more populous and in closer touch with Europe. But when the Midwest felt the winds of reform, Illinois threw itself into the battle. By no means the sole influence, Jonathan B. Turner was nevertheless the energizing spirit behind the land-grant movement in the prairie commonwealth.

Turner was born in 1805 on a rocky farm near Templeton in western Massachusetts.[27] He went to New Haven at the age of 22 and spent two years in preparatory study before entering Yale, where he received a traditional classical education. In 1833 he cut his senior year short and left with President Day's blessing for Illinois College in Jacksonville. He served 15 years in this frontier reflection of Yale, but was miscast as a professor of rhetoric and ancient languages and resigned under pressure.

A restless visionary with a tendency to fanaticism, Turner was far more than an educational reformer. He had been reared in a Congregational family that had no "saving knowledge" of Christ and in a town that was slipping into Unitarianism.[28] His older brother Asa reacted by entering the Congregational ministry, and

---

[26] Earle D. Ross, *Democracy's College: The Land-Grant Movement in the Formative Stage* (Ames, Iowa, 1942), 20-34.

[27] Carriel, *The Life of Jonathan Baldwin Turner,* is the best source on his life, but to be used with caution. My page references are to the 1961 edition, hereinafter cited as *J. B. Turner.*

[28] George F. Magoun, *Asa Turner: A Home Missionary Patriarch* (Boston, 1889), 23, 26-27, 29-30, 38.

Turner himself became a Congregational minister in Illinois, where he had charge of two churches for seven years. But what he admired most in Congregationalism was its flexibility. The autonomy afforded each church gave him freedom to develop his liberal views.[29] Turner had been at Yale when Nathaniel W. Taylor developed a theology that emphasized human rather than divine agency in salvation, and he himself often sounded like a western echo of Emerson and Thoreau. Casting his lot with the party of Hope, he denounced lingering vestiges of Calvinism ("the bastard and leprous progeny of the old Papists and despots of Europe") for a liberal American faith which he called the creed of Christ.[30]

Religion was Turner's abiding and central interest, and he believed that his many writings on the subject would be his lasting monument. In fact, this concern was the wellspring of most causes he agitated — mesmerism, spiritualism, mental telepathy, psychiatry, Mormonism, universal law, race questions, monetary philosophy, mechanical inventions, inland waterways, removal of the national capital, and opposition to slavery. Turner trenchantly commented on slavery and other political issues in the *Illinois Statesman*, which he launched in 1843. To save space for editorial opinion he asked readers to imagine as actually taking place "a certain due proportion" of fires, thefts, and murders.[31] Unsatisfactory *news* service led to the paper's demise in 1844. Meanwhile, the courageous professor had offended so many patrons that he found it expedient to withdraw from Illinois College in 1848. For the next several years he devoted himself to horticultural, entomological, and agronomic experimentation, published his findings, and proved that the Osage Orange hedge could be cultivated so as to provide suitable material for fencing the Illinois prairie.

Turner plunged headlong into the crusade for universal education in the 1830's and demonstrated at that time a penchant for thinking in national terms. Later he focused his attention on agricultural education, only to find himself locked in combat for ex-

[29] Theodore Calvin Pease, *The Frontier State, 1818-1848*, The Centennial History of Illinois, II (Chicago, 1922), 441.
[30] Carriel, *J. B. Turner*, 50.
[31] Franklin W. Scott, ed., *Newspapers and Periodicals of Illinois, 1814-1879*, Collections of the Illinois State Historical Library, VI (n.p., 1910), lxxiv.

isting resources with a formidable adversary — the normal-school advocates. A system of common schools required a multitude of teachers, and their training was essential to the completion of democracy's foundations. Turner allied with the normal-school movement out of necessity and as a transitional stage on the road to an industrial university. Thus at different times he emphasized the various lines along which education advanced in Illinois and the nation. Despite his eccentricities, one constant underlay Turner's educational evangelism — a romantic impulse which drove him to seek perfection. This strain reached a peak during the land-grant agitation when Turner declared that industrial education would create a true farmer,

a man who has such an intimate knowledge of all the hidden processes of nature . . . such fullness, breadth, amplitude and power of mind on all practical subjects of industry, morals, policy and faith as would cause all the school-men and professors of our day to hang their heads and blush for shame in his presence — a hard-handed, able-bodied, strong-minded, whole-souled, all-knowing, all-conquering man, worthy of himself and of the God who made him such — not a mere machine to hold plows and feed pigs. This and this only is the true farmer when the millenium [sic] of labor shall come — as much above all other professions in the natural and necessary development and vigor of his intellect, as he now is in the natural health and vigor of his body or as farmer Adam was before the fall above that same fallen farmer now.

When a true mechanic had similarly arisen, the lie would be given to the prevalent humbuggery that industrial pursuits were not favorable to the highest intellectual and moral development, "and the whole world will find out at last that intelligent labor is the friend not the foe of mind, and that Almighty God was not mistaken when he put the first man in the garden instead of the academy, and made his own son a carpenter instead of a Rabbi."[32] These lofty visions led Turner to assert that the progress of learning would leave "no secret of nature or art we cannot find out; no disease of man or

[32] Jonathan B. Turner, "The Millenium [sic] of Labor," an October, 1853, address at the State Fair, reported in Illinois State Agricultural Society, *Transactions*, I (Springfield, 1855), 59. R. W. B. Lewis, *The American Adam: Innocence, Tragedy, and Tradition in the Nineteenth Century* (Chicago, 1955); Henry Nash Smith, *Virgin Land: The American West as Symbol and Myth* (Cambridge, Mass., 1950); and Leo Marx, *The Machine in the Garden: Technology and the Pastoral Idea in America* (New York, 1964) describe the intellectual and cultural context which Turner reflected.

beast we cannot understand; no evil we cannot remedy; no obstacle we cannot surmount; nothing that lies in the power of man to do or to understand, that cannot be both understood and done."[33] His utopianism indelibly stamps him as a man of his rather than our times, and history has dealt harshly with the naive faith he cherished.

Turner gained an early if limited prominence in Illinois as an advocate of tax-supported public schools. But his ideas about scientific agricultural education lagged behind those advanced by such men as Norton. In 1848 he exposed his folly ("I know of no one," he said, "who has a greater capital in that line to spare than myself")[34] by recommending that an agricultural school be annexed to an existing classical college. He thought that chairs of chemistry and botany might be filled by someone already on the faculty, but he proposed the addition of a professor of "the green earth" who would make agricultural and horticultural experiments on a farm attached to the college.[35] At the time he was not alone in desiring to hitch agriculture to the old-time education. Ideas on the subject were developing rapidly, however, and within a few years he recanted.

Turner did this in the address of November 18, 1851, which clearly marks his debut as a leader of the Midwestern industrial education movement. The occasion was an invitation extended him by the Buel Institute, an agricultural society of nine northern Illinois counties which called a convention at Granville in order to secure the establishment of an agricultural university and thus to block the renewed effort of the private colleges to divide the College and Seminary funds among themselves.[36] As the featured

[33] *Prairie Farmer*, Oct. 27, 1866, 267.
[34] Turner to President Jonathan Blanchard of Knox College, [1848], as quoted in Powell, *Movement for Industrial Education*, 357.
[35] *Ibid.*, 357-62.
[36] No good evidence substantiates the assertion that Turner first formulated his plan in an address at Griggsville on May 13, 1850. The speech allegedly given at Griggsville is identical with the one delivered at Granville. In the early 1850's Turner himself referred to his plan as the one enunciated in the latter year: "As regards *my plan* as it is called, but as I should prefer more properly to say the plan of the Granville Convention . . ." is a good example of his contemporaneous statements. See Turner to Bronson Murray, Dec. 1, 1852, Burt E. Powell Papers, Box 7, University of Illinois Archives. On this confused subject, see Carriel, *J. B. Turner*, 68-94; Powell, *Movement for Industrial Education*, 17n; and *Prairie Farmer*, Aug., 1852, 383.

speaker at the Putnam County Farmers' Convention, Turner combined strong diatribe against the traditional college with vigorous
espousal of reform. He asserted that society was divided into a
small professional class whose educational needs the existing colleges served well and a large industrial class which lacked an education specifically adapted to prepare them for their life pursuits.
He ridiculed the parallel course as a canoe launched alongside the
steamship of the regular college, one on which farmers and mechanics would not embark.

His proposed remedy drew heavily on other men's ideas. He
envisioned a national system of education, basic to which was "a
National Institute of Science, to operate as the great central luminary of the national mind, from which all minor institutions should
derive light and heat, and toward which they should, also, reflect
back their own."[37] Turner differed from Bache in thinking the
Smithsonian Institution adequate for this purpose. In addition,
Turner wanted a university for the industrial classes in each state.
These institutions were to cooperate with the Smithsonian and form
the apex of a system of public education in every commonwealth.
Although they were to stress the utilitarian, Turner would exclude
no type of practical or theoretical knowledge except the " 'organized
ignorance' found in the creeds of party politicians, and sectarian
ecclesiastics . . . mistaken by some for a species of knowledge."[38]
Turner treated the inclusion of a classical department as a question
of expediency which he was willing to have answered either way,
but he considered research in agriculture and the mechanic arts
mandatory. Annual experiments were to be conducted, and each
university was to have a museum to display models of useful im-
plements and machines and a branch patent office. Professors were
to be men of practical ability who would instruct mostly in winter
months. Commencement was to be State Fair on the campus —
a gala with exhibitions and lectures pertaining to practical pursuits.

For Turner, industrial universities were the only possible solution to the existing caste system and prerequisite to national eco-

[37] Jonathan B. Turner, *A Plan for an Industrial University for the State of Illinois, Submitted to the Farmers' Convention at Granville, Held November 18,
1851* (n.p., 1851), 9.
[38] *Ibid.*

nomic advancement. He had not considered how to realize a national system of state universities, however, and he therefore went
only as far as recommending establishment of an industrial university in Illinois. For this purpose Turner thought the federal aid
previously given in the College and Seminary funds was adequate.
But that grant had to be placed beyond the reach of party or sect
to insure that it would be wisely used. Turner proposed that the
Governor nominate to a board of trust five men who would elect
twelve additional members. This self-perpetuating body would be
responsible to the people for employing the existing endowment to
erect Illinois Industrial University.

Turner was more an agitator than an original thinker. He
lacked the social realism of Howard and Greeley, the scientific precision of Pugh and Johnson, the research and university ideals of
Bache and the Lazzaroni. The superb timing of his rhetorical onslaught was the key to its effectiveness.[39] His address marks the
emergence of an organized movement for industrial education in
Illinois. The assembled farmers approved Turner's plan and initiated a campaign to publicize and enlist support for it. They also
called another convention for Springfield to coincide with the legislative session in 1852. Despite sectarian educators who denounced
Turner as a dangerous visionary, many newspapers in Illinois commended the Granville Plan. It also caught the attention of agricultural intellectuals throughout the country who had long tried to
rouse the sluggish rural masses. A number of farm and horticultural
journals beyond Illinois gave Turner a sympathetic hearing. The
U.S. Patent Office, at the urging of Senator Stephen A. Douglas
and Congressman Richard Yates, reprinted the address in its annual report.[40]

Shortly after the Farmers' Convention, however, Turner modified the Granville Plan. The *Prairie Farmer* and attitudes it represented furnished the main incentive. This influential Chicago journal was the chief weapon in John S. Wright's spirited campaign to
improve life on the prairie. Wright, like Turner, emigrated to Illinois from Massachusetts in the early 1830's. The chief organizer

---

[39] Ross, *Democracy's College,* 38.
[40] *Report of the Commissioner of Patents for the Year 1851, Part II: Agriculture,*
33 Cong., 1 Sess., Senate Exec. Doc. No. 118 (Washington, 1852), 37-44.

of the Union Agricultural Society, he threw the Society's newspaper behind school reform in 1840. Three years later he became sole owner and appointed as editor J. Ambrose Wight, a Vermont emigrant with a passion for bringing religion and education to the frontier. They made the *Prairie Farmer* as much an educational as an agricultural journal, devoting it to their battle for public schools and a normal school. These goals attracted farmers who cared little for agricultural science and teachers who favored a normal school over an industrial university.[41]

Wright apparently came out publicly for a separate scientific agricultural university at the same time as Turner. In November, 1851, the *Prairie Farmer* said: "We think we can see what is needed. A sort of Scientific Agricultural University where agriculture and all its related sciences shall be thoroughly mastered in the same manner as law, or divinity, or medicine are now mastered in their respective educational institutions." Nevertheless, Wright wanted an agricultural normal school. He differed from Turner, who said at Granville that use of the College and Seminary funds for any purpose other than an industrial university illegally perverted them. Moreover, Wight found Turner's antisectarian thrusts especially offensive. Hence the *Prairie Farmer* did not print the Granville Plan. After Turner publicly criticized this lapse, Wight editorially commended Turner for defining the issue but urged Illinois to await the lead of older states in establishing industrial education. The *Prairie Farmer* said that an institution for the study of science bearing upon industrial arts would not aid all the people equally. It recommended that Illinois appropriate a small sum for a university and devote the College and Seminary funds to a normal school.[42]

Under the pressure of these events Turner changed the Granville Plan in two significant respects. He abandoned his belief that the existing sums derived from the federal government were adequate to his design. Apparently he reached this conclusion after failing to get the teachers of Illinois to agree to combine a normal

[41] Lloyd Lewis, *John S. Wright, Prophet of the Prairies* (Chicago, 1941), 56-61 and *passim*.
[42] *Prairie Farmer*, March, 1852, 105-6; June, 1852, 291. The November quotation is at p. 494.

school with an industrial school. Since teacher-training was likely to benefit from the College and Seminary funds, Turner made a new appeal for federal aid. To a communication on hedges published in the *Prairie Farmer* in March, 1852, he added: "And I am satisfied that if the farmers and their friends will now but exert themselves they can speedily secure for this State, and for each State in the Union, an appropriation of public lands adequate to create and endow in the most liberal manner, a general system of popular Industrial Education, more glorious in its design and more beneficent in its results than the world has ever seen before."[43]

The general precedent of land grants for education dated from 1787, and the 1840's were rife with suggestions to enlist federal support for science, agriculture, and education. President Alden Partridge of Norwich University in Vermont offered an impressive scheme in 1841. He petitioned Congress to appropriate $40,000,000 to be paid out of the proceeds of the sale of public lands for the purpose of establishing a national system of education to train practically useful men. Partridge appears to have made the first definite proposition that Congress distribute the *proceeds* of the sale of public lands to the states in proportion to their representation in Congress.[44] Seven years later John S. Skinner, a pioneer in agricultural journalism, petitioned the federal government for state subsidies to be used in founding schools for agriculture and the mechanic arts. Soon thereafter Marshall P. Wilder of Massachusetts urged that part of the *proceeds* of the sale of public lands be appropriated to improve agriculture, and on January 6, 1852, Governor Washington Hunt of New York had recommended that some *proceeds* from the sale of land for taxes be appropriated to establish an institution for the advancement of agricultural science and mechanic arts.[45] Turner urged Congress to grant for this purpose *public lands* themselves, and that is perhaps the extent of his original contribution to the Morrill Act.

[43] The quotation is at p. 114.
[44] "Memorial of Alden Partridge," 26 Cong., 2 Sess., House Exec. Doc. No. 69, II (Washington, [1841]), 4-5.
[45] "Memorial of J. S. Skinner," 30 Cong., 1 Sess., Senate Misc. Doc. No. 120 (Washington, 1848); *Prairie Farmer,* April, 1852, 170; *State of New York, Messages from the Governor, IV (1843-56),* ed. Charles Z. Lincoln (Albany, 1909), 604.

Second, Turner abandoned the emphasis on science and research in his 1851 address for a low utilitarianism that possessed wider appeal. The industrial convention which met at Springfield on June 8, 1852, endorsed the shift. Governor A. C. French informed the General Assembly which met in special session at the same time that the state's interest justified fostering science to promote agriculture. But he did not publicly support the Granville Plan, and he hoped that legislators would not overlook a normal school in disposing of the $149,678 in the College and Seminary funds.[46] John A. Kennicott presided over the gathering that aimed to secure this sum for an industrial school. A self-taught horticulturist and practicing physician who lived not far from Chicago, he regarded Turner's ideas as "God-like . . . the best thought of the 19th Century."[47] Kennicott admitted spokesmen of the Illinois colleges; they wanted the territorial land grant entrusted to "Regents of the Industrial University of Illinois" to support six itinerant professors who would teach practical subjects in existing sectarian schools. The friends of concentration defeated this proposal and then adopted a Memorial written by Turner which urged the legislature to use the available land-grant funds to meet the need of the industrial classes by founding one institution in which there should be a department of normal-school teaching. He omitted all reference to scientific agriculture, and asked that Illinois make a beginning on a scale to justify an appeal with other states to Congress for an appropriation of public lands for the purpose. The convention approved the Memorial, thus endorsing the idea of a new land grant and giving hostages to the normal-school people.[48]

This development spurred sectarian schoolmen's opposition to what they regarded as a visionary scheme of a mammoth manual-labor college, but it convinced Wright that Turner now aimed at providing good teachers for the common schools. The *Prairie Farmer* therefore found itself able by September to support the

[46] *Illinois Senate Journal* (1852), 9-10.
[47] As quoted in Powell, *Movement for Industrial Education,* 146.
[48] Jonathan B. Turner, *Industrial Universities for the People, Published in Compliance with Resolutions of the Chicago and Springfield Conventions. And Under the Industrial League of Illinois* (Jacksonville, 1853). Later references are to the text reproduced in Powell, *Movement for Industrial Education,* 365-426. On the Springfield convention, see Powell, 400-404.

"Turner Plan" as the normal-school idea. The journal urged use of the College and Seminary funds to establish a teacher-training institution. The addition of professors of practical agriculture and of mechanics would yield the industrial university advocated by Turner.[49] Although the plan failed to impress the state legislature, the proposal struck a responsive chord among proponents of agricultural science and education elsewhere. Congressman Yates brought the Granville address before the June convention of the U.S. Agricultural Society in Washington. In August, Horace Greeley, long an advocate of practical agricultural education, printed part of Turner's remarks with favorable comment in his New York *Daily Tribune*.[50] It is essential to note, however, that the Granville Plan had undergone major modification since its original statement in 1851.

Harsh and narrow utilitarianism emerged triumphant at the November convention held by industrial education leaders in Chicago. Bronson Murray of Ottawa, a native New Yorker who had spent two terms at Columbia College and practiced civil engineering before settling on 1,600 acres in Illinois, presided over the gathering. This convention admitted only professed friends of education for the producing classes and schoolteachers. After discussing the desirability of including the manual-labor system, phonetics, and co-education in the university, delegates approved the Granville Plan in general and announced that an essential feature was a department for educating common-school teachers. They emphasized that no person connected with the university was to be privileged or disprivileged by his political or religious opinions. In Turner's absence, the barbarian wing of educational reform viciously attacked the classics. Speakers asserted that it would *never* be necessary or expedient to teach the dead languages in the industrial university, and Seth Paine bitterly denounced "the incubus of the languages of Greece and Rome, sitting like an evil bird on the car of progress, and blighting the young intellect of the age — marrying it to the corruption of

[49] *Prairie Farmer*, Sept., 1852, 428-29, 442. See also the important letter from Samuel Adams to Turner, July 26, 1852, in the Rare Book Room, University of Illinois Library.
[50] Yates to Turner, June 25, 1852, Jonathan B. Turner Papers, Illinois Historical Survey, University of Illinois; Powell, *Movement for Industrial Education*, 38.

centuries, long since entombed, but constantly dragged from the sepulchre of the past, to blast the buds of promise in the present."[51]

Sniffing victory, delegates to the Chicago meeting prepared for it. They appointed a committee to devise a workable plan for a university and agreed to establish an Industrial League as the means of securing such an institution in Illinois. The membership certificate of the League bore illustrations of the Crystal Palace and the Smithsonian Institution. In addition, they decided to memorialize Congress for a land grant to endow industrial universities in every state. The conviction that their plan would prevail because true induced a buoyant optimism.[52]

A fourth industrial convention met at Springfield on January 4, 1853, in order to be on hand when the General Assembly might dispose of the College and Seminary funds. At this time Kennicott, Murray, and Turner helped organize the Illinois State Agricultural Society, which was thereafter an alter ego of the Industrial League in the campaign for an industrial university. In addition, the delegates adopted a Memorial in which Turner emphasized the need to imitate Europe in use of the state to promote polytechnic and agricultural schools for the purpose of insuring continued productivity. Acknowledging that common schools were the country's hope, the statement declared that a normal school was essential to an industrial university. The document petitioned the General Assembly to memorialize Congress for an appropriation of public lands valued at no less than $500,000 to each state to endow industrial universities. The total expenditure involved fell far below the amount proposed by Partridge. The universities established were to cooperate with each other and with the Smithsonian "for the more liberal and practical education of our industrial classes and their teachers, in their various pursuits for the production of knowledge and literature needful in those pursuits, and developing to the fullest and most perfect extent the resources of our soil and our arts, the virtue and intelligence of our people, and the true glory of our common country."[53] In early February, the General Assembly unanimously re-

[51] *Prairie Farmer*, Feb., 1853, 55.
[52] *Ibid.*, Jan., 1853, 5-6; Feb., 1853, 55-57, 60-61.
[53] "Memorial of the Industrial Convention of the State of Illinois," *Illinois Reports* (1853), 142.

solved to call upon Illinois' congressional delegation to seek passage
of a law donating land for these purposes.[54] The Memorial contained no reference to science and research, the foremost goals in
the program of the Lazzaroni, but nevertheless Illinois was the
first state to petition Congress for land grants to endow industrial
universities.

Since the Memorial was ahead of public opinion, the Industrial
League began a campaign to arouse support for their objectives
within and beyond Illinois. The League employed all the existing
means of persuasion, with Murray providing the money and Turner
the energy. Turner hired Reuben C. Rutherford to lecture and
authorized the gifted speaker to collect his $600 annual salary by
selling League memberships. Both men stumped the state. Turner's
foes — and he had many, for he engaged in many causes besides
education and never with moderation — set fire to his barn at
Jacksonville in an unsuccessful attempt to prevent him from addressing the Springfield State Fair in mid-October. Rutherford
found no subject less attractive to the popular mind than education.
The people refused to join any onslaught against the old-time denominational college, and feared the prospect of an industrial university without religion.[55]

In addition, the cause of the industrial university made little
headway because Illinois had finally turned to the task of establishing public schools. At a Bloomington convention devoted to this
cause late in 1853, spokesmen attacked Turner and organized the
Illinois State Teachers' Institute (later, the Illinois State Teachers'
Association, and now the Illinois Education Association). They
agreed to work for a free-school law, a normal school, and an office
of Superintendent of Public Instruction. Early the following year
the legislature created this position. Although friends pushed Turner for the job, Governor Joel A. Matteson appointed Ninian W.
Edwards, who alienated the Industrial League when he immedi-

---

[54] But the General Assembly changed the key clause to read: "for the more
liberal and practical education of our industrial classes and their teachers; a
liberal and varied education, adapted to the manifold wants of a practical and
enterprising people. . . ." *Illinois House Journal* (1853), 416; *Illinois Senate
Journal* (1853), 311.
[55] *Prairie Farmer*, Jan., 1855, 24-25; Powell, *Movement for Industrial Education*,
69-71, 135.

ately set out to advance the common schools and to secure a normal school to train teachers.

A year later the League sought to regain the initiative. Meeting at Springfield in January, 1855, it devised an ingenious proposal for joint sponsorship of a university by the state and a self-perpetuating group of practical educators. This draft bill named six Industrial Leaguers, including Turner, Murray, and Kennicott, to the original board of trustees, and provided for popular election of six more. The university would feature a normal-school department and include agricultural and mechanical departments, with others added later so as to offer education in "all useful practical literature and scientific knowledge." The framers also envisioned three funds to finance a university located in the center of the state. The six named trustees were privately to raise a donation fund of $20,000. The Seminary and College funds were to create a normal-school fund and a university fund respectively. As soon as the trustees had the donation fund in hand, the state was to pay $20,000 from the university fund for use by the agricultural and mechanical departments. For each additional $10,000 the charter trustees raised, the state would pay a like sum to the university until the College and Seminary funds stood empty. The draft bill explicitly provided that the privately raised donation fund was to support all expenses of agricultural and horticultural experimentation and that state funds were to support only instruction, never experimentation. The authors' capitulation to the popular disregard for pure science could not have been more complete.[56]

Only one member of the appropriate legislative committees opposed the bill, but the measure contained objectionable features and stood no chance of adoption.[57] Instead, the legislature recognized

[56] The text of the draft bill is in the *Prairie Farmer,* June, 1855, 193-95. Kennicott outlined the idea of giving control to the Illinois State Agricultural Society and the Industrial League in a letter to Turner, Dec. 5, 1854, Powell Papers, Box 4. Earlier, Turner had selected a site at Peoria which his collaborators were going to purchase and hold in reserve. They acted covertly. Turner to Murray, July 4, 1854, Powell Papers, Box 4.

[57] *Prairie Farmer,* June, 1855, 190-91. Committee members praised the union of a normal school with practical education and attributed the idea to Francis Wayland, Joseph Henry, Henry P. Tappan, and President Edward Hitchcock of Amherst College.

the state's duty to provide free schools for all white children in Illinois, and the law enacted in 1855 necessitated teacher-training. At Chicago the following year Turner informed the Illinois State Teachers' Association that the League would cooperate in organizing a normal school "whether we ever get an agricultural department to it or not."[58] Unity between the industrial education and normal-school forces freed the General Assembly to establish Illinois State Normal University early in 1857. It received the interest on the College and Seminary funds. At the time the League released its claim on this money there was no assurance of obtaining fresh aid, for no one had yet introduced into Congress a bill on land grants. Turner gave in because he had no alternative, but he hoped to convert the normal school into an industrial university.

Not long thereafter the forces that had been accumulating induced Morrill to offer the Agricultural College Act to the House. The Industrial League's campaign beyond Illinois contributed to the result. In accordance with the General Assembly's instructions of 1853, Senator James Shields and Congressman Elihu B. Washburne introduced into their respective chambers on March 20, 1854, the Illinois resolutions calling for a land grant to endow industrial universities. Shields carelessly urged establishment of such an institution only in Illinois.[59] But the time was not ripe anyway, for President Pierce had just vetoed a bill granting public lands to aid the indigent insane. For the next few years Illinois reformers, along with many from other states, flung themselves into the national movement. Perhaps zeal distinguished the Illinois group, which was slow in agreeing among themselves as to the type of school wanted. Congressman Yates told Turner to omit all reference to connecting industrial universities with the Smithsonian, whose officers wanted

[58] William L. Pillsbury, "Historical Sketches of the State Normal Universities and the University of Illinois," in Superintendent of Public Instruction of the State of Illinois, *Seventeenth Biennial Report* (Springfield, 1889), xc. See also *Illinois Teacher*, I (1855), 354.
[59] *Congressional Globe*, 33 Cong., 1 Sess., 678, 686. Washburne followed the language of the Illinois General Assembly rather than the Memorial of the Industrial League with regard to the purpose which the colleges were to serve. "Industrial Universities: Resolutions of the General Assembly of Illinois Relative to the Establishment of Industrial Universities, and for the Encouragement of Practical and General Education Among the People," 33 Cong., 1 Sess., House Misc. Doc. No. 31 (Washington, 1854).

no part of agricultural utilitarianism. As late as October, 1857, the
League had no bill ready to submit to Congress.[60]

Two months later, on December 14, 1857, Morrill introduced
the measure that became the College Land Grant Act. He proposed
that each state receive 20,000 acres of public land valued at a minimum of $1.25 an acre, or land scrip in that amount, for each
member it was entitled to send to Congress. All proceeds from the
sale of land or scrip were to form a perpetual fund, the interest of
which was to endow in each state "at least one college where the
leading object shall be, without excluding other scientific or classical studies, to teach such branches of learning as are related to
agriculture and the mechanic arts, in such manner as the Legislature of the States may respectively prescribe, in order to promote
the liberal and practical education of the industrial classes in the
several pursuits and professions of life."[61] Although many Illinois
writers have argued otherwise, no good evidence supports the assertion that the Illinois reformers, needing an Eastern sponsor of *their*
draft, enlisted Morrill. In all likelihood they could not have recruited a spokesman and written a bill for him in the brief interval
since October.[62]

Morrill hardly required spurring from the Midwest, for he was
especially interested in agricultural science, and once said that as
a hardfisted blacksmith's son he could not overlook the mechanics
in any scheme designed to enlarge educational opportunity. He did
not need to be original, but could draw upon many familiar ideas
for inclusion in his measure. He may have borrowed his phrase,
"to promote the liberal and practical education of the industrial
classes in the several pursuits and professions of life," from a similar
one in the 1853 Memorial of the fourth industrial convention. How-

[60] Yates to Turner, April 14, 1854, quoted in Edmund J. James, "The Services
of Richard Yates to Public Education," *Journal of the Illinois State Historical
Society,* V (Jan., 1913), 484.
[61] *Congressional Globe,* 35 Cong., 1 Sess., 1697. Morrill had introduced into
Congress in 1856 a bill asking the Committee on Agriculture to look into establishing both a national board and schools of agriculture, the latter to be patterned after West Point and Annapolis. *Ibid.,* 34 Cong., 1 Sess., 530.
[62] The claim for Turner and Illinois is made by Carriel, *J. B. Turner,* 141-43;
James, *Origin of the Land-Grant Act,* 27, 35; Davenport, "History of Collegiate
Education in Agriculture," 48-52; Nevins, *Illinois,* 25-26; Powell, *Movement
for Industrial Education,* 90-95.

ever, he differed from most Illinois reformers if not Turner himself
in refusing to exclude classical studies from agricultural and mechanic arts colleges. In proposing federal subsidy, Morrill combined Turner's idea of an endowment in lands with Partridge's plan
of distribution according to congressional representation. As a Ver-
monter who had been appointed to the Board of Trustees of Norwich University, Morrill knew Partridge's ideas, and as a delegate
to a U.S. Agricultural Society meeting in 1856 he had heard Turner's scheme discussed. Morrill was neither original in his proposals
nor was he merely the mouthpiece of Turner and the Industrial
League.[63]

The College Land Grant Bill precipitated sharp conflict in
1859, but Congress virtually ignored the educational issues it posed.
The question of state rights and fear of centralized government
prompted strong opposition. Southern lawmakers particularly denounced the bill as a bribe to secure compliance with the federal
will. Some people from western states opposed the subsidy to colleges on the grounds of land policy. They attacked the bill as a speculators' scheme, arguing that bestowal of immense acreages upon
colleges (as well as railroads) would glut the market, depress prices,
and enable capitalists to acquire large tracts. These fears acquired
special force from the provision to give scrip rather than land itself
to the states lacking public land within their borders. The states
had to sell their scrip, and purchasers could use it to "locate" any
unappropriated U.S. lands subject to private entry. As a result, the
non–public-land states dreaded exploitation by greedy Eastern mo-
nopolists. In addition, Western foes arraigned the mode of distribution for favoring older populous communities at the expense of
younger commonwealths with the greatest educational need.[64]

A few active supporters rather than mass public demand secured passage of the Morrill Act. At least 12 state legislatures joined
Illinois in instructing their delegates in Washington to approve the

[63] William Belmont Parker, *The Life and Public Services of Justin Smith Morrill*
(Boston, 1924), 261-63; Ross, "The 'Father' of the Land-Grant College," 171-72.
[64] Paul W. Gates, "Western Opposition to the Agricultural College Act," *Indiana
Magazine of History*, XXXVII (March, 1941), 101-36. Estimates held that
not more than 580,000 out of 6,060,000 acres would go to states having public
lands within their borders.

measure, although Ohio later reversed itself and urged that Congress grant land only to actual settlers. Rather than endorse the bill and facilitate absentee ownership, the legislatures of Michigan, Wisconsin, Minnesota, and Iowa asked federal lawmakers to grant them lands to endow colleges on an individual basis. But the agricultural societies fired a barrage of resolutions at Capitol Hill, and prominent men rushed there to lobby for the bill. Veterans from Massachusetts, New York, and Pennsylvania were especially active; Kennicott but not Turner was there from Illinois.[65]

The House approved the measure by 105 to 100 in April, 1858, and the Senate by 25 to 22 in February, 1859, with the vote revealing a sectional alignment. The deep South unanimously rejected the bill, the public-land states opposed it by 55 to 33, and a few border commonwealths along with New England and the Middle Atlantic states provided the strongest backing. Illinois had practically no public land remaining within its borders and entertained no new fears of absentee ownership. Its congressional delegation neither fought nor worked for adoption. In the House the bill was backed by four to three; in the Senate Trumbull voted aye and Douglas paired in its favor.[66]

President Buchanan vetoed the College Land Grant Bill, primarily on the grounds that it exercised federal power unconstitutionally. Morrill strongly denounced the veto message and charged that it would "start a tear from the eye of more than one manly boy."[67] The 1860 election and its aftermath, not the Congress, overrode Buchanan. Although the Republican party platform endorsed land grants for homesteads and a Pacific railroad, it preserved silence on federal aid to agricultural colleges. The omission reflected continuing popular indifference to if not suspicion of agricultural education. However, zealots for the cause never ceased agitating. During the campaign Turner got both Lincoln and Douglas to promise they would sign an agricultural college bill if elected, a pledge that cost the candidates nothing.[68]

[65] *Congressional Globe,* 35 Cong., 2 Sess., 1414; True, *A History of Agricultural Education,* 103; Ross, "The 'Father' of the Land-Grant College," 173-75.
[66] Gates, "Western Opposition to the Agricultural College Act," 121-22.
[67] *Congressional Globe,* 35 Cong., 2 Sess., 1414.
[68] Carriel, *J. B. Turner,* 143-44; John Y. Simon, "The Politics of the Morrill Act," *Agricultural History,* XXXVII (April, 1963), 107.

On December 16, 1861, Morrill reintroduced his earlier proposal with two modifications. He raised to 30,000 the number of acres for each member of a state's congressional delegation, and required beneficiaries of the statute to offer military training. The South's withdrawal from Congress ended the constitutional opposition, but the military crisis along with emphasis on economic legislation resulted in the Morrill Bill receiving little attention. Western legislators who feared land monopoly and absentee ownership provided the main opposition, with John Fox Potter of Wisconsin active in the House and James H. Lane of Kansas arousing foes in the Senate. In 1862, however, Congress passed the bill by wide margins. The Senate adopted it on June 10 by 32 to 7, the House by 90 to 25 a week later. Two Illinois representatives supported and four opposed the measure, with Senators Trumbull and Browning voting aye. Political wisdom dictated that Lincoln accept the bill, which his interpretation of the Constitution did not prevent him from signing on July 2, 1862. Lincoln, however, had no special concern for or understanding of industrial education, and it is unwarranted to treat him as another Illinois architect of the College Land Grant Act.

In the Morrill Act the federal government gave higher education an unsurpassed endowment which eventually amounted to 17,430,000 acres. Each state could select 30,000 acres of public land for each legislator it sent to Washington in 1860. The entire proceeds from the disposition of this bounty were to be invested at 5 per cent, and the returns used to endow in each state that accepted the legislation within two years at least one college where "the leading object shall be, without excluding other scientific and classical studies, and including military tactics, to teach such branches of learning as are related to agriculture and the mechanic arts, in such manner as the legislatures of the states may respectively prescribe, in order to promote the liberal and practical education of the industrial classes in the several pursuits and professions of life."[69] Nothing in the legislative history of the bill illuminated the meaning of that language. In the debate, Morrill alone in his address of April 20, 1858, had focused on education. His main concern was the American agricultural backwardness which resulted in declining farm produc-

[69] *U.S. Statutes at Large*, 37 Cong., 2 Sess. (1861-62), chs. 130, 504.

tivity, and he sought a remedy by imitating Europe and establishing special schools for farmers where the conduct of experimentation would lead to agricultural science. In other respects Morrill was vague. Unlike Buchanan, whose veto declared that agricultural colleges would interfere with existing colleges by developing scientific and classical studies to attract students, Morrill did not think the new education would challenge the old. He announced that "Our present literary colleges need have no more jealousy of agricultural colleges than a porcelain manufactory would have of an iron foundery [sic]. They move in separate spheres, without competition, and using no raw material that will diminish the supply of one or the other."[70] A good deal of time and controversy would ensue before the nation decided what type of colleges should be founded on the Morrill Act.

[70] *Congressional Globe,* 35 Cong., 1 Sess., 1694; James D. Richardson, ed., *A Compilation of the Messages and Papers of the Presidents, 1789-1897* (10 vols., Washington, 1896-99), V, 546-47.

CHAPTER THREE

The Auction and
the Champaign "Elephant"

THE MORRILL ACT inaugurated a new era in American higher education by forging a link between the national government and the academic world. Yet the immediate effect of the legislation threw the burden of responsibility on the states. The 1862 statute required acceptance within two years, a deadline later extended, and it allowed five additional years to provide a college of the designated type. Three states accepted the College Land Grant Act in the year of its passage, with Iowa moving first, on September 11. Illinois consented on February 14, 1863, and 13 additional commonwealths joined her before that year ended. A total of 36 states assented to the law by 1870. Their action imposed heavy new obligations upon the states, for if the federal subsidy was too large to refuse it was too small by itself to support a college.

[59]

The devastation of the Civil War and Reconstruction conditioned the launching of the land-grant era in American education. The Morrill Act itself vigorously affirmed the nation's democratic faith at the time of the Union's gravest crisis, but the task of translating the grand vision into workable reality came during the ensuing spiritual and economic dislocations. The states established institutions on the College Land Grant Act by the political process, and lax morality if not cynical corruption characterized the politics of the period. Moreover, the prevailing social thought of the mid-nineteenth century aggravated these postwar evils. In place of the older belief that the state and its citizens must collaborate to promote the common weal, a new doctrine regarding the public welfare had arisen during the Jacksonian era. It restricted the state and exalted the free individual. *Laissez-faire* liberalism taught that unrestrained individual competition promoted the public interest by the automatic operation of a benevolent but invisible hand. This attitude along with the shoddy public morality of the age had unfortunate consequences in the founding of colleges and universities under the Morrill Act. In Illinois, rival groups gathered like sharks around the carcass of the land grant, and Illinois Industrial University received its baptism in bloody political waters.

Although notably laggard in taxing itself to support advanced learning, Illinois lost little time in accepting the 480,000 acres of scrip which constituted its share of the lands awarded by the 1862 law. The scramble to gain this prize began within the state as soon as the General Assembly met in 1863. Although the religious denominations had tried for a decade to forestall industrial education, two sectarian colleges now rushed to put their sickle into the movement's harvest. At the opening of the session, delegates from the counties which contained Knox and Shurtleff colleges introduced a bill to establish agricultural schools for northern and southern Illinois. This was a thinly disguised attempt to divide the land grant between two old-time colleges. In proposing to annex agricultural education to Knox and Shurtleff, the bill clearly violated the provision of the Morrill Act which required establishment of institutions whose *leading object* was to teach branches of learning related to agriculture and the mechanic arts. Friends pressed the bill so urgently that it was on the verge of passing the Senate on February 14. On that day, however, the General Assembly merely accepted the federal donation and recessed until June 2.[1]

The sectarians had caught the Illinois leaders of the industrial education movement off guard. Turner explained his napping by saying that he had not wanted to touch the land grant until the strong feelings aroused by earlier agitation had subsided.[2] A more likely reason is that the erratic flame of his zeal was burning low. At any rate, he and 12 co-workers immediately sprang to life. Resorting to an old technique, they called the "friends of agriculture" to meet in Springfield on June 9, a few days after the legislature would reconvene. Representatives of the denominational colleges also attended this industrial convention. They argued for the pending bill to divide the federal subsidy between Knox and Shurtleff on grounds designed to please the farmers of Illinois, namely, that the division between two widely separated colleges would best promote agriculture in a state whose climate and soil varied greatly from north to south.

Agriculturists dominated the Springfield gathering, however, and Turner was their leader. He had to prevent the General Assembly from acting hastily and gain time for arousing public opinion. The old warrior therefore obtained from the convention a Memorial which asked the legislature to delay disposal of the land grant. Looking forward two years to the point at which pressure could be applied most effectively, Turner also induced the delegates to appoint a committee to collect facts relative to the proposed institution. The Springfield Committee was to contain one person from each of the 13 congressional districts in Illinois. Apart from Turner, the members who became closely identified with Illinois Industrial University were Luther W. Lawrence, John P. Reynolds, and Willard C. Flagg. The Springfield Committee received a mandate to report its findings to the Committee of Agriculture when the General Assembly met in 1865. These achievements proved ade-

[1] *Illinois House Journal* (1863), 621; *Illinois Senate Journal* (1863), 67, 141, 164, 258, 276, 331; *Illinois Laws* (1863), 64. The vote was 62 to 0 in the House, 15 to 2 in the Senate. The text of the bill is in the *Prairie Farmer,* July 11, 1863, 17.
[2] *Prairie Farmer,* Feb. 7, 1863, 81.

quate for the time being. By a stroke of good fortune Governor Richard Yates prorogued the legislature on June 10.[3]

It appeared certain that Illinois would establish a university on the proceeds of the land grant in 1865, and in the interim the contending parties mobilized their forces. The real struggle occurred between rival factions within what can loosely be called the agricultural community, but two outside challenges arose. Representatives of Chicago mechanics who desired an industrial school in the metropolis bid for the benefits. And religious considerations affected the maneuvering, even though the denominational colleges had no chance of victory after Knox and Shurtleff failed in 1863. The influence of religion in American life was declining when the Morrill Act stimulated nonsectarian higher education by inducing state governments to found colleges of a new type. Moreover, the fund was too small to divide among all church-related schools, and farm leaders had the law on their side in insisting that no offspring of the 1862 act be tied to the corpse of the old "monkish" system. No, the sectarians could not hope to win, but nevertheless religion aroused hopes and fears. Denominational leaders reminded their large following that infidelity must inevitably accompany state-supported higher education. Spokesmen for the industrial university, notably Turner, denounced sectarianism as baneful.

The industrial education strategists, having regained the initiative at Springfield, enjoyed advantages for the impending conflict. Now it became apparent as never before that agriculture enlisted their deepest concern, and agriculture was still the state's primary economic activity. The farming community possessed an efficient organization in the Illinois State Agricultural Society, the Illinois State Horticultural Society, and the Industrial League. They also felt a proprietary right to the proceeds of the Morrill Act, for whose paternity Turner now repeatedly claimed credit. The agriculturists gained added strength by speaking with one voice on the two leading issues which aroused debate: whether to found one or more colleges, and the proper method of locating any institution authorized.

[3] *Ibid.*, June 20, 1863, 385-86. Others named to the committee were Henry D. Emery, W. H. Rosevelt, Albert C. Mason, Lewis Ellsworth, William Kite, Thompson Chandler, and N. M. McCurdy.

The majority of persons interested in the subject insisted on erecting one agricultural college and refused to consider affiliating it with any existing institution. The State Agricultural Society and the State Horticultural Society agreed on this point at their annual meetings held in connection with the harvest festivals in 1863, as did the agricultural convention which convened in Springfield the following January. About this time the Illinois State Teachers' Association recommended the same goal. These groups consciously avoided discussing the character of the education to be offered in the agricultural college. Turner choked off one attempt to consider these issues by urging that details be left for the trustees to settle later, and he did not encourage consideration of the state's financial responsibility for higher education when he advised people to go slow in building the university in order to avoid all need for additional taxes.[4]

Organized agriculture rather quickly arrived at the conclusion that the college should be located by an appointive commission rather than by law. The formulators of this position urged that a commission would afford all sections of Illinois equal opportunity to bid, thus securing the best possible bargain for the state in return for the benefits which location would give the community that obtained the university. Perhaps this remarkable decision rested on the unstated assumption that the General Assembly was more susceptible to corruption than a smaller body, but the rationale offered for the policy explicitly asserted that "selling" the location to the highest bidder would promote the public interest. In fact, however, the agriculturists jeopardized the common weal by concerning themselves solely with form rather than substance. Their conclusion reflected the *laissez-faire* ethic, and there is no evidence that anyone in Illinois ever raised the vital question of how the location could best serve educational purposes.

Their failure is more noteworthy in light of the fact that the rapid proliferation of colleges in the mid-nineteenth century had occasioned continuing discussion over proper location. Growing urbanism imparted special urgency to the matter, and a few hardy

[4] *Prairie Farmer,* Oct. 10, 1863, 225, 228; Dec. 26, 1863, 411-12; Jan. 9, 1864, 2, 24; Jan. 16, 1864, 33; Jan. 23, 1864, 50.

souls began to challenge "the naive American assumption that small towns in the forests were as suitable for the life of the mind as large cities."[5]   No one took more pains over location than Horace Bushnell, the great Congregational theologian, who devoted several months to the search for an ideal site for the college that developed into the University of California at Berkeley. "The site of a university," wrote Bushnell, "is to be chosen but once. Once planted, it can never be removed; and if any mistake is made, that mistake rests on the institution as a burden to the end of time."[6]   Bushnell determined that the location must be near the center of population and public influence in California. He also wanted proximity to San Francisco for its library facilities, and because he believed that provincial vices were more brutalizing and coarser than urban vices. He therefore concluded that he must find a suitable place on the northeastern circuit of the Bay of San Francisco, and he carefully evaluated the wind, water, topography, and aesthetic qualities of the areas which he thought suitable. He did not recommend Berkeley, but his zeal exemplified Bushnell's belief that "The university is the womb in which society is shaped. . . ."[7] No hint of such consideration graces the Illinois records.

The agricultural leaders demanded the establishment of one separate agricultural college and location by commission rather than by legislative enactment. Doubtless they would have succeeded were they able to agree on a specific site. But that they could not do. Their reluctance to discuss educational policy spared them the need to think in terms of the educational merits of various locations. They gave no voice to the pastoral ideal designed to save impressionable youths from noxious urban influences, nor did they bother to assert that an agricultural college had to plant its roots in rural surroundings. Although some evidence suggests that differences within the inner circle over locations designed to favor one or another faction prevented agreement on a precise site, it was their emphasis on the commission method which kept agriculturists from

[5] The phrase is from Perry Miller's Introduction to his edition of Philip Schaff, *America: A Sketch of Its Political, Social, and Religious Character* (Cambridge, Mass., 1961), xxiv.
[6] As quoted in William Warren Ferrier, *Origin and Development of the University of California* (Berkeley, 1930), 162.
[7] *Ibid.*, 175, and see also 157-85.

making a recommendation. That was the one gap in their otherwise united front, and through that breach rushed the willful men from Champaign-Urbana.

During the summer of 1864 the mechanics challenged the agriculturists and the idea of founding one college. Francis E. Eastman, a state representative from Chicago, informed Governor Yates that the bill introduced in 1863 violated the Morrill Act by providing for agriculture and ignoring mechanic arts. He urged that half of the land-grant proceeds be used to establish a polytechnic school in Chicago. In 1863 Eastman had induced the House to pass a bill calling for a joint committee to report plans for disposal of the federal donation, and Yates therefore appointed a commission to study the question. The Governor named to it three Chicagoans: a Methodist minister, a dry-goods merchant, and John C. Burroughs, a Baptist clergyman connected with the old University of Chicago; three downstate men interested in denominational colleges: Judge C. B. Lawrence of Galesburg, the home of Knox College, Julian M. Sturtevant of Illinois College, and Cyrus Edwards of Alton, the seat of Shurtleff College; and Kersey Fell of Bloomington and General I. N. Haynie of Cairo. The agriculturists denounced Yates for courting the labor vote, for the insult of awarding them no member on the committee, and for ignoring the Springfield Committee appointed to study the same question. The chastened Yates then added Clark Robinson Griggs of Urbana and Turner to the Governor's Committee. Turner refused to serve.[8]

Lines tightened that autumn. Early in September the Governor's Committee asked applicants for the land grant to submit written statements. The *Prairie Farmer* regarded the appeal as an invitation to the sectarian colleges to divide the federal gift among themselves. Presumably at Griggs's urging, the Governor's Committee visited Champaign-Urbana late in October to discover what local citizens were willing to do to obtain the university. One reporter wrote that the visitors were believed unanimously to favor locating the college in the twin cities.[9]

The agricultural community consolidated its ranks when farm-

[8] *Prairie Farmer,* Aug. 6, 1864, 84; Aug. 13, 1864, 100, 163; Aug. 27, 1864, 129; Sept. 10, 1864, 162; Oct. 8, 1864, 233; *Illinois House Journal* (1863), 534-35.
[9] *Prairie Farmer,* Sept. 10, 1864, 168; Nov. 12, 1864, 312.

ers came together for the autumn fairs. The State Horticultural Society met at Rockford, the State Agricultural Society at Decatur. They affirmed both the need to establish only one institution and the indivisibility of the industrial classes. But some members revealed the hollowness of the boast in rebuffing the proposal for a polytechnic school. They argued that the Morrill Act included mechanic arts only insofar as these applied to its basic purpose — agricultural education.[10] Both assemblies appointed committees to report on the subject of an agricultural college. The Decatur parley was the eighth in a series of industrial conventions dating back to Granville in 1851, and it instructed its committee to frame a bill for organization of a university and disposition of the land grant. This Decatur Committee drafted the bill which established Illinois Industrial University. Its members were A. B. McConnell, William H. Van Epps, and John P. Reynolds, President, past President, and Corresponding Secretary respectively of the Agricultural Society; B. G. Roots, a farmer of Tamaroa, Perry County, who became active in industrial conventions in the early 1860's; and Turner. In the fall elections the agricultural press urged people to support only candidates who agreed with the Agricultural and Horticultural societies' stand. In November Yates asked the Governor's Committee to disband in order to avoid collision with the Springfield Committee, the existence of which he claimed to have discovered after naming his own group.[11]

The Springfield, Rockford, and Decatur committees met jointly in Springfield on December 6, 1864, under the chairmanship of Reynolds, a member of all three. Turner, Flagg, and Roots held posts on two committees. The main purpose was to consider a bill to present to the legislature, but the first business was to hear a large delegation of mechanics from Chicago headed by A. D. Titsworth. These emissaries pleaded for equal division between a metropolitan polytechnic college and a downstate agricultural college. Their main argument was the imperative need to reform the

[10] *Ibid.*, Sept. 10, 1864, 162-63.
[11] Illinois State Horticultural Society, *Transactions for 1863*, VIII (Alton, 1864), 118, 121. The Rockford Committee consisted of G. W. Minier, Willard C. Flagg, C. N. Andrews, Jonathan Periam, B. F. Long, C. D. Wilbur, and John P. Reynolds. Illinois State Agricultural Society, *Transactions*, V (Springfield, 1865), 986-87; *Prairie Farmer*, Nov. 19, 1864, 328.

education of apprentices. The committees replied that each college established on the land grant was to teach the same branches of learning, and that the donation was insufficient to support two institutions. The point was well taken, for the state's 480,000 acres of scrip would yield only about $16,800 a year. The mechanics returned to Chicago and drafted a bill to present their views to the General Assembly. The *Prairie Farmer* considered the challenge formidable.[12]

The agriculturists assembled in the capital city also entertained two proposals to locate the university. Roots urged delegates to fix the site at Irvington, near Centralia in southern Illinois. He offered in return the Illinois Agricultural College building, some $60,000 in cash, and "considerable land." The legislature had chartered this private-state venture in 1861 and given it the 4.5 unsold sections of the original 72 sections of College and Seminary lands. President Thomas Quick of the Board of Trustees secured the location in his home town, private subscriptions enabled the purchase of a 560-acre farm, and sale of the remnant of College and Seminary lands brought $58,000. J. W. Scroggs of Champaign bid for the university by offering a large building with ten acres of land in adjacent Urbana, all of which he valued at $100,000. The committees refused to recommend any location. They wanted the choice of a site left to a commission and were willing to approve one as far north as Chicago or as far south as Cairo provided it went to the highest bidder.[13]

The Decatur Committee's draft of a bill to establish an industrial university also received careful consideration at the joint Springfield session. Later, the Executive Board of the Illinois State Agricultural Society perfected the 18 sections of this measure for presentation to the legislature. On January 10, 1865, John L. Tincher of the legislative district which embraced four counties southeast of Champaign — Douglas, Coles, Vermilion, and Edgar

---

[12] *Prairie Farmer,* Dec. 17, 1864, 385, 389. The flood of land and scrip on the market had driven the price to about 70 cents an acre. The realized proceeds were to be invested at 5 per cent.

[13] George W. Smith, "The Old Illinois Agricultural College," *Journal of the Illinois State Historical Society,* V (Jan., 1913), 476-77; *Prairie Farmer,* Dec. 17, 1864, 385. The $58,000 was subsequently lost when the bank owned by the Board's treasurer failed.

— introduced into the House a bill for "An act to provide for the organization, endowment and maintenance of the Illinois Industrial College." John T. Lindsay moved the same bill (although "University" replaced "College" in the title) in the Senate three days later. Section 11 provided for a commission to locate the institution. It directed state legislators from each Illinois congressional district to appoint one member to this body, which was to receive proposals and make the award. That section alone prevented enactment of the bill in 1865.[14]

Champaign and Chicago interests united to obstruct the provision for location and thus the entire bill. On February 10 a Cook County representative introduced a substitute for Section 11 which the House adopted. The amendment charged the board of trustees of the university with locating the institution at Urbana as soon as Champaign County conveyed to the board in fee simple and free of incumbrances certain properties with a stated value of $160,000. The Urbana-Champaign Institute building constituted the main attraction of this offer, which also included the Institute's immediate grounds and a 140-acre farm.[15]

The proposal of Champaign County culminated a process which nineteenth-century frontier communities found especially familiar. Men who were essentially speculators in land won favor in localities by promoting town and educational development while holding out economic incentive. Jonathan C. Stoughton, a Methodist minister who arrived in the two towns from Freeport, Illinois, in 1859, was such a person. He represented a company which hoped to establish seminaries at various points in the state, and outlined a plan to purchase land between Champaign and Urbana, erect a seminary building, and leave that as a gift to the twin cities when the company finished selling the adjacent home sites. On July 2,

[14] *Illinois House Journal* (1865), 122; *Illinois Senate Journal* (1865), 136; *Prairie Farmer,* Dec. 17, 1864, 385; Jan. 14, 1865, 20. The text of the bill is in the *Prairie Farmer,* March 18, 1865, 182-83. The individual contribution of the five members of the Decatur Committee has been impossible to determine. Writing to Reynolds in late 1864 or early 1865, Turner said: ". . . if I should make the first draft it would be so much like me, that every man in the state from Galena to Cairo, would swear that I wrote it; and this is undesirable in such a document." Burt E. Powell Papers, Box 4, University of Illinois Archives. On the authorship, see the *Prairie Farmer,* Aug. 25, 1866, 118.
[15] *Illinois House Journal* (1865), 807-8.

1860, Stoughton and two partners executed a contract with six residents of Champaign County. The company stated that it owned 194 acres between what are now Wright and Lincoln streets on the west and east and Springfield and University avenues on the south and north, eight acres of which they reserved for the seminary building and its grounds. (The land apparently cost slightly over $19,000 and the estimated expenditure for the seminary plot and a completed building was $40,000.) The six local parties to the contract agreed to secure an acceptable subscription list of $40,000, with signatories promising to pay 15 per cent of their pledges in cash and giving notes for the balance. They received in return lots in the tract equal in value to the amount of their subscriptions. At $200 each the lots were exorbitantly priced, but nevertheless the deal seemed attractive. Stoughton's group promised to turn over the seminary building and its eight acres to the stockholders when the subscriptions were completely paid. Presumably no one could lose. Although the scheme had educational potential, the promoters had no intention of teaching anything. They offered merely to construct a building designed for educational purposes. Stoughton commended the venture from local pulpits.[16]

In addition, the undertaking promised to further important civic needs. Construction of the Illinois Central had created a serious gap between the two towns. Urbana, the county seat, dated from 1833 and contained only 75 buildings two decades after its founding. The railroad line came through two miles west of the courthouse the following year, stimulating a settlement around the depot which formed the nucleus of West Urbana. The new community, renamed Champaign in 1860, grew much more rapidly than the old and numbered 3,258 souls in 1858. Although jealousy prevented the two little villages from incorporating as one town, residents nevertheless desired to close the aperture between them. Nature intensified the nakedness of that breach, for the towns occupied a prairie wilderness which "stretched away in billowy vastness like a congealed ocean," and neither trees, nor hills, nor water

[16] Burt E. Powell, *Semi-Centennial History of the University of Illinois, I: The Movement for Industrial Education and the Establishment of the University, 1840-1870* (Urbana, 1918), 197-200.

relieved the monotony, although the flat expanse turned into a slough at certain seasons.[17]

Residents hoped also to share in the patronage awarded by the state government. They knew that times were ripe for agricultural colleges, and in 1860, shortly before the signing of the contract with Stoughton and his partners, Urbana spokesmen offered the seminary building which existed only in their imagination to an educational convention at Bloomington for use as an agricultural school. They said the structure would be erected at an expense of $100,000. Early in 1861 60 local citizens petitioned the legislature to establish a state agricultural school and declared that stockholders of the Institute proposed to donate their building and its grounds to Illinois for the purpose. In February, 1861, the General Assembly chartered the Urbana-Champaign Institute as "a seminary of learning, comprehending an agricultural, or other departments, as the public may demand."[18] Nine persons constituted the Board of Trustees of a corporation whose capital stock consisted of the seminary plot. Bishop Matthew Simpson, like Stoughton a Methodist, laid the cornerstone on August 6, 1861, but the Civil War delayed completion of the structure. Nevertheless, passage of the Morrill Act stimulated the appetite for patronage. For this reason Griggs induced the Governor's Committee to visit Champaign County in 1863 and Scroggs put in a bid for the location to the joint committees meeting in Springfield the following year.

Shortly thereafter, Stoughton's company announced its refusal to convey the building under construction to the persons on the subscription list until they had paid their pledges in full. These signatories were indeed delinquent, but the threat ruined the chance of using the seminary structure to bait a hook for the General Assembly to take. The Board of Supervisors of Champaign County therefore committed the taxpayers they represented in order to rescue the private enterprise. They agreed to provide $24,000 to obtain the edifice of the Institute upon the understanding that Illinois would locate the industrial university there. In addition, the Super-

[17] The quotation is from Brink, McDonough & Co., *History of Champaign County, Illinois* (Philadelphia, 1878), 20n. See also Natalia M. Belting, *The Beginnings: Champaign in the 1850's and 1860's* ([Champaign], 1960), *passim*.
[18] *Illinois Private Laws* (1861) (Feb. 21), 25.

visors appropriated $15,000 either to buy a farm to augment the offer or to use in securing the location. The officials appointed a committee to submit the county's bid, and arranged to distribute $5,000 among its 12 members to facilitate their task. The Supervisors also named a committee to secure legislation authorizing the county to borrow money and issue bonds for these purposes.

Champaign County leaders demonstrated their legislative skill well before the introduction of the substitute Section 11. On January 20 the General Assembly appointed a joint select committee to investigate the advantages of Champaign and Urbana. Senator Washington Bushnell headed the 12 legislators who visited the little community of fewer than 5,000 souls. Bushnell's report, a prime example of promotional literature, bore little relation to reality. The committee praised the county's location in Illinois by describing it as situated halfway between north and south and midway between Bloomington and the eastern border. "The general appearance of the country," said the document, "is unsurpassed in the west, for the beauty of its landscape, the richness and variety of its soil, interspersed with groves of fine timber and streams of pure water." The report described the building, five stories of brick and stone with a four-story wing, as "beautiful in its architectural proportions, and very imposing in its appearance."[19] In cold fact, however, the grounds of the Institute contained one sycamore and two or three widely separated cottonwoods, and an early trustee said, "the building had an appearance suggesting that, as a stake, it had been driven into the ground."[20] The pawn of speculators, the structure was Champaign County's white elephant.

The authors of the amended Section 11 sought the lion's share of the land grant for Champaign County, but they also offered incentive to the Chicago mechanics and the southern agriculturists in order to win their backing. The substitute passage empowered the board of trustees to establish a department for the mechanic arts in Chicago, provided the metropolis furnish suitable buildings

[19] "Report of Joint Select Committee to Visit Champaign County," *Illinois Reports* (1865), I, 319-20.
[20] Thomas J. Burrill to F. Fink, Jan. 10, 1906, Burrill Papers, Box 1, Botany Department Correspondence; Joseph O. Cunningham, "The Genesis of Our Campus," *Alumni Quarterly*, IX (Jan., 1915), 19.

and grounds free of cost and donate at least $100,000 for the purpose. In addition, the critical section authorized the board to establish a department of agriculture in the southern part of the state whenever people there supplied suitable buildings and lands. These divisions encouraged Albert C. Mason to introduce a bill calling for establishment of separate agricultural and mechanic arts colleges in northern, central, and southern Illinois. In the outcome, the General Assembly failed to enact any bill establishing institutions on the Morrill Act in 1865.[21]

Veterans rehashed many familiar arguments in the two years which elapsed before the legislature met again, and made only a few points significant for the future. Although the State Agricultural Society reaffirmed its confidence in the proposed draft to organize the university (known as the Farmers' Bill), the Buel Institute, which had sponsored the Granville convention, denounced it for vague generalities that left too much to discretion. The Buel Institute unsuccessfully tried to devise a new organic law with strict controls to protect the interests of farmers and mechanics, an ominous portent.[22]

Meanwhile, Willard C. Flagg, having thought about the subject as a member of the Springfield and Rockford committees, published *The Illinois School of Agriculture*.[23] He knew much about European and American agriculture for his 35 years, and as a Yale graduate was familiar with Samuel W. Johnson's attempt to give farmers the latest results of applied science. He urged the creation of one central agricultural institution which would emphasize theory and the sciences allied to agriculture and a number of subordinate schools and experimental farms throughout the state which would stress practical agriculture. He regarded manual labor and special short courses as valuable for younger and older practical farmers respectively.

Turner reagitated old issues in a pamphlet entitled *Industrial University Education* and in an 1866 address at the Monmouth

[21] The Senate voted 12 to 12 on Feb. 6, the House approved an amended measure by 45 to 35 on Feb. 10, but the Senate later refused to consider this version by a vote of 9 to 12. *Illinois Senate Journal* (1865), 147-48, 411, 886; *Illinois House Journal* (1865), 807-10, 1000-1001.
[22] *Prairie Farmer*, Oct. 14, 1865, 285; Dec. 23, 1865, 444; July 14, 1866, 24; Aug. 4, 1866, 76; Aug. 25, 1866, 117-19; Sept. 8, 1866, 156.
[23] [Alton, 1864].

County Fair. Characteristically, he combined bitter invective against the old education with vigorous advocacy of the new. He himself published the essay which the U.S. Commissioner of Agriculture had requested when that official refused to issue it in his Department's report. For all his ostensible radicalism, however, Turner was stationary if not regressive in thought. The changed political situation in Illinois enabled him for the first time since his 1851 Granville address to stress the role of science. He insisted that the Morrill Act required the colleges to teach the principles and sciences underlying all practical arts rather than merely the agricultural and mechanic arts themselves. He wanted all land-grant universities to be part of a national system of education with its center in the Smithsonian Institution and the U.S. Department of Agriculture. He met the argument that land-grant schools would have nothing to teach, since no science of agriculture yet existed, by reiterating his scheme for developing such a science. He desired farmer-observers who would work in each county under direction of the state universities, the latter being closely connected with each other and with Washington. He envisioned the whole nation as constituting one vast experimental farm. "Set all the millions of eyes in this great republic to watching and intelligently observing and thinking," declared Turner, "and there is no secret of nature or art we cannot find out; no disease of man or beast we cannot understand; no evil we cannot remedy; no obstacle we cannot surmount; nothing that lies in the power of man to do or to understand, that cannot be both understood and done."[24]

These ideas dated their author. Reliance upon untrained investigators revealed an attitude toward science which characterized the period of Jacksonian democracy in which Turner came of age. In both Europe and the United States, however, later events demonstrated the inadequacy of this approach and the need for professionalism. Norton and Johnson, for example, preached such a doctrine at Yale years before 1866. Moreover, had Turner familiarized himself even slightly with the Smithsonian Institution's development he would have known that its directors aimed at higher

[24] The quotation is from his Monmouth address, *Prairie Farmer*, Oct. 27, 1866, 267. Turner earlier gave a brief statement on industrial universities in a speech in Morgan County noted in the *Prairie Farmer*, Feb. 24, 1866, 115. He published his pamphlet at Chicago, 1864.

scientific goals than directing the researches of workaday farmers. Nevertheless, Turner's thought was not consistently regressive. He emancipated himself from the romantic infatuation with the manual-labor system which possessed many contemporaries. In characteristically picturesque utterance he warned against reviving in the industrial universities an inefficient practice, "where fifty boys are put behind a hundred asses to learn to plow at the public expense, and all alike are to be taught industry by being forced to work under conditions that render work profitless, needless and disgusting to any man or boy of good hard sense."[25]

Sectarian educators made one last bid for the land grant shortly before the General Assembly convened in 1867. Presidents of leading denominational institutions — Augustana, Chicago, Eureka, Knox, Lombard, Monmouth, Northwestern, and Wheaton — met on October 29-30 in the rooms of John C. Burroughs of the University of Chicago. They formed the Illinois College Association and considered a report submitted by President Jonathan Blanchard of Wheaton. A staunch and opinionated neo-puritan who had formerly headed Knox College, Blanchard perhaps furnished the drive behind the group. He aimed at securing division of the land grant among many colleges on the grounds of Illinois' agricultural diversity as well as religion. Everyone knew that he desired only to keep advanced learning under denominational auspices. Blanchard proposed the establishment of Illinois Agricultural and Mechanical College, in reality a central board of higher education in the guise of a "single college." Although it lacked real authority, this cumbersome body of over a hundred ex officio members (including the Governor, the presidents of all agricultural societies in Illinois, and presidents of the private colleges) was to meet periodically to perform certain functions. Existing colleges which annexed a model farm and appointed a professor to teach agriculture exclusively — Turner himself had urged this idea upon Blanchard in 1848 — would become branches of the unified system administered by the board. The plan ordered the legislature to pay out income from the land grant to the branches, each of which could teach its own sectarian doctrines without raising church-state conflicts.

[25] *Prairie Farmer,* Oct. 27, 1866, 267.

The Illinois College Association approved Blanchard's outline with two dissents. President William S. Curtis of Knox voted against it, and President Wallace of Monmouth saw no reason why the industrial university, a professional school, should challenge the existing colleges. He thought it right for men with knowledge of scientific culture to direct the new institution. President Julian M. Sturtevant objected by letter. Although he later said that denominational rivalries paved the way for state sponsorship of higher education in Illinois, he now feared the Chicago gathering would excite the jealousy of the farmers and mechanics. But the other presidents observed that Sturtevant was eager to obtain the location for Morgan County.[26] After adjourning, the heads of the church-related colleges apparently exerted no further effort to influence the legislature.

Location again constituted the main bone of contention when the General Assembly met in 1867. The events of 1865 made clear that the law establishing the university and not a commission would specify the site, and throughout the following year interested parties prepared for the legislative maneuvering. In the final event Bloomington, Champaign-Urbana, Jacksonville, and Lincoln actually bid for the institution. Chicago was perhaps the most important of the other frequently mentioned contestants which made no offer. Jacksonville came better prepared than any aspirant except the twin cities. Jonathan Turner and Julian Sturtevant worked during 1866 to secure the agricultural college for the seat of Morgan County. When voters defeated a proposal to levy $300,000 by taxes for the purpose in the autumn, a committee of citizens undertook to raise the sum by subscription.[27]

[26] *Ibid.*, Nov. 10, 1866, 299; Nov. 24, 1866, 329; Julian M. Sturtevant, *An Autobiography*, ed. J. M. Sturtevant, Jr. (New York, 1896), 188-89, 236-37.
[27] This paragraph and a few that follow draw on Clark Robinson Griggs to Wallace N. Stearns, April 23, 1906, typewritten letter, Edmund J. James Papers, University of Illinois Archives; "Clark Robinson Griggs and the Location of the University," *Alumni Quarterly and Fortnightly Notes*, I (Oct. 15, 1915), 17-22, which contains information Allan Nevins obtained in an interview with Griggs; Allan Nevins, *Illinois* (New York, 1917), 30-40; Fred H. Turner, "Misconceptions Concerning the Early History of the University of Illinois," Illinois State Historical Society, *Transactions for 1932*, Illinois State Historical Library Pub. No. 39 (n.p., n.d.), 75-85; Powell, *Movement for Industrial Education*, 211-71; and the official journals of the Senate and House.

These efforts spurred Champaign County to intensify its plans. The Board of Supervisors arranged a referendum in October on bonding the county for $100,000 to obtain the location, and the electorate approved by 4,601 to 1,085 votes. In November the people elected Clark Robinson Griggs to the House to present their proposal. He became the executive agent of a committee appointed to carry out the local campaign. The inducements included the new seminary building and its grounds, and 970 acres of farm land acquired to facilitate agricultural operations. Champaign County appropriated $5,000 for use by the committee authorized to secure the location, the two towns and local citizens provided more than half again as much, and in addition the Board of Supervisors made available $40,000 for the expense of the campaign in Springfield.

Griggs was a skillful manipulator of men. A Massachusetts legislator before his removal west, he had farmed near Urbana and then became a sutler in the Civil War, during which he made a fortune by selling confiscated cotton. At the time he was Mayor of Urbana and a promotor of a railroad linking Danville and Pekin by way of Urbana and Bloomington. He spent a month after his election in a quiet tour of the state. Avoiding Bloomington, Jacksonville, and Lincoln so as not to alarm rivals, he solicited support of House members. He saw nearly half of the representatives and garnered some 15 pledges. Griggs got the ear of Governor Oglesby and Lieutenant Governor Bross and made both the Republican and Democratic state chairmen paid servants of the Champaign County committee. Perhaps more important, he learned much about the cities which desired legislation to aid their special interests from the General Assembly: Chicago wanted laws to develop its parks and boulevards, southern Illinois a new penitentiary, Springfield and Peoria a new statehouse. He noted these details for leverage in bargaining, meanwhile puncturing the balloons of other claimants: Chicago would grow fast without the university, Jacksonville and Bloomington were already enjoying the fruits of state patronage. Griggs pleaded that Champaign County and eastern Illinois had not yet received government favors, and at Pekin and Danville he reminded citizens that location at Urbana would stimulate the railroad between their towns. The Danville, Urbana, Bloomington, and

Pekin line also promised to render Champaign-Urbana accessible from the east and west.

In addition, Griggs induced the Champaign County committee to engage several spacious rooms in the Leland, Springfield's largest hotel, for the duration of the legislative fight. Here he, the chairmen of both political parties, who had quarters adjacent to his, and others from Champaign-Urbana lobbied incessantly. They spent generously from their slush funds, providing drinks, light refreshments, oyster suppers, quail dinners, and theater tickets for members of the General Assembly and their constituents. On one occasion they hired a special train and took legislators to the twin cities to see the proposed site. This zeal alone impressed many lawmakers, and some of them finally voted for Champaign merely because Griggs and his colleagues had worked so hard.

Not trusting completely to these means, Griggs jockeyed himself into a critical position in the House. The legislative journals do not bear out in detail his later recollection, but it is probably essentially true that Griggs maneuvered into a leading role for the speakership and then traded it for chairmanship of the Committee on Manufactures and Agriculture and the privilege of naming all its members. The bills on location had to go to this Committee, and Griggs therefore controlled their fate.

Senator John L. Tincher of Danville introduced the old bill (originally drafted by the Decatur Committee) into the Senate on January 10, three days after the General Assembly opened. Its Section 11 located the University at Urbana. Griggs moved the same bill in the House the following day. On January 17 Morgan County tendered its offer, and a week later the General Assembly empowered communities to tax themselves and vote bonds as necessary to bid for the institution. This enabling act induced citizens of McLean and Logan counties to raise funds and make offers for Bloomington and Lincoln respectively.

Early in February, with only these four bids in hand, the General Assembly appointed a joint legislative committee to visit the sites to ascertain the cash value of the proposals and the validity of property titles. The committee's report of February 16 ranked Jacksonville first, Bloomington second, Lincoln third, and Champaign-Urbana fourth.[28] The committee appraised the Morgan County offer at $491,000. The items included the Berean College building in Jacksonville, 206 acres of land, $250,000 worth of bonds, and Illinois College. Sturtevant and Turner had devised a plan which called for the industrial university to absorb Illinois College, and the committee estimated the latter's building, library, equipment, 31 acres, and $90,000 endowment fund as worth $176,000 (which comprised part of the $491,000).

Bloomington and McLean County were a close second with a proffer evaluated at $470,000. The package contained $400,000 in bonds, 143.5 acres of land, and $35,000 in freight. Part of the acreage was adjacent to Illinois State Normal University, and local promoters intended to merge the industrial university with this institution. Observers never conceded the town of Lincoln much chance, but the legislative visitors estimated the proposition of Logan County at $385,000. The entire sum, except for $35,000 in freight, consisted of bonds, and hence it would have been impossible to commence instruction without further delay.

Champaign County marched far to the rear, with an application evaluated at $285,000. The committee assigned the following price to the component parts: freight on the Illinois Central, $35,000; shrubs and trees, $2,000; bonds, $100,000; the Urbana-Champaign Institute building, $75,500; and 980.5 acres of land, $72,500. The legislator's appraisals of the four overtures were roughly accurate, and the inducements held out by Champaign County had actually cost about $207,000.[29] But certain aspects of this appeal had merit. The building, derisively called the "Elephant," testified that instruction could begin promptly. Jacksonville could make the same pledge, but no competitor offered as much land as Champaign, and that was a decided advantage for an agricultural school.

The committee made no recommendation, leaving the choice to the General Assembly. The issue was decided in hotels and corridors, where Griggs and his companions reaped a return on their

[28] *Illinois Reports* (1867), I, 443-45.
[29] This tricky question is treated carefully in Powell, *Movement for Industrial Education*, 268-70, and in Turner, "Misconceptions Concerning the Early History of the University of Illinois," 82-84.

zealous labor. "Persons from Champaign" exerted much effort to get the press to push their case. They insisted that $450,000 rather than $285,000 was the real value of the county's offer, and emphasized that eastern Illinois was entitled to some state patronage. Now, apparently for the first time, they called attention to the fitness of the area for an agricultural college. Griggs spent freely, giving rise to charges of bribery. A supervisor and some taxpayers of Champaign County publicly denounced the methods used by the local promoters.

Griggs sat on the bills in his committee until his lobbying and bargaining for votes assured him victory, and finally permitted consideration of the enabling act on February 20. The chamber amended it at the last minute to permit establishment of a polytechnical branch in Chicago, but specified that none of the federal donation was to be used to erect the branch campus. When the vote came, Governor Oglesby and Attorney General Robert Ingersoll took seats near Griggs to symbolize their support. A member called up the bill to locate the university at Jacksonville and the House defeated it. A member called up the bill to locate at Bloomington and the House defeated it. A member called up the bill to locate at Lincoln and the House defeated it. With these formalities over, the House agreed to locate the institution at Champaign-Urbana and passed the Organic Act establishing Illinois Industrial University by a vote of 67 to 10. The Senate passed the measure five days later. It first tabled an amendment which said the act should not be void for having ignored McLean County's bid of $180,000 more, "nor by reason of its having been passed by a combination with the new state house, canal and southern penitentiary 'ring.' " Nevertheless, the Senate approved by a vote of 18 to 7. Governor Oglesby signed the statute on February 28.[30]

The immediate upshot was corrosive bitterness and ugly charges of bribery which threatened the future of the University. Fingers of accusation pointed at Griggs, "The prime minister in the weaving of the tangled web." The charges of corruption laid against Champaign County have never been substantiated, and

[30] *Illinois House Journal* (1867), II, 324-25, 441-42, 446-51; *Illinois Senate Journal* (1867), 1050-52.

perhaps other competitors also soiled their hands. Both the ethos of the period and the attitude toward education combined to produce the result. But considerations of transient wrath and even dishonesty (if that is what occurred) weigh little in the balance alongside the location itself. As Bushnell said, a university, once planted, can never be removed, "and if any mistake is made, that mistake rests on the institution as a burden to the end of time." Both the rural nature of the site and the drabness of the environment were to impose severe handicaps on the University as the nation became more urban. And yet, unless one was an environmental determinist, the location was no insurpassable barrier to academic distinction.

The Organic Act directed the Governor to appoint 28 persons (5 from each of 3 judicial divisions and 1 from each of 13 congressional districts) to the Board of Trustees.[31] Its ex officio members were the Governor, the Superintendent of Public Instruction, the President of the State Agricultural Society, and the Regent of the University. At their first meeting on the second Tuesday in March, 1867, the Trustees were to elect a Regent to head the institution. The authors used "Regent" to avoid the evils associated with the office of President in the ante-bellum college. The Decatur Committee set the term of the Regent at six years, the same as the trustees, but the General Assembly reduced it to two years without recorded debate.[32] A short term represented the academic equivalent of frequent elections in politics, and it reminds us that Jacksonian democrats called the University into being. The enabling law ordered the governing body to appoint a Treasurer and Recording Secretary and authorized it to name a Corresponding Secretary. His duties were to aid the progress of science by circulating information about experiments and the industrial and economic statistics of Illinois.

The statute called upon the Trustees to manage the University so as "to teach, in the most thorough manner, such branches of learning as are related to agriculture and the mechanic arts, and military tactics, without excluding other scientific and classical stud-

---

[31] *Illinois Laws* (1867), 123-29. As enacted, Section 12 of the Organic Law related to the location.

[32] *Illinois House Journal* (1867), II, 439.

Eliphalet Nott gained prominence as a foremost American educator during his presidency at Union College in Schenectady, New York, from 1804 to 1866. He trained Wayland and laid consecrating hands on John M. Gregory.

Francis Wayland, President of Brown University (1827-55) and a leading reformer of higher education before the Civil War. Wayland's ideas strongly influenced the first curriculum at Illinois.

Jonathan B. Turner (1805-99), a visionary and broad-gauged reformer who led the Illinois land-grant forces in the 1850's.

The Smithsonian Institution building in Washington, D.C., in 1865. Jonathan B. Turner regarded the Smithsonian Institution as a central luminary of science with which all of the state land-grant institutions should be affiliated.

Alexander Dallas Bache, chief of the scientific Lazzaroni and leader of the forces which worked in the 1850's for a national university and a national academy of sciences.

Justin S. Morrill, the Vermont congressman whose second bill to establish land-grant colleges received the approval of President Lincoln in 1862.

A view of the campus in 1874 from the new University Hall. At the upper left is the original Urbana-Champaign Institute building facing north on University Avenue. At the right is the Mechanical Building and Drill Hall on Springfield Avenue. The Boneyard Creek (with its bridge) crosses the center of the picture, and the horse-drawn vehicles are tied to a fence on Green Street.

John M. Gregory, first Regent of Illinois Industrial University (1867-80).

Authorities and students in front of the "Elephant" about 1868. Thomas J. Burrill is on the left in front of the door. Willard C. Flagg and John M. Gregory are third and fourth from the left respectively.

The south side of Main Street in Champaign about 1870.

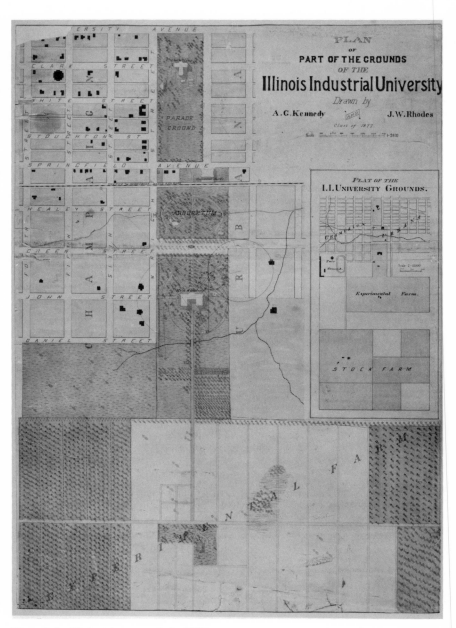

Plan of the University grounds in 1877.

A broadside advertisement, probably first used in 1877 and sent to every post office in the state. The original measures 11⅜ by 17¼ inches.

ies."[33] They were to arrange the curriculum so that students could attend school during six autumn and winter months and either return home or remain at the University during the remainder of the year. But the farmers who wrote the bill proscribed loafing and paid high regard to the dignity of work. "No student," declared the Organic Act, "shall at any time be allowed to remain in or about the University in idleness, or without full mental or industrial occupation."[34] An individual had to be 15 years old and pass an examination in common-school subjects for admission.

The authors demonstrated their revulsion against the old-time learning by prohibiting the conferring of degrees and diplomas and by banning use of Latin. They considered parchments inscribed in Cicero's language to be meaningless symbols of the hated classical college. The statute therefore specified that students who attended the University for at least one year should receive certificates of scholarship which described in English the grades they earned in courses taken. All labels and nomenclature were to be in English so far as possible.

The enabling legislation extended new educational opportunity to farmers primarily, but did not completely overlook other previously disadvantaged groups. Though the act said nothing about women and by implication did not envision them as students, many people in the industrial education movement favored co-education. The authors' silence on race was significant. The 1863 draft bill for establishment of the University had explicitly provided for admitting any white Illinois resident.[35] In light of the Emancipation Proclamation and the Thirteenth Amendment, however, the University would be open to men of all races.

Governor Oglesby lost no time in naming the 28 appointees to the governing body. Understandably, they came overwhelmingly from Republican ranks and main-line Protestant denominations. The church affiliations which can be identified reveal a sprinkling of Presbyterians, Congregationalists, Methodists, and at least one Episcopalian, one Christian, and perhaps one Unitarian. Baptists

---

[33] *Illinois Laws* (1867), 125.
[34] *Ibid.*, 126.
[35] *Prairie Farmer,* July 11, 1863, 17.

predominated, having somehow gained nine seats. John C. Burroughs and Isaac S. Mahan were clergymen of that faith, Luther W. Lawrence a Baptist minister and farmer, and Thomas Quick a leading Baptist trustee. Farmers constituted the largest single occupational group, perhaps as many as two thirds. But it is hard to be precise, because many members combined other gainful activities with agriculture, horticulture, or stock-breeding. Lawyers numbered six, bankers two, and there were a few schoolmen, two college presidents (Burroughs of the University of Chicago and Quick of Illinois Agricultural College), a county official, a builder and contractor (John M. Van Osdel), and a physician and newspaper editor (J. W. Scroggs). The appointees ranged from 33 to 62 years, and their median age was about 49. Collectively, therefore, they had formed their basic attitudes during the Jacksonian period.

While a number of trustees deserve the obscurity which envelops them, a few merit special notice. General Mason Brayman of Springfield drew on his Civil War experience to shape the military program in the University. Alexander M. Brown of Villa Ridge, a Hanover College graduate and lawyer-judge, defended disinterested learning. He found opponents in a group obviously appointed to defend the horticultural interest: Matthias L. Dunlap of Champaign, Samuel Edwards of Lamoille, and Orson B. Galusha of Morris. Although a member of no faction, Willard C. Flagg brought his Yale background and deep concern to bear on developing a science of agriculture. Samuel S. Hayes of Chicago was no doubt named to the Board because of his prominence as a Democrat. Joseph O. Cunningham, an Urbana lawyer, perhaps owed his place to the belief that a college needed close watching by local residents. Emory Cobb had amassed a comfortable fortune from telegraphy before settling down at Kankakee. The Board met in Springfield soon after Governor Oglesby announced its composition.

These men inherited an especially difficult task. The demand for a reconstruction of higher education had culminated in the Morrill Act, and this federal carrot had finally tempted reluctant Illinois into moving. Thereupon several interest groups struggled to monopolize the benefits of the national aid, with Turner and his cohorts writing their ideas into the new law. They were ardent spokesmen of economic and educational principles which had come to full flower during the heyday of Jacksonian democracy some two decades earlier. The university which existed in their mind's eye was a center of utilitarian education for the producing classes. It was poles apart from the old-time college and from the type of university demanded by men like Tappan or the Lazzaroni, who were far more familiar with European developments and more aristocratic in their outlook. The Organic Act which established the University embodied a social policy rather than an educational philosophy, and its limitations became apparent as the work of organizing the University got under way in the following years.

CHAPTER FOUR

In the Midst of a Great Conflict

RIVAL CONCEPTIONS OF HIGHER LEARNING struggled for mastery in the United States in the last third of the nineteenth century. The old-time college remained entrenched, its disciplinary ideals eloquently championed by Princeton's James McCosh and Yale's Noah Porter. Leading architects of the modern university, notably Charles W. Eliot of Harvard and Daniel C. Gilman of Johns Hopkins, advanced the ideals of science, research, and utility. Meanwhile, the land-grant colleges challenged both older educational purposes and privately controlled universities. These public institutions followed no single master plan, although Andrew D. White quickly gained special distinction for Cornell University.

Illinois' power to influence the emerging American university

[84]

lay with the Board of Trustees on March 12, 1867, when Governor
Oglesby presided over its initial meeting in the House of Representatives at Springfield. The main task of the 26 members present —
selection of a Regent — involved the larger issue of the nature of
the education to be fashioned at Champaign-Urbana. In choosing
a Regent, the governing body revealed its own limitations and the
difficulty of finding educators qualified to chart a new course.
Matthias L. Dunlap named Daniel J. Pinckney, a Mount Morris
clergyman who had campaigned for public schools and therefore
admirably suited Dunlap's plans. Thomas Quick nominated President John M. Gregory of Kalamazoo College in Michigan, a former
Baptist minister. John C. Burroughs proposed Norman N. Wood,
a Baptist clergyman of Jacksonville and former President of Shurtleff College, where he had taught philosophy and theology and
proved unpopular. The fourth candidate was J. L. Pickard, a Bowdoin College alumnus and Superintendent of Schools in Chicago.[1]

Dunlap seemingly underscored the slate's lack of distinction
by moving that any member of the General Assembly was competent
to hold the office of Regent. His real purpose in affirming good
Jacksonian doctrine was to oppose any old-style clerical president
and especially Gregory. Immediately after receiving appointment
to the Board, Quick and other Baptist trustees had asked their co-
religionist, whom they knew to sympathize with industrial education,
if they could present his name. Gregory told Burroughs he had "no
very earnest desire" for the job, but "Mr. Quick said you had no
other Baptist name to present, and it seemed to me it might be duty
to go [sic] if God opened the way." After Burroughs withdrew the
candidacy of Wood, whom he had used as a stalking-horse, Gregory
won 16 votes on the first ballot to 5 each for Pinckney and Pickard.
An attempt to push Pinckney failed and Gregory then got a unanimous vote. His choice severely disappointed leaders of the industrial
education movement, and it would have been characteristic for
Turner to complain, "O Lord, how long, how long? An ex-superin-

[1] Board of Trustees of Illinois Industrial University, *First Annual Report* (Springfield, 1868), 15-16. Hereinafter, the published reports of the Board of Trustees
will be cited by giving the number of the volume and the year of publication:
e.g., *1st Report* (1868).

tendent of public instruction and a Baptist preacher! Could anything be worse?"[2]

Gregory's second thoughts weighed against acceptance. He considered the two-year tenure hazardous, wanted the $3,000 salary raised, and viewed with alarm a "Report of the State Industrial University Committee" in which Turner charged fraud in location at Urbana. Greogry tried to secure an honorable release but accepted after the Trustees allayed his fears of sectional strife and promised to pay him $4,000, a figure he insisted on.[3] The Regent began work in Kalamazoo on April 1, 1867. He turned immediately to preparation of a curriculum report and financial matters. On the latter he took counsel with Brayman, Cobb, and Cunningham, but ignored Brayman's advice never to look to the state for funds. Instead, Gregory asked the Governor to raise the matter of a $25,000 to $30,000 appropriation with a special session of the legislature. Oglesby thought it impolitic, for in securing the location the Champaign County people had assured lawmakers that the endowment was sufficient to operate the University.[4]

The Regent assumed his place as President of the Board after formal presentation to it on May 7 in Champaign-Urbana. The high point of this meeting, at which 25 trustees clumsily made arrangements for an autumn opening of the University, came on May 8 when Gregory set the intellectual compass of Illinois Industrial University. As head of a Committee on Course of Study and Faculty appointed by Governor Oglesby the previous March, Gregory had concentrated since his appointment on basic issues of educational policy. He knew his own mind and, desiring no interference from conservatives or progressives on the Board, wrote a report with little assistance from members of the Committee: Newton Bateman,

[2] Gregory to Burroughs, Kalamazoo, March 7, 1867, John M. Gregory Papers. These papers are in the University of Illinois Archives, as are all other unpublished materials unless otherwise indicated. The only authority which I have found for the Turner quotation is Allan Nevins, *Illinois* (New York, 1917), 44-45, and it is undocumented.

[3] Gregory to Quick, Kalamazoo, March 18, 26, 1867; Gregory to Newton Bateman, March 18, 1867, Gregory Papers.

[4] Gregory wrote from Kalamazoo in mid-April to Brayman, Cobb, and Cunningham. Brayman's advice is in Gregory to Cobb, April 26[?], 1867; Gregory to Oglesby, April 22, 1867; Gregory to Cunningham, April 26, 1867, Gregory Papers.

Superintendent of Public Instruction; Brayman; Flagg, who had a vital interest in agricultural education; and Samuel S. Hayes.[5] The whole career of the 45-year-old educator lay behind his remarks.

Born on July 6, 1822, in Sand Lake, New York, Gregory came from English stock which had settled in New England before removing to the lovely region east of Albany. His mother, who named him John Milton after her favorite poet, died in his youth. The common schools, hard work, and religious discipline nurtured the frail lad, whose father, a farmer and tanner, released him from service upon realizing that his son would never earn a livelihood by manual labor. For three years the young man taught school and attended Poughkeepsie Academy.

In 1842 Gregory entered Union College at Schenectady, then at the noontide of its prestige under Eliphalet Nott. As a student he won election to Phi Beta Kappa in the classical program at a time when the Scientific Course carried Nott's approval. Gregory joined Equitable Union (later Delta Upsilon), one of six secret societies in the College. Here Nott had pioneered in accepting fraternities as inevitable and tried to render them open and useful. Gregory's organization was literary and social rather than convivial in nature, and followed strict temperance principles. It appears to have convinced him that secrecy served no useful purpose in a college society. Gregory also participated in the Philomathean Society, oldest of the literary groups at Union. The beautiful College on a wide plateau in gentle hills along the Mohawk River, the first in America to follow a coherent architectural plan, appealed to Gregory's keen aesthetic sense. But Nott himself left the most lasting impression on him. A towering personality who successfully reformed collegiate discipline as well as the curriculum, Nott kindled "high purposes and noble resolves" in countless Union graduates who gained distinction and laid consecrating hands on John Milton Gregory.[6]

---

[5] Gregory to Quick, March 26, 1867; Gregory to Pickard, March 19, 1867; Gregory to Bateman, March 28, April 24, 1867, Gregory Papers. Later, however, Gregory said that he had sought advice from his colleagues. See *7th Report* (1875), 66.

[6] John M. Gregory, "College Secret Societies," *Present Age*, I (March 16, 1882), 163-64; Gregory, "Dr. Nott," *Michigan Teacher*, I (May, 1866), 159.

After his graduation in 1846 Gregory studied law for two years before experiencing a spiritual crisis. Concluding that his conversion at 13 had not been genuine, he entered the Baptist ministry at Hoosic Falls, New York, late in 1847. At that time Gregory opened a diary in which he kept strict spiritual accounts for a quarter-century.[7] A year later he married a second cousin, Julia Gregory, whose discontent with the local church induced her husband to accept a call to Akron, Ohio. Gregory abandoned the pulpit after five years, partly at his wife's prompting and perhaps because it confined him. However, he remained an occasional preacher and devoted layman, although his morbid introspection and quest for personal perfection gradually diminished.

Gregory moved to Michigan, and as head of the literary department in his brother Urian's Detroit Commercial College established a curriculum that combined elements of both the classical and parallel courses at Union College. But he saw public education as the great need and quickly moved into a commanding position in a tight network of common-school advocates. He joined the Michigan State Teachers' Association soon after its formation in October, 1852, helped found the *Michigan Journal of Education* in 1854 (and edited it until 1859), and won election as President of the MSTA in 1854. Understanding the uses of power, he gained the office of State Superintendent of Public Instruction on the Republican ticket in 1858. His decisive triumph derived partly from a reputation earned in advocating temperance, abolition, and Christian unity in the religious press.

Not an original thinker, Gregory typified the second wave of ante-bellum architects of the common schools. He drew on the ideas of the pioneers: Horace Mann, Henry Barnard, Michigan's John Pierce, and European writers. He insisted on universal education as vital to democracy and envisioned the public-school system as an integrated whole extending through the university. Desiring to avoid mere intellectual culture and to train active mental power, he stressed the need to substitute study of nature and facts — common

[7] Allene Gregory, *John Milton Gregory: A Biography* (Chicago, 1923), copiously quotes Gregory's diary, which has not been located. See also Harry A. Kersey, "John Milton Gregory as a Midwestern Educator: 1852-1880" (unpublished doctoral dissertation, University of Illinois, 1965).

things — for the exclusive study of books. But for Gregory the great end of education lay in molding character.

As Superintendent of Public Instruction Gregory was the real executive of the State Board of Education, which assumed control of Michigan State Agricultural College in 1858. He gained valuable experience but erred in allowing the Board to become mired in detail and in singlehandedly transforming a four-year program which emphasized science into a two-year technical course. His reorganization embittered old friends of agricultural education in Michigan. Enrollment dropped by half and most students opposed his re-election to the superintendency. The State Board of Agriculture gained authority in 1861 and returned the College to its original curriculum.[8]

However, Gregory's career suffered no eclipse. In 1862 he narrowly missed winning the nomination for the U.S. Congress but regained the superintendency. Two years later he accepted the headship of Kalamazoo College when President James A. B. Stone and his wife Lucinda were forced out because of bitter conflict they aroused. Baptists regarded Gregory, who had always defended private colleges as necessary supplements to public higher education, as the best man to save the situation. He accepted in order to bring his whole influence to bear for Christian learning and in his inaugural address defended *The Right and Duty of Christianity to Educate*. Baptists recognized his success in his new post when Madison (later Colgate) University conferred an honorary doctorate of letters upon him in 1866. But persistent strife and an annual deficit of a third in his $1,500 salary, which he tried to offset by selling "shares" at half a dollar each to Baptist Sunday school children, made him receptive to the Illinois offer.[9]

A close student of Gregory's career down to the May evening when he appeared before the Board could have anticipated much about his plans. A product of a classical education, Gregory deeply respected the wisdom of the past. A man keenly attuned to the

[8] Madison Kuhn, *Michigan State: The First Hundred Years, 1855-1955* (East Lansing, 1955), 26-27, 47-64, and *passim;* Superintendent of Public Instruction of the State of Michigan, *Twenty-third Annual Report* (Lansing, 1860), 13-15.
[9] Charles True Goodsell and Willis Frederick Dunbar, *Centennial History of Kalamazoo College* (Kalamazoo, 1933), 38-72, 76-80, 86. Gregory's inaugural address was published at Kalamazoo, 1865.

times (and trained by the forward-looking Eliphalet Nott), he realized that a new educational order demanded to be born. Gregory was decidedly more evangelical than such titans of university reform as Eliot, Gilman, and White. Unlike them, however, he had not traveled in Europe and had no appreciation of the German university's significance for American higher education. But the slightly built, bespectacled educator with quick nervous energy possessed an eager willingness to learn.

Gregory began by reordering the language of the Morrill Act to demonstrate that its chief aim was "the liberal and practical education of the industrial classes."[10] Rather than teach manual trades to the masses, land-grant colleges were to afford the few a thorough comprehension of the principles that underlay industrial rather than professional pursuits. The education these studies required was as systematic and complete as that for the professions, though different.

The curriculum designed to realize these goals restated educational reforms which were up to 40 years old. Ideas advanced by James Marsh of Vermont and Eliphalet Nott in the 1820's and by Francis Wayland in the 1840's and after were the leading influences on Gregory, although he did not acknowledge his debt. (The only authorities he named were John Stuart Mill and Sir William Hamilton.) In effect, Gregory proposed that the six departments and 15 courses he recommended be divided into regular and parallel courses, but he avoided using those terms. Five suggested departments related to newer branches of learning, and these Gregory described first. The Agricultural Department embraced courses in agriculture and in horticulture and landscape gardening. The Polytechnic Department contained courses in mechanics, civil engineering, mining and metallurgy, and architecture and fine arts. The Military Department included military engineering and military tactics. The Department of Chemistry and Natural Science attempted to yoke basic science (chemistry, mineralogy, geology, and natural history) with applied science and utilitarian pursuits. The Department of Trade and Commerce provided, in addition to requisite literary and natural science studies, political economy, com-

[10] His remarks are in *1st Report* (1868), 47-64. The quotation is at p. 47.

mercial geography, commercial law, commercial correspondence, bookkeeping, and the history of commerce.

Gregory then gave extended consideration to the Department of General Science and Literature. In discussing the principles that controlled selection of subjects for this version of the old regular curriculum, Gregory revealed his commitment to the faculty psychology. Dividing knowledge into four grand divisions, he said that each affected culture in two ways. First, each afforded a certain type of mental exercise. Natural sciences cultivated the powers of inductive reasoning. Mathematics developed abstract thought and deductive reasoning. Linguistics and philology trained the faculty of discursive reasoning. The philosophical and speculative sciences strengthened the reflective faculties. Second, each division affected culture by the stimulating power of its ideas. Natural sciences aroused eager curiosity about physical facts and their underlying natural laws; mathematics failed to stimulate most mature minds; language strongly affected thought by facilitating the creation and exchange of ideas; and philosophy and history attracted and stimulated the best human intelligence.

Gregory defended the seven courses he assigned to the Department of General Science and Literature by saying they would fit students to master the special courses in the other five departments or prepare them for life's duties. The seven studies were mathematics; natural history and chemistry; English, modern, and ancient languages and literatures; history and social science; and intellectual and moral philosophy. These liberal arts had practical value, and although "Latin will not help a man to hold the plow, nor will mental philosophy teach how to fatten hogs,"[11] the Industrial University was founded to furnish liberal and practical rather than common education.

These seven subjects comprised the University Course, enrollment in which was the minimum required for regular standing. Admission to this program required the preparatory studies offered by better public schools, including Latin but omitting Greek in favor of more mathematics than existing colleges demanded. However, students would enjoy elective freedom. They could supple-

[11] *Ibid.*, 55.

ment the University Course with technical studies, add any of the seven liberal arts offerings to special work without entering the University Course, or merely choose specific courses as desired.

His curricular ideas revealed Gregory as a traditionalist responding to the demands of the age. He wanted to arrest the swinging of the educational pendulum at a golden mean, avoiding the old sterile learning at one extreme and the new utilitarianism at the other. He tried to save the best of the past and to meet practical needs. He designed Illinois Industrial University to extend the sphere and multiply the advantages of the old education for the benefit of others besides the learned professions and to fix work related to agriculture and mechanic arts upon basic advances in the underlying sciences. He was a prophet in envisioning a comprehensive university.[12]

In addition, Gregory urged adoption of the manual-labor system, contending that it promoted health, inculcated habits of industry, united learning with labor, dignified work, and enabled students to earn their own way. For Gregory, belief in compulsory manual labor as a distinctive feature of the new education constituted an article of faith. The failure of the Fellenberg manual-labor system by the 1840's had not demonstrated the impracticality of this venture. It had merely convinced many pioneer land-grant college presidents that its true application remained to be found. Now the felt realities of the times as well as pedagogical doctrines suggested a plan of vocational education combining mental discipline and physical culture with financial aid. Gregory knew well the successful manual-labor scheme at Michigan State Agricultural College, which served as the model for several universities, and he proposed to make it the keystone at Urbana. But the notion that manual labor provided a special means of moral and cultural uplift was a fantasy contradicted by all experience, and the compulsory labor requirement soon became a source of trouble in the University.[13]

The Regent's criteria for the faculty emphasized university rather than college ideals. Eminent and intensive scholarship at

[12] Edmund J. James, "The Life and Work of Dr. John Milton Gregory," *Alumni Quarterly,* VIII (Oct., 1914), 248-51.
[13] On the larger context of Gregory's belief, see Earle D. Ross, "The Manual Labor Experiment in the Land Grant College," *Mississippi Valley Historical Review,* XXI (March, 1935), 513-21.

least in one's own department and a thoroughly tested ability to teach were listed in that order as the two indispensable qualities; gentlemanly character and culture also counted. The instructional corps of 15 departmental chairs and four lecturers was to consist of professors, assistant professors, lecturers or nonresident professors, and tutors. Gregory believed that the educational system he outlined would enable the industrial classes to recapture lost status.

Gregory's curriculum report horrified some trustees, but they agreed unanimously to publish his remarks in order to test public reaction. They also postponed the opening of the University to the first Monday in March, 1868, to give time needed to ripen novel plans. At the May meeting the Trustees organized in other ways for the task ahead. They formed ten standing committees to deal with various aspects of the work, and established an Executive Committee of nine members which was to meet quarterly under Gregory's chairmanship. To this body Gregory appointed and the Board approved Cobb, Cunningham, Dunlap, Mahan, J. H. Pickrell, Quick, Scroggs, and Van Osdel.

Preparations for the opening occupied the summer. Gregory shouldered chief responsibility, but the Executive Committee — three of whose members lived at the seat of the University — met in Urbana three times and set a bad precedent by meddling with details and supervising the improvements being made to the building and grounds. The Board had authorized the expenditure of $7,850 to dignify the entrance of the Institute building with stone steps and a portico, rearrange some of its rooms, and erect outbuildings. Gregory sought Frederick Law Olmsted, architect of Central Park in New York City, to landscape the campus. Olmsted advised that horticulturists lay out the grounds immediately around the University and that further work await a plan for building needs for the next half-century. Gregory regarded pleasing buildings and grounds as essential to the success of the University, but his colleagues on the Board were aesthetically as well as financially impoverished, and the campus therefore grew with little regard for plan or beauty.[14]

[14] Gregory's closest ally in aesthetic matters was perhaps Van Osdel, a builder-architect who had designed and erected fine buildings in Chicago and later published *The Carpenter's Own Book* (1833). He drew the plans for the steps and portico.

Financial considerations were uppermost in these months. The Board redeemed $20,000 in bonds and reluctantly decided to sell land scrip in an overstocked market. In May and November the Trustees disposed of three parcels amounting to 380,000 of its 480,000 scrip acres. These transactions brought $250,192, an average of 66 cents an acre. (One contract for 100,000 acres went to Gleason F. Lewis, a speculator whose acquisition of nearly 5,000,000 acres of college scrip gave him a practical monopoly.) Later, Illinois sold 74,480 acres at a better return. The University averaged 70 cents an acre on all scrip sold, which was midway between Brown University's low of 42 cents and Virginia's high of 95 cents an acre. Management of the scrip reflected credit on the governing body, which invested the proceeds primarily in Illinois bonds bearing interest at no less than 6 per cent.

However, Illinois flouted the Morrill Act's ban on locating land in other states with their scrip. The conscious decision to choose 100,000 acres in western states rather than in timber land represented a serious lost opportunity, for Cornell cleared nearly $5,000,000 from its Wisconsin pine lands. Gregory and Trustee Moore C. Goltra located 15,973 acres in Minnesota during the summer of 1867, but the difficulty of doing so led Gregory to conclude that Kansas and Nebraska offered better prospects. Goltra then entered 9,340 acres in Nebraska. Ultimately these 25,000 acres brought more than the 455,000 scrip acres, but taxes became a drain while waiting for the located land to appreciate in value. Although the Morrill Act spurred Illinois to establish a public university, the inadequate endowment it afforded left the institution as financially naked as the poorest old-time college.[15]

Accordingly, the University made strenuous efforts to advertise, with Gregory bearing the brunt of the burden. He was not alone among contemporary educators in mobilizing support for his institution, but he may have excelled in the skill and persistency with which he sought to possess the public ear. Having long

[15] Gregory to Brayman, Chicago, May 17, and St. Paul, Aug. 2, 1867, Gregory Papers; *1st Report* (1868), *passim; 2nd Report* (1869), *passim; 3rd Report* (1870), 92; *4th Report* (1872), 77; Paul W. Gates, *The Wisconsin Pine Lands of Cornell University: A Study in Land Policy and Absentee Ownership* (Ithaca, 1943), 29-30, 42-43.

watched American colleges "languish through a feeble infancy for lack of that public sympathy which their Presidents and Faculties took too little care to win," he was determined not to allow Illinois to suffer in that way. Since popular opinion was likely to be dangerous where the public mind was filled with erroneous ideas about land-grant schools, Gregory sought to enlist on his side the power and influence of the newspaper press and citizens of Illinois. "Everywhere," he said of his visits to farmers' and teachers' groups, religious and social gatherings, county and state fairs, "I laid before them the great and noble public aims which filled my own mind, and which I believed ought to influence theirs."[16] An excellent extemporaneous speaker, he told a Quincy State Fair audience in 1867 that the University would be equal to but different from the older colleges in quality, and afford knowledge of basic scientific principles related to agriculture and industrial arts as well as mastery of their applications. Special schools, particularly in agriculture, had been arranged so as not to interfere with the general course. He promised that the University would increase and diffuse agricultural science, but admitted that the proposed program would not please everyone.[17]

In mid-October a conflict over educational policy erupted. Dunlap challenged Gregory in the Executive Committee for control of the curriculum. Contending that federal and state law designed the University to operate during winter months for the industrial classes, he proposed that a 12-week session devoted to common-school subjects begin in December. The 15-year-olds eligible for admission needed such elementary work and could also select additional studies allied to agriculture or the mechanic arts. The University should employ teachers for this program with an eye to making them regular professors when the University opened in March. In addition, Dunlap recommended that free evening lectures on practical agriculture and on mechanic arts commence in December.

Dunlap was a veteran of the movement for industrial educa-

[16] *8th Report* (1877), 193; see also John M. Gregory, "The American Newspaper and American Education," *Journal of Social Science*, XII (Dec., 1880), 61-68.
[17] Chicago *Tribune*, Oct. 10, 1867.

tion in Illinois, and to save hard-won gains he had felt it necessary to stop Gregory. He diametrically opposed the Regent on fundamental issues. Dunlap wanted an agricultural trade school with low admissions standards. He desired no elective system; favored co-education, about which Gregory had been discreetly silent; and strongly disliked the manual-labor system. One of the best-known men in Illinois, Dunlap had long been involved in politics, was prominent in agricultural and horticultural societies, and since the mid-1850's had been agricultural correspondent for the Chicago *Tribune*. He could not be denied a hearing, and the Executive Committee therefore called a special Board meeting for November 26. The Trustees apparently agreed to rebuff Dunlap before they assembled in Urbana. Organized agriculture in the persons of President A. B. McConnell and Secretary John P. Reynolds of the Illinois State Agricultural Society helped isolate the critic — temporarily. The governing body shelved Dunlap's proposal of an early opening without even considering it, but agreed to sponsor a winter short course starting in 1869.[18]

The November meeting afforded an invaluable opportunity to consider plans that the Trustees had been unprepared to resolve earlier. First, the Board adopted bylaws for itself. In many cases these formalized existing practices. At their first day's session in March the Trustees had unanimously acknowledged dependence on divine blessing in their work and resolved to commence each day's proceedings with a scripture reading and prayer, after which one of the Baptist clergymen on the Board had invoked God's aid in the name of Jesus Christ. Now they made the reading of scripture and prayer the first order of business. In defining the duties and terms of their officers, the bylaws made the Regent President of the various faculties and of the Board and empowered him to debate and vote on all issues before the governing body. Dunlap tried to reduce the great authority given Gregory by putting agricultural affairs under the Executive Committee. The Board was to appoint and remove at pleasure the instructional staff and other employees. A two-thirds vote of the members was necessary to amend the bylaws.

[18] Richard Bardolph, *Agricultural Literature and the Early Illinois Farmer* (Urbana, 1948), 60-63; Willard C. Flagg to Newton Bateman, Alton, Nov. 21, 1867, Gregory Papers.

Second, the Trustees adopted a military training plan which grew out of the lack of trained Union officers during the Civil War. The proposal envisioned close federal-state cooperation. Its author was Major Joseph H. Whittlesey, a retired West Point graduate directed by the War Department on April 4, 1867, to devise a system of collegiate military instruction. The following October Whittlesey furnished Brayman an outline of a program for Illinois adapted from one he had devised for Cornell at the request of Andrew D. White, and in November Whittlesey recommended a national program to the Secretary of War. General Brayman now offered these recommendations for his Committee on Military Department.

The Whittlesey-Brayman Report proposed to make Illinois Industrial University a miniature West Point. It provided for a graduate of the U.S. Military Academy to become the highest-ranking person at the University after the Regent. The military professor was to supervise a course of military studies. Whittlesey wanted the War Department to prescribe the course, and he corrected Brayman when the latter put it under University authority. Although Whittlesey did not intend to make the program obligatory, Brayman hoped to put the institution on as complete a military footing as possible.

West Point became a model to imitate. Classroom work adapted from the Military Academy was to take four to five hours weekly, with compulsory drill extra. Rigidly enforced camp regulations were to govern all student life except for the time spent in civilian studies. Merits and demerits were to count in determining military grades. Brayman urged that students wear a cadet uniform always, and that the best cadets command the University Battalion. He praised the plan as a means of recruiting career officers and facilitating college discipline. The Trustees unanimously approved the recommendation.[19]

[19] Whittlesey to Brayman, Winchester, Va., Sept. 5, Oct. 19, [Dec. 13], 1867; Whittlesey's printed "Circular to Presidents, Members of the Faculty, and Trustees of Colleges of the United States," May 20, 1867, all in the Gregory Papers; *1st Report* (1868), 80-86. Gregory later lobbied for the Whittlesey Plan in Congress, but feared "that the West Point men will oppose it, as likely to injure that Institution." Gregory to Brayman, Washington, Jan. 7, Feb. 7, 1868, Gregory Papers.

Third, Gregory now suggested that only two programs be offered at the outset. He desired a three-year agricultural and horticultural course for poorly prepared students, thus conceding as much to the backwardness of agricultural science as to Dunlap. In addition, he wanted a four-year general education offering. For the latter he outlined 44 term courses. He assigned a third of these to 11 separate science subjects and the remainder to other studies, including three terms of the classics (Horace and Cicero) and of both French and German. In addition, he provided for rhetoric, English literature, and modern philology. He arranged the junior and senior years to emphasize history and the social sciences, logic, mental and moral philosophy, and "Elements of Criticism."[20] In reality, Gregory was combining the old regular and parallel programs and giving the whole a somewhat modern content. His profusion of courses meant that he could not hope to achieve genuine university academic standards.

Gregory believed that diligent students could master an industrial course while taking the 44 courses he prescribed, but wanted their extra work to come from 17 optional offerings. These included five courses in Greek, three in Latin, two in English literature, and one each in chemistry, astronomy, ancient history, "Butler's Analogy," the science of education, social science, and "Evidences of Christianity."[21] The Trustees approved these proposals.

Fourth, the Board set student costs and hired a faculty. An empty treasury ruled out the offer of free education, and tuition was fixed at $15 for Illinois and $20 for out-of-state pupils. The visitorial body required $10 for matriculation, and term fees of $4 for a room and $2.50 for incidentals. Gregory labored against odds to recruit a strong faculty, for the classical colleges had trained few men for the industrial universities. He failed to find a professor of practical agriculture. Available men were likely to be New Eng-

---

[20] Gregory had studied Lord Kames (Henry Home), *Elements of Criticism* (1st ed., 1762) as a text in moral philosophy under Nott at Union College. The book dealt with rhetoric and aesthetic criticism.

[21] Two of these courses focused on books which dominated the teaching of religion in American colleges from the late eighteenth century until after the Civil War: Joseph Butler, *The Analogy of Religion, Natural and Revealed* (London, 1736); William Paley, *A View of the Evidences of Christianity* (3 vols., London, 1794).

landers out of the old mold. William M. Baker and George W. Atherton, whom the Board appointed professors effective the following March 1 at salaries of $2,000 each, were of this stamp.[22] Baker had spent three years at Bowdoin College and one at Bangor Seminary and served as a Civil War chaplain before becoming Principal of the Springfield High School. Atherton had graduated from Yale in 1863 and served in the Union Army. Gregory unquestionably intended Baker for English and Atherton for history, but slyly secured their appointments without naming their duties.

These preparations dismayed Dunlap, who boldly attacked in the Chicago *Tribune* under his familiar pseudonym, "Rural." He condemned the Regent's inexperience in practical studies, insisted that the curriculum was not sufficiently utilitarian, and invited the Trustees to reassert their authority. The cream of the joke, lamented a *Tribune* editorial, was that Gregory and his faculty were "all preachers, not very powerful ones at that." Other newspapers joined the assault, although only Scroggs from the Board joined Dunlap at this time. Gregory missed the point in viewing "Rural's" abusive charges as personal and refused to defend himself publicly, but he gained some support, notably from the Chicago *Standard,* a Baptist publication. This battle on the eve of the University's opening symbolized the serious conflict over the nature of the "new education."[23]

Monday, March 2, 1868. A small band of hopefuls — some 50 men — entered Illinois Industrial University that morning. Before the term's end the number rose to 77, over half of whom (45) were Champaign County residents. Gregory, having anticipated hundreds, concluded that Dunlap's criticisms had diverted many from enrolling. The raw youths took preparatory work mainly, along with Latin (which 30 chose), mathematics, rhetoric, and natural philosophy.[24] Despite initial disappointment, Gregory soon

[22] Harvard started paying its professors $4,000 and its assistant professors $2,000 in 1869.
[23] Chicago *Tribune,* Dec. 18, 1867; Jan. 18, 1868; Chicago *Standard,* Jan. 2, 1868; Gregory to C. C. Buell, Feb. 4, 1868; Gregory to Quick, Feb. 6, 1868; Gregory to Brayman, March, 1868, Gregory Papers.
[24] In Dunlap's letter to William Matthews, Jan. 23, 1868, Gregory had evidence of Dunlap advising a father not to enroll his son. Gregory Papers. *3rd Report* (1870), 72; "Rural" in the Chicago *Tribune,* Nov. 18, 1868; "A Professor" in the Chicago *Tribune,* Feb. 18, 1870.

believed everything was going as "merry as a marriage bell," and a lusty optimism marked the inaugural ceremonies on March 11. Trustees, townspeople, and guests from other parts of the state gathered in the fourth-floor chapel in the wing of the "Elephant." The motto "Learning and Labor" in evergreen letters crowned a picture of farmer George Washington in the hall,[25] and the religious flavor of the exercises contrasted strongly with the opening of Cornell the following October and of Johns Hopkins in 1876. At the former, President White stressed the nonsectarianism of the institution and described the blight of intolerance in denominational colleges. At the latter, all prayer was consciously omitted as inappropriate and Thomas Huxley, Darwin's "bulldog," spoke. At Illinois, however, a choir commenced the exercises with a selection entitled "How Good Is He the Giver," an Urbana minister read from the scriptures and a Champaign clergyman offered prayer, a quartet sang "Lord, Forever at Thy Side," the choir and audience sang an original ode set to a familiar hymn tune, and a clergyman pronounced the benediction. Omission of these Christian rites would have brought criticism.[26]

Gregory's inaugural address followed long and florid remarks by Newton Bateman. The Regent, having announced his educational policy the previous May, now defended himself from adversaries and broke no new ground. His performance was therefore anticlimactic. The University was the child of a great popular movement for the liberal education of the industrial classes, said Gregory, who at this point praised Turner. But two major difficulties beset the institution, and Gregory devoted himself to analyzing these. First was the internal problem, "to make true scholars while we make practical artisans, not in one or two arts, but in the whole round of human industries." In short, the task was to unite learn-

[25] Before the inauguration the University seal contained "Farmers and Mechanics" surrounding the motto "Onward and Upward." On March 11, after the ceremonies, the Board made "Learning and Labor" the University's motto and substituted "Illinois Industrial University" for the other phrase in the design of the seal. *1st Report* (1868), 29, 40-42, 125. Gregory's attachment to the concept no doubt inspired the change.
[26] Morris Bishop, *A History of Cornell* (Ithaca, 1962), 88; Hugh Hawkins, *Pioneer: A History of the Johns Hopkins University, 1874-1889* (Ithaca, 1960), 69-70; *1st Report* (1868), 149-82.

ing with labor, and to do so by relating special courses of instruction to a fundamental liberal education course (the core curriculum in science, literature, and art).

An external and more difficult problem came from public opinion. Since the University was the child of popular will, Gregory tried to rout certain common fallacies in regard to industrial colleges. He insisted that the University was not designed as an academy for working-class children. Admitting that the age demanded practicality, he explained that in a mobile society where careers were not fixed, the education which developed brainpower was most practical. Therefore language and books still remained the chief avenues of knowledge. Let us not react against the old tyranny which compelled every seeker of liberal learning to study the classics, said Gregory, by establishing "a counter tyranny to decree that no one shall study the classics." Gregory answered zealots who insisted on prescribing favorite topics by saying that the student who knew what he wanted ought to be free to choose his own path. The University should spread its table with every form of human knowledge and bid the ardent young men of Illinois freely to the feast. Gregory then sketched the promising triumphs which would attend success. Labor and learning would be indissolubly married at the University's altar, thus elevating labor to honor and making it more productive. The result would establish the University as the "West Point for the working world," and greatly promote America's national power. Lastly, success would illustrate the practicality of universal education. "Let us but demonstrate that the highest culture is compatible with the active pursuit of industry, and that the richest learning will pay in a corn field or a carpenter's shop, and we have made universal education not only a possible possession, but a fated necessity of the race. Prove that education, in its highest form, will 'pay' and you have made for it the market of the world." This argument returned to haunt Gregory when the public later decided that the education offered at the University did not in fact "pay." When all that he envisioned had come to pass, said Gregory in concluding, "The light which has heretofore fallen through occasional rifts, and on scattered hill tops, will henceforward flood field and valley with the splendors of a noontime sun, and the quickened intellect of the race will bloom with new beauty and burst into a richer fruitage of industrial arts."[27]

Gregory's failure to show wherein the "new education" was new underlay the Chicago *Evening Post*'s declaration that the "parcel of decayed or otherwise incapacitated preachers" who headed the University had not the remotest comprehension of the demands of modern civilization. But after a festive inaugural dinner — "gotten up in the highest style of Central Illinois, hog and hominy," snapped the *Evening Post* — the Trustees enjoyed the treat of Dunlap's ostensible capitulation. Both a group of Urbana residents and a special committee of the Board had just finished criticizing his childish independence and breach of propriety. Dunlap, thus confronted, apologized and gave Gregory his hand in reconciliation. The Trustees publicly expressed undiminished confidence in the Regent.[28]

The romance of novelty wore thin between the autumn of 1868 and the summer of 1873. As President and Regent, Gregory enjoyed immense power. He called the faculty into being, no easy task when his first choices for professorships in chemistry, mathematics, and mechanical science declined. By persistence and some compromise in his standards, however, Gregory assembled a staff. He appointed Willard F. Bliss, an alumnus of Phillips Exeter and Harvard who had taught Latin and studied the classics in Germany, to teach agriculture. Bliss was at the time farming in Illinois. He named A. P. S. Stuart, an assistant in chemistry at Harvard from 1865 to 1868, Professor of Theoretical and Applied Chemistry. As assistant professors he hired Thomas J. Burrill of the Urbana public schools to teach natural history and botany; Edward Snyder, a native Austrian, for bookkeeping and German; and Samuel W. Shat-

---

[27] *1st Report* (1868), 174-82. The quotation is at p. 182.
[28] The quotations are in Burt E. Powell, *Semi-Centennial History of the University of Illinois, I: The Movement for Industrial Education and the Establishment of the University, 1840-1870* (Urbana, 1918), 304. See also "Memorandum in the Dunlap Case," March, 1868; "Report of Special Committee in the Matter of M. L. Dunlap," March 11, 1868; a holograph sheet of resolutions produced by the Urbana committee, of which Thomas J. Burrill was a member; Brayman to Bateman, Dec. 3, 1868, all in the Gregory Papers; and *1st Report* (1868), 132.

tuck, an alumnus of Norwich University and an Army veteran, for mathematics and military tactics. He paid this rank $1,200.[29]

Gregory's early appointments brought protest from the Methodist editor of the *Northwestern Christian Advocate* (Chicago), who demanded formal recognition of his denomination. "All that any reasonable man will ask," Gregory countered after explaining that insistence upon a Methodist would be duplicated by other denominations, Masons, and political parties which claimed to embrace large numbers in the state, "is that this University shall not be made to serve the interests of any particular class or sect but be fully devoted to the great interests of Science and of education. . . . At all hazards we must resist all claims of representation of any sect or denomination." Gregory added that he himself was not a Baptist within the University. Religion nevertheless exerted an influence: Gregory tried to secure balance among the denominations, and tacitly assumed that faculty members should be Christian and Protestant.[30]

Like White at Cornell, Gregory also employed prominent nonresidents to overcome provinciality and stretch his funds. He enlisted John A. Warder of Cincinnati, a well-known pomologist; Edward Eggleston, the novelist and pioneer social historian, then a Methodist minister of Evanston; and John Wesley Powell, a science teacher at Illinois Wesleyan and curator of the natural history collection at Illinois State Normal University. In May, 1867, the University had given Powell $500 in return for a promise of specimens to be collected on a scientific expedition to the Rocky Mountains. That venture brought Powell fame, and in preparation for a repeat performance Powell secured funds from Normal University late in 1867. The following March Gregory made Powell Professor of Natural History, an appointment Powell dared not announce lest it cost him his subsidy from Normal. It is not clear whether Gregory expected Powell to teach, but the Trustees put him on service, paid him $600 in salary, and sent him at his request to conduct his

[29] *Harvard Graduates' Magazine* (March, 1916), 533-34; Clifford K. Shipton (Custodian of the Harvard University Archives) to author, Feb. 16, 1966; "University Faculty in 1869-1870," *Alumni Quarterly*, VII (Oct., 1913), 266-71.
[30] *Northwestern Christian Advocate*, Jan. 8, 1868; Gregory to Thomas M. Eddy (editor of the *Advocate*), Jan. 30, 1860; Gregory to Edward Eggleston, May 4, 1868, Gregory Papers.

second expedition on the understanding that he would be a representative of Illinois Industrial University.[31]

The Faculty formally organized itself on March 13, 1868, soon after instruction began. Professors Atherton and Baker met with Regent Gregory and announced that no changes were necessary in the plan Gregory had earlier outlined. A year later the Faculty agreed on an order of business for its meetings. On these occasions the professors mainly concerned themselves with administering the curriculum and with student discipline. The officers of instruction exerted little influence on policy.[32]

Gregory groped uncertainly for a meaningful academic structure, his task complicated by the launching of a new type of institution at a time when the differentiation of knowledge agitated higher education. Departments, schools, and colleges therefore emerged slowly and with little conscious design. The department, defined as a single study taught usually by a single professor and assistants, constituted the basic unit. In 1870-71, departments were also arranged into colleges, each described as an entity offering a combined course made up of the subjects needed for one or a group of related callings. By 1872 four colleges and three independent schools had appeared, and for years they constituted the University's organizational framework. The colleges were Agriculture, Engineering, Natural Science, and Literature and Science. Each was subdivided into two or more schools. In addition, schools of Commerce, Military Science, and Domestic Science and Arts existed.[33]

[31] Powell resigned in 1869 "on account of his continued detention with his expedition," but a year later personally reported to the Trustees on the botanical specimens and Rocky Mountain animals he had collected for them. The University declined a renewed invitation to share costs and results of still another expedition. Gregory to Orson B. Galusha, Kalamazoo, May 13, 1867; Gregory to Bateman, March 18, 1868, Gregory Papers; *1st Report* (1868), 32, 38-39, 127, 145; *2nd Report* (1869), 39-40; *3rd Report* (1870), 70; Helen E. Marshall, *Grandest of Enterprises, Illinois State Normal University, 1857-1957* (Normal, 1956), 118-26.

[32] "Faculty Record," I, 14, 18. This is one of three handwritten volumes of the same type.

[33] "Faculty Record," I, 101, 103, 104 (April 8, 26, 29, 1872) shows the establishment of the College of Literature and Science. The remainder of the story is worked out from the Board's published reports, the official catalogues, and other data. The Board reorganized the College in 1873 but did not officially endorse this structure until 1877. *6th Report* (1874), 69-70; *9th Report* (1878), 44-45.

The thin trickle of students widened steadily after the disappointing first term, reaching 112 in 1868-69 and 400 in the year ending in 1873. The achievement was remarkable, for the nation's private colleges did not enjoy a spurt in growth until more than a decade later, and the few public schools in Illinois produced a shortage of college freshmen. Thus, the University could not afford to be choosy. Its examination for admission covered arithmetic, grammar, geography, orthography, and history. Standards were low because the (public) school system of the state ruled out high standards, and therefore most students pursued preparatory work at Urbana. Accordingly, authorities narrowed the elective liberty Gregory had promised in order to prevent its abuse. Early catalogues suggested course sequences; later ones recommended programs for each college, in one of which all pupils were expected to enroll. Nevertheless, students remained free to select as they pleased from available offerings.

Agricultural education, ironically, made no headway at Illinois or in other land-grant colleges for decades. Critics held Gregory's emphasis on liberal education responsible, but the real reason went deeper. The University could not yet train agricultural scientists, and farm lads had no need of a university to learn practical agriculture. Initially, students could pursue a course in agriculture or horticulture which included collateral arts and sciences and lasted either two, three, or four years. Pupils performed daily farm duties under the direction of Jonathan Periam, an agrarian reformer who briefly held the position of Superintendent of Practical Agriculture,[34] but their main instruction came from Bliss. He read and commented in class on Samuel W. Johnson's recent book, *How Crops Grow* (1868). Those registered found these sessions wearisome, and Bliss, aware of his deficiency in chemistry, resigned in June, 1870.

Shortly thereafter the College of Agriculture arose. Its schools of Agriculture and Horticulture offered courses lasting four years. To head the former Gregory appointed Manly Miles of Michigan, an outstanding agricultural scientist whom he had earlier brought

[34] Periam was a practical farmer and social reformer who saw education as the hope of rural folk. He resigned in 1869, at odds with the course Gregory was steering, became active in the Granger movement, published *The Groundswell* (St. Louis, 1874), and later edited the *Prairie Farmer*.

to Michigan State Agricultural College as Professor of Zoology and Animal Physiology. A former practitioner of medicine, Miles kept in close touch with Lawes and Gilbert, the agricultural experimenters at Rothamsted in England, and in 1865 became the first professor of practical agriculture in the United States. He supervised the Michigan State farm, using it as a laboratory rather than a money-maker, and won recognition for systematic experiments with animal feeding and fertilizers. Now Miles intended to spend the autumn and winter at Urbana and the remainder of his time at East Lansing, and for a couple of years, during which he lectured for the University both at its seat and before farmers throughout Illinois, he actually kept a foot in both camps.[35]

Meanwhile, Gregory failed to find a horticulturist and in 1870 named Burrill to this professorship. Burrill added it to his duties in botany. A year later the University laid the foundations of veterinary science with the appointment of Dr. Heinrich J. Detmers, a graduate of Berlin's Royal Veterinary College who had taught and practiced in Germany before emigrating to Illinois in 1865. He instructed students in the free clinic he operated. But Gregory apparently undervalued his field while paying lip service to its importance. Detmers left in 1872.[36] Hence the College relied for the bulk of its teaching on other faculty members and on special lecturers, especially the speakers at winter farmers' institutes. Courses in agriculture and horticulture enrolled 68 out of 277 students in 1870-71, the number dropped to 62 out of 406 in 1873-74, and it plummeted thereafter. Illinois farmers found the program valueless, as the Hillsboro *Journal* revealed in describing the University's attempt to make scientific farmers: "They take the young men out in the spring of the year and compel them to sit on the fence with kid gloves on their hands, umbrellas over their heads and fifteen cent cigars in their mouths, and there watch the men who are employed to do the work. . . . This is hard on the young gentlemen but they learn to farm, you know, and that is what the institution is for."[37]

[35] "Sketch of Manly Miles," *Appleton's Popular Science Monthly,* LIV (April, 1899), 834-41; Kuhn, *Michigan State,* 60-61, 81, 96-100, 137.
[36] Frederick P. Bayles, "Dr. Henry J. Detmers, His Life History in Germany and in the United States," MS. loaned to me by Mr. David Huehner, a distant relative.
[37] As quoted in the *Illini* (a student newspaper), Feb., 1875.

Engineering education began to eclipse agricultural education almost from the start. The nation hungered for men who could design and construct machines, railways, and factories, and the apprentice system could not train them. In 1867 the Board had authorized trustees from the Chicago area to establish a polytechnical department of the University in Chicago but not to use University funds or property for the purpose. Later, several parties induced the Chicago Common Council to pledge that it would issue $250,000 of 7 per cent bonds as endowment if the General Assembly empowered it to do so and if the Board would permanently locate its mechanical branch within a half-mile of the city's geographical center. The Board agreed to these conditions in November, 1868, but the Chicago *Tribune* opposed burdening the taxpayer and urged that private enterprise support technical and professional education. Since no more was ever heard of the proposition, the College of Engineering developed downstate. Gregory's original curriculum report provided the organizational basis for the polytechnical branch and its subordinate units, the departments of Civil Engineering, Mechanical Science and Engineering, Mining and Metallurgy, and Architecture and Fine Arts.[38]

Only the former two departments experienced growth in early years. Civil engineering had emerged as an experimental study before the Civil War, and now Shattuck built on those foundations in teaching the subject. Mechanical engineering did not get under way at Illinois until Stillman W. Robinson arrived on January 1, 1870. A Vermont farm boy, Robinson left a machine-shop apprenticeship to study civil engineering at the University of Michigan, served with the U.S. Lake Survey and on the Michigan faculty, and published several engineering papers before Gregory found him. He tried to combine scientific and practical instruction, and succeeded notably in making shop instruction part of collegiate technical education. Civil engineering attracted 54 students and mechanical engineering 37 in the spring of 1872, and that progress underlay the opening of the Mechanical Building and Drill Hall, the first new building erected at the University, the previous autumn.

Gregory made science prominent in the curriculum but prob-

[38] Chicago *Tribune,* Nov. 20, 1868; *1st Report* (1868), 22, 27; *2nd Report* (1869), 41-45.

ably had no firm grasp of the field. Natural philosophy was branching into physics and chemistry at the time, and natural history into botany and zoology. This fluidity helps account for Gregory's difficulty in devising a suitable organization for the sciences. What started as a Department of Natural and Mechanical Philosophy evolved into physics and mechanical engineering, and both became part of the College of Engineering. Chemistry and natural history formed the core of the College of Natural Science. The former, a prestige science organized into a school, aimed at enabling students to apply principles of chemistry to any of the related arts and to fit them for original research. In a four-year program consisting of 36 courses, 13 were required in chemistry as well as ten hours of laboratory work a week beginning in the middle of the first year. Stuart aroused enthusiasm for the subject, and the new chemistry class numbered 50 in the fall of 1870. But few took advanced work. The School of Natural History aimed at preparing practical geologists, collectors and curators of museums, and superintendents of scientific explorations and surveys. Its load was carried by Burrill, who had gone as a botanist with Powell on the latter's first expedition to the Rockies, and Don Carlos Taft. An Amherst College alumnus who joined the faculty in the spring of 1871, Taft taught zoology and geology. Lectures, textbooks, and summer excursions furnished the mode of instruction. In 1869 Burrill and a half-dozen students surveyed and collected flora and fauna throughout Illinois. Yet enrollments in the School remained small.

Gregory's curriculum report had stressed the Department of General Science and Literature, and the first catalogue outlined a four-year liberal arts course. Critics forced a modification, but 10 of the 15 departments listed in the second catalogue still embraced traditional subjects. History and social science along with five language and literature departments (English, French, German, Latin, and Greek) and mathematics each offered courses of three years. Mental and moral science consisted of one year. Thus, students who combined the two obtained a progressive version of the ante-bellum curriculum. Although utilitarians compelled further change, these studies found a home in the College of Literature and Science which emerged in 1871-72. Its announced purpose was to fit students for the general duties of life, especially for writing, editing, and teaching in higher institutions, and to give agricultural and engineering students the literary side of their education. Few pupils took the recommended full course (20 in 1872, for example), but nearly every matriculant received instruction in the College.[39]

The bulk of its activity went on in two schools, Ancient Languages and Literature, and English and Modern Languages, and in both the study of language took precedence over the study of literature. Baker drilled his English classes in grammar and philology with a view to offering them the advantages of Latin and Greek, and had 70 students in the spring of 1871. The previous fall they had petitioned the Board for lectures on English literature. Snyder drew large numbers to German, and French was occasionally offered. About 10 per cent of the students took Latin and almost none Greek. Gregory had engaged his college classmate, Joseph F. Carey, as Professor of Classics in 1871, but in 1873 the Board dismissed Carey and replaced him with an instructor in order to deemphasize the classics.

Three departments offered courses in the College. Mathematics was the province of Shattuck, who gave his whole time to the subject after March, 1871. The catalogues listed a three-year course ending with differential and integral calculus and the calculus of variations. Gregory, listing himself as Professor of Philosophy and History, taught these subjects after Atherton resigned on January 1, 1869. Carey taught ancient history and Gregory later periods so that all students could attend history lectures. The offering of the Department of Mental and Moral Science remained pretty constant for several years. The one-year course designed for seniors included a quarter-term of mental philosophy which also considered the philosophy of education, one term of moral philosophy which gave some attention to logic, and one term of history of philosophy which also treated logic. Few students advanced to these courses, but nine enrolled in mental philosophy in 1871-72.

The College of Literature and Science also included Com-

[39] *Circular and Catalogue of the Officers and Students of the Illinois Industrial University* [Champaign, 1869?], 4-12, 14. Hereinafter, these publications will be cited as *Catalogue,* followed by the appropriate inclusive years: e.g., *Catalogue,* [1869].

merce, originally a department and later an independent school. Its one-year course emphasized bookkeeping and ended with commercial law and political economy. Snyder, a man of liberal culture and a popular teacher, elevated the subject above the ordinary and found an eager audience.

Most students down to 1873 remained on campus only briefly. With special permission they could concentrate in one department or take more than three courses each term. The majority selected subjects at random rather than following recommended sequences, for they lacked the preparation to use the elective system wisely. However, classical and literary studies were not crowding out scientific and practical pursuits in this period. In 1872, for example, 68 students were enrolled in the College of Agriculture, 37 in Mechanical Science and Engineering, and 20 in the College of Literature and Science. At the same time English literature enrolled 192, bookkeeping 120, and Greek 3.[40]

In addition, all but the physically disabled students were required by the compulsory labor system to work an average of two hours a day, five days a week. They formed in military squads and toiled under faculty supervision on the University farms and gardens or in the shops for 8 and later 12½ cents per hour. Most of the effort went into campus beautification projects. Gregory praised the system despite the fact that it posed difficulties from the start. It was hard to provide tasks for all the students and to get them to work effectively and economically.

Some people viewed the developments between 1868 and 1873 as a betrayal of industrial education. Prominent among them was Dunlap, who in the fall of 1868 broke the truce with Gregory which he had made under pressure the previous March. He used the Chicago *Tribune* to condemn dreamy theorists for creating a village academy supplemented by manual labor. Denouncing Latin as the symbol of all that was wrong, "Rural" suggested that the real producers tear Gregory away from his sermons to attend chemistry and agricultural lectures. Several trustees castigated these "quack appeals . . . to prejudice," and a *Tribune* editorial said that the Uni-

[40] *5th Report* (1873), 66-67; *6th Report* (1874), 70; *7th Report* (1875), 55, 70.

versity was not designed to teach practical farming but to enlarge the boundaries of science. Nevertheless, Samuel Edwards got the visitorial authorities to affirm that the Board's duty was to make the University "pre-eminently a practical school of Agriculture and the Mechanic arts," and Dunlap's continued attacks led influential trustees to ask the Governor not to reappoint him to the governing body.[41]

The controversy clouded the Board's appeal to the legislature in 1869 for $163,000 to support agriculture, horticulture, and engineering. Nothing was asked for either literary or classical subjects or the College of Literature and Science. Speaking to the Illinois State Horticultural Society in December, Turner scored Gregory for failure to comprehend the intended purpose of the University. The General Assembly gave Gregory a hearing early in the year and appropriated $60,000 for the University, but a substantial majority criticized the institution for being conducted as an ordinary classical school. A condemnatory resolution passed in March stated that the University's leading object should be to teach learning related to agriculture, horticulture, and the mechanic arts, and it directed the Board to adapt the institution to the educational wants of future farmers and mechanics.[42]

Meanwhile, at its annual March meeting in Urbana, the Board vindicated the University against the charge of diverting itself from its primary design. Dunlap, Edwards, and Galusha fought this resolution and tried to translate the General Assembly's chastisement into new policies. Galusha attempted to have the curriculum rearranged along the lines of the legislative resolution, but instead the Board merely made tuition free to those who studied exclusively in the Agricultural, Polytechnic, or Military departments. Edwards tried to secure Turner's election as Regent. Though the Trustees

[41] Chicago *Tribune,* Sept. 30, Nov. 4, 13, 18, 19, 25, 1868; *2nd Report* (1869), 52; Cunningham to Brayman, Nov. 23, 1868; Brayman to Bateman, Dec. 3, 1868; Bateman to Brayman, Dec. 14, 1868; Gregory to Brayman, Dec. 21, 1868, Gregory Papers.
[42] *2nd Report* (1869), 58; *Illinois Reports* (1869), I, 384; *Illinois Laws* (1869), 33-34; *Illinois State Journal,* Jan. 20, Feb. 5, 1869. The House passed the appropriations bill 44 to 32, the Senate 20 to 4. The House adopted the condemnatory resolution by 49 to 12 and Dr. Scroggs of Champaign voted with the majority. *Illinois House Journal* (1869), II, 608; III, 329-30. The concurring Senate vote is not given in the *Illinois Senate Journal* (1869), II, 655, 718.

re-elected Gregory and reaffirmed their confidence in him over Dunlap's open opposition, they reduced his authority by terminating his membership on all but two committees and by making all the departments directly responsible to the Board. The governing body also ordered Gregory's remarks about Dunlap's scurrilous newspaper criticism expunged from the record. Dunlap won an important victory by securing a decision to end the compulsory manual-labor system which he and others including Turner bitterly opposed. Practical pursuits were so central in the utilitarian trade school which Dunlap envisioned that there was no need to counterbalance the theoretical with the practical.[43]

Gregory retreated slightly but did not yield, and dissatisfaction therefore became widespread. The Constitutional Convention of 1870 entertained two proposals inimical to the University. Turner, restless as always, now envisioned the Industrial University as a branch of a larger creation. He urged Illinois to establish a new institution specializing in agriculture which would constitute one of four national universities, each geared to a regional economic specialty. The President of McKendree College revived the idea that all colleges in Illinois comprise one university system. They would receive payment from the state for each diploma granted and be uniformly administered by a central board of higher education.[44]

"Rural" hurled reckless charges in the press and inspired horti-

[43] *2nd Report* (1869), 79-90. Although the "Faculty Record," I, 8, shows that a reorganization had made the system voluntary in the fall of 1868, this does not seem to have been the case. At the time of Dunlap's victory in 1870, the manual-labor system seemed to be succeeding in the colleges where it was being tried, and for several years thereafter the University retained Gregory's cherished plan on a voluntary basis. Authorities now distinguished between educational labor, a part of the curriculum for which no wages were paid, and ordinary remunerative labor. Most of the latter was done in the areas of horticulture and the machine shop, with over $5,000 being paid out to students in the fiscal year ending in March, 1872. The system collapsed before Gregory resigned, and his successor at Urbana had no use for it. During the 1880's the manual-labor system in its essential features was abandoned throughout the nation as administrative difficulties persisted and as the increased scope of technical education shifted the task of instruction to the laboratory and seminar room as adjuncts to the classroom. In the motto "Learning and Labor" the University was left with a quaint relic of a bygone stage in the evolution of higher education. *5th Report* (1873), 143; Ross, "The Manual Labor Experiment," 523-28.

[44] *Journal of the Constitutional Convention of the State of Illinois* (Springfield, 1870), 196; *Debates and Proceedings of the Constitutional Convention of the State of Illinois* (Springfield, 1870), 176, 193, 194, 236, 250.

culturists to urge a utilitarianism dangerous to the farmers' own interests. At Dixon on January 27, 1870, the Northern Illinois Horticultural Society denounced the elective system and the exclusion of women and insisted that students take full courses in agriculture and the mechanic arts before any other subjects. Resolutions passed by the student body criticized the Dixon pronouncements, the Faculty publicly defended the University's path, and the Chicago *Tribune* said that classical studies could not legally be excluded. On March 2 the State Horticultural Society met at Bloomington, heard Turner and others unjustly criticize the University, and appointed a committee to visit Urbana.

Gregory scorned the "pitiable delusion" of his foes when the Board met a few days later, and vowed to bury the University before allowing it to become a trade school. The Board beat back an attempt to reorganize the curriculum around ten schools each offering a three-year course in industrial education. Gregory thought the crux of the trouble was ancient languages, to eliminate which would serve no good purpose, violate the law, and effect no saving. The Board sent five of its number to see what students were actually studying, and they reported favorably. At Decatur that fall the Bloomington committee informed a convention of horticulturists that students were not abusing their freedom. Delegates concluded that the University desired to inaugurate a new era in the life of the laboring classes.[45] By the autumn of 1870, then, the University had weathered a crisis. Gregory had held as much ground as possible, but not without compromising.

The opening of the University to women in September, 1870, was one of his strategic retreats and one phase of a new era. Horticulturists Dunlap, Edwards, and Galusha had long urged admission of girls. Gregory did not oppose educating women but thought the sexes should be segregated for this purpose. He temporized by arguing that physical facilities and special courses for women were lacking and that admission of females would lower scholarship. In March, 1870, the Board had agreed to admit women as soon as

[45] Chicago *Tribune*, Feb. 2, 18, 28, March 1, 1870; Gregory to Brayman, Feb. 10, 24, 25, 1870, Gregory Papers; *3rd Report* (1870), 38, 65-68, 70-73; "Faculty Record," I, 49-50; *Illinois Reports* (1871), I, 428-30; *Prairie Farmer*, Oct. 8, 1870, 317.

housing could be furnished while refusing to commit itself to co-education in principle. In August, after the crisis, the Executive Committee decided by five to four to admit qualified women whose parents provided proper homes for them. Gregory expediently voted with the majority, and 15 women entered that autumn. Though not in the very vanguard, the University was among the pioneers of co-education. In the winter of 1871 President Andrew D. White visited it in order to determine the advisability of admitting women to Cornell.[46]

Outward harmony after 1870 masked a continuing antagonism over the University's failure to break more boldly with the past. Dunlap ceased his criticism, however, the Trustees unanimously re-elected Gregory to a third term in March, 1871, and at the same time the General Assembly appropriated $125,000 for the biennium, more than double the 1869 figure. One could read a lesson in the purposes for which funds were awarded. The largest sum ($75,000) was half of the estimated cost of a new main building, given on the understanding that the remainder would come later. The General Assembly also authorized $25,000 for a Mechanical Building and Drill Hall. The rest was for chemistry, horticultural and agricultural experiments, and books and apparatus relating to industrial pursuits. Literary, historical, and classical studies got nothing, and $50,000 requested for a chemistry laboratory was denied. Since Gregory wanted Illinois to compete with the best Eastern institutions, the Trustees therefore decided to sell the rest of their scrip and the land previously located in Minnesota and Nebraska. Turner buried his prejudices against the University under the cornerstone which he laid for the new main building on September 13, 1872, at which time he emphasized the importance of educating students in an institution whose spirit was broad, industrial, scientific, American, and truly Christian.[47]

[46] Gregory's ideas on co-education were unsettled. In September, 1867, he told the Illinois State Horticultural Society that he had earlier believed in making the sexes classmates but went on to offer practical reasons for not admitting women to the University. The Society adopted a resolution that both sexes should be treated equally in admission. Illinois State Horticultural Society, *Transactions for 1867*, I (Chicago, 1868), 85-86. See also *3rd Report* (1870), 84-85; *4th Report* (1872), 62, 117-18; and Bishop, *Cornell*, 146.
[47] *Illinois Laws* (1871), 142-43. The text of Turner's address is in the *4th Report* (1872), 353-60.

But hopes for the future were soon blasted. At chapel exercises celebrating the University's fifth anniversary in March, 1873, inquisitive trustees and a visiting legislative committee learned by a show of hands that nearly every student was pursuing studies relating to the industries. Such questioning revealed the desire to make the University serve practical purposes, and economic collapse whipped this feeling to new intensity. The crisis for the University came several months before the Panic of 1873 began in September. At the time Gregory, just re-elected Regent, had departed to spend the summer in Europe. General farm distress had prevailed for two or three years before depression struck, and the Chicago fire of 1871 added a cruel loss. Thus in 1872 the General Assembly reneged on its promise to provide additional funds to complete University Hall, going up just south of Green Street. Early in 1873 the University asked and received much less from Springfield than it had two years earlier (the General Assembly appropriated $62,550), and the legislature refused to reimburse the Board for the $60,000 spent from endowment to complete University Hall.[48]

More significant was an act to regulate the University which the General Assembly passed on April 15. This reduced the Board of Trustees from 32 to 11 members, nine of whom the Governor was to appoint from the three grand judicial districts to serve with himself and the President of the State Board of Agriculture. Samuel Edwards had been urging such a move since March, 1869, and experience with an unwieldy membership led his fellow trustees to request the legislature to reduce their number the following year. As originally introduced, the bill called for election of trustees by the people and had the support of the Northern Illinois Horticultural Society. Financial hardship facilitated enactment of a measure that aimed at economy as well as efficiency. In addition, the bill deprived the Regent of a place on the governing body. To be sure, some persons wanted to curb Gregory's role. But they were also moving with a national trend to deny university presidents membership on boards of control. The reorganization also subjected the University to much closer state regulation. It directed that U.S. endowment

[48] *Student* (a student newspaper), March, 1873; *Daily State Journal* (Springfield), March 10, 1873; *Illinois Laws* (1873), 16, 18.

funds invested in federal and state bonds were not to be changed without express permission of the General Assembly and that the Governor approve all warrants for the expenditure of appropriated funds. Not least important, the act ordered all University students to study "such branches of learning as are adapted to promote the liberal and practical education of the industrial classes in the several pursuits and professions of life, without excluding other scientific and classical studies," and including military tactics for male students.[49]

This restrictive enactment became effective July 1, and Governor John L. Beveridge met with the reorganized Board in Urbana nine days later. Most of the members were carry-overs, and they elected Emory Cobb President. Reynolds of the State Agricultural Society secured adoption of a resolution that agriculture and the mechanic arts were primary and other studies secondary objects of the University, and the Trustees appointed a committee to report a curriculum in keeping with this decision. The Board also adopted bylaws which increased the powers and duties of the President at the expense of the Regent.[50] Gregory cheerfully accepted his altered status upon returning in September, but deplored the legal fetters upon students' academic freedom as contrary to the spirit of American institutions.

He saved his fire until December, when notables gathered to dedicate University Hall. On that occasion U.S. Commissioner of Education John Eaton described Illinois as the most successful in its administration of 37 Morrill Act institutions and arraigned the state for deficiency in supporting public education. He noted that 388 students had attended the University in 1870, when the college-age population in Illinois was over 200,000. These remarks were a foil for Gregory, who recalled that he had accepted the post at Illinois because he thought the Trustees had shared his desire to build an

---

[49] *Illinois Laws* (1873), 16-18. The act passed the House 86 to 26, the Senate 33 to 7. The Superintendent of Public Instruction was not a member of the reorganized Board. After 1860 the percentage of college and university presidents holding membership on boards of control decreased, especially in state universities. See Earl James McGrath, "The Evolution of Administrative Offices in Institutions of Higher Education in the United States from 1860 to 1933" (unpublished doctoral dissertation, University of Chicago, 1936), 12-13, 45.

[50] *6th Report* (1874), 168-69.

industrial university rather than a simple agricultural or technical school. The grandeur of this design, which the motto "Learning and Labor" best symbolized, did not exceed the University's resources. Gregory insisted that the animating spirit of the University had been a hemisphere apart from the old institutions. "We are in the midst of a great conflict," he declared, "— the battle of the ages."[51] His impassioned rhetoric reflected the depth of the controversy over competing philosophies of education. Gregory believed that scientific and technical studies would win in free competition with classical and literary ones. His opponents, apostles of democratic and utilitarian learning, were less certain. Taking no risks with the wisdom of the people, they had consolidated their victory in statutory enactment.

[51] *7th Report* (1875), 73.

CHAPTER FIVE

The University Takes Shape

MANY FORCES SHAPED THE UNIVERSITY during the remaining seven years of Gregory's tenure, for then as now higher education was caught in an intricate web of relationships. The state universities, dependent upon the public for tax dollars as well as students, felt particularly exposed to extraneous pressures. They never enjoyed the luxury of developing autonomously, and only vain conceit could have tempted universities to believe that they shaped society more than society shaped them. Admitting these realities, some features of university life were less amenable to constraints than others.

The policies devised for Illinois Industrial University by its governors constituted perhaps the most potent single influence on the institution. These were hammered out collaboratively by the Board of Trustees and its chief executive agent, the Regent. Gregory and the Board preserved outwardly friendly relations and agreed on many subjects, but unfortunately a serious lack of harmony over fundamental issues characterized their dealings down to 1880. Both parties did their duty as they saw it, and both, viewed from different perspectives, were "right." Judged by the needs of the time, however, Gregory was more right than the Board. An evaluation of the Board's and the Regent's respective roles in four important areas reveals much about the history of the University. It also casts doubt on the principle of entrusting ultimate control to a group of nonresidents possessing no real familiarity with educational issues.

Opposing conceptions of higher education constituted the major issue separating the Trustees and the Regent. Gregory never agreed with the Board's desire to train men for immediate usefulness, but his difference with the governing body increased after 1873 as he gained a new vision of a true university. The key to understanding the conflicts between Gregory and the Board lies partly in the experience each brought to the task, but even more in the extent to which they developed on the job. The evidence shows that the Trustees learned little after 1873, Gregory much.

Almost without exception the Trustees came to their duties poorly prepared to determine educational policy. The composition of the supreme tribunal, which remained fairly stable from 1873 to 1880, severely limited its effectiveness. As a group they resembled their predecessors in political and religious affiliations (except that Presbyterians now prevailed) and in means of livelihood. Collectively they were young, averaging about 43 in 1873, and had come of age with the revolt against the old classical learning. Experience, not the college classroom, had been their main teacher.

The President of the Board was Emory Cobb, a wealthy man prominent in the business life of Kankakee and in national activities of the Protestant Episcopal Church. He impressed contemporaries as genial yet decisive. Daniel B. Gardner served with Cobb on the Executive Committee. He had been a member of the Ohio Senate before arriving in Champaign, and in 1860 became the town's first Mayor. Gardner went on the reorganized Board in 1873, and thereafter both his position and his proximity tempted him to meddle with Gregory's executive duties. Alexander M. Brown acted as Gregory's alter ego on the governing body. Roswell B. Mason, a former Chicago mayor brought to his duties an impressive record as an engineer in the construction of canals, railroads, and bridges. Scottish-born Alexander McLean, Mayor of Macomb, was the only immigrant on the Board. He began three decades as a member in 1876.

Perhaps the most remarkable individual in this group was John J. Bird (Byrd), a 29-year-old Negro. Appointed by Governor John L. Beveridge as of March 1, 1873, Bird attended his first meeting on March 11-12, his last on September 12-13, 1882. In between, he held a commission as police magistrate in Cairo, Illinois, from April 29, 1873, to July 1, 1879, absented himself from 27 out of 40 Board sessions, and did not complete his second term as a trustee. He participated little in the meetings he attended, but in 1875 his colleagues named him to inform Gregory of the latter's re-election as Regent. Both his appointment and service are shrouded in mystery which contemporary newspapers do not readily dispel, but surely Bird must be among the earliest if not the first Negro trustee of an American university not founded avowedly for Negroes.[1]

The lives of the members after they joined the Board did little

[1] Franklin W. Scott, ed., *The Semi-Centennial Alumni Record of the University of Illinois* ([Urbana], 1918), 969-82, has brief biographical data on individual trustees. It has been supplemented with material drawn from other sources too numerous to cite. Bird probably supplied the information about himself in Scott, p. 970, which says that he was born in Cincinnati in 1844, edited and managed newspapers from 1882 to 1896, was in the mail service of the postal department from 1881 to 1912, and organized and superintended the first free-school system for Negroes in Illinois. An effort to follow up many of these leads proved unavailing. However, on Bird's offices, see Philo J. Beveridge (the Governor's secretary) to George H. Harlow (Secretary of State), March 4, 1873, appointing Byrd [*sic*] a trustee, in the Executive File; Bird's acceptance of July 5, 1873, in the Governor's Correspondence; and "Justices of the Peace, 1873-89, Counties A-L," 8, all in the Illinois State Archives, Springfield. Dr. Wayne C. Temple kindly furnished this information. Bird died suddenly on June 1, 1912, in Springfield. His death certificate in the Sangamon County Clerk's Office, Springfield, Vol. 10, 257, lists him as colored and a custodian at the statehouse. On Feb. 23, 1966, the Rev. W. R. Stewart of St. John's A. M. E. Church in Springfield informed the author by letter that individuals affiliated with that church over a period of 50 years testified to the fact that John J. Bird "was a member of St. John A. M. E. Church and was an American Negro citizen."

to widen their competence for the task in hand. Prominence in local communities gave individual members confidence in the soundness of their judgments without necessarily affording them any redeeming insight into the deeper forces agitating the nation's intellectual life. By themselves the governing powers were ill prepared to devise a pattern for an American university, and for many reasons hesitated to follow Gregory's lead. Perhaps the most that can be said for the Board of Trustees is that it roughly mirrored the public's wishes.

Gregory, on the other hand, enjoyed the advantage of a superior education. He wanted to yoke the best of the past in fruitful union with the demands of the present, and his emphasis on science alone — he used the word almost as a talisman — showed his eagerness to move with the times. And more important, his official duties schooled him in contemporary needs. He wrote and lectured across the land on educational issues, remained active in the National Educational Association after relinquishing its presidency in 1868, spurred collaboration among the land-grant colleges, and lobbied for various educational causes in Washington. He relied upon Andrew D. White of Cornell for advice, but apparently not upon Charles W. Eliot of Harvard nor upon Daniel C. Gilman of Johns Hopkins.[2]

Gregory learned most about university ideals from Europe, but unfortunately his lessons came late in life. He first went to Europe in 1869 at age 47, primarily to study the role of practical and scientific education on the Continent. In France and Germany he discovered that dense populations necessitated agricultural science, and Justus von Liebig, the German organic chemist, informed him that agricultural science augmented land values by improving soil fertility. Gregory also saw how Germans sent itinerant lecturers out to demonstrate the new truth found by experimentation in agricul-

[2] The Cornell University Archives has some 16 letters from Gregory to White from 1860 to 1884. Kathleen Jacklin (Associate Curator and Archivist of the John M. Olin Research Library at Cornell) graciously furnished me copies. White visited Champaign-Urbana in 1871 to study the effectiveness of coeducation and spoke at commencement in 1873. Gilman visited Gregory at Illinois in 1876, but there is no record of Gregory-Gilman correspondence at Johns Hopkins. J. Louis Kuethe (Assistant Librarian of Johns Hopkins) to author, Feb. 18, 1966. Indices of the Charles W. Eliot correspondence at Harvard show nothing from Gregory. Clifford K. Shipton (Custodian of the Harvard University Archives) to author, Feb. 16, 1966.

tural schools. He felt vindicated to learn that Europeans believed it advisable to unite agricultural and polytechnical schools with university education.

Six more trips to Europe before 1880 made the Illinois educator increasingly aware of what the Old World could offer the New. He participated in an official capacity at the Vienna Exposition in 1873 and at the Universal Exposition in Paris in 1878. At the former, which he described in articles published in America, he found Germany's display of the industrial arts an important example of government's effect on education. Both world's fairs intensified his belief in the wealth-producing power of the mechanic arts and in the relation of industrial-scientific education to national welfare. On these voyages he also purchased books, scientific apparatus, and art works for the University.[3]

However, the full significance of the European university dawned on Gregory only after he visited the University of Berlin in 1879. The ocean separating him from the Trustees permitted boldness as he outlined the grand vision which Illinois should embrace. He wanted the state to have a true university, "a place where knowledge and science are discovered and perfected, as well as a center for its dissemination." Its aim should be to lead well-prepared students to the summits of learning rather than to conduct numerous immature minds along lower paths, for leaders of thought rather than masses of students made the true university. Witness Berlin. Gregory therefore urged enlargement of the faculty so that professors at Illinois would have ample time for research. He regarded no man worthy of a faculty appointment who would not "eagerly employ every leisure hour allowed him in the prosecution of his studies and in the advancement of science."[4] Gregory insisted that the scientific needs of the nation would not permit Illinois to go another quarter-century without one institution to represent the higher learning. Though greatly in advance of the ideas that had underlain Gregory's first curriculum report in 1867, these views were still premature for

[3] *6th Report* (1874), 105-6; John M. Gregory and Osborn R. Keith, "Report on the Paris International Exposition of 1878," *Illinois Reports* (1879), IV, Sec. H. Several of Gregory's articles in 1873 are in the Gregory Scrapbooks.
[4] *10th Report* (1881), 184.

Illinois in 1879. The Trustees never caught his progressive spirit and considered the Regent visionary and impractical. He in turn regarded them as limited in outlook.[5]

The Regent and the Board frequently differed over the remedy for the economic difficulties which pressed the University closely in these years. The general depression which began in September, 1873, caused acute financial hardship until the end of the decade. Enrollment reached a high of 406 in the academic year ending in June, 1874, but then declined and took five years to regain the former figure. More serious than the resulting loss of student revenues was the shrinkage of income from the University's endowment. As bonds matured they were refunded at lower rates of interest. By 1877 the University's annual income was $3,500 less than its annual expenditure.[6] In general, Gregory's solution emphasized the need to increase receipts; the Board's, the need to decrease expenses.

Gregory began searching for new funds well before the panic hit. He went to Washington in 1872 as a delegate to the agricultural convention called by the U.S. Commissioner of Agriculture. Those present discussed the need for further congressional aid for the colleges established on the land grant, one of several educational purposes for which various interests were seeking federal funds. Gregory urged the government to divide the proceeds of the sale of public lands into thirds, and to distribute the money among the states to support schoolteachers or libraries, normal-school work, and state colleges and universities. He wanted the donation for the latter purpose apportioned to each state on the basis of its population and area, a formula different from that of the Morrill Act. This new college bill failed to pass Congress. However, both it and the renewed bid for a national university inspired passionate outbursts by defenders of vested interests. Eliot, jealous for Harvard, denounced government aid to higher education as an "insidious and irresistible enemy of republicanism," the essence of which was breeding a race of self-reliant freemen. Eliot's comments no doubt severely taxed the

[5] Thomas J. Burrill to Edmund J. James, May 16, 1914, James Papers.
[6] *9th Report* (1878), 45.

patience of Gregory, who publicly excoriated similar remarks by President McCosh of Princeton as baseless and mean-spirited.[7]

The main hope of financial relief lay closer to home. An increased appropriation from the General Assembly was one possibility, but the subject divided Gregory and his employers. The latter decided to ask for $25,000 in 1875 rather than the $16,000 Gregory recommended. There is no discernible reason for Gregory's caution at this time. Later, however, the Regent was bolder than the Board, which rejected some of his proposals as impolitic. They did endorse Gregory's suggestion that the state give the University a regular income from a tax on the assessed valuation of taxable property as Michigan had done in 1873 and Wisconsin three years later. The Board asked for a one-twentieth mill tax. However, they reduced Gregory's request in the last two biennia of his administration. The legislature gave $29,500 in 1877 in addition to $40,000 for a chemistry laboratory and $5,000 for a greenhouse and botany laboratory. Two years later the General Assembly granted $24,500 after the University requested only $20,500. Most of this money (apart from buildings) went for maintenance, repairs, and taxes on western lands, and not one cent to support expenses of instruction.[8] An explanation, perhaps a justification, for the Board's caution is found in the popular discontent in Illinois which found outlets in the Grange and the Illinois State Farmers' Association. Jonathan Periam, the former Superintendent of Practical Agriculture at Urbana, no doubt expressed a prevailing attitude toward the University in saying that the people were steadily working to infuse a spirit of practical effort into "the fossils, or worse," who had mismanaged it.[9]

The sale of land presented a second possible means of relief. The authorities agreed to dispose of the public lands located pre-

[7] [U.S. Department of Agriculture], *Proceedings of the National Agricultural Convention, Held at Washington, D.C. February 15-17, 1872*, 42 Cong., 2 Sess., Senate Misc. Doc. No. 164 (Washington, 1872), 21-24; Charles W. Eliot, "National University," National Educational Association, *Journal of Proceedings and Addresses, 1873* (Peoria, 1873), 107-20; James McCosh, "Upper Schools," *ibid.*, 19-35, 43-44; *7th Report* (1875), 68-69.
[8] *8th Report* (1877), 92, 105, 151, 203; *Illinois Laws* (1875), 14; *9th Report* (1878), 10-11, 20-21; *Illinois Laws* (1877), 17; *10th Report* (1881), 135, 137-38; *Illinois Laws* (1879), 50.
[9] Jonathan Periam, *The Groundswell: A History of the Origin, Aims, and Progress of the Farmers' Movement* (St. Louis, 1874), 508.

viously in Minnesota and Nebraska, but found no market. Raising costs to students constituted a third alternative. Gregory insisted on the necessity of this course, and the Board contended that the institution should be kept as inexpensive as possible. After long resisting, the Board raised the incidental fee effective in September, 1880.[10]

Finding no way to increase income, the Board tried to effect savings. Salaries became their main target. One trustee recommended a 25 per cent cut in 1873 and 20 per cent the following year. This brought a decision that faculty members were henceforth to receive no additional compensation either for extra time given to departmental duties during the regular year or vacations or for non-departmental services. The crisis came in 1877. Early in that year the governing body chose to ask for a legislative appropriation to build a chemistry laboratory rather than to sustain salaries, and in September Gregory demonstrated to the Board by comparative data the low salaries paid by Illinois. He asked that any necessary decrease begin with himself. The Board decided that the faculty should absorb the annual deficit of $3,500 and reduced by 10 per cent the salary of the Regent and all full professors.[11]

Beyond immediate economic difficulties lay the deeper challenge of popular attitudes toward the University. Educated people still favored the private liberal arts college, and even the industrial classes did not yet see the value of the institution intended for them. Gregory therefore intensified his desire to win public opinion to his side, knowing that success along this line was the key to larger enrollments and appropriations. Apart from authorizing modest sums for a purpose they approved, the Trustees left the task to others.

The University employed the printed word as one method of publicity. Gregory and the Faculty carefully prepared the catalogue with a view to attracting students, resisting the temptation to inflate merit. They condensed this material into circulars, and at the depth of the depression the Trustees blanketed the post offices of the state with these and large posters advertising the Industrial University. Authorities spent most of their budget for printed media on news-

[10] The incidental term fee, doubled to $5 a term in 1872, now went to $7.50 a term. *5th Report* (1873), 67, 156; *10th Report* (1881), 231.
[11] *6th Report* (1874), 105; *7th Report* (1875), 101, 117; *8th Report* (1877), 191.

paper advertisements, especially in the agricultural press. To reach the public schools they also advertised in their own student publications. Inevitably the campus newspaper became a vehicle of public relations rather than an independent organ of student expression.

Campus visitations became grist for the publicity mill. The Illinois Press Association met in Urbana in 1872, for example, and Gregory printed their favorable comments and distributed them to newspaper editors throughout the state. Participation in international fairs was another conscious promotional device. Vienna convinced Gregory of the worth of exhibiting at the Centennial Exposition in Philadelphia in 1876. Nearly 10,000,000 people attended the American show at which the University's display emphasized engineering, natural history, chemistry, and agriculture. Tanaka Fujimaro of the Japanese Ministry of Education reported to his government that the presentation of what he called the Illinois Institute of Technology "held first rank among the exhibits of the state."[12]

Public addresses lay at the heart of the campaign for favor. Gregory, never strong physically, assumed the brunt of the burden. He was better attuned to the new dimensions of higher education than the Trustees or the Faculty, and his spirit was dauntless. Once when weather prevented horse travel he hiked two hours and crossed a swollen stream to keep a speaking date in the country. The physical toll impelled Gregory to cease these labors before his term ended. He claimed success for these endeavors, but the harsh fact is that the University made little progress in gaining popular recognition before he resigned.[13]

Failure to distinguish between legislative and executive functions in government of the University was perhaps the most debilitating factor in Gregory's dealings with the Board. The Trustees had not yet learned to confine themselves to formulation of policy, a fault basically attributable to the nation's continuing inability to devise a satisfactory method of administering higher education. The

[12] U.S. Department of State, Diplomatic Dispatches from John A. Bingham to William M. Evarts, No. 631, Sept. 24, 1877. Microfilm from National Archives in the State Historical Society of Wisconsin. I am indebted to Mr. Maynard J. Brichford (University of Illinois Archivist) for this reference.
[13] This subject is treated at greater length in Winton U. Solberg, "The University of Illinois Struggles for Public Recognition, 1867-1894," *Journal of the Illinois State Historical Society,* LIX (Spring, 1966), 11-16.

supreme governing body therefore erred in miring itself in a Ser-
bonian bog of detail. To cite illustrations at random, it insisted upon
granting summer leave to each individual faculty member, formally
approved resolutions for such items as a hand bell and a lawnmower,
and once authorized $8 to buy erasers. Even more grievous, the
Board interfered with the Regent's executive responsibilities. Daniel
B. Gardner of Champaign meddled constantly, and at critical junc-
tures the Executive Committee overrode Gregory.

The smoldering tension erupted at the annual Board meeting
in March, 1875. On the eve of the gathering Gregory privately
asserted that he was still by law and usage the chief executive officer
of the University, despite the revised bylaws of 1873 which had
ended his membership on and presidency of the Board of Trustees.
Believing that his powers were worsening as compared to Cobb's, he
told Alexander M. Brown, his confidant on the Board, that all reports should be communicated to the Trustees through the Regent.
In his view, the President's authority consisted of presiding over
Board and Executive Committee meetings and signing warrants.
Gregory suggested dispensing with the Executive Committee or replacing Cobb as President of the Board.[14]

Appointment of Manly Miles either aggravated the difficulty
or constituted its crux. It is impossible to be certain because someone has destroyed critical pages in Gregory's Letterbook. Apparently, however, the Executive Committee, over Gregory's strong opposition, named Miles as Professor of Agriculture and Instructor in
Agricultural Chemistry at a total salary of $3,000, a third more than
any other professor received. At some undetermined time before or
after the appointment in June, 1875, Gregory soured on Miles, the
object of a five-year pursuit. Perhaps Miles offended mainly by insisting on the supremacy of agriculture in the work of the University.
At any rate, the hiring of Miles made for an intolerable situation, and in March, 1876, Gregory announced his own intention to
resign.[15]

---

[14] Gregory to Alexander M. Brown, March 6, 1875, Gregory Papers.

[15] Pages 466-90 covering the period from Nov., 1874, to March, 1875, have been
ripped from the Letterbook. See also *8th Report* (1877), 137; and R. L. Brown
(class of 1875), "John M. Gregory — an Appreciation," 2, A. G. Allen Research
File, 1898-1920.

He wanted to regain ascendancy over the University, but was quite prepared to leave if necessary. The local climate disagreed with members of his family (Mrs. Gregory, a sickly woman who died in 1877, had absented herself from Urbana for 14 months), and other fields beckoned him. Both California and Missouri were considering Gregory to head their universities, and he thought he might go to Berkeley if asked.[16] His letter of resignation arraigned the Board for interference which violated common university practice in appointments and threatened to be a perpetual source of trouble.[17] By forcing the issue Gregory won a complete victory. Opinion within and beyond the University rallied behind him. In return for his decision to remain, the Trustees fired Miles and redefined the lines of authority. The amended bylaws empowered the President to conduct Board and Executive Committee meetings, sign warrants, and communicate orders concerning University administration to the Regent. The bylaws also gave the Regent authority to nominate all faculty members for appointment by the Board and to supervise all subordinate officers under direction of the governing body and its Executive Committee. [18]

A year later the Board took another needed administrative step. It devised bylaws for the Faculty and officially recognized the structural framework which had evolved earlier. The bylaws defined and organized the University Faculty, entrusting it with general control of discipline and studies subject to the Board's direction. They made similar arrangements for the four colleges and the schools. These bylaws provided for the senior professor in each college to become its dean unless the general Faculty ordered otherwise. Early in 1878 the Faculty of the University elected the senior

[16] Gregory to Andrew D. White, June 1, 10, 1875, Gregory Papers, and White Papers at Cornell (the latter are necessary to supplement the former); J. P. B. in the Chicago Baptist publication, the *Standard*, Dec. 16, 1875, wrote that California was casting eyes at Gregory. Daniel C. Gilman resigned at Berkeley on March 2, 1876, and the Board of Regents elected John LeConte to succeed him on June 1, 1876. There is no official evidence in University of California records that authorities there considered Gregory for the job. J. R. K. Kantor (Archivist of the University of California, Berkeley) to the author, Dec. 14, 1965.
[17] *8th Report* (1877), 173; Gregory to S. Stanton, March 30, 1876; Gregory's manuscript letter of resignation, Gregory Papers.
[18] Champaign County *Gazette,* March 29, 1876; *Illini,* April, 1876; *8th Report* (1877), 185, 189-90, 192.

man in each college to head it. The deans formed a sort of advisory committee which the Regent called occasionally to meet with him. After 1873 Shattuck served as business manager, and in 1879 the Faculty elected Burrill (then the senior faculty member and Dean of the College of Natural Science) Vice-President of the University. Burrill's statement that almost to a man the faculty respected Gregory tells us about all that can be discovered on the subject. Certain periods saw exceptions, Burrill added, and near the end of Gregory's term an undercurrent of dissatisfaction and opposition existed in one influential but unnamed quarter. Several indications suggest that Edward Snyder was no strong supporter of Gregory.[19]

No adversity forced Gregory to abandon his initial hope that "a splendid good" might arise at Urbana, and the University laid solid academic foundations in some areas before he resigned. The state law of 1873 which specified the branches of learning to be pursued was one influence on this development. On March 12, 1874, the Trustees ordered the curriculum adjusted to the statute. They directed students to select at least one of three subjects carried each quarter from a group of courses related to agriculture and the mechanic arts. These included mathematics, natural sciences, bookkeeping, and cognate technical studies such as soils, drawing, the construction and use of machines, carpentry and joinery, bridges, rural law and economy, and military science. The rule required individuals who chose only one of the former to take another study from a second group designed to promote the liberal and practical education of the industrial classes. This category embraced history, modern languages and literature (English, French, and German), political economy, and constitutional and international law. Anything taught in the University, and therefore ancient languages, was permitted for the third course. In the face of this restrictive ruling, the University now reasserted that it had always aimed at allowing as much freedom as possible in the selection of studies.[20]

[19] *9th Report* (1878), 44-45; "Faculty Record," I, 249, 294; Burrill to Edmund J. James, May 16, 1914, James Papers. Gregory's communication to the Faculty from Europe hints at tensions within the instructional staff and suggests the principle of rotation in office in the choice of deans and a vice-president. See "Faculty Record," II, Sept. 19, 1879 (no pagination in this volume).
[20] *7th Report* (1875), 100; *Catalogue, 1875-76*, 22. For the 1873 law, see pp. 115-16 above.

The character of the student body also shaped the course of academic progress. The University received poorly prepared tyros because it arose before the state possessed an adequate system of secondary education. Chicago boasted but one high school (with 495 students) in 1868, and two years later the whole of Illinois had only 108 public high schools — about one per county.[21] Gregory met the situation in three ways. First he recommended a progressive raising of admissions standards starting in 1873. The proposal was premature, and by 1876 Gregory became convinced that the University must require a preparatory year so that it might offer advanced work and avoid losing students. The institution itself would provide those who failed its entrance examinations a year of preliminary work. These studies would not count toward the 36 credits needed for full certification. The beginners paid the costs of their own instruction and had certain privileges, but were not regular University students. This program grew into a Preparatory School, a regressive step which long gave the University the flavor of an academy. A large proportion of the student body pursued elementary work — 114 out of 388 students in 1876-77; 131 out of 434 in 1879-80 — and teachers hired for their competence in preliminary studies gained a foothold which enabled them to teach University subjects.[22]

A third, more helpful solution lay in improving the public-school system so that the University could receive qualified students and develop along true university lines. This required effective articulation between the schools and Champaign-Urbana, and the two methods employed for the purpose enormously stimulated secondary education in Illinois. The University named as examiners the better-graded schools and high schools with sufficiently good courses to prepare students for college. Their staffs were permitted to receive and conduct examinations for admission to the University, which reserved the right to make final decisions. Moreover, Illinois along

[21] Department of Public Instruction, City of Chicago, *Fourteenth Annual Report of the Board of Education for the Year Ending July 3, 1868* (Chicago, 1868), 120-21; Superintendent of Public Instruction of the State of Illinois, *Eighth Biennial Report*, 1869-70 (n.p., n.d.), 2.
[22] "Faculty Record," I, 99, 199-200; *5th Report* (1873), 70; *8th Report* (1877), 21, 30, 172; *10th Report* (1881), 136.

with other state universities in the Midwest borrowed the system of accredited schools which Michigan instituted in 1871. Under this plan, the University admitted graduates of certain schools without further examination after the Faculty had inspected and certified the school as offering acceptable collegiate preparation. This device enabled the University to preserve its own standards while at the same time taking its place as the capstone of the state system of public education. In 1876 the Princeton High School was the first to be accredited, and then other communities rushed to gain the accolade of recognition. As late as 1880, however, the Faculty believed it had no right to admit private schools to its accredited list.[23]

After 1873 the student body became more diversified than in earlier years. Most counties in Illinois sent one son or daughter to Urbana. Altogether, more than a dozen states were represented, and pupils entered from Armenia, Germany, Greece, Japan, and England, primarily to study agriculture. The first women, 15 in number, enrolled in 1870, and their ranks rose to 90 three years later. That proportion, somewhat less than a fourth, remained fairly constant until Gregory's last year, when it increased appreciably. Few students were the minimum legal age (15), but one claimed to have entered at 13, and some were nearly 30. Those unknown to the Faculty needed a certificate of good moral character. Since few matriculants remained four years, they seldom got beyond introductory work, which went by the old name of daily recitation. Great enthusiasm for studies seems to have prevailed.

A spirit of pride in initiating the reform of higher education animated students, who cheerfully shouldered the normal load of three courses which each met five times a week during the three quarter-terms that made up the University year. Better students could carry additional subjects with special faculty permission, and many did. Beyond the academic schedule, chapel, military drill,

[23] In 1873 the University started allowing admission by County Superintendent's Certificate. Authorities at Urbana furnished questions, and candidates who passed creditably received a certificate from the County Superintendent of Schools. This admitted them on a trial basis, for their matriculation was withheld until the student passed the regular examinations of the first term. See *6th Report* (1874), 56; *8th Report* (1877), 71-72; *9th Report* (1878), 30; "Faculty Record," II, April 30, 1880. See also Joseph Lindsey Henderson, *Admission to College by Certificate* (New York, 1912), 50-58.

laboratory and shop work, and manual labor (optional after 1870) demanded the students' time.

The elective principle initially destroyed the division of the student body into four classes, but gradually this leading aspect of the ante-bellum collegiate system re-emerged. Late in 1871 the Faculty appointed a committee on the classification of students into years, and shortly thereafter the groups that entered and completed four years of work at the same time began to acquire a cohesiveness that revived the sense of class. In 1876-77 the catalogue first ranked the students from freshman through senior.[24]

Students criticized the grading system as useless in the spring of 1877. The following October the Faculty told instructors to abandon marks and hold their students to good work by exhortation, although professors might privately record grades. Students were to receive credit for a course by passing a final examination at which at least one faculty member besides the regular instructor determined the grade. An earlier practice of inviting citizens to attend final examinations by notices published in newspapers had by this time died out. In the spring of 1879 a student attacked the stress on memory and cramming, and Gregory admitted that the criticisms were basically valid.[25]

The four colleges furnished the framework within which most of the academic development occurred, but the College of Agriculture constituted an exception. Here the exalted expectations which attended the launching of a school with Morrill Act funds turned to bitter disillusion early in the decade. Agriculture was a mass of empiricism, and progress awaited development of a science of the subject.[26] Meanwhile, agricultural education steadily declined under the operation of causes beyond immediate control.

The instructional program suffered the worst reverses. Not until a decade after the University opened was a professor obtained who gave continuity to the course offerings. In 1874, before the

[24] "Faculty Record," I, 88.
[25] *Ibid.,* 57, 172-73, 236-38; *Illini,* May, June, 1877; April, May, 1879.
[26] For Gregory's clear comprehension of this fact, see his address to the farmers' institute in 1869, "Agricultural Facts and Theories," *2nd Report* (1869), 123-28.

Board hired Miles, Gregory appointed to a chair in agricultural chemistry Charles W. Silver, an 1872 graduate who completed his studies at Halle. A year later Silver made way for Miles, whose firing left a vacancy filled in 1877. In the interim Gregory resorted to expedients to plug the holes. Students got what they could from the regular staff in cognate areas, and successfully petitioned for veterinary science, which Frederick W. Prentice began to teach in 1873. A graduate of veterinary schools in Edinburgh and London, he sent to Paris for one of Dr. Auzoux's famous papier-mâché models of a horse and worked in a small building erected for his use. Most of the agricultural instruction came in short, intensive sessions. Students participated in the farmers' institutes, and in the spring term of 1875 all seniors, including women, had to attend a special series of lectures by local professors and visiting agriculturists, including Bliss, Flagg, Miles, and George E. Morrow.

Morrow became Professor of Agriculture at Illinois on January 1, 1877. He was primarily a farm journalist rather than a practical farmer or an agricultural scientist. While serving in the Civil War the Ohio farmer's son discovered the facility of his pen and sold stories to New York and Cincinnati newspapers. Discharged for reasons of health, he entered the University of Michigan, and while a law student contributed regularly to *Western Rural*. After graduating in 1866 he removed to Chicago with that newspaper, and later edited and co-owned the *Western Farmer* in Madison, Wisconsin. He left an Iowa Agricultural College professorship for his new post in the belief that agricultural education would thrive best in a university. He already enjoyed national prominence earned by his writings and his promotion of farmers' organizations.[27]

After the Board formally recognized the College of Agriculture in 1877, Morrow became its first Dean the following year, a post he held until 1894. He regarded teaching as his primary obligation and eagerly sought to attract students. But Morrow could do nothing to overcome the aversion to scientific agricultural education which plagued Illinois along with other land-grant institu-

[27] [Thomas J. Burrill], "Memorial Address on George E. Morrow," [April 8, 1900], Burrill Papers, Botany Department Correspondence, 79-93; Stephen A. Forbes, "The Life and Work of Professor George E. Morrow," April 8, 1900, Agriculture Dean's Office.

tions. Enrollments in the College of Agriculture declined from a high of 79 in 1871-72 to 17 in the autumn of 1879, when not more than five were expected to finish the four-year course. And worse was yet to come. This situation induced the University to institute a short course which permitted students to learn about technical agricultural subjects exclusively for a year. It also guaranteed Morrow ample time for duties beyond the classroom. He performed a valuable service by using his considerable powers as a publicist to keep alive faith in agricultural education during the dark night of despair.[28]

Outside the classroom, however, the University gained national prominence in its efforts to deal with the problems of agricultural research, extension, and organization of the land-grant schools. Willard C. Flagg inspired much of the University's research achievement. In 1867 the Board of Trustees had elected Flagg, one of their number, to the position of Corresponding Secretary. Flagg had definite ideas about the conduct of this office, which had been designed as a University-affiliated directorate of science for the state. He immediately gathered a mass of statistical, scientific, and historical data, and published material on past and present Illinois agricultural practices in the Board's *First Annual Report*. In addition, he outlined there desirable future investigations to be made in soils, meteorology, botany, zoology, and entomology. He urged the creation of a statistical bureau and the holding of annual agricultural conventions. Moreover, he advocated the establishment of experimental stations throughout the state where farmers would conduct tests under direction of University personnel and perhaps with the aid of a chemist from a local high school.[29] In light of what Yale's John P. Norton had discovered about the defects of this system in Scotland, this proposal from a Yale graduate was oddly regressive.

The Board organized the University for experimentation soon thereafter. Late in 1870 the Executive Committee retained 13 acres of land for the campus and divided the remainder into a Stock Farm, 410 acres lying south of Mount Hope Cemetery, and an

[28] *5th Report* (1873), 14; *8th Report* (1877), 34-35; *10th Report* (1881), 196.
[29] *1st Report* (1868), v-xii.

Experimental Farm, 200 acres running north of the burial ground. In the latter they reserved about 70 acres for field crops and gave over the remainder to horticulture. The plan of supervision left much to be desired. The Trustees thought more in terms of running a model farm for profit than in advancing the science of agriculture. Having taken the power of managing the farm from the Regent and the Faculty (really Bliss), the Board retained control through its Committee on Agriculture. To supervise the Stock Farm they chose as Head Farmer E. L. Lawrence, a Belvidere resident who had managed a farm since he was 14. As an economic incentive, they offered Lawrence a maximum rather than a minimum salary if receipts warranted. The surplus went to his employers.[30]

Flagg received appointment as Superintendent of Experiments on the Experimental Farm at an undetermined date in the spring of 1871. He therefore became director of investigations begun on April 12 when small plots were sown with corn and other seeds to test fertilizers, methods of cultivation, and varieties of grains, grasses, and roots. Manly Miles had given Gregory the idea that induced the launching of this research. Miles envisioned a systematic series of experiments, and drew upon Lawes and Gilbert, the English researchers at Rothamsted, for his critical point that experimental plots of no less than one-twentieth of an acre produced the best results.[31]

Both Flagg and Miles wanted to establish several centers of research like the one at Champaign-Urbana and to coordinate their work. In this way the empirical data needed to develop a science of agriculture could be amassed. Hence Flagg recommended that experiments be conducted at seven places throughout Illinois under the supervision of University trustees who lived in these localities. Miles opposed him on the grounds that good experimentation required special training. They agreed, however, that agricultural experiment stations were vital, and in December, 1870, the Board asked the General Assembly to provide money for these facilities. Flagg also persuaded Gregory to use his prestige to call a meeting of land-grant institutions "for the purpose of organizing, consulting

[30] *4th Report* (1872), 61, 65, 119.
[31] *Ibid.*, 65-66, 126, 227-28; *5th Report* (1873), 111-18.

and co-operating in the great work of advancing the cause of Agricultural knowledge and education, especially by experimentation with similar crops under similar conditions, at all the Agricultural Colleges."[32] The result was a Convention of Friends of Agricultural Education which assembled in Chicago on August 24-25, 1871. The 29 persons present from 12 states included college presidents, professors, and representatives from farm newspapers. They elected Gregory to preside. Miles took the leading part in deliberations, and Flagg quietly managed the proceedings from the wings.

The Chicago gathering was a landmark in the development of agricultural education in the United States. Delegates focused their attention on cooperative investigations. For the report of a Committee on Experiments which he headed, Flagg drew heavily on recommendations he had made earlier to the Board of Trustees relative to experiments in meteorology, mechanics, physics and plant growth, industrial chemistry, mining and metallurgy, animal breeding and feeding, and soils. Those present adopted his proposal that various land-grant colleges conduct similar experiments. These required planting corn in hills and drills, uniformly applying manures to adjacent plots, and testing the variation of soil on neighboring pieces of ground.[33]

Collaboration of the type required by these efforts raised broad policy questions. Should the agricultural colleges engage in research? Gregory believed the country demanded that they should, even though the Morrill Act made their main object teaching. Miles and E. W. Hilgard favored ignoring the public's impatience over how slowly research produced useful results, but Flagg thought it essential to recognize popular wants in order to win confidence. What should be the relation of land-grant schools to each other and to other institutions? That question led to debate over a permanent organization. Some contended that the agricultural colleges should affiliate with the National Educational Association and serve general purposes. Gregory and Flagg argued that they should go their separate way and emphasize agricultural experimentation. Flagg moved the formation of an organization to advance industrial edu-

---

[32] *4th Report* (1872), 215; see also 123, 298-99, 312; *5th Report* (1873), 118. The convention is fully reported in the *4th Report* (1872), 215-351.
[33] *4th Report* (1872), 315, 318, 320.

cation. Delegates laid his resolution on the table with the under-
standing that the convention's officers pursue the matter. The
American Association of Agricultural Colleges and Experiment
Stations was eventually the outcome.

Equally significant was Flagg's resolution that the example of
Europe made it desirable to establish at least one agricultural experiment station in each state. The Chicago delegates adopted the motion and authorized Gregory to appoint a committee consisting of
one member from each state with a land-grant college to memorialize their legislatures and Congress to this effect.[34] This decision
induced the U.S. Commissioner of Agriculture to call an agricultural
convention at Washington in 1872, the first of several national gatherings which culminated in 1887 with passage of the Hatch Act
establishing agricultural experiment stations.

Despite Illinois' achievement at Chicago, the Board of Trustees
could not give intelligent direction to the University's own research.
Flagg returned from the convention to initiate in the spring of 1872
experimental plots to compare fertilizers, methods of cultivation,
rotation of crops, and varieties of the same crop. But after he
stopped directing research in 1873 (when he became President of
the Illinois State Farmers' Association), confusion and inertia prevailed. The Board authorized the Head Farmer to make, with
Gardner's consent, any experiments his funds justified. On the Experimental Farm Lawrence continued Flagg's tests. After simple
but exhaustive experiments in feeding cooked and raw foods on the
Stock Farm, Lawrence — who once announced that the best cure
for hog cholera was drinking new warm milk — concluded that the
preferred way to feed cattle was to give them corn in a sheltered
yard! He drove relentlessly to realize maximum profits.[35]

A condition of chaos greeted Manly Miles on his arrival for
duty in 1875, and now the Board returned to the Professor of Agriculture the "general management and superintendence of the agricultural interest, including the farm."[36] Miles insisted on running
the Experimental Farm solely for laboratory purposes, and made
noteworthy research contributions during his brief tenure. Drawing

[34] *Ibid.*, 221, 297-315, 343.
[35] *7th Report* (1875), 106, 114; *8th Report* (1877), 108, 132.
[36] *8th Report* (1877), 162.

upon French and German practice, he conducted the first experiments with silage in the United States. In September, 1875, he covered several earthen pits which he had filled with cornstalks and broomcorn seed and found that cattle readily ate the resulting silage. His published results created great interest. Miles also proposed to put from two to five acres into a permanent series of small plots for studying the cultivation of Indian corn. This advice systematized his previous recommendation that had led to the planting of one-twentieth-acre plots on April 12, 1871.[37]

Morrow's research followed lines laid out by Miles and other predecessors. Under the loose direction of a committee of the Board he possessed ample authority to proceed as he wished. In the summer of 1879 Morrow visited Lawes at Rothamsted and observed French agricultural practices, but brought back no new ideas. In that year he commenced on a "piece of land more than usually well adapted for such a test" what he "designed to be a long continued experiment to show the effect of rotation of crops, contrasted with continuous corn growing — with and without manuring, and also the effect of clover and grass in rotation." Morrow's research program emphasized Indian corn, the Illinois staple, and built on foundations laid by Miles and Flagg. The piece of land he used was in the vicinity of and perhaps part of the ground where Miles had conducted his experiments. The area became known as the Morrow Plots, now the oldest permanent agricultural test plots in the United States. Miles originated the idea, but loss of favor with the administration prevented the perpetuation of his name.[38]

In these same years Burrill was conducting research which eventually brought him an international reputation. During the summer of 1871 he conducted microscopical observations at Cobden, Illinois, with a view to determining the cause of pear and apple

[37] *Ibid.*, 152-54; Alfred Charles True, *A History of Agricultural Experimentation and Research in the United States, 1607-1925,* U.S. Department of Agriculture, Misc. Pub. No. 251 (Washington, 1937), 149; Miles, " 'Ensilage' of Fodder: Preserving Green Feed by Burial," *Cultivator and Country Gentleman,* XLI (1876), 627-28; Miles, *Silos, Ensilage and Silage* (New York, 1889).

[38] *10th Report* (1881), 232, and see also 47-58, 218-19. Flagg referred in 1874 to Plat No. 1 as "south of the road, and immediately east of the barn," a location which was probably south of the present Morrow Plots. See *7th Report* (1875), 15, 106. Manly Miles explicitly proposed a permanent series of plots in 1875. See *8th Report* (1877), 153.

blight and why grapes and stone fruits rotted. On the campus he directed investigations on grounds north of Mount Hope Cemetery. His Experimental Orchard and Forest Plantation flanked the Experimental Farm on the west and east respectively. In the former, some 30 acres, Burrill planted 1,200 varieties of apple trees as well as pears and other orchard fruits in 1869. In the latter, some 20 acres first established in 1871, he experimented with timber trees. Illini Grove, a remnant of the original plantation at the corner of Lincoln and Pennsylvania avenues, stands today as a memorial to Burrill's labors. Students set out 10,083 forest trees and made 40,000 apple and 7,000 pear grafts in 1872. Burrill supervised the greenhouse and ornamental planting around the University, and also had charge of a Botanical Garden and Horticultural Grounds, both of which ran south from University Hall toward the cemetery. The latter contained experimental and vegetable gardens. Attempts to raise produce for market and for canning did not succeed.[39]

The University's contribution to the education of ordinary farmers originated in the attempt to plow new truth back into the soil. Illinois pioneered in agricultural extension, although Kansas Agricultural College preceded it by one year in organizing a farmers' institute. The Board agreed to sponsor free lectures on practical subjects under Dunlap's prodding in 1867, and modeled the first program held at Champaign-Urbana two years later after the Yale plan of 1860 with which Flagg was familiar. The 1869 Agricultural Lectures and Discussions brought scientists and farmers together for addresses and discussion in the hope of uniting theory and practice, or "Learning and Labor." The initial offering attracted a small audience and afforded students richer fare than usual.[40]

Thereafter the University organized farmers' institutes during midwinter at various places throughout the state as well as at Champaign-Urbana. The Trustees paid for advertising and speakers' costs and asked local communities to furnish the hall. Admission was free. The entomologists, orchardists, chemists, veterinarians,

[39] *3rd Report* (1870), 44-45; *5th Report* (1873), 81-82, 96-109; *6th Report* (1874), 89, 92-94. The *7th Report* (1875), 15, has a diagram of the campus showing the location of the various farms and orchards.

[40] Alfred Charles True, *A History of Agricultural Education in the United States, 1785-1925,* U.S. Department of Agriculture, Misc. Pub. No. 36 (Washington, 1929), 119; *1st Report* (1868), xi; *2nd Report* (1869), 120.

and other "live scientific men" imparted little new knowledge, and the gatherings reflected a combined Chautauqua and Grange. Miles, Turner, Burrill, and Professor Stuart spoke on applied science; Flagg often lectured on the political and economic problems of farmers; Van Osdel on rural architecture; Snyder on agricultural bookkeeping; Professor Baker on ancient agriculture; Professor Carey, the classics teacher, on plows and plowing; and Gregory on general and ennobling themes. These programs brought out only a few of the more progressive farmers, but the number of institutes rose from three in 1870 to seven in 1873. Illinois' modest success spurred Iowa State, Cornell, and Michigan State to organize similar programs. But economic depression induced the Board to cut off financial aid to extension late in 1873.[41]

The University revived the lectures in 1878 after Flagg rejoined the Board and after leading agriculturists expressed a determination to secure an appropriation from the General Assembly for the purpose. Morrow now became the guiding spirit behind farm extension. He proposed to have the presidents of the state agricultural, horticultural, and dairy associations along with editors of leading agricultural newspapers speak at Urbana, thus giving a new public relations cast to the plan. But he also recommended three weeks of free agricultural and veterinary lectures to precede the farmers' institute. The Board approved both recommendations.[42]

During the 1870's engineering education moved forward throughout the nation as decisively as agricultural education marked time, and Illinois registered particularly noteworthy achievements. Stillman W. Robinson, who had long been the senior professor, became Dean of the College of Engineering in 1878. In this decade the Department of Mining and Metallurgy made no headway, while that of Civil Engineering developed steadily but unspectacularly. Far more exciting and significant were the advances in Mechanical Science and Engineering and in Architecture and Fine Arts.

[41] Flagg printed as much material as possible from the first five years of institute proceedings in the Board's annual reports. See the 2nd to 6th Reports (1869-74). See also W. J. Beal, History of the Michigan Agricultural College (East Lansing, 1915), 158.
[42] 10th Report (1881), 197, 199, 212; John Hamilton, History of Farmers' Institutes in the United States, U.S. Department of Agriculture, Office of Experiment Stations, Bulletin No. 174 (Washington, 1906), 29.

When Robinson took up his duties at Illinois in 1870, mechanical engineering was just emerging as a branch of study. Worcester Polytechnic Institute, founded in 1868, was the first American school to link teaching in mechanic arts and the process of manufacturing to science and mathematics. W.P.I. established a machine shop in which students could learn the essentials of a trade while producing articles for commercial sale. However, the shop was regarded as a laboratory and not expected to pay its own way. The instruction in shop work at Worcester made no improvement on the best apprentice training of the day.[43] The Russians, however, devised a more profound solution to the problem of manual-shop training about this time. There is no evidence that Robinson knew of the latter system, but he independently developed a similar pedagogy and his contribution should be evaluated in light of the Russian experience.

A royal decree created the Imperial Technical School in Moscow on June 1, 1868, and there Director Victor Della Vos devised a substitute for the apprentice method of training. The School's original distinction between *instruction* and *construction* shops (the latter filled orders for sale) led Della Vos and his assistants to discover their novel technique. In working out an instructional program to prepare students for the construction shops, they analyzed the mechanic arts scientifically and based their course of training on the results. The Russian system involved the following component parts: organizing a separate instruction shop for each distinctive art or trade, such as joinery, wood-turning, and blacksmithing; providing separate work places and tools for each student; analyzing each step involved in the mastery of a trade and arranging them in progressive order; and combining drawings, models, and tools into a series of graded exercises by which a student could, under supervision, advance toward required standards of skill. Strict regimentation was part of the method, which was the product of an autocratic and militaristic culture. The success of the pedagogical innovation brought an end to the construction shops.[44]

Although the Imperial Technical School exhibited at the Vi-

[43] Charles Alpheus Bennett, *History of Manual and Industrial Education, 1870-1917* (Peoria, 1937), 311-13.
[44] *Ibid.*, 14-20, 40-47.

enna Exposition in 1873, it influenced the United States only after participating in the Centennial Exposition three years later. President John D. Runkle of the Massachusetts Institute of Technology, coming upon the Russian models at Philadelphia, immediately saw them as the solution to the problem of shop instruction. In August he persuaded his governing board to authorize instruction shops for mechanical engineering students and to establish a School of Mechanic Arts for individuals who wished to follow industrial pursuits rather than become scientific engineers. In addition, Runkle proposed to reunite manual and mental training for the liberal education of all students. Both the Russians and Runkle spurred Calvin M. Woodward to found the St. Louis Manual Training School of Washington University on June 6, 1879. For some time Woodward had been searching for methods of teaching tool work with no immediate vocational goal and of relating this instruction to liberal education. Long before Della Vos bedazzled visitors to Philadelphia, however, Robinson had pioneered along similar lines at Champaign-Urbana.[45]

In 1870 Robinson announced that his aim was to qualify men to design, construct, and superintend machinery, and for this purpose he sought to combine severely scientific and thoroughly practical instruction. The former included mathematics, mechanical philosophy, physics (the latter two were listed separately), chemistry, analytical and applied mechanics, drawing, and liberal arts subjects desired by individual students. For the latter Robinson immediately won authorization to establish a machine shop. He regarded it as a means of "practical culture," a place for teaching in six months what an apprentice would take three years to learn. But the shop was also to operate commercially, making instructional apparatus for the University and for sale. Instruction rather than profit was the shop's prime purpose, however, for it was the equivalent of a laboratory in the natural sciences.[46]

[45] John D. Runkle, "The Manual Element in Education," [Massachusetts] Board of Education, *Forty-first Annual Report, 1876-1877* (Boston, 1878), 185-92; Bennett, *History of Manual and Industrial Education,* 320-21; Charles Penney Coates, *History of the Manual Training School of Washington University,* U.S. Bureau of Education, Bulletin No. 3, 1923 (Washington, 1923), 7-17; Lawrence A. Cremin, *The Transformation of the School: Progressivism in American Education, 1876-1957* (New York, 1961), 27.
[46] *Catalogue, 1869-70,* 10-12; *3rd Report* (1870), 110-11.

Robinson taught the engineering subjects and physics, primarily by lectures and recitations, using Silliman's *Physics* as a textbook. The course in physics attracted 24 students in 1873, the largest number in the Department except for manual training. In that year Robinson was teaching four to six hours daily and supervising the shop. Gregory therefore recommended appointment of a physics professor as soon as funds allowed. Late in 1873 the Physical Laboratory and Lecture Room in the new University Hall opened, and the following year laboratory work was introduced. Students performed experiments in physics one day a week, and Robinson conducted more complicated "illustrations" one evening a week. He attracted large audiences, and emphasized practical application of principles. Advanced classes performed or observed "the higher physical experiments." Illinois was not the first school to use the inductive method in teaching physics, but it moved along with progressive institutions.[47]

In the machine shop at the southeast corner of Wright and Springfield streets, Robinson, who patented about 40 inventions during his lifetime, taught the design and construction of machines. He first directed students in the manufacture of working equipment, the most important item being an eight-horsepower steam engine, after which they made from working drawings "several pieces of philosophic and other apparatus of fine character. . . ."[48] These included a helioscope, an Atwood's machine to measure the flow of fluids, models of a truss bridge and a truss roof, and a machine invented by Robinson which graduated thermometer scales.

The machine shop scored an immediate popular and financial success. Hearing of the enthusiasm Robinson aroused by uniting learning and labor, young apprentices rushed to Champaign-Urbana to become "scientific mechanicians." As a result the Mechanical Building and Drill Hall, dedicated in the fall of 1871, was the first substantial building erected after the University opened. With a larger student-made steam engine and other equipment, the

[47] *6th Report* (1874), 166; *Catalogue, 1874-75,* 49. Benjamin Silliman, *First Principles of Physics, or Natural Philosophy, Designed for the Use of Schools and Colleges,* was first published in Philadelphia, 1859. At Illinois and elsewhere, the terms "natural philosophy" and "physics" were often used interchangeably until about 1870.
[48] Superintendent of Public Instruction of the State of Illinois, *Eighth Biennial Report,* 104; *4th Report* (1872), 279.

shop provided more labor than the farms and also returned a profit. Thermometer-graduating machines and a device invented by Robinson for trimming photographs sold in quantities; hay presses, a 40-horsepower steam engine, a pattern for a coffee mill, and other items found ready markets. For a time the shop operated a half-day a week and all summer for commercial purposes, but Robinson insisted that it not be expected to pay its own way.

At Urbana as at Moscow, practical instruction originated for the purpose of supplementing theoretical and technical instruction. Robinson, like Della Vos, wanted to teach design, drawing, and shop practice as quickly as possible. He therefore took no more than seven students per class, and closely supervised their work on assigned topics for two hours each day. He tried to furnish each individual a complete set of tools and workbenches for their separate labors in wood, brass, and iron. Robinson required pupils to keep summer journals during the three consecutive summers before their senior year in which they described machinery, manufacturing methods, and rare mechanical operations observed in their travels. He demanded a thesis of students who completed the course. The program was exacting, but of course Robinson could not regiment his charges as could Della Vos.[49]

Robinson was advancing along lines parallel to Della Vos, and it appears that he arrived independently at essentials of the famous Russian system early in the 1870's. This accomplishment may account for Gregory's failure to mention the display of the Imperial Technical School at Vienna in 1873. The general excellence of European technical schools demonstrated at Vienna did impress Gregory, and also convinced him that Robinson's Department, however expensive, would greatly influence Illinois' manufacturing interests. From Europe he urged Robinson to seek advice from other Americans about better equipment for the Physical Laboratory. By 1875 Gregory was justified in declaring that "the success of our School of Mechanical Engineering stands unrivalled on this continent."[50]

[49] *4th Report* (1872), 105; Bennett, *History of Manual and Industrial Education*, 15, 46; *Catalogue, 1871-72,* 36, 37; *6th Report* (1874), 98-99; *8th Report* (1877), 141.
[50] *8th Report* (1877), 138, and see also 141; *6th Report* (1874), 160; *7th Report* (1875), 91.

The following year the Russian technical display created "so great a sensation in the east," according to Gregory, an official judge of the educational exhibits at Philadelphia, that Illinois did not escape the impact.[51] The chief influence, however, seems to have been an attempt in the next couple of years to perfect Robinson's system in light of that devised by Della Vos. The University now laid new stress on shop exercises designed to acquaint students with the proper use of tools for different purposes, and it more carefully divided the mechanical laboratory into shops for pattern-making, blacksmithing, moulding and founding, bench work for iron, and machine tool work for iron. In the elementary shop students drew every piece before executing it; in advanced shop they designed and constructed complete machines.[52]

Robinson's achievement brought him international recognition by 1878. "We are none too soon in the field in this great department of education," said Gregory after seeing the brilliant display of the Russian technical schools at the Paris Exposition that year. But in September Robinson departed, driven by the salary cut of 1877 to Ohio State University and a job paying him $450 a year more than Illinois. Gregory then obtained Selim H. Peabody for the post, offering him $1,800 — Robinson's salary. Peabody successfully held out for $2,000.[53]

The hoary apprentice system was demonstrating its inability to train architects when the American university began to emerge after the Civil War. Illinois vies with two other institutions as a pioneer in architectural education. Massachusetts Institute of Technology began a two-year program in design, construction, and professional practice when Boston architect William R. Ware started offering a course in September, 1868. Andrew D. White took special interest in the field, and Cornell established a four-year School of Architecture as a branch of the College of Civil Engineering in 1871. Gregory laid the foundations for architecture at Illinois in 1867 in calling for a Course (Department) of Architecture and Fine Arts in his curriculum report. The Chicago architect and trustee, John M.

[51] *9th Report* (1878), 105.
[52] *Catalogue, 1876-77,* 35; *Catalogue, 1877-78,* 31-32.
[53] *9th Report* (1878), 105-6.

Van Osdel, has been credited with inspiring Gregory's decision, but in all probability Gregory's alertness to the changing role of education accounted for his recognition of the need for university training of architects.[54]

However, the Illinois school rested on weak foundations until 1873. At the outset studies in architecture came under the Department of Civil Engineering. James W. Bellangee taught architecture and mechanical drawing from 1869 to 1871. Harold M. Hansen, a Swede who had studied at the Preussische Bauakademie in Berlin, replaced him. The first student to register for the course offered by the Department of Architecture, which existed only in the catalogue, was Nathan C. Ricker. At the age of 26, possessing $750 in savings and a burning desire to learn, Ricker arrived in Urbana on January 21, 1870. It was midnight, and he slept on the dormitory floor.

In chapel the next morning Gregory announced that a master workman who felt the need of intellectual training had just enrolled in the University. The student exemplified Gregory's confidence that the "new education" would unite learning and labor. Back in Maine, where he was born on an Acton farm in 1843, Ricker had made himself a competent wood-worker and by strict discipline had taught himself Latin, French, geology, and botany. He built piano cases for some time after coming of age and then emigrated to La Harpe, Illinois, where an uncle had gone. There Ricker became a building carpenter and purchased a half-interest in a wagon and blacksmith shop. When a vacationing student told him about Illinois Industrial University late in 1869, he immediately sold his business interest and struck out for Urbana.[55]

Ricker studied rendering, drawing, and design with Hansen and filled the gaps in his education by reading. In the following academic year he had charge of the carpenter shop and taught

[54] Mark L. Peisch, *The Chicago School of Architecture: Early Followers of Sullivan and Wright*, Columbia University Studies in Art History and Archaeology, No. 5 (New York, 1964), 8, credits Van Osdel, following Turpin C. Bannister, "Pioneering in Architectural Education," *Journal of the American Institute of Architects*, XX (July, 1953), 8. See also Morris Bishop, *A History of Cornell* (Ithaca, 1962), 160-61; Samuel C. Prescott, *When M.I.T. was "Boston Tech," 1861-1916* (Cambridge, Mass., 1954), 94-95.

[55] Nathan C. Ricker, "The Story of a Life" (typewritten MS. autobiography, Urbana, 1922); Ira O. Baker, "Nathan Clifford Ricker, '72," *Alumni Quarterly*, VI (April, 1912), 97.

wood-working. The next summer, after the Great Fire, he obtained in a Chicago architect's office "a great practical training, perhaps not equalled since the burning of Rome."[56] That fall Hansen failed to return and Gregory asked Ricker to take responsibility for architecture and drawing. Ricker taught and examined himself and three fellow students. Discerning his promise, Gregory offered him a permanent job if he would complete his course and travel abroad for six months. To enable him to sail for Europe with Gregory in late March, the Board granted him a certificate of scholarship for a full course in architecture on March 12, 1873. Ricker thus finished three months before the first architectural student graduated from M.I.T., and became the first American graduate of a collegiate program in architecture.[57]

Ricker bypassed Paris, the mecca of American architects since the 1860's, for Berlin and the Bauakademie. It was Hansen's school, and Hansen's pupil wanted to observe the instructional methods and use the excellent library to acquaint himself with the best standard works on architecture and art. Director Richard Lucae registered the traveler as a special student from "Champaign in North America," and Ricker's stay convinced him he had been right in regarding the exacting German way of teaching architecture as superior to the French. At the Vienna Exposition, which he visited at Gregory's request, the technical exhibit of the Christian Brothers and the Russian system of shop practice impressed him. Vacation travel and the trip home by way of France and England afforded firsthand evidence of architectural monuments. He returned with a keen awareness of the deficiencies in his own training.

Ricker became Head of the Department of Architecture that fall. Determined to excel, he found the difficulties of pioneering immense. For a dozen years he alone taught architecture, and in addition offered engineering courses, directed the wood-working shop, and designed University buildings. Neither curricula nor textbooks existed, and the public, perhaps in the Midwest especially, regarded architects as useless. Many scoffed at the idea of educating architects in an environment where cornfields rather than magnifi-

[56] Ricker, "The Story of a Life."
[57] *6th Report* (1874), 109, 112; Ricker, "The Story of a Life."

cent public buildings dominated the landscape. Ricker, perhaps capitalizing on a liability, regarded isolation more as a quality of mind than an inescapable fact of geography.

He stamped his ideas on the reorganized curriculum, which emphasized both construction and aesthetics. Ricker's scientific interest in stresses and strains and his definition of the architectural needs of the Midwest, and not the Department's connection with the College of Engineering, led to the attention given construction. For this purpose Ricker introduced a course in graphic statics in 1874; he said he was the first to offer the subject in an American architectural program. These foundations underlay Ricker's pioneering work in advanced structural design two decades later, after the Chicago skyscrapers created a demand for individuals trained in the new technique of steel-skeleton construction. In addition, Ricker laid much importance on aesthetics. He taught the subject mainly by indirection, offering one course in aesthetics and four in the history of architecture.[58]

At the outset Ricker taught by lecturing, only to conclude that American students were unprepared to profit from this method. Since textbooks were unavailable, he made his own by blueprinting his lecture notes for distribution. Some 2,000 pages were soon in use. At this time he began translating French and German architectural books, a labor of love to which he often devoted whole summers, making classics available and winning wide recognition for himself.

Ricker made practical training a main ingredient of his Department starting in the fall of 1873. Some trustees conducted the new Head to the wood-working shop and announced that the Board "expected him to make the damned thing pay."[59] But he had better ideas. He must have been familiar with Robinson's innovations before 1873, but Vienna inspired him, and he determined to adapt the system of shop practice for mechanical engineers to wood-working for architects. He therefore announced that students

---

[58] *Catalogue, 1874-75,* 34; Ricker, "The Story of a Life." The catalogues do not show a course in graphic statics, but Ricker published *Elementary Graphic Statics and the Construction of Trussed Roofs* (New York, 1884). See also *13th Report* (1887), 150-51.
[59] Ricker, "The Story of a Life."

would be required to make general and detailed drawings of German plaster casts of architectural subjects, and to acquire a practical knowledge of construction by a full course of shop practice, ten hours a week during the first year and one term during the second. Here they were to make models to scale from drawings of the various elements of buildings and from original designs for stairs. The one term of manual training in carpentry and joinery introduced soon developed into a full year's course, and individual workbenches and sets of tools were made available.[60] After 1876 the catalogue description of the shop practice added the phrase, "The system is similar to the Russian system, so much admired at the Centennial Exposition, but more comprehensive, and applied to building rather than Mechanical Engineering."[61] Later, Ricker said that Robinson deserved credit for originating the so-called Russian system of manual training in mechanical engineering in the United States early in 1870, and that he himself had adapted it to architectural education.[62]

In 1875 the University instituted a Builder's Course in the School or Department of Architecture. This one-year program, which copied a German model, aimed at accommodating carpenters and mechanics unqualified for the regular architectural training. It featured architectural drawing and the theory and practice of stair-building. On March 11, 1877, the Board authorized a School

[60] *Catalogue, 1874-75,* 34-36, 56. See also *13th Report* (1887), 153.
[61] *Catalogue, 1876-77,* 42.
[62] A controversy over credit for introducing the Russian system into the United States apparently developed between Ricker and Runkle. Ricker said that Runkle was favorably impressed with some 20 pieces of wood-work he saw on a visit to the University of Illinois in 1875, but later claimed credit for introducing the Russian system into the United States and then asked whether any documentary evidence showed that the Russian system was in use "under this distinctive name" at Illinois before August 14, 1876, when his governing board approved it for M.I.T. Robinson and Ricker had introduced essentials of the "Russian system" before 1876, but of course not under that name, over which Runkle made a great point. Both Ricker at Vienna and Runkle at Philadelphia were greatly impressed with what they saw of the Russian system. The Russians, a more formal people than the Americans, were excellent at displaying their results. Robinson arranged no exhibit. See Ricker, "Statement on Manual Shop Training," 2-page holograph MS.; and J. A. Chamberlain (Director of Manual Training, Washington, D.C., Public Schools) to C. A. Bowser (Superintendent of Champaign Schools), Dec. 7, 1893, both in Ricker-Runkle Controversy File, 1893.

of Art and Design to bring together art courses originally introduced
for female students and courses in clay-modeling and design which
Gregory sponsored on the grounds that excellence in manufacturing
depended upon them. Peter Roos, former Head of the Boston Art
Academy and a teacher of drawing and design, directed the
School.[63]

The Department of Architecture averaged about eight students
a year during its first decade, and early produced graduates who
gained national and even international distinction. Clarence H.
Blackall (class of 1877), who went to Boston and designed the first
steel-framed building erected there, was the first of a distinguished
line. After Robinson resigned, Ricker became Dean of the College
of Engineering.

The College of Natural Science emphasized the two branches
of study embraced by the schools comprising it — Chemistry and
Natural History. Chemistry was the prestige science of the day, and
A. P. S. Stuart laid the foundations for a strong department. He
brought with him from Harvard the spirit of organized student laboratory work, and required an original investigation as well as a
written thesis from advanced pupils. When he resigned in 1874 to
enter banking, Henry A. Weber, an Otterbein College alumnus who
had studied with Liebig, became Instructor of Chemistry. He too
emphasized laboratory practice in all the curricula offered by the
School, and introduced work in chemical physics. The clearest indication of success in this area was the opening in 1878 of a Chemistry
Laboratory designed by Ricker. The building's size and facilities
were superlative.

The School of Natural History faced greater problems than its
companion, for chemistry was a relatively advanced discipline compared to botany, zoology, and geology. These were the three large
departments of natural history, whose heyday in America lasted over
a century and began coming to an end about 1830. But the new
order did not emerge in a day. When Illinois Industrial University
opened, the doctrine of design, which taught that everything in
nature had a purpose and indicated God's goodness, still prevailed.

[63] 8th Report (1877), 91, 183; 9th Report (1878), 21, 30; Catalogue, 1875-76,
41; Catalogue, 1876-77, 62-64; "Faculty Record," I, 228.

Botany and zoology continued to be offered as "natural history," although Harvard's Asa Gray and Louis Agassiz pointed toward the rise of specialists in botany and zoology. But before 1870 botany at Harvard went little beyond the gross morphology and elementary classification of the flowering plants and ferns, and Gray devoted little attention to cryptogamic botany. Laboratory exercises and the microscope were almost unknown in the most advanced schools. Modern geology had emerged, however, and the better colleges appointed men to separate chairs in that field or in mineralogy.[64]

Natural history experienced uneven development at Illinois in early years. The University failed to obtain the Bromby Collection only because the specimens in mineralogy, geology, and conchology proved worthless. Strangely, the Trustees tabled a motion to ask the General Assembly to remove the state geological collection to Urbana and to have the state geologist lecture there. But in 1869-70 Gregory engaged Professor Sanborn Tenney of Williams College for a series of 30 lectures on the relations of zoology to the pursuits of mankind.[65]

Shortly thereafter Don Carlos Taft joined the faculty and taught zoology and geology until 1882. Highly individualistic, the youthful Taft had suddenly formed the idea while at a dance in his native New Hampshire that he was not making the best of his life. He left the dance and his girl, went out into the night resolving to do better, and worked his way through Amherst and Union Theological Seminary. Later Taft settled in Elmwood, Illinois, where he was the Congregational minister and taught in a local academy. The unpopularity of his liberal sermons drove him into teaching geology as his main work. Through all these years Taft also kept trying to master his vanity, and succeeded so well that he prided himself on his complete indifference to his dress. Eccentricities probably robbed Taft of a wholly successful career at Illinois during Gregory's administration. But Taft served the institution faithfully, and endeared himself to students, who affectionately called him "the great uncombed."[66]

[64] William Martin Smallwood, *Natural History and the American Mind* (New York, 1941), 215, 350-53, and *passim*.
[65] *3rd Report* (1870), 39, 94, 107.
[66] Ada Bartlett Taft, *Lorado Taft: Sculptor and Citizen* (Greensboro, N.C., 1946), 1-3; *4th Report* (1872), 133; *5th Report* (1873), 68, 146, 152; *Catalogue, 1870-71*, 33, 35.

Botany, Burrill's province, was an entirely different story. It developed under the inspired touch of a truly remarkable individual. His career deserves a full biography, but the leading details must suffice. He was born on April 25, 1839, at Pittsfield, Massachusetts, of parents who had emigrated from Britain with their families when very young. Economic hardship drove his father, an expert weaver, to remove to Stephenson County in extreme northern Illinois when Thomas Jonathan was nine. The boy grew up on a farm between Freeport and Rockford, working with his father and six brothers and acquiring an education in private schools taught in log dwellings and in the organized district school. At 19 he went to high school in Freeport, but homesickness and sensitivity to his rustic clothes prompted his leaving after three weeks. The next year, more determined but less confident, he returned to high school, going this time to Rockford to avoid facing his Freeport acquaintances.[67]

After a stint of schoolteaching Burrill entered the State Normal University at Normal in April, 1862. The institution was one of the best teacher-training schools in the nation, and also the center of important scientific activity in Illinois, especially in natural history. Burrill's botany teacher was Joseph A. Sewall, who had studied under Gray and Agassiz at Harvard and was a physician. Sewall was curator of the museum of the State Natural History Society located at Normal.[68] The annual meetings of the Society in neighboring Bloomington brought together the leading scientific men of the state. This environment evidently stimulated Burrill's interest in natural history. Upon graduating in 1865 he began teaching in Urbana, and two years later went as botanist on the first Powell expedition to the Colorado Rockies. His collection of plants from this trip founded the herbarium on the campus.[69] Temporarily employed to teach algebra when the University first opened, Burrill had almost immediately been appointed Assistant Professor

[67] Thomas J. Burrill, "Boyhood Biography, a Personal Sketch," typewritten MS., Burrill Papers; Stephen A. Forbes, "Thomas Jonathan Burrill," *Alumni Quarterly and Fortnightly Notes,* I (July 15, 1916), 410-11. I am indebted to this excellent article in my treatment of Burrill.
[68] Gregory tried to hire Sewall to teach chemistry when the University opened.
[69] The statement that the University had a herbarium of dried plants collected by the Powell expeditions (*Catalogue, 1870-71,* 33) seems to have been missed by Forbes and others.

of Natural History and Botany to fill the vacancy created when Major Powell did not take up his chair at Urbana. Two years later he was promoted to a professorship in botany and in horticulture.

When Burrill joined the staff, the study of bacteria in botany was still in the primitive stage. It had long been known that diseases attacked plants, at times very destructively. Fire blight, a contagious disease of pear, apple, quince, and other trees, was a major problem for fruitgrowers and therefore for Illinois. Although different investigators had already discovered that microorganisms caused other types of diseases in plants, no one had satisfactorily explained the cause of pear blight. In fact, bacterial diseases of plants were far rarer than fungus diseases, and bacteria had not been generally suspected of causing disease before about 1850. It was not until 1872 that Ferdinand Cohn started presenting a complete study of the then known kinds of bacteria, and Robert Koch obtained the final proof of the bacterial cause of anthrax only in 1876.[70]

Burrill immediately singled out for study the new field of plant pathology. He recognized it as a little-understood and challenging area of botanical inquiry, but may have focused attention on it out of a desire to stop the scourge which proved so costly to Illinois orchardists. Burrill loved science, but less for its own sake than as an agency of human welfare. A profound religious faith underlay both his science and his humanitarianism. His research and his teaching were inseparably entwined, and it is instructive to recall that despite his considerable achievement as a scientist he suspended his investigations whenever they conflicted with his duty to his students.

The courses Burrill began to offer in 1868-69 demonstrated his advanced ideas. He started with a term of structural and physiological botany and went on to two terms of systematic botany in which he taught the use of the microscope, fungi and vegetable diseases, and the virtually uncultivated field of cryptogamic botany. In an entomology course for sophomores, he paid attention to the habits of insects injurious to vegetation and the means of checking their ravages. He was probably the first to teach plant pathology, a sub-

[70] Professor Donald P. Rogers of the University of Illinois, in a letter of March 16, 1965, helped me place Burrill's work in botany.

ject taken up at Harvard in 1875, and the first to use microscopes in botanical instruction. He obtained instruments in 1868 and 1869, and announced their availability in the catalogue of 1869-70. The University furnished several more for student use by 1876.[71]

When he began his study of fire blight, Burrill leaned to the belief that fungi were the source of trouble. In 1869 he told the first farmers' institute, "it is pretty generally believed that the parasitic fungi are not in the first instance a predisposing cause of disease or decay; but it is known that they materially influence both, after causing great loss and alarming destruction."[72] Four years later he had concluded that the fungi indeed caused the disease, and in 1877 reported that evidence for the theory of the fungus origin of the fire blight of the pear and the twig blight of the apple was well founded. He observed that a sticky, brownish matter which exuded from affected limbs was entirely made up of "minute oscillating particles," which he did not then recognize as bacteria.[73] But a year later, having identified the moving atoms as bacteria, Burrill reported success in reproducing the pear disease by inoculating healthy trees with bacteria free of fungi. He found that the disease spread from the point of origin, and microorganisms could be discovered in advance of the discolored portions of tissue. "Does it not seem plausible that they cause the subsequently-apparent change?" he asked. "It does to me, but this is the extent of my own faith; we should not say the conclusion is reached and the cause of the difficulty is definitely ascertained. So far as I know the idea is an entirely new one — that *bacteria* cause disease in plants — though abundantly proved in the case of animals."[74]

In the summer of 1880 Burrill experimented to see if these

---

[71] *Catalogue, [1869]*, 5-6; later catalogues show that the courses changed very little throughout the decade. See also Charles F. Hottes, "Personal Recollections of Dr. Thomas J. Burrill and the Bacteriology of His Time," typewritten MS., Carl Stephens Papers. Neil E. Stevens, "The Centenary of T. J. Burrill," *Scientific Monthly*, XLIX (Sept., 1939), 288-89.

[72] *2nd Report* (1869), 327.

[73] Burrill, "Aggressive Parasitism of Fungi," Illinois State Horticultural Society, *Transactions for 1873*, n.s., VII (Chicago 1874), 219; Burrill, "Pear Blight," Illinois State Horticultural Society, *Transactions for 1877*, n.s., XI (Chicago, 1878), 114, 116.

[74] Burrill's comment in "Discussion on the Reports" (on General Horticulture — Fourth District), Illinois State Horticultural Society, *Transactions for 1878*, n.s., XII (Chicago, 1879), 80.

organisms were the really active agents or simply contributory causes of destruction. He inoculated 69 trees on the campus with the blight and established the role of the bacteria in producing disease. He published his results in a national science journal and in the Board's reports, but two years elapsed before he found time to describe the bacterial species (*Micrococcus amylovarus*) which he had shown to be the cause of blight.[75] His explanation for the long delay after 1878 in announcing his significant conclusions is a revealing commentary on the man's sense of responsibility and on the status of science in the University. "Other interests at the same time so engaged my attention and time," he wrote, "that the work was not so extensively prosecuted as I heartily wished it had been, after becoming gradually convinced of the possible complete demonstration of the perplexing problem."[76] His reference was probably to the turmoil and the extra duties occasioned by Gregory's resignation.

Americans generally accepted Burrill's conclusions at once, and in 1885 J. C. Arthur of Geneva, New York, verified the work and carried it somewhat further. Anton de Bary, a foremost European botanist, was slower to note and accept Burrill's findings. But in 1911 an authority on the subject credited Burrill with discovering that pear blight could be attributed to bacterial origin and nothing else, and the Society of American Bacteriologists congratulated Burrill on founding the science of plant pathology in working out the cause of pear blight. Burrill's contributions to science brought him world-wide fame and gave the University great distinction.[77]

Despite the 1873 statute defining preferred studies, the College of Literature and Science continued to aim at furnishing a liberal

[75] Burrill, "Anthrax of Fruit Trees; or The So-Called Fire Blight of Pear, and Twig Blight of Apple, Trees," American Association for the Advancement of Science, *Proceedings,* XXIX (Salem, Mass., 1881), 583-97; Burrill, "Blight of Pear and Apple Trees," *10th Report* (1881), 62-84; Burrill, "The Bacteria: An Account of Their Nature and Effects, Together with a Systematic Description of the Species," *11th Report* (1882), 93-157; Burrill, "New Species of Micrococcus (Bacteria)," *American Naturalist,* XVII (March, 1883), 319-21.

[76] Burrill, "Anthrax of Fruit Trees," 588. Burrill omitted this statement from the article in the *10th Report,* an adaptation of his essay in the AAAS *Proceedings.*

[77] Erwin F. Smith, *Bacteria in Relation to Plant Diseases* (3 vols., Washington, 1905-14), II, 7-9; Eugene Davenport, "Dr. Thomas Jonathan Burrill Memorial Address," Illinois State Horticultural Society, *Transactions for 1916,* n.s., L (n.p., 1917), 74.

education. It made explicit its desire to train teachers for higher education, especially industrial institutions, but said nothing about training teachers for the schools. In addition to the studies in its School of Ancient Languages and Literature and in its School of English and Modern Languages, the College emphasized history and philosophy. Science courses and mathematics were recommended in various curricula, but departments in other colleges taught these offerings. Inevitably, many students took part of their work in the College of Literature and Science, but the individuals who enrolled with an intention of finishing there were either undecided on their future or wanted a liberal education. As a result the College acquired a distinctive character. "It especially favors female students," Gregory said in 1879, "by affording them fields of education appropriate to their wants and tastes."[78] About this time 40 per cent of the student body was registered for nontechnical courses, the majority of whom were women studying literature. The College therefore possessed handicaps in winning support from a utilitarian-minded, male-dominated legislature.[79]

Edward Snyder was the senior professor in the College, and the Faculty elected him Dean in 1878. Snyder had fine qualities, but was perhaps not the person to gain ground for literature and science. Born in 1835 in Austrian Poland, he had been an instructor of history and languages at a military academy in Europe, fought with the Austrian Army, and with the Union Army after emigrating in 1862. Before joining the Illinois faculty he taught in St. Louis and in a high school at Carlinville. An impressive man who was the University's military commandant for eight years and a strict disciplinarian always, Snyder concentrated on modern languages, primarily German, and introduced Italian in 1878. In later life he expressed no regret at having sacrificed scholarly ambitions to devote himself to helping young people with understanding and advice.[80]

James D. Crawford, a Williams College alumnus, had charge of ancient languages. In 1874 the Board appointed him as an instructor, thus de-emphasizing the classics. Late that year the Faculty

[78] *10th Report* (1881), 198.
[79] *13th Report* (1887), 45.
[80] Thomas Arkle Clark, "Edward Snyder — a College Memory," *Alumni Quarterly*, I (April, 1907), 61-68.

resolved that Latin and Greek could be substituted for other languages and for the first year of English, and in 1878 it required Latin for admission to the College. However, the campus newspaper termed the study of ancient and even modern languages a waste of effort because they were not sufficiently useful. English literature nevertheless remained popular. When Baker died in 1873, Gregory induced Trustee Brown to promote the former classics professor Joseph F. Carey, Gregory's college chum, for the vacated chair. But the Board appointed Joseph C. Pickard, a graduate of Bowdoin College. Pickard instructed 200 students in the year ending in June, 1875.[81]

Gregory taught history, political economy, and philosophy, and was the most effective teacher in the College if not in the University. Apart from offering a course in American history for those deficient in the subject, he perpetuated the ante-bellum tradition by instructing the senior class. He made himself their moral and ethical guide, giving them much more than knowledge of the subject being covered. On one occasion the students petitioned for a class in "Gregonometry." When the Regent announced in 1877 his inability to continue teaching in addition to his other duties, the Board refrained from asking funds for a professor to replace him on the grounds that the General Assembly was not likely to appropriate money for history.[82]

His courses, except for history, reveal Gregory as a moderately progressive thinker, and shed light on the man and the University.[83] He valued history highly for its illustrations of character and morality, and saw in it the hand of God working toward predestined ends. Though Gregory realized that historical events illustrated the working of cause and effect, his teaching stressed memorization of important facts relating to time and place. Unfortunately, he had a vested interest in this old method, having emphasized it in his books, *The Hand-Book of History and Chronology* and its companion, *The Map of Time*. While the three Adamses — Henry at Harvard,

---

[81] *6th Report* (1874), 167; *7th Report* (1875), 90, 117; *8th Report* (1877), 126; *Illini*, April, 1877.

[82] "Faculty Record," I, 91; *9th Report* (1878), 60-61; *10th Report* (1881), 135. The Board also refused to seek funds for a physics professor.

[83] Lecture notes by Gregory and by his students for the courses he taught are in the Gregory Papers.

Charles Kendall at the University of Michigan, and Herbert Baxter at Johns Hopkins — were initiating a new era in the study of history by offering seminars which aimed at providing a scientific comprehension of underlying forces, Gregory continued to drill his pupils in concrete facts. However, Andrew D. White also emphasized chronology, and like Gregory hoped that a knowledge of inert facts would be a springboard to understanding.[84]

The Regent worked out in his classes in the 1870's the views published in *A New Political Economy* (1882). The book demonstrated Gregory as a traditionalist who embodied the best new ideas. He regarded economic science as a static system governed by natural laws, and described wants, work, and wealth as the three primary economic forces. No apologist of *laissez-faire,* he came close to repudiating the notion of immutable economic laws. In fact, however, he showed how the science of pure economics applied to the conditions introduced by social and national factors. He therefore accepted the need to limit monopoly and acknowledged labor's right to organize. He was moving closer to the historical and institutional approaches which soon engaged the best minds in economics.[85]

Gregory expounded Scottish Realism in his moral and mental philosophy classes. Adherents of this school had long insisted that there were innate ideas in the mind which nonetheless required full employment of the senses for their realization, and it was only after the Civil War that the Common Sense philosophy began to lose its dominant position in American higher education. Gregory's receptivity to new ideas, especially in science, made him a liberal spokesman of Scottish Realism. On the critical problem of the relation between mind and matter, he abandoned the dualism between the two and insisted that "the study of the nervous system constitutes a necessary part of mental science."[86] Study of the physiology of the

[84] *The Hand-Book* was published in Chicago, 1867; *The Map* at about the same time. It was available as a wall chart. See also Gregory's articles, "The Study of History," *Illinois Teacher,* XIV (June, 1868), 194-95, (Aug., 1868), 268-71; and Walter P. Rogers, *Andrew D. White and the Modern University* (Ithaca, 1942), 136.

[85] The book was published in Cincinnati. I am indebted to Robert L. Wagner, "The Economic Thought of John Milton Gregory," unpublished course paper written for the author.

[86] Gregory, "Syllabus of Lectures on Mental Science, to Senior Class of Ill. Ind'l. University," 7, Gregory Papers.

brain constituted part of his course. These emphases demonstrate that Gregory was moving with leaders of thought in this field, and not long thereafter James and Dewey led the attack on Cartesian dualism. Gregory carefully avoided all reference to intuition and innate ideas, traditionally regarded by Scottish Realists as the source of moral truths. Though Gregory accepted the faculty psychology, he was unwilling to say that the conscience was an independent faculty which dispensed absolute moral values. Conscience was for him a complex faculty; he attributed the origin of ethical standards to empirical sources and regarded all moral judgments as relative. On the question of causation, which divided intuitionists from empirical philosophers, Gregory followed closely the "association" or empirical doctrine of Hume and Mill. With respect to moral obligation, Gregory taught that the laws of God contain their own rewards for those faithful to them. He waived the question of the soul's immortality, insisting that science could shed no light on the problem. Gregory welcomed the "undeniable truths" unearthed by Darwin. He saw no difficulty in reconciling biological evolution with Christianity and did not insist upon a separate creation of man. He believed, however, that a single, universal intelligence was the directing force behind the evolutionary process.[87]

Gregory introduced pedagogy as part of the instruction in mental philosophy. He had pioneered in making the subject a part of higher education at the University of Michigan in 1860, and now regarded the "science of education" as applied philosophy. He apparently considered the study as a vital ingredient of a liberal education, and therefore under him the University never consciously trained teachers for the public schools, although many graduates entered that desperately needed work.[88]

The College of Literature and Science also included three independent schools. The School of Military Science served as a vehicle for courses, but the compulsory military training program over-

[87] Gregory is interpreted as among the most forward-looking of the moral philosophers in the 1870's by J. David Hoeveler, Jr., "Philosophy at the University of Illinois, 1868-1880," unpublished seminar paper written for the author.
[88] R. Freeman Butts and Lawrence A. Cremin, *A History of Education in American Culture* (New York, 1953), 287. Gregory published *The Seven Laws of Teaching* (Boston, 1886).

shadowed it. The School of Commerce became an embarrassment, but not because students avoided it. Shattuck replaced Snyder as its Head in 1873, and two years later Fernando Parsons took over. He extended the one-year course by offering bookkeeping instruction to preparatory students and by allowing students a second year in which to simulate business and banking operations with college currency. This fatuous play-acting illustrated the perils of uniting learning and labor, and Gregory admitted that the Morrill Act had not contemplated such a result. Parsons resigned in 1880 because of his salary, and the administration unfortunately debated whether to continue the course.

The School of Domestic Science, however, broke new educational ground. When Illinois admitted women in 1870, it was among the first institutions after the Civil War to do so. At the outset the girls selected from the courses ordinarily available. But Gregory believed that higher education for women must recognize their distinctive duties, and in 1872 announced an intention to establish the next year a school to "provide a full course of instruction in the arts of the household, and the sciences relating thereto."[89] He envisioned a four-year curriculum the same as that in the School of English and Modern Languages with domestic economy replacing mathematics in the sophomore and junior years. Gregory's ideas on liberal education for women were advanced. They made Illinois a leader in the field. Although both Iowa State College and Kansas State College among the land-grant schools preceded Illinois in introducing home economics (in 1869 and 1873 respectively), their work was of the cooking- and sewing-school variety.[90]

Before the School could open, however, other courses considered especially appropriate for women appeared. These consisted primarily of music and fine arts, although elocution also was introduced with women allegedly in mind. The Trustees confessed to making music available merely because ladies desired it, and added,

[89] *Catalogue, 1871-72,* 52.
[90] Mabel Newcomer, *A Century of Higher Education for American Women* (New York, 1959), 12-14; Annie Tolman Smith, "Progress of Education for Women," *Report of the Secretary of Interior,* 42 Cong., 2 Sess., House Exec. Doc. No. 1 (Washington, 1872), 514-16; Isabel Bevier, *Home Economics in Education* (Philadelphia, 1924), 120-23.

"Music constitutes no part of any University course of studies. . . ."[91]
Hence, students had to pay fees for piano and organ lessons to a
woman instructor, who also earned a pittance for directing the
chapel choir. Freehand drawing and wood-carving were also presented as being peculiarly adapted for female students. Gregory
visited the School of Design at Cooper Institute in New York City
to borrow ideas in this area. Later, when the University enlarged
its art instruction so as to train designers for industry, officials ruled
that persons who studied art for aesthetic rather than utilitarian
purposes (the women) must pay fees, while others (the men) need
not.

Gregory desired as a teacher and preceptress a lady who could
comprehend "the grandeur and importance" for American civilization of special education for women. He hired for this purpose
Louisa C. Allen, a 22-year-old graduate of Illinois State Normal
University who was affiliated with Peoria County Normal School.
She had been born in Kentucky and reared on an Illinois farm. A
family friend and trustee, J. H. Pickrell, recommended her to Gregory. It is hard to understand why he considered her especially fit
for a job to which he attached such importance. True, she expressed
enthusiasm for education in domestic economics. But she listed her
strongest points as elocution, physiology, and botany in that order.
Somehow she must have impressed him as possessing a capacity to
grow in the job. On June 10, 1874, the Board appointed her an
instructor at $1,200. In accepting she asked for $300 more, and
Gregory made her some sort of promise. Then he defined her job
as overseeing all female education and organizing a department by
developing a scientific system of instruction based on Catharine
Beecher and Harriet Beecher Stowe's book, *The American Woman's Home.*[92]

The instructor prepared for her new responsibilities during the
summers of 1874 and later, according to a daughter, by studying in

[91] *Catalogue, 1879-80*, 80.
[92] Allen to Pickrell, March 9, 1874; Allen to Gregory, May 23, 1874; Gregory to
Allen, May 15, 28, June 6, Sept. 5, 1874, Gregory Papers; *7th Report* (1875),
117; *8th Report* (1877), 124. *The American Woman's Home: Or, Principles
of Domestic Science; Being a Guide to the Formation and Maintenance of
Economical, Healthful, Beautiful, and Christian Homes* was published in New
York, 1869.

England, visiting New England women's colleges, and by special work with prominent scientists at Harvard and nearby. In 1874 the University opened the School of Domestic Science and Arts, which Miss Allen accurately termed "the first college course of high grade in domestic science organized in the United States, if not in the world." Against formidable obstacles of hostile opinion and lack of precedents she taught and prepared the full course of study announced in the catalogue of 1875-76. This aimed at making women the educational equals of men and "enabling them to bring the aids of science and culture to the all important labors and vocations of womanhood."[93]

The four-year curriculum combined technical studies beginning midway in the sophomore year with liberal arts instruction. Chemistry, anatomy, and physiology formed the foundations of the technical studies. Their principles were applied especially to courses in food and dietetics and to hygiene. Professor Allen believed that a desirable purification of national life must commence in the home, and had great confidence in the uplift which might ensue when women were educated to a knowledge of "the strong moral influences exerted by good bread, wholesome food, and healthful, attractive homes."[94] Health and sanitary reform also enlisted her energies. She lectured on the anatomy, physiology, and hygiene of the female pelvic organs, convinced that women become invalids for lack of knowledge on the subject. In addition, the School's technical studies included Household Aesthetics, a combination of interior decoration and woman's dress. Household Science treated heating and ventilation, culinary utensils, and impurities of food. Domestic Economy embraced household expenditure, management of servants, and care of children. A course in Usages of Society touched on etiquette. In Household Architecture, Ricker lectured, Burrill taught landscape gardening, and the girls learned to care for plants. Moreover, students had to write an original thesis to complete the curriculum.

Apart from the School, Miss Allen introduced calisthenics for

[93] Louisa C. Allen Gregory, "The School of Domestic Science of the Illinois Industrial University," U.S. Bureau of Education, *Industrial Education in the United States: A Special Report* (Washington, 1883), 279. The description of the domestic science curriculum that follows draws upon this article.
[94] *Ibid.*

the women of the University. More than a third of the girls got excused from these compulsory exercises with wands and dumbbells, apparently because parents opposed them. The highly touted drill was a focal point for campus visitors. Miss Allen also looked after the interests of her sex, girls who boarded in homes or furnished their own house ("The Convent") because the Trustees saw no hope in asking the General Assembly for a women's dormitory. Miss Allen was officially made Preceptress in 1878. In that year the School became part of the College of Natural Science, an indication that domestic science was taking precedence over liberal arts.

Gregory and Allen won at least moderate success with their pioneer attempt to combine liberal and practical education for women. The number enrolled in the School of Domestic Science rose from 6 in 1875-76 to 18 in 1879-80, by which time six students had earned degrees in the curriculum. The School may have attracted women to enter the University. Along with others, Gregory praised both the work and Miss Allen. Yet the Gregory-Allen experiment was premature. Contemporaries easily found legitimate targets for ridicule: the utopian reform aspirations, and the "scientism" which envisioned a Zentmeyer grand microscope (to test for food impurities) along with a Chickering grand piano in every household. At least one student charged that Miss Allen was "utterly ignorant" of the principles of housekeeping and cooking. Unfortunately, however, the conduct of the principals made it impossible to judge the School on its real merits. Surely the Trustees knew in 1879 that Gregory, now a widower, was courting Professor Allen when he appealed to them to make her a full professor and raise her salary the $300 promised earlier. The Board merely granted a promotion with no additional pay. Three months later, on June 17, 1879, Gregory married Louisa Allen and took her on a honeymoon to Europe.[95]

A good deal of confusion attended the awarding of symbols of graduation at Illinois in the 1870's. The problem originated in the revolt against the degrees and diplomas of the old-time college. The

[95] Emma Sickles to Edmund J. James, July 19, 1910, James Papers; *Illini*, June, 1877; *10th Report* (1881), 160, 166.

framers of the act establishing the University regarded such instruments as meaningless relics of the past and prohibited the awarding
of them. Instead, students were to receive certificates of scholarship
showing the precise grades earned in courses actually studied. But
these documents lacked currency, since other land-grant colleges had
continued the common practice of awarding degrees. Graduates of
Illinois found that their lack of diplomas handicapped them in seeking jobs, and believed that the University lost students and public
respect because of its odd custom. It was this issue which first enlisted the interests of the organized alumni, for football had not yet
arisen. A handful of early graduates formed the Alumni Association
at commencement exercises in 1873, and the Board of Trustees
blessed the group by attending an alumni gathering in the chapel
in June, 1876. That fall the alumni and students petitioned the
General Assembly to authorize the Board to confer degrees, and the
legislature obliged the following May. Although a Trustees' committee disapproved of granting these documents, it bowed to the
wishes of the alumni. Accordingly, it recommended that various
bachelor's degrees be awarded, but advised consultation with other
land-grant schools so as either to do away with degrees or to secure
uniformity in awarding them.[96]

The University therefore called a conference which met at Columbus, Ohio, in December. The presidents and other delegates
from 18 state universities and colleges chose Gregory to preside and
discussed many educational topics. In the main address, Gregory
said that the use of degrees was so interwoven with the educational
system that it had to be continued and made more trustworthy. He
urged the uniform awarding of the bachelor of arts (B.A.) degree
for the old classical course as modified; the bachelor of science
(B.S.) for the scientific course; the bachelor of letters (B.L.) for
English literature and modern languages; the bachelor of philosophy
(Ph.B.) for social sciences, history, and philosophy; and the B.S.
degree for all technical courses. The only fixed guides were that
college studies should equal the work of four academic years, con-

[96] Franklin W. Scott, ed., *The Alumni Record of the University of Illinois* (Urbana, 1906), xii; *Illini*, Dec., 1877; *8th Report* (1877), 41; *9th Report* (1878),
41-42.

tain due proportions of language, mathematics, history, science, and philosophy, and that the B.A. degree should be reserved for the classical languages. Beyond that, each institution should be free to determine its own policy, remembering that equivalency rather than identity of studies was essential. Conference participants adopted most of Gregory's proposals, although they lacked authority as an agency of accreditation or standardization.[97]

After Columbus, the University continued granting certificates to non-degree candidates who enrolled for a year or more while insisting that students had to complete prescribed courses in order to earn degrees. The requirements for all bachelor's degrees were to be as nearly as possible equal in amount and value. The B.S. (with the name of the school inserted after the degree) was to be awarded graduates of courses in the colleges of Engineering, Agriculture, and Natural Science (including Domestic Science); the B.L. to graduates of the School of English and Modern Languages; and the B.A. to those from the School of Ancient Languages and Literature. Master's degrees in science, letters, and arts, and equivalent degrees (such as C.E. for Civil Engineering) were to be awarded to those who passed examinations on a year of prescribed postgraduate study and presented an acceptable thesis or to graduates who submitted a thesis "after a term" of successful practice.[98]

The new requirement occasioned great confusion but imposed more order on the curriculum. It demonstrated that degrees were harder to obtain than full certificates. Most seniors had some deficiency to remove before qualifying for a degree, and in the ensuing scramble many students changed their programs in order to graduate in four years. A number had to stay a fifth year to obtain a bachelor's degree. In June, 1878, however, 27 students received B.S. degrees, 14 B.L.'s, 3 B.A.'s (two of whom were Gregory's offspring), and 6 won master's degrees. Full certificates went to 25 students, partial certificates to 4. The reform was desirable, but ex-

[97] "Faculty Record," I, 212-13; *Illinois Laws* (1877), 216; *Proceedings of the Conference of the Presidents and Other Delegates of the State Universities and State Colleges, Held at Columbus, Ohio, December 27 and 28, 1877,* U.S. Bureau of Education, Circular of Information No. 2, 1879, Appendix B (Washington, 1879), 180-83, 192.
[98] "Faculty Record," I, 232, 245-47; *9th Report* (1878), 80.

ternal pressure had been necessary to overcome the Board's revulsion against a vestige of the traditional liberal arts college.[99]

Academic development at Illinois Industrial University through 1880 contributed to the emergence of the American university and helped determine what type of education would evolve under the Morrill Act. The latter task fell primarily to the individual states, since the act itself had been phrased in generalities and the various interests which provided the impetus for its passage were divided in their expectations. Illinois developed a comprehensive university, both in devoting its land-grant proceeds to one campus — as did Wisconsin but not Michigan — and in encompassing most of the studies then offered in higher learning. In a relative sense the achievement at Urbana was considerable. If the humanities lagged, botany, chemistry, engineering, and architecture obtained solid foundations. The University led in the effort to unite the land-grant colleges and to bring them into closer relations with the federal government.

From another perspective, however, one wonders about the progress. The ideal of a comprehensive university resulted in spreading the University far too thin, and much of the work done was undoubtedly of poor quality. It could be argued that this condition mattered little, since not much earlier Agassiz had charged Harvard with dispensing the dregs of learning, and the academic level at Illinois would certainly rise. What then? Would a new conception of education provide unity and a sense of purpose such as the old college had enjoyed? No one at Urbana had yet answered that question.

[99] "Faculty Record," I, 258-60; *9th Report* (1878), 93-94.

CHAPTER SIX

The Gregorians

A UNIVERSITY PROPERLY EXISTS for its students, and an academic program is essential to transmitting knowledge. But education involves far more than courses of instruction. It depends partly on what students bring to the learning process, and thus reaches back to the home. In addition, the cultural and physical environment in which a school operates will invariably shape the education it furnishes, as will the tone and spirit prevailing within the institution itself. Good education may not require a teacher and a student on opposite ends of a log, but if the two inhabit private worlds that intersect only in formal instruction, education will at best be incomplete.

From the beginning both higher authorities and students at

Urbana recognized that education transcended the classroom. Officials designed facilities to serve more than strictly instructional purposes, and imposed various requirements both to make the University an orderly and harmonious community and to enlarge the lives of students. The pupils accepted with little resistance the demands levied upon them. They tended automatically to respect constituted authority, a fact which is essential to an understanding of nineteenth-century higher education. But they also found two ways of coping with an externally imposed system which had disagreeable features. They created their own comfortable student world in which literary societies, fraternities, a campus newspaper, and sports figured significantly. And they gradually, even reluctantly, brandished a weapon to make their lot more tolerable: student power.

The Gregorians, the students in the period to 1880, were fairly homogeneous in their backgrounds, attitudes, and expectations. Most were raw Illinois youths reared in homes of conventional piety, little (if any) literature, and no intellectual atmosphere. Their horizons were bounded by Protestant certainties, Fourth-of-July democracy, crude manners, and aesthetic unawareness. They were aggressively egalitarian. One student even greeted Gregory on the campus the day after first meeting him with a breezy "How di-do, Doc?"[1]

Certainly they possessed a tremendous will to succeed. They knew that education in America was a social and economic escalator, and many either went to college to escape the farm or discovered while there that education was an exit from rural life. After the ceaseless drudgery of farm chores, hard academic work was like a lull in the noonday shade. Even more vital, contemporary social attitudes fed the flame of their ambition. Belief in self-help and the will to mastery became dominant springs to action in the period of swift social and economic transformation after the Civil War, as revealed in the literature of the time. William Makepeace Thayer had published *The Pioneer Boy and How He Became President* in the year after the Morrill Act. Horatio Alger issued *Ragged Dick* in the year the University was founded, and Orison Swett Marden

[1] Arthur Peabody to William C. Langdon, Aug. 21, 1918, Edmund J. James Papers.

followed Alger with such books as *Pushing to the Front* (1894) and *Rising in the World* (1896). Inevitably, students approached education with these themes ringing in their ears.

In some ways a strong faith in the platitudes of the day proved helpful, for most students found the pathway to success difficult. They arrived in Urbana poorly prepared by an inadequate school system, and often had to drop out to teach or find other ways of raising the money to continue their education. Normally the students who lacked culture had not positively rejected it, and at best they displayed an admirable determination to rise above the limitations of background and to cut through the fog of contemporary shibboleths.

Students matriculated in a University situated in a rustic retreat. The community's best links with the outer world were the Illinois Central and the Danville, Urbana, Bloomington, and Pekin railroads, and the telegraph line first strung from Chicago in 1870. Nevertheless, isolation laid a heavy hand on Champaign and Urbana. These bleak provincial towns occupied a seemingly endless expanse of flat, unbroken prairie. Only a partial eye could call the towns lovely, and yet some 8,000 souls called them home. The business houses and churches were almost all of wood, and the cheaper grade of scantling frame at that. No streets were paved, but Main Street in each village was half-planked. The only sidewalks were wooden. Cattle and pigs pastured where they pleased. Since there was no artificial drainage the whole area became on occasion a slough or a mud bog. "Drowned in the mud, the mud, the mud," sang students in the late 1870's.[2] But the soil constituted one of the most fertile agricultural areas in the entire world, and many found the immense, rich black prairie hauntingly beautiful. The flaming orange-red sunsets were dramatically impressive.

Champaign-Urbana and their environs offered little wholesome recreation. The Boneyard was still a favorite haunt of swimmers and fishers. The Salt Fork and the Sangamon River were more attractive, but in those days a few miles was a long way. Distance deprived students of the hills, woods, and water except on festive occasions. Nor did the community have much to offer. The life of

[2] "Sagamores of the Illini: Roland Ray Conklin," *Alumni Quarterly,* VIII (Oct., 1914), 273.

townspeople centered in their homes and churches, and local congregations did not warmly welcome students who attended religious services. Hostility between town and gown was a familiar fact of higher education, but perhaps disillusion with the University abetted it in this case. After capturing the location in order to enrich themselves, residents had soured when the institution's slow growth dashed their hopes. In 1873 Governor Beveridge publicly insisted that the Board of Supervisors was legally and morally obligated to levy taxes to pay the $11,500 interest on Champaign County's endowment bonds held by the University.

The students lived in a fairly self-contained academic world. The campus occupied an "island" between the two towns, and at the start only a few houses were in the vicinity. Student life was austere. The original building served dormitory as well as other purposes. Each student room, about 12 feet square and equipped with nothing but a flue, was shared by two occupants who provided all furnishings, including a stove. They bought coal by the hod and scavenged for kindling wood. Although a Negro cook kept a boarding table on the ground floor of the building, most students "batched" for reasons of economy. Some lived on 50 or 60 cents weekly, eating mush and milk or mush and beans and treating themselves rarely to bread and pie bought in the dormitory from a student salesman. The closest stores were in the villages a couple of miles away. To reach Champaign or Urbana one either walked or took the interurban street railroad which ran by the campus every half-hour. Horse-drawn vehicles remained in use until electric cars replaced them in 1890.

The pace of the University was geared to hard work. The daily schedule kept students busy with programmed activities from dawn to dusk. Poverty as well as the lack of organized sports and social clubs made hard study the main alternative. And yet these conditions did not last long. Expansion of the student body and destruction of the old main building brought an end to the dormitory era in 1881. Students then took rooms and ate in boarding clubs in houses near the campus.[3]

[3] Isaac S. Raymond, "The Beginning," *Alumni Quarterly*, VI (July, 1912), 193-96; Joseph O. Cunningham, "The Genesis of Our Campus," *Alumni Quar-*

Gregory's aesthetic sensitivity must have made him acutely aware of the shortcomings of his adopted home and state, even though Edgar Lee Masters exaggerated when he said of Illinois at a slightly later period, "There was no culture, you know, in Spoon River."[4] Gregory knew that most students, reared on farms and in ugly small towns, had never seen a really beautiful man-made object. But rather than loathing and despising the limitations of time and place, as did Masters' Archibald Higbie, Gregory determined to lift students above their environment. He must have proposed establishing an art gallery soon after arriving in Urbana, for there was talk of erecting a building for the purpose as early as 1868. But his fateful visit to Europe in 1873 kindled in him an urgency to realize the project. He had always stressed the value of the fine arts as a means of elevating taste; now he began also to emphasize their vital influence on the useful arts, especially architecture, drawing, and design.[5]

After the Board denied his optimistic request to appropriate $1,500 for an art museum in 1874, Gregory himself raised the money. He lectured on the history of art and devoted his fees to a fund which he increased by taking up a subscription among local residents and faculty members. Over 60 persons ultimately contributed more than $3,000. This demonstration of good will impressed Jonathan Turner, who now thought the fine arts might be the way to help the agricultural classes out of their terrible plight! That summer Gregory went at his own expense to the art capitals of Europe, especially Paris, where he purchased plaster copies taken from the originals of ancient and modern statuary and busts.[6]

Some copies of the masterpieces reached Urbana whole, but

terly, IX (Jan., 1915), 18-21; Frances A. Potter, "Those Early Days," *Alumni Quarterly and Fortnightly Notes,* I (Oct. 15, 1915), 23-28; Natalia M. Belting, *The Beginnings: Champaign in the 1850's and 1860's* ([Champaign], 1960), 23-41; *7th Report* (1875), 73.
[4] Edgar Lee Masters, *Spoon River Anthology* (New York, 1946; 1st ed., 1915), 194. Masters was born in 1869; his fictitious village of Spoon River was compounded of Petersburg and Lewistown, Illinois, as known in his boyhood.
[5] *2nd Report* (1869), 54; *7th Report* (1875), 47, 91-92.
[6] *8th Report* (1877), 91, 92, 105, 193; *10th Report* (1881), 41; Turner to Gregory, May 30, 1874, as quoted in the *Illini,* June, 1874. The Trustees did authorize $75 to fit up a room in University Hall to house the art collection. *7th Report* (1875), 102.

others arrived shattered. One observer thought that the bushels of fragments resembled Armaggedon or the Last Judgment. But Gregory and Don Carlos Taft donned work clothes to reassemble the pieces, aided by James Kenis, a Belgian artist brought from Chicago who joined the staff, and Taft's 14-year-old son Lorado. Young Taft's blood had already been fired by Gregory's lectures on art, which opened a new heaven and earth to his imagination, and now he became an expert in fitting together shards. Years later, when Lorado Taft enjoyed distinction as a great American sculptor, he ascribed the beginning of his career to these two events.[7]

The Art Gallery formally opened on New Year's Day, 1875, in a large room on the third floor of University Hall. Dark maroon walls provided a dramatic background for the white casts. Even trained gallery-goers found the exhibit impressive. There stood the Laocoon group, Venus de Milo, Venus de Medici, Gibson's Venus, Discobolus, Thorwaldsen's Cupid, and ten more full-sized statues, mainly Greek and Roman. The Apollo Belvidere, the Dying Gladiator, Diana the Huntress, Venus d'Arles, and the Sleeping Ariadne were a few of the 42 reduced-size casts. In addition, there were 68 full and 28 reduced-size busts of famous persons of all ages from Homer to individuals then living. (The only Americans were Franklin, Washington, Lincoln, Stephen A. Douglas, Clay, Webster, and James Fenimore Cooper.) The collection also contained busts of 23 ideal heads, many bas-reliefs, and medallion heads. There were 127 photographs of famous paintings, 92 photographs of Italian and Swiss scenes, and 388 lithographs of historical portraits. Both the objects displayed and the historical sketch in the accompanying *Catalogue of the Art Gallery* announced Gregory's conviction that America had not yet produced significant art.[8]

The Gallery brought the University great distinction. The Chicago *Tribune* reported, "This grand collection is now the largest west of New York," and visitors came from afar to view it. Some questioned the utility, and one man said the statuary would be more

[7] Allene Gregory, *John Milton Gregory: A Biography* (Chicago, 1923), 271-72; Ada Bartlett Taft, *Lorado Taft: Sculptor and Citizen* (Greensboro, N.C., 1946), 3-4.
[8] *Catalogue of the Art Gallery, Illinois Industrial University: Comprising a Brief Description of Each Cast and Picture with an Introductory Notice of the Various Schools of Art* (Champaign, 1876).

valuable if ground into lime dust and scattered over the ground. The *Illini,* the campus newspaper, veered to the other extreme and regarded the Gallery as part of a new national artistic awakening. Perhaps the best tribute came from a student who said of the Art Gallery, "It opened a new epoch in all our lives."[9]

Books took on extra importance in Champaign-Urbana. Perhaps the geographical isolation and lack of local libraries gave the University a special incentive to acquire the printed word. Gregory always emphasized the library's strong attraction in drawing and retaining students, and made its welfare an object of primary concern. Armed with $1,000 authorized for the purpose, he himself purchased in New York 644 of the 1,000 volumes with which the University opened. The collection had a general cultural character, comprising 180 volumes of modern history and biography, 133 of science, 60 of philosophy, 30 of ancient history, 20 of historical romances, 14 of poetry, 10 of English literature, 178 miscellaneous volumes, and three sets of encyclopedias. These books, however inadequate for launching industrial education, reflected Gregory's personal interests. In addition, the original holdings consisted of 283 volumes of U.S. government documents and 116 unnamed books obtained by gift.[10]

As soon as classes commenced, expansion of the library became a basic goal. Now the buying concentrated in the fields of agriculture, engineering, and the natural sciences, thus righting the balance. About this time the University began receiving some 70 American, English, French, and German periodicals. These dealt primarily with agriculture, but also with engineering, science, and literature.[11] The number of books climbed steadily: the library possessed 3,646 volumes in 1870 and 10,600 six years later. This rate of growth considerably exceeded the average rate of growth for American college and university libraries in the two centuries down

[9] Chicago *Tribune,* Jan. 2, 1875; *Illini,* March, 1876; Mary Larned Parsons (class of 1878) to Mary C. McLellan, n.d., Mary Larned Folder, Alumni Morgue.
[10] *1st Report* (1868), 75, 102, 124. For a catalogue of early holdings, see *ibid.,* 209-15; *2nd Report* (1869), 41-43; and *3rd Report* (1870), 127-63.
[11] For representative lists, see *3rd Report* (1870), 159-62, and *8th Report* (1877), 27.

to 1931, which was a doubling in size every 15 years. The growth at Urbana put Illinois in sixty-seventh place among the nation's college and university libraries in 1876. In that year Rutgers, founded over a century earlier (1766), owned 14 more books than Illinois. Only 29 collegiate institutions in the country could boast of more than 20,000 volumes. Yale had 114,200, Harvard almost twice as many.[12]

Behind this achievement lay the money provided by the General Assembly, supplemented briefly by the use of matriculation fees. Between 1869 and 1875 the legislature gave $5,000 a year for both the library and for either scientific apparatus or museum material. The law specified that the books purchased were to treat agricultural or mechanical subjects. Somehow the authorities found nearly $5,000 each year for the library alone, but only about 20 per cent could be used to buy books. When the General Assembly granted nothing for the library in 1875, the pace of acquisitions immediately slackened. Although the state usually granted $1,500 a year for books starting again in 1877, the University had lost ground. Its library holdings rose only from 10,000 volumes in 1875 to 12,550 in 1880.[13]

From the start the University broke with the ante-bellum collegiate customs of keeping the collection of books locked up for all but a few hours a week and of not circulating volumes. After 1873 the Illinois library occupied a central and accessible room on the second floor of University Hall. It opened five days a week after morning chapel until 4 P.M. and from 7 to 9 P.M., on Saturday afternoons from 2 to 5, but not on Sundays. Students used the place constantly, and yet in 1873 the Faculty denied their request to make it available on Saturday evenings.[14] Lending policies were comparatively liberal for the time: while only faculty members could officially charge books, students actually checked them out for their own use in the name of the librarian or a teacher. Henry M. Douglas, who doubled as an assistant teacher of ancient languages and

[12] *4th Report* (1872), 71; *8th Report* (1877), 27; Fremont Rider, "The Growth of American College and University Libraries — and of Wesleyan's," *About Books,* XI (Sept., 1940), 4-5, 9.
[13] *8th Report* (1877), 92, 105; *9th Report* (1878), 42; *10th Report* (1881), 175, 221.
[14] "Faculty Record," I, 44, 127.

as Librarian from 1869 to 1871, projected a catalogue to include individual entries for periodical articles. Since he classified Neander's *Planting of the Christian Church* among books dealing with agriculture, it may be well that he did not finish the job. His successor, James D. Crawford, also a classics teacher, made no haste to provide even a written catalogue, though an excellent printed catalogue served the Art Gallery. Students kept up a running fire of criticism about the deficiency.[15]

The military program strongly influenced the University for years after it opened, often disastrously. The authorities employed military rules to promote student discipline and required all male students to drill an average of two or three hours weekly. Perhaps (but not certainly) Illinois interpreted the Morrill Act as requiring land-grant colleges to make military tactics compulsory. The Faculty unquestionably regarded the obligation as one imposed by Illinois law, and for a decade the state alone sponsored the military program. Students shouldered state-supplied arms and bought their own uniforms, a West Point–type outfit with distinctive I.I.U. buttons. A faculty member had charge of drill — Edward Snyder succeeded Atherton and Shattuck in 1870. A veteran of the Battle of Solferino, Snyder organized the University Battalion with student officers and in 1871 took 123 uniformed men to do guard duty in Chicago after the Great Fire. Enthusiasm for the program led to completion of a Drill Hall in 1871, and Gregory concluded that military education was on balance advantageous. At the request of John A. Logan of Illinois, a distinguished Civil War general and a former Chairman of the House Committee on Military Affairs, he drafted a plan calling on land-grant colleges to furnish training equal to that given at the U.S. Military Academy. As he had in 1867, he lobbied in Washington for enactment of such a measure.[16]

[15] Nathan C. Ricker, "The Story of a Life" (typewritten MS. autobiography, Urbana, 1922); *4th Report* (1872), 72; *Illini*, Jan., May, 1878; Feb. 2, 1885.
[16] "Faculty Record," I, 134; *4th Report* (1872), 69, 346-47; *Army and Navy Journal*, Feb. 24, 1872, 451. Gregory outlined a national system of military education supported by Congress at the agricultural convention in 1872, but opponents stoutly resisted and tabled the proposal by a vote of 39 to 24. See [U.S. Department of Agriculture], *Proceedings of the National Agricultural Convention, Held at Washington, D.C. February 15-17, 1872*, 42 Cong., 2 Sess., Senate Misc. Doc. No. 164 (Washington, 1872), 68-74.

Snyder, commissioned an honorary colonel in the Illinois State Militia in 1873, successfully managed the Military Department by ability and zeal. He kept minor dissatisfactions from becoming serious after the novelty wore off. Many students resented a requirement which few could escape, although in 1875 the Board did authorize conscientious objectors to be excused from drill. But there were rewards to stimulate interest. In 1874 the Battalion went by special train to participate in dedication of the Lincoln monument at Springfield. Cadets who excelled in drill were admitted in the middle of their sophomore year to military classes which lasted two years and furnished officers for the cadet corps. After 1873, when two graduating seniors were commissioned in the Illinois State Militia, other graduates could anticipate commissions. A few years later opinion within the University credited the Military Department for its beneficial influence on campus life. In a published article Gregory defended collegiate military training against its many critics throughout the state and nation. He contended that it promoted discipline, physical culture, unity in the student body, and gentlemanly conduct.[17] Shortly thereafter, however, he had good reason to regard the cadet corps as a source of grave disorder.

Church and college, so closely allied before the Civil War, gradually worked out a new relationship in the late nineteenth century. Some sectarians hoped that denominational colleges might continue undisturbed in their old ways after the Morrill Act, and some secularists would gladly have eliminated religion from the state agricultural and mechanical colleges. But such a division was unthinkable. The nation was still Protestant and church-going, and insisted that education divorced from religion threatened moral disaster. The people of Illinois — whose leading denominations were Methodist, Baptist, and Presbyterian — never doubted that the old faith should be perpetuated at Urbana.[18]

[17] "State Militia Commission Records 1861-1875," Vol. A, Adjutant General's Records, Illinois State Archives, Springfield; B. H., "Our Military Department," *Illini*, Feb., 1879; John M. Gregory, "Military Drill in Colleges," reprinted in *Illini*, June, 1879, statedly from *National Journal of Education,* May 15, 1879. I have been unable to locate such a journal.
[18] The reconstruction of religion in higher education after the Civil War is a neglected subject. But see Winton U. Solberg, "The Conflict Between Religion

The University was at the outset avowedly Christian but non-sectarian. Theoretically it opened its doors to all beliefs and to none; actually it was a Protestant institution. The state Constitution of 1870 was simply not considered relevant. It guaranteed liberty of conscience and the "free exercise and enjoyment of religious profession and worship" as constitutional rights. "No person," declared the fundamental law, "shall be required to attend or support any ministry or place of worship against his consent."[19] The authors of that instrument had eliminated Bible-reading from Illinois public schools, but their silence on religion in the colleges underscored the general conviction that higher education should possess a specifically Christian component. In the nineteenth century the constitutional separation of church and state merely intensified the close alliance between religion and the people.

Gregory tacitly assumed that his appointees should be Protestant Christians, although he insisted that a university could not be founded on a sect. In 1868 he did not know the religious affiliations of three of his nine faculty members, but Presbyterians and Congregationalists apparently became most numerous and many denominations were represented. Some professors with divinity degrees had been clergymen and continued to preach, and a few were resolutely evangelical. In an 1873 address Governor Beveridge accurately described the staff as a "christian Faculty."[20] But the Faculty never opened its meetings with prayer.

The student body was also Protestant. Methodists were most numerous in the University as in the state, a significant fact in light of this denomination's earlier suspicions about intellectualism. Presbyterians and Congregationalists ranked second and third in num-

and Secularism at the University of Illinois, 1867-1894," *American Quarterly*, XVIII (Summer, 1966), 183-99; Hugh Hawkins, "Charles W. Eliot, University Reform, and Religious Faith in America, 1869-1909," *Journal of American History*, LI (Sept., 1964), 191-213; and Earle D. Ross, "Religious Influences in the Development of State Colleges and Universities," *Indiana Magazine of History*, XLVI (Dec., 1950), 343-62.

[19] *Debates and Proceedings of the Constitutional Convention of the State of Illinois* (Springfield, 1870), 1732-61; Francis Newton Thorpe, ed., *The Federal and State Constitutions* (7 vols., Washington, 1909), II, 1014.

[20] *7th Report* (1875), 77; Gregory to Edward Eggleston, May 4, 1868, Gregory Papers. The faculty's religious preferences have been discovered from a wide variety of sources as well as from folders in the University Archives on individual professors.

bers attending, and both groups emphasized the intellect. The Baptist and Christian churches were not represented in proportion to their size in the population. The atmosphere was uncongenial to Jews, agnostics, and Roman Catholics. Jews and agnostics were somewhat rare in Illinois at the time, and the children of Catholic immigrants concentrated in Chicago were not yet ready for college. But the Protestant character of the University made these groups unwelcome, a condition that long persisted.[21]

Chapel was the heart of the religious program and daily attendance became officially compulsory in the autumn of 1868. At a bugle's blast men formed military ranks in the halls and women (after gaining admission) assembled in the library for the march into a room bearing the inscription:

> There is nothing so kingly as kindness
> There is nothing so royal as truth.[22]

Gregory usually officiated at the brief ritual. He offered prayer and led both a responsive New Testament reading and recitation of the Lord's Prayer. In talks which Gregorians vividly recalled in later life he encouraged students to live nobly and emphasized the power of ideals in shaping lives. This ceremony was much less distinctly religious than the holy worship which had characterized the antebellum period and still obtained in many colleges. Trustees usually attended chapel when the Board met in Urbana and often spoke; Gregory advised on studies, warned against disorder, and informed his charges about contemporary events. Students themselves frequently gave informal or formal addresses.

The Sabbath remained God's holy day of state. Students were expected to attend some local church in the morning and to participate in divine service at the University in the afternoon. Gregory's sermon-lectures at this worship won praise for their common sense,

---

[21] My conclusions about student religious preferences are based on many fugitive sources, extrapolations from the religious situation in the state of Illinois at the time, and student religious preferences at the turn of the century.

[22] "Faculty Record," I, 4-6; James M. White to David Kinley, May 13, 1924, Kinley Papers. The original University building contained a chapel. After 1873 the ceremony took place in a room variously labeled "chapel" and "auditorium" in University Hall. The inscription was in this building.

liberality, and freedom from dogma.[23] Ideally, students spent the remainder of the day quietly. To avoid profaning the Lord's day, the University celebrated its tenth anniversary on March 10 when March 11 fell on a Sunday in 1877.

The religious features of commencement imitated those of an earlier era. Gregory or a clergyman gave a baccalaureate address the Sunday before the midweek graduation exercises. But campus revivalism never took root at Urbana in these years, even though it manifested itself elsewhere until late in the nineteenth century. Among the reasons were the fresh educational start made by the University, the major reorientation of revivalism after the Civil War, and the nature of the student body. Undoubtedly the more pious youths avoided what the public regarded as a secular school and went to church colleges. Although of conventional Protestant backgrounds, few students (less than ten out of 846 graduates in the period ending in 1894) entered the ministry.[24] The University did not influence American culture through the pulpit. This fact undoubtedly perpetuated the public's suspicion of the University as irreligious, for the number of ministers trained by a college had long been a key criterion of Christian education.

No formal inducements were held out toward Christian life, but "the whole tendency and spirit of the institution," as Burrill once wrote, were "favorable to that end."[25] At Illinois as elsewhere the Young Men's Christian Association pioneered in interdenominationalism and also promoted conversions. After originating in London, the society spread in the early 1850's to the United States,

[23] Presumably Sunday morning worship was expected from the outset. In 1868 the Faculty required attendance at Sabbath afternoon worship in the University, and in 1873 directed the Regent to tell students they were "expected to attend some church on the Sabbath and request them to do so." "Faculty Record," I, 5, 127. Henry M. Beardsley, "Dr. Gregory and the Students at Illinois," *Alumni Quarterly*, VIII (July, 1914), 164-65. One series of "lectures" considered: Is there a God? Is the human soul immortal? Is the Bible of divine authority? Was Jesus of Nazareth more than a mere man? Is Christianity true? Is religion necessary? *Illini*, Nov., 1875.

[24] These conclusions are based on biographical data in Franklin W. Scott, ed., *The Alumni Record of the University of Illinois* (Urbana, 1906), and various catalogues. No doubt other students became ministers or missionaries without my discovering it, but the number cannot have been large.

[25] Burrill to the Rev. Harry Willard, March 4, 1903, Provost's Office Papers.

where an evangelical test for membership was added. Michigan and Virginia established the first university chapters before the Civil War, and after Appomattox the Y found its greatest strength in state and private universities. At Illinois a group of students and one faculty member, probably Burrill, started meeting together for weekly Bible study and prayer about 1870. On February 3, 1872, they formed a YMCA patterned on the intercollegiate organization, a branch of which already existed at Illinois State Normal University near Bloomington. No doubt partly to offset suspicions of irreligion, University authorities granted use of a room and permission to hold devotional meetings Sunday mornings and one weekday evening. Since Illinois, unlike Michigan, refused to allow the two sexes to form one society, women held their own occasional prayer meetings. Formation of the YWCA was delayed. Late in the 1870's the men's Y sponsored as a student in the University an Apache Indian, Carlos Montezuma, who became a physician. It was 1875 before Librarian Crawford requested the purchase of a Bible before any other new book, saying it was "needed frequently for reference."[26]

The tone of University life was pious in a neo-puritanical way. Smoking was considered an evil and drinking an abomination. Early in 1870 the Board asked the Executive Committee to seek a state law prohibiting sale of intoxicating liquor within a radius of three miles of the campus, a distance that included downtown in both Champaign and Urbana.[27]

Student reactions in these years show that Gregory's personal effectiveness in chapel and at divine service could not forestall boredom and discontent. The first request for excuse from chapel came in December, 1869, but the Faculty would grant relief only for conscientious scruples. Gregory either privately or publicly rebuked absentees who could not provide good explanations. He could sus-

[26] William H. Morgan, *Student Religion During Fifty Years: Programs and Policies of the Intercollegiate Y.M.C.A.* (New York, 1935), 6-7, 18-19; Richard C. Morse, *History of the North American Young Men's Christian Associations* (New York, 1922), 17-18; Scott, *Alumni Record* (1906), 6; *Illini*, Dec., 1878; Feb. 29, 1892; Henry Wilson, "Report of the General Secretary to the Board of Directors University of Illinois Young Men's Christian Association," April 10, 1929, Kinley Papers; *8th Report* (1877), 127.
[27] *3rd Report* (1870), 84.

pend incorrigible offenders.[28] Yet professors rarely attended an exercise they imposed on students; the latter complained of that fact and openly manifested their displeasure. The method of assembling in military units stimulated a competition in rudeness. The loud applause in chapel drew criticism from the *Illini* editor, who unconsciously expressed a desire to separate holy from profane things. Years later the class of 1874 retrospectively begrudged the moments spent in chapel, and a history of the class of 1878 perhaps explains why. Its stress on material wealth as the test of a worthwhile life suggests that many success-oriented students considered the rite a waste of precious time and Christian ethics an embarrassment in their push to the front. Moreover, Gregory's emphasis on chapel exercises as "the central element and chief factor in our system of discipline," which led him to urge all faculty members to attend, cannot have deepened piety.[29]

Although secular attitudes were evolving within the shell of old forms, the University won praise for its religious character. In 1878 the *Northwestern Christian Advocate,* a Methodist journal published in Chicago, asserted that the state universities which succeeded best were under "real, if covert, control by church influences." It cited Illinois under Gregory as proof "that state schools are successful and trusted by the people in proportion as they are guided by teachers cultured by the church."[30]

The vexatious article of collegiate discipline admitted of no easy solution after the Civil War. Attitudes changed slowly if at all. President Samuel Spahr Laws of the University of Missouri insisted that all university government must come from above and that any reliance on student participation or honor was fallacious. President John Bascom of the University of Wisconsin also considered student discipline a faculty prerogative, although he thought it unwise to enforce rules rigidly. In the late 1880's a flood of periodical articles

[28] "Faculty Record," I, 42; II, Nov. 14, 1879.
[29] [Charles P. Jeffers], "The Retrospect of Seventy-Four," typewritten poem, Alumni Association, Class of 1874 (University Archives); E. M. Burr, ed., *Class History of the Class of 1878* ([Urbana], 1911); "Faculty Record," II, Sept. 19, 1879.
[30] "Education by the State," *Northwestern Christian Advocate,* April 3, 1878.

and stirrings on various campuses testified to widespread interest in improving internal collegiate discipline and government.[31] But significant reform had begun earlier. Basic to the reconstruction of higher education initiated at Harvard by Eliot was his desire that students substitute internal for external discipline. In his 1869 inaugural address he emphasized the need to apply the principle of freedom to the choice of studies and called for revision of the University's rules and regulations. "The best way to put boyishness to shame is to foster scholarship and manliness,"[32] observed Eliot, who did not stress reform of discipline. The next year the University launched "the most comprehensive scheme of student self-government ever attempted in the United States" in the nineteenth century.[33]

Gregory, responsive to the "yeasty heaving" of the period in which the modern American university began to emerge, was instrumental in inaugurating this bold departure. Even before Eliot, he applied the principle of freedom to both the elective system and to undergraduate discipline. "No question more concerns the future of American colleges," he wrote, "than that of the government of students." Americans would not consent to European laxity in collegiate discipline, but the spirit of the age demanded re-evaluation of traditional modes of government, for young people questioned all authority and were impatient with restraint. Gregory therefore decided, as he explained in an article published a decade after the

[31] Jonas Viles, *The University of Missouri: A Centennial History, 1839-1939* (Columbia, Mo., 1939), 175. Laws was President from 1876 to 1889. Merle Curti and Vernon Carstensen, *The University of Wisconsin: A History, 1848-1925* (2 vols., Madison, 1949), I, 385. Bascom was President from 1874 to 1887. About 1870 interest in student self-government arose contemporaneously with the beginnings of the revolution in higher education, gaining momentum in the following decade and after. For a fuller discussion, see Winton U. Solberg, "The University of Illinois and the Reform of Discipline in the Modern University, 1868-1891," American Association of University Professors, *Bulletin,* LII (Sept., 1966), 305-14.

[32] Charles W. Eliot, *Educational Reform* (New York, 1909), 11-14, 18-19; Samuel Eliot Morison, *Three Centuries of Harvard, 1636-1936* (Cambridge, Mass., 1936), 344.

[33] Henry Davidson Sheldon, *The History and Pedagogy of American Student Societies* (New York, 1901), 256-57. William E. Drake asserts that student government was probably first initiated at Illinois. See *The American School in Transition* (Englewood Cliffs, N.J., 1955), 327.

event, to start "An Experiment in College Government" at Illinois in 1870.[34]

Actually, student government did not begin as he recalled. Gregory had asserted his ideal in the first catalogue, which announced: "The University is designed for *men,* not *children,* and its government rests in an appeal to the manly feeling and sense of honor of its students. It has but one law, and that is, Do Right."[35] Nevertheless, the Faculty found it necessary from the start to exercise traditional disciplinary measures. The official record for the first term is silent on the subject, but during the academic year commencing in September, 1868, it shows that the Faculty, in addition to requesting the mayors of Champaign and Urbana to enforce laws barring minors from billiard halls and saloons, suspended two students who withdrew from the University without permission, expelled three pupils for wrongdoing, and authorized two others, one of whom denied having had anything to do with the "public woman," to remain in school on condition that they promise to avoid saloons and spend their evenings studying.[36]

The dormitory gave rise to most of the disciplinary problems. In September, 1868, the Faculty devised a semi-military organization to govern it. Hall Sergeants selected from and by the residents were to supervise halls, inspect rooms, and report to an elected Adjutant who was responsible under the Regent for the building's order and cleanliness. Opposition to student officers was made "a grave offense against college discipline." The plan extended similar control beyond the dormitory by requesting boardinghouse keepers to be certain that student lodgers were at home during evening study hours.[37]

The following March 4 the Faculty appointed a committee to improve the discipline of the University building. A week later the Board of Trustees formally committed the government of the Uni-

[34] *International Review,* X (June, 1881), 510-18. The quotation is at p. 510. Gregory used his reports to the Board of Trustees for much of this article.
[35] *Catalogue, 1868,* 20.
[36] "Faculty Record," I, 14-18. One of the expelled students had also written a "malicious" letter to the *Illinois State Journal* (Springfield), which somehow fell into Gregory's hands. An appeal to outside authority by a student was a serious matter.
[37] "Faculty Record," I, 4, 5, 12.

versity to the Regent and Faculty, and directed them to prepare rules for governing students and maintaining order. These were to rest on the authority of the Faculty until approved by the Trustees. The Board made the students subject to the Regent and empowered him to enforce the disciplinary rules.[38]

Accordingly, the Faculty adopted detailed regulations affecting dormitory discipline and conduct elsewhere in the University. The result was two dozen bylaws which affected personal conduct, care of property, attendance, admission and dismissal, and student rooms. The rules revived ante-bellum college practices by regarding every matriculant as pledged to obey the officers and laws of the University and as "bound, in honor, to promote, in all suitable ways, its interest and success." They forbade unnecessary noise in halls and public rooms, use of alcoholic drinks, and visiting of saloons as well as billiard and gambling houses. Nearly half of the rules pertained to the dormitory. After completing the legislative task which necessity and the Board required of them, the Faculty formally voted to strike from the catalogue the statement, "It has but one law, and that is, Do Right."[39]

Professors managed the University under the system thus established. They supervised conduct in chapel, classrooms, and laboratories, and in the small community which offered little in the way of diversion, they effortlessly learned of student intimacy with vice. As before, the governmental problem centered in the dormitory, where the raw, pulsating energy of rural youths confined to close quarters sought periodic release. Control of the dormitory required constant surveillance, an irksome task for professors.

The solution lay in transferring responsibility from the governors to the governed, and Gregory's proposal to this effect at chapel in 1870 constituted the heart of his experiment in college government. Nott's disciple believed in maximum freedom for students, but he also sought to make the best of an existing situation. He offered an elaborate rationale, reminding his charges that they were not children but citizens who needed to become familiar with

[38] *Ibid.,* 21; *2nd Report* (1869), 90.
[39] The bylaws appear with somewhat different categories but otherwise essentially the same in the *Catalogue, 1869-70,* 31-32, and the *5th Report* (1873), 60-62. "Faculty Record," I, 28, 29, 30, 31, 33 (the source of the second quotation).

the duties and practice of government. He appealed to the "conscious manhood" of students who refused to be governed as mere boys and girls. Gregory believed that the majority of good elements in a college community lacked the organizing zeal of the evil minority which combined for nefarious purposes. Hoping to mobilize decency against disorder, he told students that they possessed more effective power to detect and prevent violations of college laws and to maintain good order than any faculty. If successful, their government "would establish new and more honorable relations between students and the Faculty, taking from the professors the disagreeable duties of a detective police, and relieving the students from an irritating espionage." In addition, a successful student government would noticeably honor the young institution. After careful consideration a unanimous vote launched the experiment.[40]

Gregory and some students drafted a constitution and bylaws which the student body adopted with Faculty approval on October 3, 1870. A preamble dedicated the College Government to the better attainment of the quiet and order essential to study. Three articles resembled provisions of the U.S. Constitution. The first conferred all legislative power, subject to the Regent's absolute veto, on a General Assembly. Another placed judicial authority in an elected five-man Council, which was to try cases and punish offenders. The third entrusted executive power to a President, Adjutant, and Hall Sergeants. These officials were to supervise roll call and chapel formations and to enforce the bylaws. The latter regulated or banned the playing of musical instruments and other types of noise, controlled the handling of slop pails, and forbade throwing trash out of windows. The bylaws also authorized punishment of any student who failed to report gross or repeated violations of the rules. Penalties consisted of fines ranging from a few cents to $5. The constitution was not to be construed so as "to prevent the right of the Faculty to make and establish any regulation they may deem necessary for the good of the Institution."[41]

[40] Gregory, "An Experiment in College Government," 512-13, 517-18; Gregory to James K. Edsall (Attorney General of Illinois), Jan. 22 [Jan. 2], 1880, "Regents' Letterbook, 1879-1894."
[41] "Secretary's Record, College Government, 1870-1881," 3-7; Gregory, "An Experiment in College Government," 513. The *Student* printed the constitution in Feb., 1872.

After 1870 the Faculty continued to supervise general conduct and to maintain a semblance of control over the students' living arrangements. In 1873, for example, they ordered residents to be in their rooms with doors open for ten minutes after chapel on certain days. However, students enjoyed almost complete jurisdiction over the dormitory. As soon as the Government began to function, the Council fined 10 of 14 persons charged with disorderly conduct in the dormitory and tried two students for countenancing rather than actually helping to tie slop buckets together as a joke. Early in 1872 the General Assembly heartily endorsed rigid enforcement of the rules and instructed the new officers to be strict; the Council later arraigned a Hall Sergeant for failing to perform his duty.[42]

The first test of wills with the Faculty exposed dangers inherent in the College Government. While Gregory was out of town, the Council indicted 11 choir members on January 19, 1872, for practicing during study hours. Pending Gregory's return, Professor William M. Baker gave the choir permission to practice again at a forbidden hour. At a trial which followed, the Council fined 15 participants in the latter episode, none of whom appeared or informed the Council that Baker had authorized the rehearsal. The convicted parties appealed to Gregory, who told them to ignore the Government. The General Assembly, with two dissenting votes, then resolved that the choir was under the College Government's jurisdiction and threatened to abrogate the Government unless the Faculty sustained the Council. At noon on the day before a scheduled hearing of the first choir offense, the impatient General Assembly suspended the Government, effective the following morning, until students heard from the Faculty about their ultimatum. To resolve the impasse, Gregory called a meeting of the Assembly, to which he brought Trustee Joseph O. Cunningham, a former county judge. Cunningham upheld the College Government, whereupon the Faculty paid the choir members' fines.

In inviting external interference, Gregory revealed only a partial understanding of the requirements of disciplinary reform. More-

[42] "Faculty Record," I, 177 and *passim;* "Secretary's Record, College Government, 1870-1881," 17, 19-20, 27-28. *4th Report* (1872), 274.

over, the Regent realized too late that a fraternity clique had forced the crisis. Leaders of Delta Tau Delta, a recently formed secret society, had used an otherwise trivial issue to seize control of the Government. When they chaffed Charles W. Rolfe, a student, about their success, he offered to undo it. Greek leaders rejected his proposition that a dozen named men remain neutral for 48 hours, but Rolfe nevertheless got a majority of students to sign a resolution condemning the fraternity's act and its authors. At that point the fraternity men obtained from a mass meeting the ultimatum which they forced upon Gregory, who subsequently admitted that he would have acted otherwise had he known of Rolfe's resolution. Rolfe's account makes it probable that the Council convicted and fined John A. Ockerson, one of its prominent members but not a fraternity man, because he opposed the strategy being devised. At the height of the crisis the clique convicted him for violating a bylaw which read: "Any student being convicted by the Council, shall pay such cost as the Council may impose."[43]

The Government enjoyed a large measure of success until 1873, when growth of the University led to adoption of a new constitution which extended the Government's scope and authority. With only a minority of students housed in the college building, dormitory discipline became subordinate to general discipline on the campus and in the local towns. Students took the initiative in securing a new fundamental charter, which the Faculty authorized and made effective *after* formally delegating governmental power to the students and reserving the right to take cognizance of cases and to resume their authority whenever the College Government failed to perform properly or to maintain good order. The Faculty refused the demand of a few students for a full and irrevocable delegation of the powers and duties conferred upon it by the Trustees.[44] Therein lay the fundamental defect of the scheme, illustrating a perennial problem of student self-government and of education. The professors

[43] "Secretary's Record, College Government, 1870-1881," 7 (the article quoted), 32-41; Charles W. Rolfe (later a professor in the University) to President David Kinley, May 9, 1922, Kinley Papers; Gregory, "An Experiment in College Government," 515.
[44] "Secretary's Record, College Government, 1870-1881," 54-60, 81; "Faculty Record," I, 143-44; *Student,* Nov., 1873; *8th Report* (1877), 139.

were willing to allow the students a large measure of freedom in the hope that the latter would make wise decisions, but they would not, they could not, abandon their power to step in when they thought the students went astray. The students wanted the substance rather than the shadow of autonomy, and therefore the idea "gradually grew into even an arrogant and imperious force, that the dominant authority, ruling and controlling the institution in all its aspects, existed rightfully and necessarily in the public opinion of the students."[45]

The Government was a republican political organization whose General Assembly included all students except first-term freshmen. At the first meeting each term the outgoing President had the privilege of nominating a list of successors — a President, Vice-President, Secretary, Treasurer, Prosecuting Attorney, and Marshal — to serve for one term each, and seven senators to serve for one academic year. Any other student could also nominate candidates. The General Assembly then selected two persons to run for each office. Although other tickets might be placed in the field independently, the President possessed a vantage point in naming officials. The usual election paraphernalia — printed ballots, ballot boxes, election judges, certified results — lent an air of reality to the proceedings, and induction ceremonies at chapel gave victors the first fruits of victory. A 21-member Senate inherited legislative power from the now unwieldy General Assembly. The Regent's veto provided the only check over the Senate's enactments. These defined misdemeanors and fixed penalties for offenses against good order and decorum both on the campus and in the twin cities, except for those acts that occurred in University rooms and buildings in the presence of college officers.

The judiciary consisted of a Chief Justice and two associates nominated by the President and confirmed by the Senate, and the Marshal, who was Chief of Police and executive officer of the Court. The Marshal exercised general surveillance over students and informed the Prosecuting Attorney of violators, who then received warrants notifying them of trial. The Court could impose fines for

<hr />

[45] Selim H. Peabody, "An Educational Experiment," National Educational Association, *Journal of Proceedings and Addresses, 1889* (Topeka, 1889), 545.

specified offenses, but it could not expel students. The judges could refer troublesome cases to the Faculty, but there was no provision for appeal by the convicted student or for pardon. The President had little power beyond presiding over the General Assembly and nominating judges, but his privilege of nominating candidates made his office vital to cliques which wanted to control campus politics.[46]

The Government contributed much to University life in subsequent years. The General Assembly provided a forum for student opinion, the offices tacitly reserved for girls encouraged female students in a masculine school, and the Senate assumed responsibility for directing the student newspaper to maturity. Even more vital, Gregory and some students believed, were other achievements. First, the Government promoted honorable and friendly student-faculty relations by taking from the Faculty the need and disposition to employ secret student detectives to ferret out wrongs. Second, it promoted manliness and honor among students by encouraging the better element to organize for their own protection. In exposing the fallacy that concealment of a comrade's crimes was a duty of good fellowship, Gregory thought the Government introduced a revolution in college life. Third, the system secured better discipline than usually prevailed in American higher education. Fourth, it offered training in self-government which was vital in a democracy, and politics added excitement to college life. Having exercised his veto but twice by 1875, both times to check poll-tax amendments, Gregory expressed full confidence in the success of an experiment which he and the *Illini* both thought was arousing widespread interest in other colleges.[47]

Unfortunately, however, the College Government substituted new problems for old and never merited the praise it received. Ironically, the system gave poor training in self-government and pro-

---

[46] The *Illini* printed the constitution in April, 1875, 204, the bylaws in May and June of that year, 232-36, 269. *The Constitution and Laws of the College Government* were separately printed in 1875. See "Publications Scrapbook, 1868-1890," 195. The best description of the operation of the Government is in Peabody, "An Educational Experiment," 540-42.

[47] On Gregory's and the Faculty's praise in these years, see *8th Report* (1877), 139; "Faculty Record," I, 281-82. On students' praise, see the *Illini*, Nov., 1874; Oct., 1875; June, 1877. Successive editions of the official catalogue were also laudatory.

moted discord. Most students were conservative Republicans by background and inclination and exhibited little interest in contemporary political issues. They resolutely believed that "political discussions should be eschewed" in everyday student life. "We have a horror of their being brought into the [literary] societies. Whenever they are called up they are argued with a strict reference to party ties, and generally end in a whirl of heated words and wild statements."[48] Moreover, students regarded political clubs as useless elements of dissension on the campus. And Gregory steered pupils away from live politics. When the Hayes-Tilden presidential contest slightly dispelled student torpor in 1876, Gregory discountenanced political demonstrations.[49]

Hence students ignored real politics to battle fiercely over play politics. Their imitation of contemporary electioneering techniques set student against student and made a mockery of self-government. In the fall of 1874 three rival tickets — the Reporter, Anti-Clique, and Dead Beet — challenged the Government's candidates, and "friends" of James R. "Windy" Mann, later minority leader in Congress, nominated him for both President and Prosecuting Attorney to insure his defeat. In the following term five parties vied for office, two in earnest, three in jest. The Reform party charged incumbents with corruption and bribery; Dress Reform candidates promised rights for women. Personal spite and abuse marred the April, 1875, elections and spilled over to disrupt joint meetings of the literary societies. After students unsuccessfully attempted to amend the constitution so as to bar fraternity members from Government office, the Board of Trustees condemned secret societies as detrimental to the scheme of government.[50]

The enforcement of laws also generated conflict and created opposition to the Government. The constant turnover in office as well as varying degrees of enthusiasm contributed to the uneven administration of justice. Since the system depended upon fines for its operating revenues, it had to secure convictions or face bank-

---

[48] *Illini,* Oct. 5, 1880. See also Oct. 20, 1880.
[49] *Ibid.,* Oct., 1876.
[50] Copies of the *Reporter,* an ephemeral publication, illuminate the fall election of 1874. See also the *Illini,* May, 1875; Nov., Dec., 1876; *8th Report* (1877), 185.

ruptcy. Moreover, students objected to being disciplined by their own classmates. Accusations of unfairness arose and were fed by rivalries between literary societies and the forbidden fraternities which operated *sub rosa*. The charge that students acted as faculty spies became increasingly serious. On one occasion a state legislator denounced the Government as a system of espionage.

Jurisdictional rivalries over internal discipline hardly promoted friendly relations between students and the Faculty. The officers who managed the Government were sensitive to interference and refused to act as puppets for their professors. For this reason the Faculty reaffirmed in 1876 that its authority extended to all offenses committed in chapel, the library, laboratories, and classrooms, and subsequently withdrew the Government's power to suspend University privileges of students. Frequently the Faculty upheld the Government when convicted offenders appealed the Court's judgments, but too often the Faculty remitted penalties and allowed students to graduate with unpaid fines. Part of the trouble lay in a system which failed to provide for review or pardon, but nevertheless students complained that Faculty interference weakened the Government's dignity and rights and made it "merely a farce."[51]

In any case, the experiment had failed by about 1878. When an opposition ring, determined to destroy the Government, attacked its legality, the Faculty finally acknowledged that the system was "an agency chosen by us for the accomplishment of the disciplinary work incumbent on us as a Faculty," and that they had all along maintained "a constant though generally silent supervision over the Students' Government." The statement revealed why intelligent students viewed self-government as a charade.[52]

But some educators, unaware of the troubles, viewed the reform

[51] *Illini*, Feb., 1879, and *passim* for the years after 1877; "Faculty Record," I, 132, 162, 184, 199-201; II, Dec. 12, 1879 (the source of the quotation). "Students refusing to pay the fines imposed by the Students' Government are suspended from University privileges," said the *Catalogue, 1877-78*, 67. "Students refusing to pay the fines imposed by the students' government are referred to the Faculty, and if found guilty of an offense, are sentenced to such penalties as the Faculty may deem proper," said the *Catalogue, 1879-80*, 80.
[52] "Faculty Record," I, 281-82; *Illini*, May, 1878; Feb., 1879; June, 1879. The chief legal objection was that the Government conflicted with an Illinois law prohibiting intimidation or punishment by mock trial. See Article 163, *Illinois Revised Statutes* (1877), 373.

as a success. It is not known whether President Julius H. Seeyle borrowed from Urbana, but the plan of student self-government which he introduced at Amherst College in the fall of 1880 partly imitated the one at Illinois. The Amherst System put a large measure of control in the hands of a College Senate, a body consisting of ten elected student representatives which met monthly with the President of the College, who possessed the power of veto, as presiding officer. Historians of Amherst are therefore incorrect in asserting that the innovation was "the first case of student self-government on record in any American college." President Frederick A. P. Barnard drew upon the experiment at Urbana when he sought to admit students themselves to participation in the government at Columbia College in New York City. Barnard had long given serious thought to the problem of discipline, and while still a professor at the University of Alabama had published *Letters on College Government and the Evils Inseparable from the American College System in Its Present Form* (1855). Now he thought the difficulty of college government would disappear if students themselves assumed responsibility for preserving good order, and when he first referred to the subject in his annual report at Columbia in 1881 he mentioned that such a plan had been successfully tried for a decade at the state University in Illinois. Other colleges made similar starts in the 1880's, but everywhere these student bodies lived a rather precarious existence.[53]

The community offered students little diversion, and academic as well as other duties left little leisure. They nevertheless set out to amuse and better themselves on their own time, and borrowed customs from the established Eastern colleges even when these were falling into disuse. Student life at Illinois in the late nineteenth century illustrates cultural diffusion, and the pattern of extracurricular activities lagged about a generation behind its prototype on the Atlantic Coast.

[53] Cornelius Howard Patton and Walter Taylor Field, *Eight O'Clock Chapel: A Study of New England College Life in the Eighties* (Boston, 1927), 56-58; Claude Moore Fuess, *Amherst: The Story of a New England College* (Boston, 1935), 220-22, 252-54; John Fulton, *Memoirs of Frederick A. P. Barnard* (New York, 1896), 366-67. The quotation is in Patton and Field, p. 57, and in Fuess, p. 220.

For a century the literary societies had been centers of life outside the classroom. No college was considered complete without two rival Greek-named clubs to enliven intellectual life. Their forensic and literary exercises and the prominent speakers they brought to the campus permitted escape from the confines of a pre-scribed curriculum. These organizations found favor with students who had been raised in the small towns of rural America on lyceum and Chautauqua lectures. But the heyday of the literary societies began to wane during the decade of the Civil War when students in established colleges lost interest.[54]

At Urbana, however, the old tradition took root and long per-sisted. Students formed two literary societies on March 7, 1868, five days after the University opened. The story that Gregory cre-ated these agencies by fiat at chapel one morning in March, 1869 — dividing students alternately into two groups by the roll, some-what like Noah loading the Ark — is touching but inaccurate.[55] He undoubtedly encouraged his charges, and perhaps suggested "Philo-mathean," the name of his Union College society, for one organiza-tion. The Adelphics and Philos hoped the newly admitted girls would enter their ranks in 1871, but Gregory vetoed the idea of intermingling the sexes, and in October the women formed the Alethenai.[56]

The weight of the past blighted the promise of a fourth group. It originated on January 28, 1870, as the Agricultural Society, with 16 members discussing corn. The club then experimented with names and subjects relating to practical pursuits and finally called itself the Scientific Association. The gifted Willard Flagg was men-tor to this special-interest organization. He guided it away from the past: in place of the jejune mental gymnastics afforded by con-ventional literary themes, the boys discussed live issues, such as rail-

[54] David Potter, *Debating in the Colonial Chartered Colleges, an Historical Sur-vey, 1642 to 1900*, Teachers College, Columbia University, Contributions to Education No. 899 (New York, 1944), 89; Frederick Rudolph, *The American College and University: A History* (New York, 1962), 137-44.

[55] Allan Nevins, *Illinois* (New York, 1917), 93. Nevins followed Raymond, "The Beginning," 194. The sources do not bear out Raymond (class of 1872).

[56] *Student*, Jan., 1873; J. F. [James Faulkner?], "Brief History of Societies," *Illini*, Jan., 1875; C. I. Hayes (class of 1873), "Early History and Reminiscenses of the Adelphic Society," *Illini*, June, 1879; "Faculty Record," I, 19; *Illini*, March 24, 1884.

road freight charges, awarded prizes for original scientific investigations, and collected plant specimens rather than books. But the decrepit ante-bellum ideal was fixed in student minds, and in 1875 the Scientific Association saved itself from extinction by becoming a traditional literary society.[57]

In early years self-culture and sociability absorbed the "lits," which met in University-assigned rooms, the men on Friday or Saturday evening from 7 to 10, the women late on a weekday afternoon. Each society raised the money to furnish its own quarters. "Come up Higher," the motto of the Philomatheans, aptly characterized the programs designed for the betterment of individual members. Participants regarded effective speech as the highway to success, for public address was still the nation's dominant literary tradition. Orations, declamations, and debates therefore dominated the evenings, and essayists read their compositions. The speakers reproved appointed critics who dished out praise indiscriminately. A good deal of fellowship and levity accompanied these solemnities. Within the club room members could cultivate friends and nourish a feeling of exclusiveness, for only about a third of the students (but most seniors) belonged to one of the societies. And what better place for a spicy burlesque on the Faculty, a deed doubly exciting in that it was sure to be investigated. An annual "sociable" climaxed by a late banquet complete with lemonade toasts highlighted the year.

But members were hardly content to remain in their own precincts tutoring each other in elocution. The literary societies contained the ablest, most prominent students, and a coterie of Adelphics and Philomatheans knew that they possessed the power to shape events. They used it to improve the University as well as themselves. As early as 1869 a committee from the two literary societies arranged for Faculty and students to celebrate the first anniversary of the University's opening in March.[58] Anniversary Day developed into a prominent collegiate ritual, and in 1874 the student groups began reaching out to influence other campus activities.

However, the immediate stimulus for some of their most im-

[57] E. E. Harden, "History of the Scientific Association," *Illini*, June, 1879.
[58] "Faculty Record," I, 19.

portant efforts came from beyond the University. Late in 1873 the Adelphic Society of Knox College invited Urbana to participate at Galesburg the following February 27 in the first interstate oratorical contest in the Midwest. From a slate of nominees chosen at a joint meeting of the three men's clubs, the Faculty selected W. W. Wharry to represent the school. He competed with speakers from the University of Chicago, Iowa State, Iowa College (Grinnell), Beloit, and Monmouth, and over 2,400 persons heard the Chicago man win with "The Heart the Source of Power."[59]

Galesburg was the catalyst for organizational arrangements which revealed the importance of forensics at the time and blazed the trail later followed by intercollegiate athletics. Delegates from participating schools founded the Inter-State Contest Association, and those from Illinois agreed to form a permanent state body to promote oratory. Accordingly, representatives from Chicago, Knox, Monmouth, Northwestern, Illinois Industrial University, Illinois College, and Shurtleff met at Bloomington on April 7 and established the Illinois Collegiate Association (later the Illinois Intercollegiate Oratorical Association). This group then urged Ohio, Indiana, Michigan, Wisconsin, and Iowa to organize similar state groups and to compete in annual regional oratorical meets.[60]

The first annual Intercollegiate Oratorical Contest took place in November, 1874, at Bloomington. The University, whose representative spoke on "National Arbitration," competed with seven other colleges in the state. In 1875 Gregory granted 50 students leave to attend the exercises at Jacksonville, where the audience numbered about 1,200 and townspeople feted the guests. The Urbana speaker won with an oration on "Church and State." The first and second prizes of $75 and $50 were substantial, and the meetings excited sharp intercollegiate rivalry. When Urbana played host to the contest in 1879, Charles G. Neely of the University took fourth place with "Education, a Bulwark of Morality." The audience numbered about 500 and the Illinois Collegiate Association lost $100. "That oratory is better than any other single thing upon

[59] *Ibid.*, 142, 145, 147; *Student*, Nov., 1873; *Illini*, Jan., March, 1874.
[60] *Illini*, May, 1874.

which to contest need not be discussed here," wrote the *Illini,* "— it is generally admitted."[61]

The first annual Interstate Oratorical Contest apparently was held at Indianapolis in February, 1875, and T. I. Coultas of Wesleyan represented the state of Illinois with "Culture, the Basis of Brotherhood." In the years to 1880, Chicago, Madison, St. Louis, and Oberlin held the competition, but no speaker from Illinois Industrial University won first place.

Rivalry with other colleges greatly stimulated the student body at Champaign-Urbana. In March, 1874, just after the first interstate meet at Galesburg, University authorities responded to a student petition for a class in elocution by hiring Jennie C. Bryant. But the professors only begrudgingly recognized the subject. The Faculty allowed students to take no more than a total of two elocution courses, and granted only half-credit for each; the University provided for Miss Bryant to be paid mainly by student fees. Despite official handicaps, however, elocution became a great popular success. Would-be orators filled five classes daily, and the bi-weekly elocution contests Miss Bryant began conducting in the chapel in November, 1874, aroused keen interest.[62]

The literary societies profited most from these challenges to excellence. In the fall of 1874 the Adelphics and the Philos, who held union meetings, established the Inter-Society Oratorical Association. Their purpose was to run campus forensic contests, and also to dominate extracurricular life. Although intense rivals, the two men's clubs wanted to exclude others from power. Thus in 1877 they refused to admit the Scientific Association to the Inter-Society Oratorical Association, and did not accept the Alethenai until April, 1879.[63]

In these years students brightened their lives in many ways. Rarely were they explicit about the need to overcome isolation or to fabricate ritual and create tradition, but one suspects that these motives figured prominently. The conduct of extracurricular ac-

---

[61] *Ibid.,* Nov., 1874; Dec., 1878; Oct., 1879; Nov., 1879 (the source of the quotation) ; "Faculty Record," I, 192.
[62] "Faculty Record," I, 154, 156, 172; *Illini,* 1874-75 *passim.*
[63] "Faculty Record," I, 172, 177, 227; *Illini,* March, 1875; Feb., 1877; April, 1879.

tivities gave rise to quarrels among the students, whose initiative and enthusiasm the Faculty always dampened with strict controls. The authorities did not trust students to behave decently and sought to protect the University's good name. They especially regulated any program designed for a public audience.

About 1874 the Adelphics, Alethenais, and Philomatheans started sponsoring entertainments and lectures by prominent speakers. They often invited spokesmen of a passing era (Henry Ward Beecher, Wendell Phillips, Elizabeth Cady Stanton), but the speakers brought contact with a larger world. This precedent later developed into the "Star Course," which featured musical presentations.

Union meetings of the literary societies proved enormously popular. Some were social and included picnics on the banks of the Sangamon; others were the big yearly forensic contests. The Inter-Society Oratorical Association first sponsored these in 1875, printing a program and charging admission. Orations were judged on thought, composition, and delivery, and most speakers avoided live issues in favor of genteel, conventional themes. They considered politics divisive. Out of 16 orations in two years, at most five focused on contemporary issues. Two dealt with Chinese immigration, one with the struggle of Ireland, one with the limitation of suffrage, and another with the necessity of education in the American republic. "Purpose, Its Relation to Character" illustrates the nature of the others.[64] For a time the contests succeeded, though students complained that faculty members took no interest. The charge was untrue: in 1879 the Faculty limited the number of union meetings to one a term, which could be either social or literary.[65]

Other campus groups either imitated or ridiculed the literary programs. The Sophomores apparently initiated class exhibitions in 1875, and these became so popular that the Faculty limited each class to one public exhibition or entertainment yearly. The Faculty even specified the term in which each class could present its show. Presumably authorities supervised all preparations, since they had earlier ordered a staff member to direct rehearsals of programs de-

[64] For 1879, see the "W. G. Curtiss Scrapbook, 1878-1882"; for 1880, the *Illini*, June, 1880.
[65] *Illini*, April, 1875; "Faculty Record," II, Nov. 21, 1879.

signed for public display and to approve programs before they were published. These conditions account for the appearance of bogus programs, crude parodies of Inter-Society Oratorical contests. One long, narrow broadside of about 1879 entitled "Senior Slop" demonstrated coarse and tasteless humor. But there was almost no ritualized class conflict in these years, although someone uprooted the senior class tree in 1879.[66]

Anniversary Day, Class Day, and Commencement all became fixed collegiate rituals. The literary societies combined their union meeting of the winter term with celebration of the University's March birthday. The highlight of the half-holiday was a chapel program. The Regent spoke and students orated and entertained. On one occasion 30 "beautiful young gentlemen" all adorned with white gloves and eyeglasses breathed soft harmony through fine-toothed combs.[67] Class Day, an exercise by seniors on the Monday before graduation, made its distinct appearance in 1874. In Eastern colleges this rite of public orations and farewells topped by a midnight feast was well developed. The proceedings were simpler at Champaign-Urbana. One year at the foot of the class tree every senior shoveled a spade of dirt around a giant boulder inscribed "Class of '76" to the accompaniment of an oration and the singing of the class song. The class of 1878 gave a more useful gift — the clock in the west tower of University Hall.[68]

Commencement was much simpler at Illinois than in the better-established colleges, and totally free of such symbols of the past as Latin and academic regalia. Otherwise, the closing exercises followed a familiar pattern. They began with a baccalaureate sermon on Sunday and ended with midweek graduation ceremonies. The original attempt to feature a visiting speaker was abandoned after one experience. In 1873 President Andrew D. White of Cornell spoke on "The Battle Fields of Science." Thereafter the Faculty relied on student orators. The Faculty wanted to control selection of participants and to have most students speak, even if the multi-

---

[66] "Faculty Record," I, 113, 193; II, Nov. 21, 1879; *Illini*, March, 1875; Nov., 1879. A copy of "Senior Slop" is in the Arthur N. Talbot Papers.
[67] *Illini*, March, 1879.
[68] "Faculty Record," I, 156; [George Rugg Cutting], *Student Life at Amherst College: Its Organizations, Their Membership and History* (Amherst, 1871), 82; *Illini*, May, 1874; June, 1876; April, 1878.

plicity of performers meant that each person could utter only 500 of the 2,000 words submitted in orations and essays for Faculty approval. The diversity of topics at graduation dramatized how thoroughly the unity of the old-time education had been shattered. The senior class insisted on choosing the speakers and easing the requirement that all graduates perform. By 1878 a nasty dispute had developed over the issue.[69]

Greek-letter social fraternities, established in the 1820's, stood on the threshold of great national growth after Appomattox. They had survived charges of undermining academic, democratic, and religious values and begun to replace the literary societies in the 1850's. Young men found them irresistibly attractive because of their professed ideals and secret rituals, and the splendid opportunities they afforded for rollicking good times. But college faculties usually resented the coming of the Greeks, and not least because of the fear that secret organizations might undermine established authority. Both Yale and Princeton, bastions of the old collegiate order, adamantly opposed social fraternities. Cornell welcomed them when it opened (and seven arose there during the first year), but many state universities, including Indiana, Wisconsin, Nebraska, California, and Illinois, long remained hostile. Students assailed official restraints by insisting on organizing clubs of their own choosing as a matter of right, and bitter controversy often resulted. It was not until the 1880's, after embattled Greeks won legislative and judicial victories and a more sympathetic public opinion, that the obstructions generally began to crumble.[70]

Meanwhile, Gregory had erected strong barriers against what he termed "the traditional tinsel of a more barbarous time." Five fraternities had already established a total of 12 chapters in private Illinois colleges when the University opened, and early in 1872 the "serpent" first entered Gregory's collegiate Eden. Spurred on by students from a neighboring college, three Philomatheans founded

[69] "Faculty Record," I, 142, 156, 180-81, 223-25, 237-38, 250, 260-62; *Illini*, Nov., 1877.
[70] Sheldon, *American Student Societies*, 215, 220-24; Rudolph, *The American College and University*, 144-50; Morris Bishop, *A History of Cornell* (Ithaca, 1962), 138; William Murray Hepburn and Louis Martin Sears, *Purdue University: Fifty Years of Progress* (Indianapolis, 1925), 66, 72, 79.

a chapter of Delta Tau Delta. The members, including James N. Matthews, the first matriculant in the University, Ira O. Baker, and James R. Mann, captured offices in the literary societies, the College Government, and the campus newspaper. Soon thereafter 14 more students joined. Although the Delts had no fraternity rival on the campus, their activities in college politics led to "pro" and "anti" Delt factions.[71]

The secret society was not officially discovered until the spring of 1876, and the revelation elicited vigorous opposition. A hundred students petitioned the Faculty to repress the fraternity. The College Government recommended changing its own Constitution so as to require all officers to abjure membership in such a group. These expressions perhaps demonstrated Gregory's skill in educating pupils to views he laid before the Board of Trustees on June 6. His criticism condemned secrecy as the main evil of Greek-letter organizations. In a free country concealment was unnecessary and a sham, and a quality which made it impossible to distinguish good from bad student clubs. Any college administrator might readily agree, but Gregory had a special reason for opposing secrecy. He attributed troubles experienced by the College Government to covert fraternity factions, and believed that these clandestine activities frustrated all hope of a successful experiment in self-government. Apart from secrecy, Gregory also declared fraternities harmful for other reasons. They substituted artificial for natural affinities among students, and when "birds of a feather" congregated together it became impossible for different types of students to educate and correct each other. Gregory also charged that fraternities placed sociability over scholarship, but he never emphasized the point.

His arraignment induced the Trustees to manifest their displeasure the following day. They passed a resolution which condemned secret societies as detrimental to student government and asked students to disband and discountenance these organizations.

[71] *8th Report* (1877), 183-84 (the source of the quotation); Ernest G. Hildner, "Higher Education in Transition, 1850-1870," *Journal of the Illinois State Historical Society*, LVI (Spring, 1963), 72; *Illini*, May 25, 1881; Stewart Howe, "Early Days of Illinois Fraternities," *Illinois Alumni News*, VI (April, 1928), 292; Ira O. Baker to J. E. Stark, April 10, 1916, Carl Stephens Papers. The biographical sketches in Scott's *Alumni Record* (1906) usually list fraternity affiliation.

The Board did not officially ban Greek-letter organizations, but the Delts found it desirable to go underground. Here they lived a tenuous existence until their charter was withdrawn in 1879. As soon as Gregory resigned, however, fraternity men attempted to make a place for secret societies at Urbana.[72]

The few student publications in existence when the University of Illinois opened were former literary society journals which had begun to report news. The *Harvard Advocate* had recently dropped essays for accounts of boat races and baseball. At Urbana, the first undergraduate publication was the *Student,* an eight-page monthly established by a few upperclassmen with Faculty approval in November, 1871. "We enter the arena of journalism in support of the New Education," it announced, perhaps reflecting Gregory's philosophy more than student sentiment. The format reflected the *Student's* contention that specialization was the true principle of education, and four departments of the paper corresponded to colleges of the University — Letters, Science, Mechanic Arts, and Agriculture. The fifth was Women's Affairs. Two editors presided over each department, which contained grimly unimaginative essays on themes ranging from "Turbine Wheels" and "The Common Potato" to "The Divinity of Christ." Announcements, a few news items, and jokes relieved the dull earnestness. In its second year the *Student* contained 12 pages and short editorials, though it still lacked an editor-in-chief. But the publication avoided controversy or politics, including the Greeley-Grant campaign in 1872, and a plea to allow dancing came the closest to questioning the administration's policy.[73]

Theoretically the *Student* was the property of the senior class, but actually it was an orphan. In March, 1873, the Faculty had officially declined responsibility for its conduct. By late 1873 many

[72] "Faculty Record," I, 211; *8th Report* (1877), 183-85; *Illini,* May, 1878. See also Gregory, "College Secret Societies," *Present Age,* I (March 16, 1882), 163-65; William A. Heath, "The Mythology of Illinois," *The Illinois,* III (May, 1912), 411.

[73] *Student,* Nov., 1871; Dec., 1873; Patton and Field, *Eight O'Clock Chapel,* 300n, errs in saying "the idea of a college daily started in the midwest" and that the *Daily Illini* of the University of Illinois was established in 1871, implying that the *Daily Illini* was the first college daily.

agreed with the correspondent who criticized the "long, stupid articles," and asked for campus news and personals rather than fare which encyclopedias served better. A few students effected reform. George R. Shawhan, James Faulkner, and Howard A. Mann, having unsuccessfully petitioned the Board of Trustees for funds to buy a press, raised $350 by subscription, obtained working space from the Faculty, and found a parent for the orphan. Shawhan, President of the College Government, induced the Student Senate to assume responsibility. The Senate appointed a committee to manage the press, and that body named Shawhan, a prominent Philomathean, editor. The Senate committee enlisted Burrill as faculty adviser so that he could intercede with Gregory.[74]

The *Student* expired in December, 1873, and the *Illini* first appeared the next January. Shawhan chose this name to give more individuality to the monthly publication which sold for $1.50 annually. He edited the paper for two years. During the rest of the decade editors changed annually. In this period the book-size journal of 30 to 40 pages an issue was a hybrid, a literary magazine trying to become a newspaper. Half the space reprinted essays composed for chapel addresses or literary society programs, a fair index of the importance of forensic and literary exercises in student life. Faculty members also contributed articles.

A second section reported campus and alumni news, carried items from other colleges, reviewed books, and featured an editorial column. Editors prided themselves on "the liberty of being outspoken in all matters pertaining to the University and its students," but the editors voluntarily made the newspaper a house organ.[75] Economic factors were one reason. The University itself subsidized the publication by purchasing both advertising space and copies, which it sent to Illinois high schools as a publicity measure. In 1875 the newspaper began operating out of quarters provided by the University on the second floor of the Mechanical Building, while the General Assembly appropriated $500 for printing equipment.

The specter of paternalistic control was another reason. In

[74] *Student,* Aug., 1873; "Faculty Record," I, 122; "Secretary's Record, College Government, 1870-1881," 83; John L. Pierce and Henry M. Beardsley, "History of the Illini," *Illini,* March 10, 1883.
[75] *Illini,* June, 1878.

1874 the professors voted to choose one of their number "for the *Illini*."[76] The stake of the students in the University's success was a third factor. One editor who regarded himself as outspoken made the point in saying that the *Illini* served "as a help to the University by making it better known."[77] Hence, editorials urged the need to keep pace with the development of higher education. They advocated such measures as decreased emphasis on the "dead" languages, employment of an elocution teacher, and substitution of degrees for certificates. The press championed spelling reform in the hope that the University might seize leadership in the Midwest of a movement initiated by the American Philological Society and endorsed by Gregory. But editors ordinarily avoided matters that might offend. Authority was to be respected, not challenged.

Yet the *Illini* faithfully mirrored campus life and provided a medium for unifying the student body. Its pages indicate that student-faculty relations were less than warm and intimate. Apparently few classroom performances impressed pupils, whose praise did not emphasize scholarly virtues. Students hailed Taft as "a good entertainer" and able teacher, and cherished the kindliness hidden beneath Snyder's austerity. They commended Gregory until late in his career for bringing his knowledge, his vision, and his character to bear upon young lives, kindling in them high purposes and noble resolves. The rare contacts outside the classroom elicited special approval. Apart from Gregory's receptions, Taft entertained students at home, once delivering a lecture on cosmogony, and Weber annually invited some students to Thanksgiving dinner. But in 1879 the *Illini* exaggerated only slightly when it said that in nearly four years there had been no gathering in which both faculty and students mingled.[78]

The undergraduate publication also served as an arbiter of student taste and conduct. It complained in 1878 of a little too much formality among students, many of whom passed each other in halls or on streets without speaking.[79] The editors exemplified and expounded the gospel of success. Consider Samuel A. Bullard.

[76] "Faculty Record," I, 168.
[77] *Illini*, Nov., 1876.
[78] *Ibid.*, Dec., 1875; Nov., 1877; Dec., 1878; Jan., March, 1879.
[79] *Ibid.*, Nov., 1878.

Editor from 1877 to 1878, Bullard was an Adelphic; President of
the YMCA, the class of 1878, and the Temperance Club; and Chief
Justice of the Supreme Court. Work, he and other editors advised;
waste no time, for the night cometh wherein no man works; avoid
billiards, for the spirit it generates will be harmful in later life; be
punctual; participate in student activities; sign a temperance pledge;
and do not hiss in chapel. This advice the class of 1880 encapsulated
in its motto, "Work and Win." Not to be outdone, the class of 1881
followed with "Earnest Effort Conquers."

Athletics took on their modern character after the Civil War
when an inherited distrust of games and diversions began to crumble
and when farm-bred youths found urban routines confining. The
gospel of physical well-being accompanied the rise of different sports
for the classes and the masses. Boating, racing, golf, cycling, baseball, and boxing provided new outlets. Baseball in the late nineteenth century best illustrated the future of sports in urban America.
The game became a national pastime and a big business. Professionals entertained paying spectators who exercised vicariously. The
forces behind these developments also shaped the character of athletics in the nation's colleges.

At Illinois in 1868 official sentiment favored "Learning and
Labor" rather than leisure and amusement. Authorities expected
students to unite studies with manual employments, and "play was
hardly worthy of consideration."[80] The Faculty forbade all boxing
and wrestling, and restricted games to specific hours.[81] The farm
boys knew nothing of such esoteric sports as football, golf, or tennis,
but they seized warm evenings to jump, race, somersault, and turn
handsprings on the campus, and on Saturday afternoons hunted
rabbit and quail in woods nearby.

The science of physical education and gymnastics gained a
foothold in American higher education in this period, and the
University's first authorized athletics were of this type. Amherst
pioneered in 1860 by appointing Edward Hitchcock, a physician,
to a chair of hygiene and physical education, and in 1878 Harvard

[80] Charles P. Jeffers, "Athletics at the University, 1869-1874," Stephens Papers.
[81] "Faculty Record," I, 64.

erected Hemenway Gymnasium. In 1870 Illinois erected a horizontal bar with a trapeze and rings beside the old main building. One student, trying to impress the ladies, lost his hold and almost his head on the new equipment, but undaunted classmates formed a Gymnastics Club nonetheless. Members secured $30 for apparatus from the Board and use of a room in the Mechanical Building and Drill Hall. They made gymnastics a great success, giving annual exhibitions, and buying apparatus with membership fees. The Faculty then intervened. It laid down detailed rules for the gymnasium room and appointed the military professor to supervise the facility. Gregory declared in 1878 that "the physical training of our college students cannot be properly provided for till the spirit of the athletic games shall be united to the steadiness of the daily drill, and all be placed under the charge of a thoroughly competent surgeon and drill master."[82]

"The steadiness of the daily drill." That was precisely what American students wished to avoid. They desired fun, freedom, and competition from their athletics. Baseball was the answer. It was then the king of American sports, and the Illini could have borrowed the game from other colleges or from professional clubs. About 1870 students chose sides for a primitive version of the game and boardinghouses fielded teams. The first athletic contest at the University occurred on May 8, 1872, when a student team defeated the Eagle Baseball Club of Champaign by 2-1. Six baseball teams existed by 1876 and others were forming. The desire for more competition created the University Baseball Association in 1878 and a call for one team to represent the whole school. That team initiated intercollegiate athletics at Illinois on October 2, 1879, in a game with Illinois College during the Intercollegiate Oratorical Contest held in Champaign-Urbana.[83] The day was fateful (but not quite fatal) for the future of higher education. "Certainly the good sense of the young men of the West," the *Illini* had said in deploring intercollegiate athletic teams in 1875, "will prevent the formation of

[82] Gregory, "Physical Training in College," *Present Age,* III (Feb. 21, 1884); "Faculty Record," II, Jan. 22, 1880.

[83] *Illini,* May, 1877; April, 1878; Nov., Dec., 1879; Donald L. Wolf, "A History of Intercollegiate Baseball at the University of Illinois" (unpublished master's thesis, University of Illinois, 1958), 5-7.

many of these. Students should have a higher aim in life than to emulate the traveling ball-players of the country." Late in 1879, however, the campus newspaper urged Illinois to imitate other colleges and form an athletic association. The die was cast.[84]

The students proposed, the Faculty disposed. However imperfect, the system worked reasonably well until about 1878. After that it became harder to resolve recurring tensions. One reason was loss of respect for Gregory. After his wife died in 1877 he invited ridicule by his courtship of Louisa Allen, a staff member 26 years his junior whom he married in June, 1879. He hung over bannisters holding long conversations with the young woman boarder at the Burrills', and frequently went the back way in making calls, dodging around among the trees. The courtship went to such an undignified extreme that Mrs. Burrill took Professor Allen to task for it. Moreover, in 1877 Gregory added membership on the State Board of Health to other official appointments, and many thought he was too aggressive in seeking state offices. Brief but sharp anti-Gregory barbs began appearing in the *Illini*.[85]

Second, it was obvious by 1878 that Gregory's vaunted experiment in student government had failed. An attack on its legality drew the acknowledgment that the scheme was designed to do the Faculty's disciplinary duty. Thereafter conditions deteriorated, and in January, 1880, the *Illini* editor charged that Faculty remission of fines turned students into spies.

Third, opposition to paternalism mounted. An 1878 order for classes to change rooms in strict accordance with three bells rung at intervals to signal rising from desks, moving, and roll call was a small matter, but opposition to the method of choosing commencement speakers was more important. A continuing dispute reached a climax late in May, 1878, when the Faculty refused to consider a communication from the senior class on the subject until all conditions were withdrawn. But the seniors did not remove the terms which the Faculty regarded as improper.[86]

[84] *Illini*, May, 1875; Dec., 1879.
[85] [J. E. Stark] to Allan Nevins, May 20, 1916, Stephens Papers. For examples of the barbs, see *Illini*, Dec., 1877; March, May, 1878.
[86] "Faculty Record," I, 243, 264, 265, 267.

The immediate precipitant of trouble that led to Gregory's resignation was the Military Department. It began a new era in January, 1878, when the U.S. Government provided the University with arms and accoutrements along with an instructor. The War Department ordered Major W. A. Dinwiddie, a cavalry officer, to Urbana, but local authorities never passed on his qualifications. Dinwiddie immediately induced the Faculty to make the military salute the regulation form of recognition between professors and students, and began competitive drills designed to perfect the cadet Battalion. Students initially favored this emulation of West Point. But relations between Dinwiddie and Snyder were poor. The upshot was that Dinwiddie challenged Snyder for authority and forced Gregory to choose between them. Gregory gave the Board deliberately vague counsel designed to get the Trustees to demote Snyder, who was never a strong supporter of Gregory, and to make Dinwiddie his ally in restoring discipline. Dinwiddie withdrew the resignation he had submitted after gaining the upper hand.[87]

During 1879 cadets lost their former enthusiasm for Dinwiddie and expressed their opposition to military training by acts of insubordination. Late in 1879 a Faculty committee (Gregory, Burrill, and Dinwiddie) reaffirmed that drill was a legal obligation and added that violations of military rules as well as acts or words which undermined the respect due to drill would bring censure and possibly expulsion from the University.[88] On January 13, 1880, the Faculty adopted eight military regulations, allegedly to remove uncertainty about requirements governing admission to military classes and eligibility for appointment as cadet officers. Most of the rules actually embodied existing usages, but one pertaining to commissions offered a significant innovation. Under prevailing practice, at least since 1875, the Governor had commissioned as captains in the militia those students who had completed the military class, obtained command experience, and "whom the Faculty of the University may recommend for their high character both as students and as

[87] My conclusion about relations between Gregory, Dinwiddie, and Snyder must remain conjectural, but the circumstantial evidence is very convincing. See "Faculty Record," I, 248; II, May 9, Sept. 29, Oct. 24, 1879; *Illini*, Feb., 1878; *9th Report* (1878), 108; *10th Report* (1881), 181.
[88] "Faculty Record," II, Dec. 5, 1879.

gentlemen."[89] Gregory, describing the system at Columbus, Ohio, in 1877, said that military students who had served as cadet captains and lieutenants and "were in good standing were recommended to the governor . . . and he issued them commissions according to their rank as a reward."[90] A total of 36 had received commissions since 1875, as many as nine in 1877 and ten in 1878.[91] But one of the January 13 resolutions said: "No student shall be recommended to the Governor for a commission except he shall be conspicuous for high character both as a student and a gentleman, and these recommendations shall not exceed five in one year unless by unanimous vote of the Faculty."[92]

This innovation alarmed the students. Editor E. E. Harden first obtained a copy of the rules on Friday, January 23, for publication in the *Illini*. A Battalion officer, he quickly assembled nearly two dozen junior and senior cadet officers to consider the change. They regarded the ruling as jeopardizing their chance of a commission and destroying the tacit agreement in effect when they entered the advanced military program. One grievance was the limitation of the number of recommendations to five. Another was the character requirement. Good character had always been demanded for both matriculation and military commissions. But students regarded the new standard as vague and sinister because it would permit a student with good character to remain in college and still be deprived of a commission on grounds that the Faculty did not unanimously consider him "conspicuous for high character."

The cadet officers therefore laid plans over the weekend to

[89] This phrase was quoted in the *Catalogue, 1875-76*, 51, and thereafter.
[90] *Proceedings of the Conference of the Presidents and Other Delegates of the State Universities and State Colleges, Held at Columbus, Ohio, December 27 and 28, 1877*, U.S. Bureau of Education, Circular of Information No. 2, 1879, Appendix B (Washington, 1879), 190.
[91] "State Militia Commission Records 1861-1875," Vol. A; "Commission Records 1875-1879 [1880]," Vol. 20, Adjutant General's Records, Illinois State Archives, Springfield. Dr. Wayne C. Temple furnished necessary copies of these records.
[92] "Faculty Record," II, Jan. 13, 1880. On June 4, 1879, the Faculty agreed that passing the military class and receiving a University degree should not be sufficient cause for a commission if high character both as a student and gentleman were lacking. See "Faculty Record," I, 293. *After* the military uprising, Gregory stated on March 9, 1880, that Faculty usage had been to require a unanimous vote and that annually some students were refused on the ground of lacking the requisite scholarship or character. See *10th Report* (1881), 221.

force the repeal of what they considered a serious injustice. At roll call on Monday morning they refused to form their ranks but presented a statement saying that they would not serve until the rule relating to the number of commissions and the need for unanimous Faculty approval was revoked. All cadet officers signed a paper to this effect save one, most likely S. Cecil Stanton, Gregory's protégé.[93]

The Monday rebellion created great confusion and disorder. The Faculty met quickly and ordered officers who remained absent from their posts removed from command. The authorities ignored the insurgents' statement of conditions on the grounds that it was not respectfully presented, and demanded an apology. On Tuesday morning the officers again refused to serve and the Faculty reduced them to privates. Nearly 200 students assembled on Wednesday evening at Eichberg's Opera House in Champaign and agreed to seek reinstatement of the officers. By week's end the greatest excitement reigned. "The faculty have got themselves into a very hot box," a Chicago newspaper reported, "having few sympathizers either among the students or citizens."[94]

Gregory devised the strategy which he claimed was essential to vindicate authority. During February he urged Washington to dispatch at once a "new officer of the right stamp" to relieve Dinwiddie and help quiet the situation.[95] He also brought pressure by writing interested parents that the united determination of their sons to withdraw from the University in a body if any cadet officer was condemned constituted an illegal combination. Perhaps parents threatened their sons. In any event, the rebels explained in writing that their earlier statement was wrongly interpreted as implying a threat and announced the belief that their only wrong was in leaving their posts. On February 16 Gregory rejected this great concession as ambiguous.[96] He wanted total submission. Accordingly, on Feb-

[93] Stanton, the son of Gregory's friend, was the only person in the class of 1880 to receive a commission. See "Commission Records, 1875-1879," Vol. 20.
[94] "Faculty Record," II, Jan. 26-27, 1880; June 6, 1881; Champaign County *Gazette*, Jan. 28, 1880; Champaign *Times*, Jan. 30, 1880; *Illini*, Feb., 1880 (the editorial by Harden gives a good account). The quotation is from a clipping in the Talbot Papers, perhaps the Chicago *Inter-Ocean* of Jan. 28 or 29, 1880.
[95] Gregory to Joseph G. Cannon, Feb. 28, March, 1880, "Regents' Letterbook, 1879-1894"; *10th Report* (1881), 221.
[96] Both documents are in the Talbot Papers.

ruary 17 the Faculty gave 22 culprits the option of signing the following statement or facing expulsion: "I hereby freely and without reserve express to the Faculty my regret for, and disapproval of, my action in leaving my command without permission, and avow it to be, as it always has been, my free and full intention to conduct myself as a loyal and obedient student of the University."[97] Fifteen students, including Arthur N. Talbot, a junior and President of the Senate (and later a distinguished professor in the University), accepted these terms, and two days later the Faculty dismissed seven who did not. One of these, A. E. Kauffman, then signed the pledge and was allowed to remain. On February 23 most of the student body unsuccessfully petitioned the Faculty to reconsider the six expulsions. The next day two of the 15, C. J. Bills and W. L. Parker, requested and received dismissal.[98]

A contemporary analysis by an unknown writer in the Champaign *Times* judiciously evaluated these events. He found the new regulation on conspicuously high character useless: it was impossible to test for character beyond the old standard of integrity and morality; anyone falling below that level should be removed from the University; moreover, enforcement of the January 13 regulation could only reflect on the character of those denied commissions. The author denied Gregory's contention that the government of the University was at stake rather than simple right or wrong. The old bylaws made four absences from obligatory military duties a basis for suspension and required the Faculty to accept valid excuses. But the cadet officers had absented themselves from duties that were not obligatory, and an apology rather than an excuse was demanded. The writer criticized the rebels for not resigning before abandoning their posts and thought they should have tendered the apology demanded. The justice of the students' cause, he added, and the fact that revolt was practically their only remedy should at least require rescinding of the rules before the students were compelled to apologize for their hasty action. It would only be fair to give the students an apology before requiring one for an act caused by wrongs inflicted.[99]

[97] "Faculty Record," II, Feb. 17, 1880.
[98] *Ibid.*, Feb. 23-24, 1880; *Illini*, March, 1880.
[99] Champaign *Times*, Feb. 28, 1880.

The *Vindicator,* a scurrilous four-page publication, appeared on February 24, the day after the Faculty refused to reconsider the expulsions. Perhaps disaffected students would have issued a clandestine sheet even if the campus newspaper had been a forum of free expression. In this anonymous paper, probably printed on the *Illini* press, angry youths lashed the entire Faculty for twisting truth and using power unjustly, and boldly ridiculed individual professors. But the main attack centered on the "valiant major" who got the "gruff old doctor" to agree to curb the independence of the captains by giving only five commissions on the excuse

> That to the good and loyal
> Are honors only due
> And if you'd have a title royal
> Their bidding you must do.

Other verses charged Dinwiddie with laming Doctor John, but the students did not exculpate Gregory. A poet acknowledged the effectiveness of Gregory's appeal to parents: the youth's sire, mad as fire, said that if

> I conspire
> He will raise me ten times higher
> Than the Methodist church spire,
> Doctor John, Doctor John.

The *Vindicator* denounced autocracy. It invited students to apply to Regent Jeremiah Mickelby Gab for admission to the Royal Russian University and termed Gregory a "snivelling old lump of perdition" who made students apologize for not standing still to be kicked. Moreover, the paper struck personal blows. It defined a Regent as "A man who builds his house of cheap bricks, bought at reduced rates, on pretense they are for state purposes, and then denies it before a committee of the legislature." The *Vindicator* called for "Faculty who will work for the interest of the University and not for their own interest." It congratulated Professor Greenhalgh and Louisa Whistletricker on their marriage.[100] These attacks reveal the type of gossip which was circulating.

On March 1 the six involuntarily dismissed students requested readmission. With some misgivings the Faculty readmitted the

---

[100] The only copy I have found is in the Talbot Papers.

penitent petitioners to full standing in their classes, but without changing existing records. Authorities immediately granted Harden leave of absence until commencement.[101] Meanwhile, Governor Oglesby put in a rare appearance at a Board meeting which reformed the Military Department. Gregory recommended that military drill be confined to freshmen and sophomores, a change he now claimed always to have wanted. He advised the election of student officers from only the sophomore and junior classes. He urged that commissions be awarded as special honors rather than regularly, and the Board ordered them recommended for merit on special examination by a Faculty committee. Lieutenant William T. Wood relieved Dinwiddie and facilitated reorganization, and an *Illini Extra* celebrated the ending of drill for juniors and seniors.[102]

In April the student body elected deposed cadet officers to the top offices in the College Government, a further slap at the Regent. On June 8 Gregory submitted his resignation. The Trustees accepted and made it effective the following September. No doubt "under the conditions all considered, *he was tired of his job*,"[103] as Burrill later explained, but the point is that students forced him to leave. Knowing that he was losing control over them, Gregory had allied with Dinwiddie to regain his authority. But his attempt to put a lid on the campus by new rules on military commissions placed cadets in a position they could not honorably accept. Loss of respect for Gregory perhaps emboldened the officers, prominent students who were active in the College Government, to defend their interests. Their actions precipitated events which Gregory handled unwisely.

Propriety prevented anyone from stating publicly the reasons for the resignation at the time, but in 1883 the Champaign County *Herald* said, "It was a coterie of smart alecks that drove Dr. Gregory away."[104] A student newspaper offered a better explanation in 1891. Gregory had shrewdly realized that the underlying cause of

[101] "Faculty Record," II, March 1, 5, 1880; June 6, 1881.
[102] *10th Report* (1881), 221, 224-25, 233; "Faculty Record," II, Feb. 19, 1880. *Illini Extra,* April, 1880.
[103] Thomas J. Burrill to Edmund J. James, May 16, 1914, Stephens Papers. See Gregory's note in "Faculty Record," II, June 4, 1880.
[104] June 14, 1883.

all the disturbance was his "mismanagement and unpopularity with the students," it asserted, and had therefore promptly resigned.[105] The circumstances of his departure ironically revealed that for all his apparent liberality Gregory was deeply committed to traditional authoritarianism and had found no solution to the persistent problem of student government. His personal failings no less than this thorny unresolved issue of higher education cost him an opportunity to remain at Illinois. But the clouds which darkened Gregory's exit must not be allowed to obscure the fact that during more than a decade as the first head of the institution Gregory had contributed significantly to defining the nature of the new American university.

[105] *Illini,* Feb. 21 [1891]. This bogus edition of the student newspaper revealed the oral tradition which a new generation of students entertained. They were making a case for the ouster of Regent Peabody.

CHAPTER SEVEN

A Question of Style

THE TASK OF SELECTING Gregory's successor challenged the governing body, but its members scarcely rose to the occasion. They needed a Regent who could resolve acute local problems — restless students, curricular sprawl, legislative parsimony, and public indifference — and at the same time constructively relate the University to the changing character of higher education in the United States. After Johns Hopkins opened in 1876, a new emphasis on graduate instruction and research became insistent. Moreover, undergraduate life throughout the nation altered in these years as the elective system and extracurricular activities made inroads on older collegiate ideals. At the same time enrollments in higher education soared.

Between 1870 and 1910 the number of college students rose four times faster than the total population.[1]

The Illinois Trustees presumably should have selected an educational leader who gave promise of guiding the University in light of the new forces at work. They named Selim H. Peabody Acting Regent on July 27, 1880, less than two months after Gregory resigned. Ostensibly they continued their search for a permanent head until the following March, when they finally elevated Peabody to the position at a salary of $3,000.[2] The appointment of the former faculty member is not readily understandable. The Trustees may consciously have selected him in order to reverse many of the directions set by Gregory, or because his success as a professor was fresh in their minds, or because he was simply the best person who would take the job. It does seem that the Illinois Trustees would not have chosen this particular man had they adequately acquainted themselves with his views, although it could be argued that in 1880 Peabody appeared to be an excellent head of the University and that no one could have predicted the collision which would hurl him from office eleven years later. The trouble is that we know little about this vital choice, for despite their power in determining the shape of American intellectual and cultural life, the boards which control higher education leave relatively little information about such matters for the historian to evaluate.

Reasonable familiarity with Peabody's career and ideas should have enabled the Trustees to anticipate much of his educational policy. Peabody was born in Rockingham, Vermont, on August 20, 1829, and traced his paternal ancestry back to the Francis Peabody who arrived at Plymouth Plantation in 1635.[3] His mother named him Selim after an Arab chieftain in a popular novel, Thomas Moore's *Lalla Rookh,* and the boy spent his early years in an austere New England parsonage. His father, Charles Hobart Peabody, was

[1] George Paul Schmidt, *The Liberal Arts College: A Chapter in American Cultural History* (New Brunswick, 1957), 182; S. Willis Rudy, "The 'Revolution' in American Higher Education, 1865-1900," *Harvard Educational Review,* XXI (Summer, 1951), 168.

[2] *10th Report* (1881), 248, 257, 361; *11th Report* (1882), 178.

[3] Katherine Peabody Girling, *Selim Hobart Peabody, a Biography* (Urbana, 1923), describes the life of her father.

a Baptist clergyman at Randolph, Massachusetts. Selim's parents intended him for the Lord, and gave the youth his first lessons out of the Bible. But his father's death in 1842 changed these plans. Luckily he got one year at Boston Latin School, paid for by a suitor of his mother, whose marriage to a poorer man temporarily ended the lad's formal instruction. Selim then worked for a farmer and a carpenter before abandoning manual labor, and, like countless other young men, briefly taught school. At 19, after joining the Baptist Church and pledging not to play games, he entered the University of Vermont.

Hard and persistent effort saw Peabody successfully through college. Shy and poor, he damaged his health by living on crackers and milk too often. He marched along the prescribed route of a traditional curriculum, excelled in mathematics and physical science, and in 1852 graduated third in his class. Along the way he made exciting discoveries of Shakespeare and Ruskin, and relished Littel's *Living Age,* a sort of highbrow *Reader's Digest.* Although Peabody made friends slowly, he joined the debating and glee clubs, and even affiliated with a secret Greek-letter fraternity, Sigma Phi. Upon graduating he married Mary Elizabeth Pangborn, an Episcopalian with a more cheerful disposition than his own.

He then began a career as a schoolteacher which lasted a quarter of a century. After serving in Vermont high schools, Peabody took a position in a polytechnical college in Philadelphia, where he joined with Republicans in support of Frémont for President in 1856. But the Panic of 1857 drove him west, and he settled in Eau Claire, Wisconsin, on a town lot given him by a relative. Peabody became a teacher and principal in Fond du Lac and Racine high schools, and in 1863 won election as President of the Wisconsin State Teachers' Association. From 1865 to 1878 he taught physics at Central High School in Chicago, except for the years 1871-74, when he was Professor of Mathematics, Physics, and Civil Engineering in Massachusetts Agricultural College, a post he resigned over a dispute with the school's President. Wherever he lived, Peabody threw himself into the religious, civic, and cultural life of his community.

During these years Peabody published a number of books for

youngsters. He designed *The Elements of Astronomy* (1869) for advanced high school students, and a series entitled *Cecil's Books of Natural History* for children. Named for the eldest of his four off-spring, the three small volumes were in a familiar genre, and the point is worth noting. A popular example of the older type of natural history book which invested plants, animals, and objects with personality was *The Tragi-Comic History of the Burial of Cock Robin* (1821), but before Peabody wrote, Samuel Goodrich, using the pen name "Peter Parley," had reformed this genre with books which mirrored the division of natural history into separate sciences. Peabody's efforts — *Cecil's Book of Birds* (1869), *Cecil's Book of Insects* (1869), and *Cecil's Book of Beasts* (1872) — were in this vein.

In 1878, after long service in secondary schools, Peabody became Professor of Mechanical Engineering and Physics at the University, a post he had declined a decade earlier when the institution opened. He demonstrated effectiveness as a teacher, and grateful physics students presented him with a gold chain and inscribed charm when he resigned on February 1, 1880, to accept a literary job in New York.[4] There he compiled a three-volume anthology of writings by and about *Heroes and Patriots of America* and began editorial work on the multivolume *International Cyclopedia* published by Dodd, Mead and Co. He had just nicely settled into this work when the call arrived from Urbana.

Peabody's qualifications to head a university were considerable, but he did not excel in the public aspects of the position. Physically he made a good appearance at the age of 51. Bald, portly, and of medium height, Peabody possessed dark eyes and wore a short beard. He could meet and impress men of influence, and express himself precisely. Yet his pen lacked felicity and he acknowledged his lack of reputation as a speaker. His meaty public addresses smelled too much of the lamp. Even people who welcomed ornate rhetoric and rich biblical imagery must have groaned at his long and stilted productions. "Let me not weary you," he once told an audience, "with my too ambitious flight, with trite figures of gardens

[4] Gregory to Emory Cobb, Jan. 27, 1880, "Regents' Letterbook, 1879-1894"; *10th Report* (1881), 220; *Illini*, Feb., 1880.

and flowers and marching hosts. Let me not lose you in the dreamy air, lulled by gentle zephyrs, the senses saturated with the sweetness of the sensuous benediction."[5] And even more vital was his personal manner. Although essentially kindly and generous, he was reserved, even abrupt and austere. Most people saw only the cool outer crust of the man, and his style counted against him. This became increasingly the case after new classes of students no longer remembered him as a gifted teacher, and when the pressures and tensions of office accumulated.

An important source of Peabody's trouble lay in the intellectual rather than the personal realm. His deepest convictions ran counter to the drift of much contemporary opinion, and, right or wrong, he became increasingly out of step with his times. Peabody made the doctrine of the fundamental law the basis of his beliefs. This postulate had emerged as a foundation of the American democratic faith during the eighteenth century. It fused together belief in the law of God and the law of Nature, enabling Americans to insist that fixed and absolute truths were given for man's guidance by Revelation and a benevolent universe, both of which could be largely if not completely comprehended by reason. The first challenges to this doctrine appeared about the time Peabody assumed control at Illinois, when Darwin's influence led men like Justice Holmes, Charles Peirce, and Lester F. Ward to attack these notions. But no doubts troubled Peabody, who expounded the best thought of an earlier era, mainly in 11 baccalaureate sermons whose original manuscripts are neatly preserved.[6] He held that a natural law of divine origin reigned supreme in both the physical universe and the human will. Peabody thought that man could, in his effort to apprehend the world about him and to recognize the good, follow popular consent, reason, and conscience as far as they went. But each was in some degree inadequate. The philosophy that mankind acquired by its own efforts needed faith as its companion. The law of God obligated humans to obey the higher imperative, and this source behind the natural law was a more exacting master than the civil law. For

[5] Selim H. Peabody, "The Use of It," MS. of baccalaureate address, 1888, Peabody Papers.
[6] The manuscripts are in the Peabody Papers, as are the manuscripts of other addresses cited here.

Peabody there could be no ultimate recognition of good other than in "the word of God's truth and in the testimony of His Christ."[7]

Less open to new experience than Gregory, Peabody ignored rather than refuted either philosophical idealism as formulated by Hegelians and other post-Kantians on the one hand or evolutionary naturalism as taught by Darwinians on the other. He saw no conflict between faith and science, and regarded the methods of each as valid within its own realm. "What care I," he told seniors in 1882, "if I have a stone or an ape for my ancestor, if only a divine law hath produced me in either case according to the wise purpose of one whose laws were ever just and good."[8] In baccalaureate addresses he urged graduating classes to adhere closely to the example of Christ's life and work and to look for evidences of the divine will in choosing a vocation.[9]

These views gave Peabody a measure of serenity in meeting the intellectual crisis of the late nineteenth century, but they also made him anxious about the future of the Republic. A conservative who valued an existing social order which was undergoing rapid change, Peabody emphasized the dangers of immigration, urbanism, social stratification, organized labor, and Roman Catholicism rather than stressing the need for creative responses to new developments. Apart from naively recommending more education as the solution, he called for recognizing the supremacy of civil and divine law as the path to stability and order. Peabody shared the prevailing reverence for constituted authority without giving equal thought to its responsibility in meeting fresh challenges.[10]

His educational ideas stamp Peabody as conservative, though in the context of the times many considered him reactionary. He thought the training of mind should dominate all education so that mankind might be "uplifted into that nobler and higher sphere of

---

[7] Peabody, "And Their Eyes Were Opened," MS. of baccalaureate address, 1887.
[8] Peabody, "The Supremacy of Law," MS. of baccalaureate address, 1882.
[9] Peabody, "The Choice of an Occupation," MS. of baccalaureate address, 1885.
[10] See Peabody's writings, especially "I Pray . . . That Thou Shouldest Keep Them from the Evil," MS. of baccalaureate address, 1883; "The Duty of the State to Higher Education," MS. of address, 1885; "Render unto Caesar the Things Which Be Caesar's," MS. of baccalaureate address, 1886; *13th Report* (1887), 175-87; "A Citizen of No Mean City," MS. of baccalaureate address, 1890; "A Still, Small Voice," MS. of baccalaureate address, 1891.

thinking, in which the most glorious element of our human life and of our human thoughts reside [sic]."[11] Accordingly, he emphasized the "growth and culture of the mind" (the Yale Report had said "the discipline and furniture of the mind") as the one principle which should control the course of study.[12] In addition, Peabody wanted the schools to form character — to put pupils on the plane of manhood or womanhood.

These views underlay the Regent's criticism of the elective system. He introduced a new prescription into the curriculum at the University, an accomplishment that gained him a national reputation. The National Educational Association made him Chairman of its Committee on Higher Education, and the Committee's report to the annual meeting in 1888 on the elective system was Peabody's fullest statement on the subject. He distinguished between what he called the emotional and disciplinary value of studies. The former made the student's interest and happiness in his courses the criterion of choice. The latter held that each separate group of studies had distinctive pedagogic value in developing mental powers or faculties, and that it was worthwhile "to strip to the conflict, to wrestle, to buffet, and to win and triumph after hard struggles and persevering, vigorous effort."[13] Peabody of course saw the real value of studies as disciplinary. Pupils should follow a curriculum arranged by experienced professionals rather than by inexperienced schoolboys. His underlying premise — the faculty psychology — was that of the Yale Report. Peabody assumed that the characteristics of the human intellect were similar in all normally constituted persons, and therefore college curricula should be arranged on the assumption of the unities of the human soul and mind. But even if one concluded that each intellect was individual, students were unprepared to judge wisely the mental training which was best for them. A man's mind was worth far more than his property, which the law allowed one to control only after reaching his majority. The same

[11] Peabody made this statement in commenting on Calvin M. Woodward, "The Function of the Public School," National Educational Association, *Journal of Proceedings and Addresses, 1887* (Salem, Mass., 1888), 236-37.
[12] Peabody, "The American University," MS. of Anniversary Day address, 1882.
[13] [Selim H. Peabody, Chairman], Report of the Committee on Higher Education, "The Elective System in Colleges," National Educational Association, *Journal of Proceedings and Addresses, 1888* (Topeka, 1888), 270.

principle should rule mental development. The report drew praise from opponents of electives, especially William Torrey Harris, the nation's foremost Hegelian and a leading educational theorist. As U.S. Commissioner of Education from 1889 to 1906, Harris enjoyed a good vantage point for espousing these views.[14]

Both Peabody and Harris were leading critics of the educational value of manual training and shop instruction, a subject frequently debated at NEA gatherings in the 1880's. The Illinoisian regarded books rather than plows or engines as the proper tools of learning, thus challenging the philosophy behind the motto "Learning and Labor." As Chairman of the NEA's Committee on Technological Education in 1886, Peabody issued a report which acknowledged the *economic* value of shop work in producing better workers while denying its *educational* value. He insisted that the proper purpose of schools was *pedagogic,* to make larger, stronger, and nobler men.[15] But the tide was running against Peabody, and when his own state pioneered in 1884 with two of the three new models of manual-training instruction, the head of the University became isolated from his constituency. In that year the Chicago Commercial Club organized the Chicago Manual Training School, a private venture; and the Baltimore School Board opened the first public manual-training school in the country. Peru, Illinois, decided to introduce manual-training courses into its high school, and that pattern became most common in the United States.[16] These developments led Peabody to criticize the high schools. He charged that in adapting their programs to the majority, they forgot to prepare

[14] *Ibid.,* 276-80; see also Lawrence A. Cremin, *The Transformation of the School: Progressivism in American Education, 1876-1957* (New York, 1961), 14-20. But Harris by no means agreed fully with Peabody. When he congratulated Andrew S. Draper on being chosen President of the University, he added that the school had not previously fulfilled its true function because it had been "run by men who had wrong ideas concerning the direction of the work." Harris to Draper, May 23, 1894, Draper Personal Letters.

[15] [Selim H. Peabody, Chairman], Report of the Committee on Technological Education, "Pedagogical Value of the School Workshop," National Educational Association, *Journal of Proceedings and Addresses, 1886* (Salem, Mass., 1887), 305-12, discussed 312-17; Peabody, "The Value of Tool-Instruction as Related to the Active Pursuits in Which Pupils May Subsequently Engage," MS. of address, 1889, published in National Educational Association, *Journal of Proceedings and Addresses, 1889* (Topeka, 1889), 98-103.

[16] Cremin, *The Transformation of the School,* 29-32.

a minority for college by furnishing "training, discipline, culture."[17]

Such a statement, hardly calculated to win popularity, illustrated Peabody's conception of leadership in a democracy. He left no discussion of the issue, but his whole career refuted the pernicious doctrine that a leader must always follow the people. Aware that the University had to retain public confidence, he also had the higher wisdom to realize that the people did not always know what it wanted. For Peabody leadership was not the art of administering a popular consensus but the duty of guiding society to a place of light. The only unforgivable crime for a democratic leader was to reject the will of the majority after it had been clearly expressed. Peabody therefore made the University a rock rather than a weather vane, and he possessed the requisite candor and courage for the task, even if he elevated honesty to the point of tactlessness. His failure in the presidency unfortunately discredited his theory of leadership and his policies.

Both Peabody's educational ideas and his conception of leadership underlay the University's relations with the public. Although an economic conservative, Peabody strongly believed in the state's responsibility for fostering education at both the school and collegiate levels. He argued that national greatness depended more on the intelligence of the people than on material wealth, and that the federal and state governments were better at offering quality education at lower cost than was any private agency. He therefore wanted increased centralization in order to make the entire national educational system more effective.[18]

But he also wanted the people of Illinois to shoulder their own burden. The Empire State of the Mississippi Valley, Illinois ranked fourth in the Union in population (exceeded only by New York, Pennsylvania, and Ohio) and took a front place in material wealth. Yet it gave paltry aid to the University. Every adjoining state except Kentucky furnished more money for higher education than

---

[17] Peabody, "The Relations of High Schools to Colleges," MS. of address, 1889.
[18] Peabody, "The Duty of the State to Higher Education," MS. of address, 1885, printed with additional information under the title "The Duty of the State Towards Its University," *12th Report* (1885), 57-72. See also Peabody's article, "Illinois, Its Present and Future Greatness," *ibid.*, 73-85.

did Illinois. The ratio of students who attended college to the total population was lower in Illinois than in the nation, even when the figures included about a third of the whole number who attended colleges outside of the state. Illinois was honor-bound by reason of accepting federal aid in 1818 and 1862 to maintain at least one outstanding center of higher learning, and yet she had never done so. Peabody's demands were small: "If the farmers of Illinois would permit the University to choose one fair ear of corn, or its equivalent, from each acre of land in corn or grain in the State," he said, "the proceeds would more than twice pay the present annual expense of this institution." Peabody urged the state to support at least one public university that would rival Harvard or Yale, Oxford or Paris, Halle or Berlin, within the lifetime of students then enrolled.[19]

The General Assembly of course did not appropriate on a scale to realize that goal, but nevertheless Peabody did relatively well at Springfield. In 1881 he asked for $55,000 and received $41,300, a sum that considerably exceeded Gregory's largest appropriations (apart from capital funds), which were $29,500 in 1877 and $24,500 in 1879. Gregory's grants were for closely specified purposes like maintenance and taxes, and never for faculty salaries. Peabody, however, obtained $11,400 for current expenses of instruction during the biennium, thereby getting the General Assembly for the first time to recognize its obligation to finance costs of teaching in the University.[20]

During each of the next three biennia the University received an average of slightly over $54,000, with an average of about $28,000 for faculty salaries. In his last two biennia, at a time when Peabody's popularity was low and declining, the University did even better. The state appropriated $68,500 in 1889, including $10,000 for a Drill Hall and $40,000 for costs of instruction. Two years later the General Assembly voted $149,300 for Champaign-Urbana. Much of the total went for construction — $14,100 for a

[19] *Ibid.*, 66-72 (the quotation is at p. 70); see also Peabody, "Report of the University of Illinois," in Superintendent of Public Instruction of the State of Illinois, *Nineteenth Biennial Report* (Springfield, 1892), 15.

[20] *10th Report* (1881), 251, 259; *11th Report* (1882), 163, 174, 182; *Illinois Reports* (1882), I, 9; *Illinois Laws* (1881), 30-31.

State Laboratory of Natural History and $70,000 for a Natural History Building. That left $65,200 for general purposes, of which $40,000 was for faculty salaries. This $65,200 represented a 162 per cent increase over Gregory's last state appropriation.[21]

Peabody's record suggests that state aid does not depend mainly on presidential popularity. Each head of the University may expect larger grants than his predecessor, but the real explanation for enlarged state aid at the end of Peabody's tenure was the fresh stimulus from the federal government. The Hatch Act of 1887 provided $15,000 a year to organize and conduct an Agricultural Experiment Station, and the Morrill Land Grant College Act of 1890 brought $15,000 a year, a sum that was to increase $1,000 annually until it leveled off at $25,000 each year. It may be too strong to say that the United States shamed Illinois into supporting its University, but certainly the state pump flowed more freely after federal priming. The year 1890 marked a critical turning point in the financial history of the institution.

Peabody assumed responsibility for publicizing the University, but it would be hazardous to attribute any increase in appropriations or student numbers to these efforts. However, the attempt to win friends now became more systematic. On September 14, 1881, the Board authorized employment of a person "to correspond for and in the interest of the University with the press of the State." The Trustees asked the faculty members to furnish this individual with reports of all experiments and matters of public interest pertaining to the University and appropriated $200 for the work. Four years later the governing body appointed a standing Committee on Publications to supervise all publications and advertisements.[22]

Peabody lacked Gregory's instinct for publicity, but he perpetuated all the previously used techniques of gaining recognition. He did not avoid the speaker's platform, though his manner was less impressive than that of his predecessor. In the campaign for students and status, the University continued to rely on printed media.

[21] These conclusions are drawn from the *11th* through the *16th Reports* and from the *Illinois Laws* (1883), 14; (1885), 28; (1887), 71, 76; (1889), 31, 54; (1891), 27, 60.
[22] *11th Report* (1882), 195 (the source of the quotation); *13th Report* (1887), 76.

Officials now advertised in Indiana, Nebraska, and Missouri newspapers as well as in the *Nation* and *Century* magazines. But most of their publicity budget bought space in the Chicago *Tribune* and *Inter-Ocean*, and the largest single sum went to the *Illini*. Authorities mailed the campus newspaper to county superintendents and high schools throughout the state. They also advertised by means of a framed placard sent to every county seat and an illuminated certificate sent to each accredited school. The pressure to tell a good story led to exaggeration in the catalogue, which ran to nearly 200 pages by 1890. In that year Peabody asked that its descriptions be modified so as to express "more clearly the actual present condition of things."[23]

The University revealed much about itself by continued participation in exhibitions. In the winter of 1881 Peabody sent to the Capitol in Springfield two carloads of material which portrayed the practical work at Champaign-Urbana. The display contained nothing from the College of Literature and Science. To be sure, in later years the institution also exhibited at educational gatherings, but reserved its main efforts for events like the World's Industrial and Cotton Exposition, which opened at New Orleans in December, 1884. At the Paris Exposition in 1889 a collection of photographs and descriptions of course work won the University a silver medal.

The quest for public favor transcended these direct publicity methods devised in earlier years. The subtle influence of the constant pressure to gain popular sympathy was best demonstrated in the University's efforts to portray itself as a nonsectarian Christian school and as no hotbed of infidelity.

The new impetus for a program of advertising arose from University alumni, who became organized and powerful at Illinois as elsewhere in the late nineteenth century. In June, 1884, a committee from the Alumni Association conferred with the Board of Trustees about better advertising the University of Illinois, and that fall some 50 graduates and former students organized the Chicago Association of State University Alumni.[24] Their goals were to promote social intercourse and to advance the welfare of their alma

[23] *15th Report* (1890), 129.
[24] *12th Report* (1885), 236; *Illini,* Oct. 6, 1884.

mater, both of which typified the efforts of American college graduates to institutionalize fellowship and to elevate a school in every
respect. If the graduates did not stress academic improvements
alone, neither did they mention athletics. Officers of the Chicago
Association were Stephen A. Reynolds (class of 1872), Charles G.
Neely ('80), Charles B. Gibson ('77), Archibald O. Coddington
('81), Judson F. Going (ex-'83: he had been expelled a day before
his graduation), and Ethan Philbrick ('81). James R. Mann ('76),
Francis M. McKay ('81), and Robert E. Orr ('82) were active
members. Early in 1885 the Chicago club announced the need to
raise the University's academic standards, attract more students and
money, and eliminate the word "Industrial" from the official title.[25]

Efforts to change the University's name constituted the first
step in the Chicago club's campaign. By the 1880's practically all
land-grant institutions were trying to exchange the label "Agricultural," which misrepresented their functions and outlook, for a title
such as "State College" or "State University." The term "Industrial," used only by Illinois and one imitator, imposed an even
greater handicap than "Agricultural," for the public interpreted it
to mean either a reformatory or a charitable institution in which
compulsory manual labor figured prominently. The Regent received many letters asking him to admit children from shattered
homes, delinquents, and incorrigibles, and teach them a trade while
keeping them from evil influences.[26]

At Illinois the attempt to alter the University's name went
back to the late 1870's. Gregory had asked the Board to seek cor-
rection in 1878, and the next year a bill for this purpose passed the
House by 93 to 10 but failed in the Senate through a supposed legal
objection. Students reopened the issue in 1880 by voting 235 to 20
to change the name, and the *Illini* editor urged them to take the
matter to Springfield if the Faculty did not.[27] But Peabody committed himself to the reform, even though it aroused bitter resistance

[25] *Illini*, Jan. 19, 1885.
[26] Earle D. Ross, *Democracy's College: The Land-Grant Movement in the Formative Stage* (Ames, Iowa, 1942), 181-82; Selim H. Peabody, "Report of the
Illinois Industrial University," in Superintendent of Public Instruction of the
State of Illinois, *Fourteenth Biennial Report* (Springfield, 1883), 14-16.
[27] *9th Report* (1878), 107-8; *Illinois House Journal* (1879), 385, 738; *Illinois
Senate Journal* (1879), 791; *Illini,* Dec. 15, 1880; Jan. 19, 1881.

in farm circles. Horticultural organizations accepted the change, but the agricultural press steadily denounced the proposal as indicating lack of sympathy for industrial education and a covert desire to transform the character of the University. Typical of the complaints was the *Western Rural* (Chicago), which looked to the time "when our Harvards will take on the character of the industrial institutions" rather than the reverse. Early in 1885 the Illinois State Board of Agriculture refused by a vote of 14 to 5 to delete the word "Industrial" from the official name of the University.[28]

But the Chicago club, a small group concentrated in the state's metropolis, played David to the agricultural Goliath. Late in 1884 the Board of Trustees requested the General Assembly to act, and on February 25 a bill, probably written by Judson F. Going, was introduced into the House. It passed by 106 to 21 on May 21 and went to the Senate, where a fierce battle opened. Peabody could have retreated in the face of the political opposition mustered there, but he wrote every senator to explain that the name actually constituted a serious obstacle to success and to show that he had developed the technical side of the University. He thought Illinois, which had made scientific education the head of the corner, was as deserving of a noble name as institutions which had built on the cornerstone of classical learning. Peabody also communicated these ideas to Jonathan B. Turner, whose name was so intimately linked with "industrial" education. Though the upper chamber passed the bill by a vote of 28 to 14 on June 10, 20 diehards in that body publicly denounced the outcome. They regarded the spirit behind the change as un-American and declared that deletion of the word "Industrial" robbed the school of its identity and put a stigma on labor. But on June 19 the corporate name of the institution legally became the "University of Illinois." Some old friends of agricultural and industrial education now abandoned all hope in the Urbana enterprise, but the Trustees widely publicized the new name and Peabody was not alone in believing that it stimulated enrollments.[29]

[28] *Western Rural*, Aug. 30, 1884; Illinois State Department of Agriculture, *Transactions for 1885*, n.s., XV (Springfield, 1886), 16.
[29] *Illinois House Journal* (1885), 770; *Illinois Senate Journal* (1885), 898, 937; *13th Report* (1887), 44-45; Peabody to Turner, June 13, 1885, Jonathan B. Turner Papers, Illinois Historical Survey, University of Illinois; *Illinois Laws* (1885), 252.

A proposal to raise endowments for the University was the second step in the Chicago club's program. After corresponding with leading colleges and universities about their practices, President Gibson informed the Trustees in March, 1886, of the alumni group's desire to solicit funds for special purposes designed to improve the University as a center of broad and liberal education. He made no mention of athletics. Gibson petitioned the Trustees to prescribe rules regulating the acceptance of endowments, and the Board appointed a five-man committee to confer with the club on the matter.[30]

Power relationships constituted a third and more significant step in the Alumni Association's betterment drive. The alumni, led by the Chicago group, wanted to reform the method of choosing the University's governing body. Supreme authority over American institutions of higher learning had become lodged in the hands of lay bodies rather than faculties well before the American Revolution, and thereafter both law and custom sanctioned this method of control. Ordinarily the governor appointed trustees in state institutions and board members co-opted their own successors in private colleges and universities. These bodies made the president *their* agent, and the faculty possessed only the rights of employees or whatever power higher authority permitted. The 1867 Organic Act which established Illinois Industrial University and the reorganization act of 1873 both perpetuated this arrangement. The latter authorized the Governor to appoint nine trustees to staggered six-year terms, and together with himself and the President of the State Board of Agriculture they constituted the University's supreme tribunal.

But Illinois alumni began demanding representation on the governing body in the 1880's. Their clamor reflected a national movement to admit graduates to a share in college government which took definite shape after 1865. In that year the Massachusetts legislature passed an act transferring the election of the Harvard Board of Overseers from itself to the graduates of the College. At least 30 colleges and universities, presumably all private institutions, followed suit before 1900, in which year Princeton, after long resis-

[30] *13th Report* (1887), 96-97.

tance, increased the size of its board of control by five, who were to be elected by alumni. The state universities continued in their old ways, however, with only Michigan (1850), Nebraska (1875), and Colorado (1876) providing for popular election of trustees.[31]

Illinois graduates, having tried unsuccessfully to get one of their number appointed to the Board, devised a new strategy in June, 1882. The Alumni Association nominated men from the northern, central, and southern divisions of the state — Frederick L. Hatch ('73), Samuel A. Bullard ('78), and George F. Kenower ('75) — and circulated petitions asking Governor Cullom to name one. In December Cullom appointed Kenower to fill a seat vacated by resignation.[32] A Belleville teacher, Kenower proved a disappointment because he attended only a few meetings of the Trustees. In 1883 Sylvester M. Millard, a Chicago lawyer, succeeded Emory Cobb as President of the Board, and before he surrendered the position in 1889 the alumni had gained new and lasting influence in that body. Governor Oglesby appointed Francis M. McKay, an Evanston school principal, to take the seat resigned by George A. Follansbee in 1886, and the following June George R. Shawhan, class of 1875 and Champaign County Superintendent of Schools, took office by appointment.

But the alumni wanted representation by legal right rather than gubernatorial grace. No one cared more about the University than its graduates, who believed that popular election of trustees every two years would be an excellent device for publicizing the institution. Yet the alumni of other state universities shared these concerns for welfare and esteem. Why, then, did the Illinois group insist on effecting a change rarely achieved by graduates of other state universities?[33] The answer must lie in the antagonism between Peabody and his foes, and the group of activists concentrated in the Chicago club of alumni was the most potent of the latter. For

[31] Samuel H. Ranck, "Alumni Representation in College Government," *Education*, XXII (Oct., 1901), 107, 109; Edward C. Elliott and M. M. Chambers, comps., *Charters and Basic Laws of Selected American Universities and Colleges* (New York, 1934), 129, 339, 367.
[32] *Illini*, Oct. 28, 1882.
[33] Elliott and Chambers reported in 1934 that Illinois was one of five American state universities whose governing board members were elected by popular vote. See *Charters and Basic Laws*, 229.

reasons which will be shown, most alumni and students became increasingly dissatisfied with Peabody starting about 1886. He favored prescribed courses and academic excellence, regarded fraternities and athletics as threats to institutional purpose, and had the disciplinarian's love for what was technically called a "quiet term." His opponents held his style as an educator against him even before they concluded that his ouster was essential to the establishment at Urbana of their model of a first-class university.

The Chicago club seized the initiative in obtaining alumni representation on the Board. Charles G. Neely introduced into the House on February 28, 1887, a bill which called for election of three trustees at each general election starting in 1888. The measure also returned the State Superintendent of Public Instruction to an ex officio seat on the Board and authorized the Trustees to appoint three members to an Executive Committee. Stephen A. Reynolds guided the proposal to a 36 to 2 victory in the Senate in April, and the House adopted the final version by 97 to 3 on May 27. Governor Oglesby allowed the bill to become law without signing it.[34]

Peabody resolutely opposed the reform, although the Board itself took only passive interest. He argued that the change would take the University into politics. To buttress his view he obtained supporting statements from ex-Governor Cullom and Governor Oglesby, and a testimonial from President James B. Angell that a similar plan had worked badly in Michigan.[35] These gestures, which may have convinced a few legislators, demonstrated surprising political naiveté. As every schoolboy knew, the University was already in politics up to the hilt. The dispute really centered on the relative merits of two different methods of choosing the policy-makers of the University, an issue on which reasonable men might disagree.

Under the old political method power rested in the hands of the Governor. The chief executive could of course make his appointments for political purposes, as the *Illini* charged Cullom with

---

[34] Francis M. McKay to Allan Nevins, Aug. 3, 1916; James E. Armstrong to Franklin W. Scott, Nov. 12, 1918, both in the Carl Stephens Papers; *Illinois House Journal* (1887), 335, 1050; *Illinois Senate Journal* (1887), 435, 654; *Illinois Laws* (1887), 306.

[35] Allan Nevins, *Illinois* (New York, 1917), 122.

doing in 1881 when he had an eye on the U.S. Senate.[36] President Bullard of the Alumni Association complained that the Regent's office had long controlled the naming of trustees, and that Peabody regarded their power as limited to endorsing his policies.[37] Bullard probably exaggerated (it is hard to be sure; heads of universities rarely leave incriminating documents), but Gregory had whispered the names of favorites into the Governor's ear and Peabody may have done likewise. It was hardly a criminal offense. Whatever its weaknesses, the old system had great merit for a public institution of higher learning. Voters could hold the Governor responsible, he could choose the most qualified residents of the state and not just alumni, and the staggered terms of the Board prevented him from making political tools of the Trustees while at the same time insuring that the governing body would roughly reflect the political temper of the state.

Under the new political method power came to rest in the hands of cliques in the Alumni Association. Ostensibly the law transferred the choice to the electorate, which voted on candidates nominated by each political party and listed on the ballot as Democrats or Republicans. But the offices were considered nonpartisan; contestants did not campaign for their posts, and neither the general merits nor the educational views of the runners came before the voters. Party preference governed the selection of trustees. Since Illinois was a bastion of Republicanism from 1887 until 1932, Republicans elected their entire slate of trustees in 17 out of 22 general elections in this period, and in two additional instances returned some candidates to the Board. The Democratic slate won only in 1890, 1892, and 1912. On both of the latter occasions Illinois gave its vote to Democratic presidents and governors (Grover Cleveland and John P. Altgeld in 1892; Woodrow Wilson and Charles S. Deneen in 1912), which made 1890 an exceptional year.[38]

Since the political tide floated trustees into office, the reform actually transferred power from the Governor to the group that

---

[36] *Illini,* March 16, 1881.
[37] Samuel A. Bullard, "Alexander McLean, Trustee," *Alumni Quarterly,* II (Jan., 1908), 6.
[38] I have drawn on a course paper written for me by Timothy Tucker, "University of Illinois Trustees' Elections: A Yardstick," for these details.

selected the candidates. The Alumni Association perhaps always intended that it should dominate the choice within each political party. Hence the new method was in fact less responsible to the electorate than the old, although it could be paraded as democratic. As a consequence the change had a narrowing influence on the University. It tended to make the ideal trustee a conventionally successful graduate who was in good standing with the Alumni Association. In 1888 incumbents Francis M. McKay, Samuel A. Bullard, and Alexander McLean won election to the Board, and soon McKay, Bullard, and the Chicago club were agitating for Peabody's removal from office.

Peabody's main goals for the University of Illinois grew logically out of his basic educational ideas. Above all he wanted to gain academic distinction for the school. To do this he stressed the need to offer students an *education* which would prepare them for careers of service to society. Peabody insisted that technical studies or any instruction designed merely to *train* individuals for earning a better living was not a college's noblest function. "A fatal error will have been committed if their training has been confined to the technical studies which, however useful they may be, are useful in only a narrow and limited scope."[39] These objectives prompted Peabody to raise admissions standards and severely curb the elective system.

Peabody worked quietly toward these ends, since he was undoing the legacy of his predecessor. Despite the state law of 1873 requiring each pupil to take at least one study each term which had direct bearing upon the industrial arts, Gregory had attempted to maintain elective freedom to the very end of his tenure. In June, 1880, he communicated to the Board the results of a plan devised to remedy the restricted freedom that resulted from requiring courses of study for degrees in several schools and colleges. To allow the largest liberty of choice consistent with state law and the University's credit, the Faculty had designed an eclectic course out of which students could make up a four-year program of 36 studies that entitled them to a certificate of graduation without a degree.

[39] Selim H. Peabody, "What Work Is Legitimate to the Institutions Founded on the Congressional Act of 1862," *11th Report* (1882), 55-63. Peabody read this paper at a convention of agriculturists in Washington, D.C., on Jan. 11, 1882.

Gregory thought the state of Illinois would never permit its chief seat of learning to revert to "the antiquated narrowness of old-time Colleges, on any such plea as the need to guard idle and worthless students from the consequences of their indolence."[40]

But Peabody deplored the laxity which enabled students to choose their own courses. The plans of undergraduates were vague and shifting, he thought, and students habitually avoided difficult studies; therefore he allowed pupils to choose only between courses of study and not between specific subjects. Once an individual enrolled in a school or college he faced a rigidly fixed program. At the same time, however, Peabody mitigated this system by urging, especially in the physical and biological sciences, the establishment of general as well as specialized introductory courses.

A number of factors conditioned the academic progress of the University. Peabody inherited an institution which lacked internal balance, and for years he combatted the suspicion that the University emphasized classics and literature by portraying the school as primarily a scientific and technical center. As a result the College of Literature and Science lost strength. Registrations fell from 33 per cent of the student body in 1881-82 to 22 per cent in 1890-91.[41] Peabody realized the gravity of the situation, and in 1886 announced that the College of Literature and Science was the one which needed "the most earnest fostering care."[42] The technical areas advanced unevenly. The College of Natural Science held its own, for chemists and teachers of natural science were in demand. The College of Agriculture languished, while student enrollments made the College of Engineering the largest in the University.

Throughout Peabody's administration the Faculty increased in size but remained relatively impotent in formulating policy. During the Regent's first year 15 full professors constituted the core of a staff of 28, and in his last year there were 24 full professors, two assistant professors, six instructors, and seven assistants on the teaching faculty. Theoretically the bylaws gave the Faculty control over

[40] *10th Report* (1881), 232, 237 (the source of the quotation).
[41] Peabody compiled statistics with a passion, and those pertaining to enrollment are scattered throughout his reports to the Board of Trustees and to the State Superintendent of Public Instruction. See especially *16th Report* (1892), 52, and Superintendent of Public Instruction, *Nineteenth Biennial Report*, 6-7.
[42] *13th Report* (1887), 139.

studies and discipline, but the President had his way on these and other matters. Perhaps the heavy teaching load — it averaged 19 hours a week in 1882[43] — contributed to the result, but the Regent's power to hire and fire no doubt weighed more heavily. The atmosphere cannot have been healthy, and in 1888 it was widely rumored that several professors were about to resign.[44]

The size of the student body remained consistently low during most of Peabody's tenure. During his first year registration fell to 379, after exceeding 400 in the two previous years. Total enrollment remained at an average of about 350 until late in Peabody's administration and then rose steadily, going from 377 in 1887-88 to 519 in 1890-91. The student body topped 500 for the first time in the winter term of 1891 and caused great rejoicing.

The sources of students shifted somewhat in this decade. The University continued to gather nearly two-thirds of its pupils from the industrial classes, but the percentage coming from farm homes fell from 52 to 45, while that coming from parents in mechanical pursuits rose from 12 to 19. At the same time students with fathers in mercantile activities fell from 23 to 18 per cent, while those from professional families rose from 13 to 18 per cent.[45] Women constituted about 21 per cent of the student body until 1886-87, after which they averaged about 16 per cent during the rest of Peabody's administration.[46]

The sluggish growth of the student body must be projected against the rapid expansion of collegiate enrollments then taking place throughout the country. Peabody did not openly worry about quantity if at all. Trustee McKay held him responsible for low registration, and the Chicago club of alumni concluded that Peabody's removal was essential to the University's progress just as the number of matriculants began soaring.[47] Peabody may have figured importantly in the matter, but many reasons account for the

[43] *12th Report* (1885), 171.
[44] *Illini,* Dec. 17, 1888.
[45] Superintendent of Public Instruction of the State of Illinois, *Sixteenth Biennial Report* (Springfield, 1886), 11. The figures compare the period 1868-82 with the period 1882-86.
[46] Superintendent of Public Instruction, *Nineteenth Biennial Report,* 7.
[47] Francis M. McKay to Allan Nevins, Aug. 3, 1916, Stephens Papers; R. E. Orr to Charles H. Shamel, March 27, 1891, Shamel Papers.

University's failure to become bigger at an equal pace with other institutions. Costs were not a leading factor, for tuition was now free in all University classes, and fees were low ($105 for a four-year course — much less than at Michigan, Sheffield, Columbia, or M.I.T.).[48] Unfortunately, however, the proportion of Illinois students who attended any college or university in the state was below the national ratio of college students to the total population. The public-school system of the state prepared very few students for college. The average Illinois high school in the mid-1880's had 80 students and 2.8 poorly prepared teachers, and only 70 per cent of the school-age population was enrolled in school in 1890. In that year official figures reported 208 high schools, but Peabody thought only 75 or 80 deserved the name.[49]

Not surprisingly, the system of examination and accreditation did not link the schools and the University. The schools used this Jacob's ladder to gain status for themselves rather than to prepare pupils for the University. In the seven years before 1883, accredited high schools sent only 156 students to the institution. Moreover, 118 of these came from Champaign and Urbana, and 18 schools on a list of over 30 sent no pupil to the state center of learning.[50] After reappraising the system in 1883, the Faculty dropped the examining schools except where staff members knew the principal. They decided also to inspect all accredited schools when the principal changed, except when the new principal came from an accredited school. The Faculty limited the effectiveness of high school graduation diplomas to one year after issue, and made them worthless for admission to the College of Literature and Science unless they certified that the applicant had the requisite Latin. In addition, the University required accredited schools to file annual reports.[51] Under these rules the list of accredited schools grew, with Peabody himself doing much of the inspecting. In 1890 graduates of 58 high schools could enter any college without examination if they presented their

[48] *12th Report* (1885), 21, 168.
[49] Superintendent of Public Instruction, *Sixteenth Biennial Report,* 251-55; *Eighteenth Biennial Report* (Springfield, 1891), xxix.
[50] Superintendent of Public Instruction of the State of Illinois, *Fifteenth Biennial Report* (Springfield, 1884), 13.
[51] "Faculty Record," II, Oct. 19, Nov. 23, 1883.

diplomas within a year after receiving them. Graduates of an additional 22 high schools could enter all colleges except Literature and Science on the same terms.

Although public schools furnished Urbana few students, the University refused to accredit private schools. The Faculty originally devised this policy in 1879 and applied it when St. Mary's Parochial School sought accreditation in 1884. Two years later the Board explicitly approved this course after denying accreditation to Bunker Hill Academy. Most of the private schools in Illinois, which in 1890 numbered 1,000 and enrolled over 100,000 students, were Roman Catholic institutions. Nothing better demonstrated the University's basic Protestantism than the erection of a barrier against the graduates of the rapidly growing parochial schools.[52]

The lack of satellites required the University to supply its own students for matriculation. Accordingly, in the spring of 1881 the Board rescinded an earlier decision to terminate the Preparatory School at the end of that year. Peabody established a curriculum for students headed for the three technical colleges which contained two terms each of algebra, geometry, and English, and one each of physiology, physics, and botany. Pupils bound for the College of Literature and Science modified this program by substituting Latin for English and also Greek for science if they intended to study ancient languages.[53]

The Preparatory School classes were simply a necessary fact of life. Their ranks averaged about 100 persons a year, by far the largest single group within the student body, and constituted the best source of University material. Members were mature — at one point the average age was 19.5[54] — and included many graduates of unaccredited schools as well as young men who considered the academy at Urbana the most suitable place to resume interrupted educations. Peabody recruited able teachers for the prep students, who displayed great vigor and earnestness. Officials continued to talk about discontinuing a department which had no proper place in the University, but it had sunk deep roots.

[52] *Ibid.*, Sept. 9, 1884; *13th Report* (1887), 86, 94; Superintendent of Public Instruction, *Eighteenth Biennial Report,* xxiii.
[53] *10th Report* (1881), 222, 225; *11th Report* (1882), 178; "Faculty Record," II, April 22, 1881; Feb. 2, 1883.
[54] Superintendent of Public Instruction, *Eighteenth Biennial Report,* 94.

Agricultural education remained in the doldrums during the 1880's, and deep disappointment with the agricultural operations of the land-grant colleges prevailed. Everywhere the number of students enrolled in agricultural courses remained low, and with good reason. Farmers could afford to indulge their suspicion of science as long as they cultivated extensively rather than intensively, and obtained as much new knowledge from agricultural journals and the reports of state experiment stations as their sons brought home from agricultural colleges. Moreover, economic incentives to farm or study agriculture remained weak, for corn, cattle, and hogs sold cheap, and persons trained as chemists, machine designers, and railroad builders commanded better jobs and wages than educated agriculturists.

But the foundations of a new era arose at the end of the decade in the Hatch Act (1887), the American Association of Agricultural Colleges and Experiment Stations (AAACES) (1887), and the second Morrill Act (1890). Gregory and Flagg had been particularly instrumental in setting in motion at the Convention of Friends of Agricultural Education in 1871 the forces that produced these results, although Peabody and Morrow did not sustain Illinois' leadership. Their attitude toward research prevented their taking a very prominent role at the three national conventions which U.S. commissioners of agriculture called in the early 1880's to discuss the agricultural colleges and experiment stations and their link with the federal government. George B. Loring assembled the first meeting at Washington on January 10-18, 1882. Representatives of colleges and stations in 21 states and territories heard a number of papers emphasizing scientific investigations and the training of research workers. The delegates seemed agreed that these tasks were as much the duty of land-grant schools as teaching when Peabody rose to challenge the conclusion. He insisted on distinguishing between the two functions because in his opinion too many colleges believed they were derelict if they did not develop science, an attitude that led to the neglect of teaching. Although he emphasized this fruitless dichotomy in considering the work legitimate to the schools founded on the Morrill Act, Peabody acknowledged that experiments were appropriate and should be fostered if they assisted in instruction even indirectly. But if not, he added, let teachers "obey the law and TEACH."[55] Technical and practical studies, he went on to say, were not the noblest function of a college, and even Latin and Greek would not harm a farmer's boy. All this was true, but not what the agricultural delegates expected to hear. Morrow shared the conviction that the primary duty of the land-grant schools was to teach. Until experimentation developed a science of agriculture, however, the agricultural colleges possessed little worth teaching.

At a second agricultural convention sponsored by Loring in Washington on January 23-29, 1883, delegates from 29 states and one territory moved to foster science. They gave their endorsement to a congressional bill to establish agricultural experiment stations in connection with state agricultural colleges. Later, however, the colleges found the measure unsuitable because it regarded the stations virtually as branches of the U.S. Department of Agriculture. Accordingly, an amended bill introduced in 1884 by Congressman William Cullen of Illinois made the federally subsidized stations departments of the land-grant colleges.

Delegates from 28 states and three territories who attended a third agricultural convention at Washington called by Commissioner Norman J. Colman on July 8-9, 1885, unanimously endorsed a resolution declaring that the progress of American agriculture required federal aid and urged Congress to pass the Cullen Bill. The assembly authorized an executive committee to promote this goal, to plan another convention, and to form a permanent organization of the agricultural colleges. Peabody became a member of the six-man group headed by George W. Atherton, formerly of the Illinois faculty and at the time President of Pennsylvania State College. Atherton's committee cooperated with Colman, and Congress passed a bill named after William H. Hatch which President Cleveland signed on March 2, 1887. It provided $15,000 a year from the sale of public lands to each of the state experiment stations, most of which were organized as departments of land-grant colleges rather

[55] [U.S] Department of Agriculture, *Proceedings of a Convention of Agriculturists, Held in the Department of Agriculture, January 10th to 18th, 1882* (Washington, 1882), 57. The text of Peabody's address, "What Work Is Legitimate to the Institutions Founded on the Congressional Act of 1862," is also given in the *11th Report* (1882), 55-63.

than as independent agencies. The General Assembly accepted the law on May 11 and authorized the University's Board to organize and conduct an Agricultural Experiment Station. Representatives of the land-grant schools and experiment stations met in Washington on October 18-20, 1887, at the call of Atherton's committee, and formed the AAACES. The Association, whose first President was Atherton, initiated systematic cooperation between the colleges and federal agencies and between the colleges themselves.[56]

Meanwhile, the College of Agriculture at Urbana had nearly expired. It did have a staff. Morrow remained Dean, and had the assistance of a veterinary science teacher and professors in cognate areas. When Frederick W. Prentice resigned the former position in 1885 to practice medicine, a subject that he had taken leave from the University to study, Peabody felt the importance of veterinary science to the livestock interest of Illinois made it imperative to name a successor. He appointed Donald McIntosh, a Scottish-born graduate of the Toronto Veterinary College, who came from Kingston, Ontario, to take up the work on January 1, 1886. The College also had a course of study designed to give an intellectual training which would make the American farmer self-reliant, imaginative and adaptable, not a mere technician like his European counterpart. The program emphasized the basic studies closely related to agriculture — botany, chemistry, entomology, geology, physics, and zoology — and the application of principles, taught in courses covering the elements of agriculture, elements of horticulture, farm engineering and architecture, animal husbandry, history of agriculture and rural law, and landscape gardening. Drawing and the use of wood-working tools also constituted part of the offering, as did political economy, history (history of civilization and constitutional history), and philosophy (mental science and logic). Morrow considered scientific study a valuable discipline of the mind and opposed narrow practical education as a reflection of the strong materialistic strain in American life.[57]

[56] [U.S.] Department of Agriculture, *Proceedings of a Convention of Delegates from Agricultural Colleges and Experiment Stations Held at the Department of Agriculture, July 8 and 9, 1885* (Washington, 1885), 140; Alfred Charles True, *A History of Agricultural Education in the United States, 1785-1925*, U.S. Department of Agriculture, Misc. Pub. No. 36 (Washington, 1929), 206-11.
[57] George E. Morrow, "Agricultural Education," *Illini*, Feb., 1877.

But the College lacked students. There were 21 enrolled in 1881-82, the number rose to a peak of 29 in 1886-87, and fell to a low of 14 in 1889-90. The year after Peabody left it sank to 11. Even these figures overstate the real situation: only eight students graduated from the College in these years, and in 1890 not one out of 175 applicants for admission intended to study agriculture.[58] Most of the students attended the farmers' short course. Instituted after Morrow arrived in 1877, the one-year program featured elements of agriculture, agricultural engineering and architecture, animal anatomy and physiology, shop practice, rural economy, veterinary science, animal husbandry, history of agriculture and rural law, and entomology or landscape gardening. Students in even a greater hurry could spend only the winter term at Urbana studying farm management, stock-breeding, and animal diseases.[59]

This instant education failed to catch hold, and in his last two years Peabody experimented with agricultural preparatory courses in the hope of recruiting students at a tender age. He proposed a two-year junior course as the alternative to the regular agricultural course. Pupils were to combine agricultural and academic studies in their preparatory and freshman years.[60]

During this same period the University relinquished its leadership in agricultural extension. Morrow had helped revive the farmers' institutes in 1878, and with one exception they continued to be held annually at Urbana through 1885. By that time the attendance numbered less than 40 and Peabody called a halt. He thought the programs interfered with the regular duties of the University.[61] But Morrow, essentially a missionary of agricultural education, wanted the University to keep in touch with farmers. He desired joint action with the State Board of Agriculture, which had begun earlier in the decade to sponsor institutes throughout Illinois at which University professors spoke. Upon his urging, the Board of Trustees agreed to allow faculty members at no cost to the University to continue par-

---

[58] Superintendent of Public Instruction, *Nineteenth Biennial Report*, 6; *16th Report* (1892), 23.
[59] See, for example, the *Catalogue, 1884-85,* 41.
[60] *16th Report* (1892), 53-54.
[61] *Cultivator and Country Gentleman*, XLIX (1884), 146. Peabody had expressed his views on interference with regular collegiate duties in 1882. See *11th Report* (1882), 221.

Louisa C. Allen Gregory, head of the
School of Domestic Science.

Manly Miles, a pioneer professor of
agricultural science, in the early
1870's.

Willard C. Flagg, a member of the
Board of Trustees and a gifted organizer and director of agricultural
experimentation.

Illinois Industrial University Battalion, 1878.

Edward Snyder, commandant of the University Battalion 1873-78, and Dean of the College of Literature and Science until 1894.

Samuel W. Stratton in his cadet officer's uniform in the early 1880's. Stratton later taught physics at the University, became the first Director of the National Bureau of Standards, and served from 1923 to 1930 as President of the Massachusetts Institute of Technology.

Professor Nathan C. Ricker, a pioneer of American architectural education.

Lorado Taft, class of 1879 and later a famous American sculptor.

The College Government at work about 1877.

University Hall, with the Chemistry Laboratory (now Harker Hall) to the left, about 1887.

The chapel in University Hall, decorated for a special occasion, perhaps Class Day, in the 1880's.

Selim H. Peabody, second Regent of the University (1880-91).

The Layfield (boarding) Club in 1889.

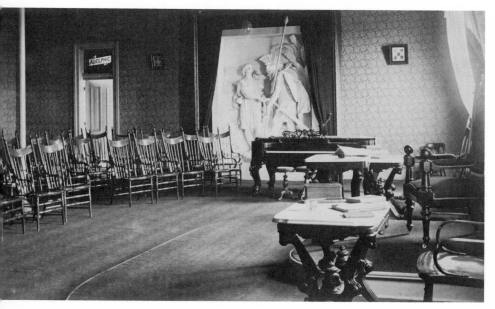

Adelphic Literary Society Hall about 1890.

Emory Cobb, a member of the Board of Trustees from 1867 to 1891 and for many years its President.

Francis M. McKay (1851-1925), class of 1881 and member of the Board of Trustees from 1885 to 1901.

The *Illini* office in the Mechanical Building and Drill Hall. Clarence A. Shamel, editor in 1890-91, is seated.

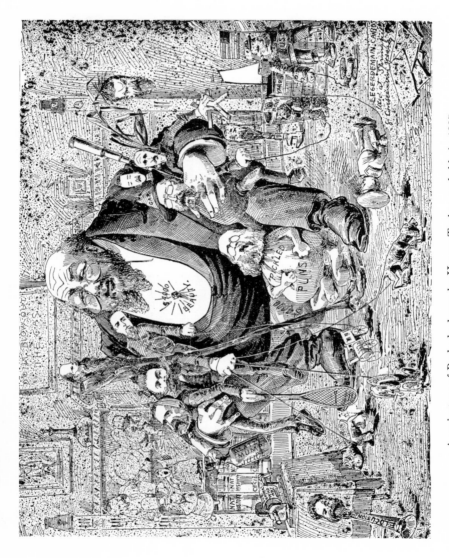

A caricature of Peabody drawn by Horace Taylor, probably in 1887.

ticipating in these extension programs held under the auspices of the State Board of Agriculture. Morrow alone made the job a significant part of his load. He attended 10 institutes in 1886 and 17 two years later, and the Board provided an assistant to free him for participation at these and at many additional farm gatherings each year. On Morrow's request for a definition of his primary obligations, the Board finally limited him to attendance at six representative agricultural institutes a year.[62]

The net result of two decades of agricultural education at Illinois was not encouraging, but federal aid from the Hatch Act provided the foundation for a new era. Late in 1887 the University's Trustees appointed Peabody and three professors as a Board of Directors for the Agricultural Experiment Station. But the next March the Trustees revised the directorate so as to bring the Station into closer relations with economic interests in Illinois. The new Board included the Regent, two University trustees, three professors, and nominees recommended by the State Board of Agriculture, the State Horticultural Society, and the State Dairymen's Association.[63]

The Station took over agricultural and allied research, mainly continuing investigations already under way. It laid out work in four areas: the cultivation of cereal grains and grasses, the feeding of animals for growth and meat product, the feeding of cattle for milk product, and the cultivation of small fruits and garden products. The directors divided the projects into those whose results might quickly impress the public and more lengthy ones. Occasionally other inquiries were added, an example being the study of ways to protect farm crops against chinch bugs. The Station's staff numbered about nine, including senior faculty members who gave part of their time to supervising the work. William L. Pillsbury of Springfield became Secretary of the Experiment Station on April 19, 1888, a job he combined with the secretaryship of the Board starting the next July 1. By March, 1891, the agency reported that it had conducted 119 experiments and published 15 bulletins as well as three

[62] George E. Morrow, "Report of the Agricultural Department," *University of Illinois Bulletin No. 2* ([Urbana], 1886), 23-24; *Cultivator and Country Gentleman,* LIII (1888), 251; *14th Report* (1889), 27, 32, 37, 134; *15th Report* (1890), 36.
[63] *14th Report* (1889), 88-89, 99-102.

annual reports. This progress in developing a science of agriculture gave legitimate grounds for believing that farmers would someday take an interest in the University.[64]

In addition to the Hatch Act, another federal subsidy marked a decisive turning point in the University's history just as Peabody's administration ended. The Morrill College Land Grant Act of 1890 culminated nearly two decades of effort to provide further congressional assistance to beneficiaries of the 1862 act. Gregory and other agriculturists had raised the question at Chicago in 1871, the agricultural convention of 1872 had adopted a resolution introduced by Senator Morrill on the subject, and Morrill had officially pressed the matter for years. Congress overwhelmingly passed a bill providing each state and territory $15,000 a year, a sum that gradually rose to $25,000 annually, and President Harrison signed it on August 30, 1890. Although the National Grange obtained a clause in the act which restricted use of the funds to "instruction in agriculture, the mechanic arts, the English language, and the various branches of mathematical, physical, natural and economic science, with special reference to their applications in the industries of life, and to the facilities for such instruction," the grant enabled Peabody to release other University resources for work in such areas as psychology, Greek, and French.[65]

Assuming the regency, Peabody found the College of Natural Science most in need of improvement and quickly effected significant reforms in the domain over which Dean Burrill presided.[66] First he abolished the cynosure of the Gregorys, the School of Domestic Science. A month after taking office Peabody told the Trustees that the School was "an experiment into darkness" and would speedily perish unless an enthusiastic devotee of the Gregorys' objectives were put at its head. A committee of the Board charged with appointing a director pleaded insufficient knowledge to act (no

[64] Ibid., 103-6, 114; 15th Report (1890), 17-18; 16th Report (1892), 63, 66.
[65] 16th Report (1892), 16.
[66] 12th Report (1885), 180. The catalogues show Burrill as Dean from 1878 until 1885, when William McMurtrie succeeded him. But Henry A. Weber actually held the deanship from October 17, 1881, to May 8, 1883, according to the "Record Book of the College of Natural Science," Oct. 17, 1881; May 8, 1883.

doubt legitimately), and asked the Regent and Faculty for a recommendation.[67] Peabody, Burrill, and Shattuck, having investigated the matter, reported that 21 of the 48 students enrolled in the School down to 1880 had taken its work for a year or less and only seven had graduated. The committee's interviews with every girl in the program convinced it that the School had been kept alive "by only the most assiduous care and the most active propagandism, even under very favorable circumstances."[68] The Faculty committee therefore recommended discontinuing the School. Its stated reasons were lack of public demand for such instruction and the difficulties of staffing and financing the operation. But Peabody's opposition lay behind the result. He obviously considered the School of Domestic Science a frivolous innovation, thereby gaining a reputation in some quarters as an antagonist of education for women. Actually, he paid women the high compliment of wanting to educate them without regard for sex distinctions. He therefore made almost no special provision for their instruction. In March, 1881, the Board adopted the committee's advice, and the nine students enrolled at the time in Domestic Science shifted into other programs.[69]

Reorganization of the two schools within the College presented a greater challenge, but Peabody soon brought about significant changes. The School of Chemistry was offering four vocationally oriented programs (chemical, pharmaceutical, agricultural, and metallurgical) in addition to a regular chemistry course when Peabody arrived. The latter involved much concentration: in four years, 15 out of 36 term courses were in chemistry, 7 in related sciences and mathematics, 6 in German, and 4 in subjects required of University seniors — mental science, logic, political economy, and constitutional history. After investigating enrollments, Peabody criticized the regular course in 1882 as unsuited to the needs of nonspecialists. Of the students who took chemistry, only about 5 per cent completed the full curriculum. The vast majority, including every student in the College of Literature and Science, most of those in Engineering, and some in Agriculture, found the regular course too fragmented and specialized. Peabody therefore proposed

[67] *10th Report* (1881), 248, 251 (the source of the quotation), 259.
[68] "Faculty Record," II, Dec. 3, 1880.
[69] *11th Report* (1882), 178.

establishment of an introductory course designed to provide the basis for a general knowledge of chemistry as part of a general education. He wanted a course lasting one quarter which would survey the entire subject rather than a fraction of it and be taught by lectures and experiments performed by the professor. Specialists could continue to pursue the regular course and give considerable time to laboratory work. Peabody's proposal of two tracks reflected his desire to educate all students in at least the rudiments of both the sciences and the humanities.[70] He early recognized the dangers of a society in which scientists and humanists could not communicate — the so-called problem of the "two cultures"— and constantly strove to prevent this eventuality.

The unanticipated departure of the two chemistry professors — Henry A. Weber and Melville A. Scovell — facilitated change. After graduating from the University in 1875, Scovell had remained on the faculty and become Professor of Agricultural Chemistry in 1880. During that summer he and Weber had begun research with funds furnished by the Board of Trustees to find a commercially successful way of making sugar from sorghum cane. They discovered a process of making sugar, syrup, and glucose from the cane, and their findings promised to open vast new opportunities for Illinois farmers. Late in 1881 they published with the Board's authorization a pamphlet describing their results. About the time it appeared officials first learned that Weber and Scovell had obtained for themselves rather than the University the patents on the processes discovered. Their action raised the unprecedented and vital question, should faculty members be allowed to benefit personally from University-sponsored research while they were on salary from the institution? Peabody thought not, and envisioned a wave of protest when the public learned that funds supplied by the state were being used to benefit individuals. In March, 1882, he laid the matter before the Board, which condemned and disapproved the action of the two professors by a vote of five to two and decided to consult the Attorney General and the Governor about legal and other aspects of the case. In June the Board concluded to dispense with the services of Weber and Scovell. The only trustee who dissented from

[70] *Catalogue, 1880-81*, 53, 57; *11th Report* (1882), 222-23.

the Board's decisions in both cases was James R. Scott, President of the State Board of Agriculture. Weber and Scovell briefly remained in Champaign, where they failed in an attempt to produce sugar from cane commercially. Out of the bitterness over the episode came a policy giving the University alone the right to patents on research conducted by investigators on the staff who used appropriated funds. The University filled only one of the two vacated positions, which went to William McMurtrie, formerly chief chemist with the U.S. Department of Agriculture.[71]

In 1882 Peabody also began a reorganization of the School of Natural History which the students helped him complete two years later. Burrill and Taft constituted the faculty of this School, and Peabody obtained the latter's dismissal. A family tradition portrays Don Carlos Taft, Professor of Geology and Zoology, as withdrawing from the University because his unconventionality led to Peabody's embarrassment. Allegedly, Peabody took a new trustee around to meet Taft and found him, barefooted, trousers rolled up, mopping his own classroom floor. Actually, however, Peabody found Taft professionally inadequate. He asked the Board in March, 1882, to ascertain whether the development of the Department of Geology and Zoology over the decade of Taft's tenure and its present condition were satisfactory, and to suggest a remedy if it found grave deficiencies. In June the Board granted Taft leave of absence to travel in England, declared his chair vacant to relieve the University of embarrassment in the situation, and directed Peabody to name a replacement.[72]

He offered the job to three men before finding a successor. First he invited Stephen A. Forbes of Normal, who declined because no provision had been made to transfer to Urbana two state agencies he headed. Next he offered the chair in zoology to David Starr Jordan, then of Indiana University and later President of Stanford University. Jordan visited Champaign and "was very little pleased with its surroundings, geographically speaking." He thought the

---

[71] *11th Report* (1882), 187, 191, 192, 209, 211, 219, 235-36, 238. Weber and Scovell's report is in *ibid.*, 71-91. See also Thomas J. Burrill, "Melville Amasa Scovell, '75," *Alumni Quarterly,* VI (Oct., 1912), 289-91.
[72] Ada Bartlett Taft, *Lorado Taft: Sculptor and Citizen* (Greensboro, N.C., 1946), 13; *11th Report* (1882), 223, 235-36.

resources for zoological work much greater than at Indiana, but compared to Bloomington, which possessed "hills and magnificent woods and some rocks and streams," he found "the 'dusty and broad Champaign' . . . wholly unattractive." He would accept if he were sure he could be content to remain five or ten years and build the Department, "or if the salary were enough larger so that if I left on account of climate, I would not make my removals at a loss." But Illinois offered only $2,000, $100 more than he was getting, and asked twice as much work, and Jordan admitted harboring "a — perhaps unreasonable — prejudice against an unbroken prairie."[73] His refusal illustrated a continuing problem of recruitment: Illinois either had to pay well to offset its environmental handicap or risk losses.

Peabody finally enlisted Benjamin C. Jillson as Professor of Zoology and Geology. A graduate of Sheffield Scientific School who had served nine years as Principal of the Pittsburgh High School before leaving Pennsylvania, Jillson won Peabody's praise for introducing laboratory work (which Taft had failed to do) but ran afoul of some pupils. In the spring of 1883 an anonymous student publication declared "Blasted Crank" Jillson ignorant of the subjects he taught and warned this "most absolutely know-nothingness in the University" that a change of climate would be good for his health.[74] A year later he resigned, opening the way for a new era in natural history at Illinois.

The Regent now appointed Charles W. Rolfe Assistant Professor of Geology. Peabody had brought Rolfe, an 1872 graduate, from the Kankakee public schools in 1881 to teach mathematics in the Preparatory School and assist Burrill. An effective teacher, he had risen to Assistant Professor in Natural History before transferring to his new chair.[75] For the work in zoology and entomology, Peabody obtained Stephen A. Forbes, one of the great names connected with the development of science at the University of Illinois.

[73] *13th Report* (1887), 19; Jordan to Stephen A. Forbes, Bloomington, Ind., July 29, 1882, Natural History Survey, Chief's Correspondence, 1871-1909. Jordan reiterated his antipathy to the prairie town in his memoirs, *The Days of a Man* (2 vols., New York, 1922), I, 245.
[74] *11th Report* (1882), 238; *12th Report* (1885), 219; [Judson F. Going], *Cecil's Book of Natural History: About the Great Ones of '83* [Urbana, 1883], 11.
[75] *12th Report* (1885), 239; *13th Report* (1887), 84.

Forbes was born on a farm in Stephenson County, Illinois, on May 29, 1844. His father died when the boy was ten, leaving the family in poverty. Under the circumstances Stephen got at best a fragmentary formal education. He attended district school until he was 14, and for the next two years studied at home, learning to read French, Spanish, and Italian. One of his favorite books at this time was the classic by Jonathan Edwards on the freedom of the will, a volume that gave to his mind "its permanent bent."[76] An ardent Republican, the youth also took politics seriously. At Freeport in August, 1858, he boldly interrupted Douglas when he thought the Little Giant used epithets unfairly. Though silenced by the men around him, Forbes found himself vindicated by Lincoln's opening remarks.[77]

He briefly attended Beloit Academy in 1860, and when the Civil War broke out enlisted at the age of 17 in the Seventh Illinois Volunteer Cavalry. Forbes fell into Confederate hands while carrying a dispatch near Corinth, Mississippi, in 1862, and spent four months in prison, industriously studying Greek. After being released and recovering his health, he rejoined his regiment, made captain at the age of 20, and saw much hard fighting. As a soldier Forbes devoted his idle hours to reading books, but his real education came from the knowledge of the world and especially of men gained during the war. Through all its storms he had "kept the solitary flame of his separate intellectual life steadily burning."[78]

Upon returning to civilian life Forbes spent a year at Rush Medical College and somewhat more time with a medical preceptor at Makanda, Illinois. But he changed his plans after becoming infatuated with botany, and from 1868 to 1871 studied natural history as an avocation while teaching school in Franklin and Jefferson counties in southern Illinois. His studies led in 1870 to the publication of his first scientific articles. The favorable impression they

[76] Ernest Browning Forbes (son of Stephen), "Stephen Alfred Forbes: His Ancestry, Education and Character," *Memorial of the Funeral Services for Stephen Alfred Forbes* [Urbana, 1930], 7.
[77] *Ibid.,* 9-10.
[78] Stephen A. Forbes, "War as an Education," *The Illinois,* III (Oct., 1911), 9. In his excellent article in the campus undergraduate magazine, Forbes depicted the impact of the Civil War upon himself and his generation of soldiers much as did Oliver Wendell Holmes, Jr.

made probably accounted for Forbes's appointment in 1872 as Curator of the Museum of Natural History at Normal. The Museum, founded by the State Natural History Society and taken over by the state in 1871, was housed at but had no organic connection with Illinois State Normal University, where Forbes had studied for one term in 1871. In 1875 Forbes directed a Summer School of Natural History and was made Instructor of Zoology at Illinois State Normal, a job that lasted three years. When the General Assembly transformed the Museum into the Illinois State Laboratory of Natural History two years later, Forbes became Director. In 1882 he also received appointment as State Entomologist, the fourth incumbent in a distinguished line. Two years later Indiana University awarded him a Ph.D., his first academic degree, upon examination and presentation of a thesis.[79]

By that time Forbes had gained distinction in more than one scientific field. Between 1875 and 1882 he had studied the microscopic life of the fresh inland waters. His writings on zoology and biology during this period established him as the leading worker in America in the study of aquatic biology. He also pioneered in investigating the fauna of the region, especially the food of fishes and of birds. Early in the 1880's Forbes turned his attention mainly to entomology, another science in whose development in the United States he figured prominently. Illinois faced the practical problem of controlling insect pests that ravaged agriculture, and Forbes understandably gained eminence as an economic entomologist. The Société d'Acclimation de France awarded him its premier medal in 1886 for his valuable scientific publications. His early writings in various disciplines stressed the interrelationship between organisms and their environment, and his interest in ecology, which made men regard him as the founder of that science, dominated Forbes's later research and writing. In addition to his other merits, Forbes wrote with great charm and lucidity. Peabody named him Professor of Zoology and Entomology effective September 1, 1884. Forbes reported for duty at the opening of the following year, bringing along the State Laboratory of Natural History and the State En-

[79] [Stephen A. Forbes], "Stephen A. Forbes," *Scientific Monthly,* XXX (May, 1930), 475; Forbes, "History of the Former State Natural History Societies of Illinois," *Science,* n.s., XXVI (Dec. 27, 1907), 892-98.

tomologist's Office, both of which legislative enactments transferred to the University effective July 1, 1885.[80]

These changes strengthened the faculty of the College and facilitated Peabody's desire to furnish both general and specialized education. Upon arriving in the School of Chemistry, McMurtrie introduced two courses in agricultural chemistry to accommodate different needs and dropped Johnson's classic texts, *How Crops Grow* and *How Crops Feed,* on the grounds that they were outmoded. He also revised the program leading to a B.S. in chemistry. Now it opened with a one-term course in general and applied chemistry which, according to Peabody, met the needs of students who did not plan to concentrate in this subject without jeopardizing those who did. The Department conducted much analytical work for the State Board of Health, and McMurtrie carried on research in the chemistry of the hog and in the fineness, elasticity, and strength of wools.[81] Although graduate chemists were in great demand, McMurtrie, a strict disciplinarian, was never a popular teacher. He assigned his beginning class in general chemistry the task of flawlessly memorizing the list of elements from aluminum to zirconium and demanded high standards. At the close of his first year a student publication termed "Billy Mc" a "growling cur" who made the chemistry laboratory a despised place. Enrollment figures support the complaint that he drove pupils away. The number of students in Chemistry fell from 40 in his first year to 15 in his last.[82]

[80] Henry B. Ward, "Stephen Alfred Forbes, a Tribute," *Science,* LXXI (April 11, 1930), 380; Harley J. Van Cleave, "Stephen Alfred Forbes as a Scientist," *Memorial of the Funeral Services for Stephen Alfred Forbes,* 24-28; L. O. Howard, *Biographical Memoir of Stephen Alfred Forbes, 1844-1930,* National Academy of Sciences Biographical Memoirs, XV (Washington, 1932), 10-17. Howard's *Memoir* includes a bibliography of Forbes's writings. About half (224 titles) of the items refer to entomology, 74 to zoology aside from entomology, 10 to botany, 20 to ecology, 52 to general natural history, and 19 to educational matters. See pp. 16, 26-54. See also *12th Report* (1885), 234, 239; *13th Report* (1887), 10-11, 160; *Illinois Laws* (1885), 23-24.
[81] *Catalogue, 1882-83,* 56, 58; *12th Report* (1885), 180, 219; *13th Report* (1887), 19. Although the University had been analyzing specimens of water furnished by the State Board of Health, Peabody wrote the Secretary of the Board to protest the Board's published statement that the University would analyze any water sent by authorities of any city, town, or village in Illinois. Peabody to John H. Rauch, Feb. 3, 1886, "Regents' Letterbook, 1879-1894."
[82] Samuel W. Parr, "Historical Sketch of the Chemistry Department," *University of Illinois Bulletin No. 25,* XIII (Urbana, [1916]), 22; [Going], *Cecil's Book of Natural History,* 12; *14th Report* (1889), 164; Superintendent of Public Instruction, *Nineteenth Biennial Report,* 7.

After McMurtrie resigned in 1888 to become Chief Chemist for the Royal Baking Powder Company, the inept John C. Jackson brought the Department to the verge of chaos. He fled in midyear and Arthur W. Palmer accepted a call to rescue it. Born in London and privately prepared for college, Palmer graduated at Urbana in 1883 and took a doctorate at Harvard three years later. He returned to the University as an assistant and won recognition for his ability, but left for advanced study in Berlin and Göttingen when Peabody passed him over as McMurtrie's successor on the grounds of his youth (he was then 27). A cable summoned him back to an assistant professorship in the fall of 1889, and a year later he became full professor. Enrollments in the Department alone hit 50 that academic year. The increased teaching burden plus Peabody's desire for two distinct courses, one each for "majors" and "non-majors," made urgent the need for another professor. The second Morrill Act provided funds for this purpose, and in December, 1890, Peabody appointed as Professor of Analytical Chemistry an 1884 graduate of the University, Samuel W. Parr, who had won a reputation at Illinois College as a successful teacher of chemistry. He left the division of labor between Palmer and Parr for subsequent arrangement.[83]

In the School of Natural History Rolfe made less progress with geology than did Burrill and Forbes with their specialties. Both the location of the University and its lack of an adequate geological collection for teaching purposes constituted handicaps. Peabody failed in the attempt to have the treasures of rocks, fossils, and minerals in the State Geological Collection at Springfield removed to Urbana where they might actively serve instructional purposes, but he and Rolfe finally purchased over 5,000 geological specimens. Perhaps more vital, Rolfe was neither an original scholar nor a producer of scholars. He contributed primarily through the classroom, teaching a prep class in botany, a sophomore course in anatomy and physiology, and three geology courses adapted to as many special needs. He offered a survey for general educational purposes, economic geology for mining engineers, and a more intensive course

[83] Superintendent of Public Instruction, *Nineteenth Biennial Report,* 7; Parr, "Historical Sketch of the Chemistry Department," 22-24; *15th Report* (1890), 15, 37, 94, 148; *16th Report* (1892), 20, 37, 43.

for juniors registered in Agriculture, Natural History, and Mining Engineering.[84]

Burrill and Forbes supplied the forward thrust to the School. The careers of these scientific luminaries bore many resemblances. About the same age, they grew up in poverty within miles of each other in Stephenson County and came under the intellectual influence of the remarkable natural history circle at Normal before joining the University. Burrill remained a devout and strait-laced Methodist whose faith in God never wavered. Forbes lost his childhood beliefs and became a rationalist and an agnostic, the first one known to have joined the faculty. Perhaps a mind given its bent by the supernatural determinism of Jonathan Edwards passed over easily to scientific determinism. Yet Forbes supported liberal religion. With his wife he initiated the movement that led to establishment of the Unitarian Church in Urbana. This act may be interpreted as the accommodation of the faculty's agnostic to a community where Protestant orthodoxy prevailed, although late in life Forbes found renewed comfort in the beliefs of his childhood.[85]

Both men, to use a phrase coined by Forbes, "worked like drayhorses and were paid like oxen."[86] Burrill taught as many as eight different courses a year, especially botany, biology, physiography (in which he introduced anthropology), and microscopy. In addition, he supervised the field work in horticulture and served as Botanist and Horticulturist of the Agricultural Experiment Station. Summers provided the time for research. His investigations stressed bacteriology and mycology and resulted in a steady stream of publications. But after the discovery of the germ theory of disease, bacteriology as a field in biology had a low average prospect of yielding fresh insights as opposed to new facts, and none of the papers Burrill published after 1883 equaled in importance those relating to

[84] *12th Report* (1885), 181; *13th Report* (1887), 138, 162; *14th Report* (1889), 167-69.
[85] Forbes wrote in 1923: "I was, and still am, a rationalist and an agnostic, for whom what is known as faith is merely assumption, often practically unnecessary, since in active life one must very often act *as if* he believed what he does not and cannot really know. . . . " But before his death in 1930 he drew a line through "and still am" and substituted "as a younger man." Ernest Browning Forbes, "Stephen Alfred Forbes: His Ancestry, Education and Character," 10-11.
[86] Forbes, "History of the Former State Natural History Societies of Illinois," 898. Forbes applied the statement to college professors of the period.

his discovery that bacteria caused disease in plants. His mycological research led in 1885 and 1887 to important publications on "Parasitic Fungi of Illinois."[87]

Burrill attracted able students and instilled in them appreciation for the meaning of research. "It seems strange," wrote one of his pupils, Arthur B. Seymour, in praising Burrill's achievements in the campus newspaper in 1880, "that our trustees do not recognize more the value of original investigation and give more opportunity for it in the various departments of the University."[88] Seymour, an 1881 graduate, spent most of his life in the Farlow Herbarium at Harvard and left the *Host Index of the Fungi of North America* (1929) as his chief monument. Franklin S. Earle, who studied with Burrill off and on from 1872 to 1879 but did not graduate, served many years as director of an agricultural experiment station in Cuba, contributed to systematic mycology, and became an authority on the culture and disease of tropical plants. George P. Clinton followed Seymour to Harvard upon graduating in 1890, was Botanist of the Connecticut Agricultural Experiment Station from 1902 to 1937, and published much on parasitic fungi of cultivated plants. Merton B. Waite, an 1887 graduate who had studied with Burrill and been an assistant to Forbes, was for years in charge of the work on fruit diseases in the U.S. Department of Agriculture. Fittingly, in 1898 he made the important discovery that bacteria which cause plant disease may be carried by insects.[89]

Forbes assumed his varied duties in 1885, and three years later succeeded McMurtrie as Dean of the College of Natural Science. He taught entomology and two courses in zoology, a short general survey and an intensive one-year course. But Forbes found the ex-

[87] *13th Report* (1887), 143-46; *14th Report* (1889), 161-63; Donald Fleming, *William H. Welch and the Rise of Modern Medicine* (Boston, 1954), 124; C. E. Janvrin, comp., "The Scientific Writings of Thomas J. Burrill," Illinois State Horticultural Society, *Transactions for 1917*, n.s., LI (Bloomington, [1917]), 197-98.

[88] *Illini*, Oct. 5, 1880.

[89] Neil E. Stevens, "The Centenary of T. J. Burrill," *Scientific Monthly*, XLIX (Sept., 1939), 290-92; Franklin W. Scott, ed., *The Alumni Record of the University of Illinois* (Urbana, 1906), 60, 103, 118-19; Franklin S. Earle Folder, Alumni Morgue; and scattered references in the Board of Trustees' *Reports*. Earle was the son of Parker Earle, a Cobden fruit-grower and a member of the Board of Trustees from 1885 to 1891.

isting natural history curriculum deficient. It appealed primarily to students who desired a general, liberal education with a biological rather than a literary basis. Forbes wanted the offering to meet also the needs of premedical students, prospective science teachers, and those eager for a career in one of the sciences into which natural history was dividing. He therefore proposed the establishment of elective courses which would enable students to engage almost wholly in laboratory practice and technical reading in their last one or two years. The catalogue announced the reform in 1886. Forbes now gave a one-term course in general zoology taken chiefly by literary students, and an intensive course which lasted two hours a day for a minimum of one and a maximum of two years. By means of a hefty text, lectures, a syllabus of each lecture (he found students incapable of taking full and trustworthy notes), frequent quizzes, and much laboratory work, Forbes hoped to make zoology "a means of mental discipline, not less efficient and valuable than the classical and mathematical studies." Perhaps he stated that goal for Peabody's benefit, but nevertheless students approved a reorganization designed to avoid recitation and permit specialization. Enrollments in the School of Natural History, which had averaged 16 a year between 1881 and 1886, averaged 42 a year from 1886 through June, 1891.[90]

Although one authority regards Forbes along with J. H. Comstock of Cornell and C. H. Fernald of Massachusetts Agricultural College as outstanding in the development of university courses in entomology, this field frustrated Forbes in the late 1880's. At Urbana the courses in entomology, one of the most difficult branches of zoology, came in the freshman year, when students could not fully profit from them. Yet Forbes hesitated to ask for a change because the complicated, fixed curriculum made it hard to alter the position of a single study.[91]

Forbes drew fewer men to entomology as a career than did Comstock or Fernald, writes one authority, though he had a re-

[90] *13th Report* (1887), 160-63; *14th Report* (1889), 164-67 (the quotation is at p. 166); "Faculty Record," II, March 9, 1886; *Catalogue, 1886-87,* 69; Superintendent of Public Instruction, *Nineteenth Biennial Report,* 7.
[91] Herbert Osborn, *Fragments of Entomological History* (Columbus, 1937), 241; *14th Report* (1889), 167.

markably fine equipment in library, laboratory, and field facilities, "and a student body the equal of any in the country."[92] He appears also to have trained fewer future research workers in his fields than did Burrill in plant pathology and mycology. A partial explanation is the official positions which made Forbes responsible for securing practical results in insect control. These needs led him to retain efficient assistants who helped produce the conclusions that Forbes published prolifically in the bulletins, circulars, and reports of the State Laboratory of Natural History and the State Entomologist's Office. Research that produced immediate benefits had obvious advantages, but the contrast between Forbes and other eminent scientists in training investigators posed a vital problem in the organization of scientific research.

The size of the College of Engineering reflected clearly the practical orientation of the Illinois students. Youngsters shunned agricultural education because they considered it the road to economic oblivion, and only a modest number pursued natural science. It is strange that chemistry and the life sciences did not attract more pupils, for they were throbbing with vitality and new ideas. Not uncommonly students struggle with inherently difficult subjects and imperfect teachers in order to be part of an exciting intellectual discipline. And besides, jobs as teachers of science in the high schools were opening. Nevertheless, students made Engineering the colossus of the campus. That College contained 99 out of the University's 352 students in 1881-82, and 252 out of 519 in 1890-91. In this period mechanical engineering attracted 586 enrollees, civil engineering 575, architecture 370, and mining engineering 39.[93] These disciplines, though not devoid of intellectual substance, were hardly bursting with new fundamental ideas. Even physics was not then revolutionizing thought as it soon would. Of course the good jobs which flourished in an industrializing and urbanizing America for

---

[92] Osborn, *Fragments of Entomological History*, 243. The distinguished group of Forbes assistants included William H. Garman, Franklin S. Earle, Thomas F. Hunt, Clarence M. Weed, Charles F. Hart, John Marten, Merton B. Waite, and Fred W. Mally. Osborn mentions many of these men, not always accurately, and other references are scattered throughout the official *Reports* of the Board.
[93] Superintendent of Public Instruction, *Nineteenth Biennial Report*, 6-7.

men technologically trained explain the vogue of engineering education.

For years Peabody taught in and officially headed the Department of Mechanical Engineering. Actually, he turned over its virtual direction to an assistant. The first was his son Cecil, an M.I.T. graduate who was Professor of Engineering at the Imperial Agricultural College in Japan (1879-81) when his father appointed him Assistant Professor of Mechanical Engineering and Physics at Illinois. *Cecil's Book of Natural History,* an attack on the Regent anonymously issued by a student in June, 1883, which blasted Jillson and McMurtrie, also denounced young Peabody. "A State University is no place for a dead beat to attempt to learn a profession at the expense of her students," declared the author, who thought the bouncing of "Jap and Jill" and "Billy Mc" might renovate the University.[94] On the very day the academic year opened in 1883, Cecil Peabody left for a job at M.I.T., stranding five classes without an instructor. His father hastily obtained Arthur T. Woods, an Annapolis graduate employed in the Bureau of Naval Construction. Woods served as an assistant professor on loan from the Navy until June, 1887, and probably returned to active duty because Peabody failed to promote him. Failing to obtain a successor, Peabody humbled himself and snatched Woods from a steamship which was ready to carry him to sea by offering a full professorship. Woods served until 1891 as Head of the Department. During these years the course of study followed lines laid out by Robinson and improved by the senior Peabody. He systematized the instruction in the machine shop, and tried to provide sufficient tools and space to prevent overcrowding in this popular facility. But Peabody demonstrated little sympathy for the commercial operations of the shop.[95]

Physics developed into an autonomous department in the late 1880's. The subject had been taught as part of the curriculum in mechanical engineering for two terms in the junior year, and it remained there when Theodore B. Comstock, who arrived in 1886 to develop a program in mining engineering, took charge. The foundations in physics had been excellently laid for Comstock. He

[94] [Going], *Cecil's Book of Natural History,* 11, 13.
[95] *11th Report* (1882), 195, 226-27; *12th Report* (1885), 207; *14th Report* (1889), 72, 157-60.

divided the class and offered both a general course and one for engineers. Upon Comstock's sudden departure in 1889, Peabody appointed a young graduate, Samuel W. Stratton, to teach the course. Stratton is another eminent scientist connected with the University of Illinois, although his fame rests upon his career with the National Bureau of Standards, which he founded and directed from 1901 to 1923, and as President of M.I.T. from 1923 to 1930.

Stratton was born on July 18, 1861, in Litchfield, Illinois. On his father's farm he early displayed a mechanical bent, and after graduating from the local high school went to Urbana in 1880, intending to stay one year as a special student in drafting and shop work. Since Litchfield High School was unaccredited, Stratton had to take entrance examinations. He scored in the 80's in six subjects and 97 in natural philosophy (physics). Peabody assigned him to the Preparatory School, where he took two terms of machine-shop practice, earned grades over 90 in ten courses except for bookkeeping (85), and decided to continue his education at the University.[96]

Upon matriculating in 1881 Stratton received University credit for five preparatory courses, which facilitated his completing most of the prescribed four-year curriculum in mechanical engineering during the next three years. He got his lowest grade in analytical mechanics (75), earned 12 marks in the 80's, 23 in the 90's (three were 99), and two 100's. In physics, which he studied for two terms during 1883-84, his scores were 95 and 98. He roomed for a year with Frank A. Vanderlip, later Assistant Secretary of the Treasury and President of the National City Bank of New York, who studied mechanical engineering at Urbana in 1882-83. An excellent student but no "grind," Stratton worked at several jobs to meet expenses and participated in campus affairs. He joined the Philomathean Society, the Telegraphic Association, the Mechanical Engineering Society, and became Captain of Company C in the military organization. In June, 1884, the University awarded him a certificate rather than a B.S. degree, for which he lacked required courses in geology, history, and mental science.[97]

[96] Samuel C. Prescott (Dean of Science at M.I.T.) to Carl Stephens, Sept. 26, 1933, Samuel W. Stratton Folder, Alumni Morgue.
[97] Stratton's academic record is contained in papers in the University's Office of Admissions and Records, but rank-in-class standings were not kept at the time. See also "Sagamores of the Illini: Samuel Wesley Stratton, '84," *Alumni Quarterly*, IX (April, 1915), 75-78.

During the next academic year, when Stratton stayed on as a resident graduate student, he registered for some courses and presented a graduation thesis, "Design for a Heliostat." In the fall of 1885 he joined the faculty as an instructor of mathematics and physics in the Preparatory School, and received his B.S. in Mechanical Engineering the following June. Subsequently he worked in Alumni Association headquarters, taught descriptive astronomy and descriptive geometry, reproduced blueprint lectures for the Department of Architecture, and in June, 1889, received an appointment for the next year as Assistant in Architecture.[98]

When Comstock unexpectedly failed to return to duty in the fall of 1889, Peabody assigned Stratton to teach physics. He proved so "thoroughly competent, energetic and inventive" that Peabody made him Assistant Professor of Physics in June, 1890, and recommended enlargement of his sphere of work.[99] Stratton moved the course into the sophomore year and added one term, making physics a full year's course. He also introduced electrical engineering into the Department of Mechanical Engineering. Students had requested this offering in March, 1886, and shortly thereafter Peabody ordered the apparatus necessary to teach it. In 1890-91 the University announced its curriculum in Electrical Engineering, the first two years of which were identical with that in Mechanical Engineering. One student enrolled in the program. During the summer of 1891 Stratton and Glen M. Hobbs, who became his brother-in-law, inspected the electrical facilities of Harvard, Yale, Cornell, and other Eastern colleges. They established an electrical engineering laboratory that fall, and in the ensuing year enrollment in the program reached 29. It rose to 87 in 1892-93.[100]

The University lost Stratton over a few dollars. Peabody made him a full professor on the eve of his thirtieth birthday in June, 1891, and increased his salary $200, giving him $1,600 a year, the lowest paid anyone in that rank (although an unfilled professorship of physical culture was also set at that figure). In the past full professors had ordinarily received the same stipend, but distinctions

[98] *13th Report* (1887), 46, 99; *14th Report* (1889), 33, 72; *15th Report* (1890), 75.
[99] *15th Report* (1890), 114, 148-49, 160.
[100] "Faculty Record," II, March 26, 1886; *Illini,* Sept. 23, 1891; Superintendent of Public Instruction, *Nineteenth Biennial Report,* 7.

were arising, based less on academic fields than experience. In 1891 14 full professors, those in English, History, and Rhetoric along with those in Agriculture, Civil Engineering, and Zoology, were earning $2,000. But six younger or newer full professors were getting $1,800. Nevertheless, Stratton aroused great enthusiasm for his work during 1891-92, during which he taught an average of 20 hours weekly, and at the end of that year the University raised his salary $200. He and a new appointee in mining engineering were the two lowest paid full professors. Stratton's youth and the low prestige of physics rather than failure to appreciate his merits undoubtedly accounted for the treatment of him. At any rate, he resigned to accept an assistant professorship at the University of Chicago, where he attained a full professorship before leaving in 1901 for Washington. Assistant Secretary of the Treasury Vanderlip, his old roommate, was instrumental in getting Stratton invited to formulate the work for the National Bureau of Standards, whose predecessor was under the control of the Treasury Department.[101]

Mathematics, considered mainly a tool subject during Gregory's tenure, remained an appendage of the Department of Mechanical Engineering until 1882-83. Shattuck and his young assistants taught pupils from all colleges within the University, but primarily engineers. Peabody, however, gave mathematics new status. The catalogue of 1882-83 listed it as a subject pursued by all students in the colleges of Engineering and of Literature and Science, and other curricula also required courses in this field. Engineers studied two full terms of mathematics, including trigonometry, analytical geometry, advanced algebra, calculus, and descriptive geometry. And all students in Literature and Science took one required year of mathematics. Peabody's reform gave impetus to the formation of a separate department of mathematics, but neither that nor a four-year program in the subject existed by the end of his regime.

By 1880 the Department of Civil Engineering rested on solid foundations built initially by Shattuck and Robinson and more

[101] *15th Report* (1890), 160; *16th Report* (1892), 101, 240, 250; F. C. Brown, "Samuel Wesley Stratton, 1861-1931," *Science*, LXXIV (Oct. 30, 1931), 428.

fully from 1871 to 1878 by John Burkitt Webb. Born in Philadelphia in 1841, Webb had distinguished himself as a student at the University of Michigan. After graduating there in 1871 he remained as Assistant Professor of Civil Engineering until he accepted a full professorship at Urbana in November of that year. An excellent man in his field, the most advanced branch of engineering at the time, Webb never aroused the enthusiasm or affection of Illinois students. Taking pride in the University's commitment to the "new education," they considered him less an innovator than Ricker in architecture or Robinson in mechanical engineering. Moreover, they found Webb exacting beyond their capacities, and resented his emphasis on the educational rather than the practical aspects of his subject. The *Illini* alluded to his great unpopularity, and Webb, who had married Gregory's daughter Mary Emmeline two years before he obtained leave in 1878 to study in Europe, resigned a year later.[102]

Ira O. Baker succeeded Webb and held the position until 1915. An Indiana native who had finished high school in Mattoon, Illinois, Baker graduated from the University with a certificate in 1874 and joined the staff as an assistant in civil engineering and physics. He inherited the headship of a Department whose courses in surveying, topography, descriptive and practical astronomy, railroad engineering, hydraulics and resistance of materials, stone work, and bridges prepared men to build the network of rails, roads, harbors, and waterways needed by a vast industrial nation. Among the able assistants Baker recruited as assistant instructors were Jerome Sondericker, an 1880 graduate who left five years later to join the M.I.T. faculty, and Arthur N. Talbot, class of 1881, who spent his professional career on the Illinois faculty. But most students aimed at better-paying jobs with railroad and bridge companies, and many ingratiated themselves with Baker to earn a favorable place in the little book he used to prepare recommendations. Baker deplored the evil influence of vocationalism upon his Department, and considered

---

[102] Ira O. Baker and Everett E. King, "A History of the College of Engineering of the University of Illinois, 1868-1945" (mimeographed MS., 2 vols., Urbana, [1947]), I, 26-62; *5th Report* (1873), 149; *Illini,* Jan., 1878; "Faculty Record," I, 290.

students who preferred formulas to knowledge as machines rather than men.[103]

Yet many graduates gained distinction in later life. John A. Ockerson, class of 1872 and a member of the Mississippi River Commission, and August Ziesing, class of 1878 and President of the American Bridge Company, completed their studies before Baker trained a host of prominent civil engineers. Albert F. Robinson, class of 1880, complained shortly after leaving Urbana that "The little we got at the University in regard to bridges does not make a *grease spot* on the paper," but he boasted of designing and building 120,000 tons of steel bridges in a decade. Lincoln Bush, class of 1888, served a number of railroad and bridge companies before joining the Delaware, Lackawanna & Western Railroad, where he devised a novel, smoke-eliminating train shed and performed the dramatic engineering feat of moving and lowering a 1,000-ton drawbridge across the Passaic River by means of sand jacks on barges. He became President of the American Society of Civil Engineers in 1928.[104]

Baker established pioneer laboratories to test cement and road materials, and conducted research for books which gave him a wide reputation, *A Treatise on Masonry Construction* (1889) and *Durability of Brick Pavements* (1891). The University's responsiveness to new problems led in 1890 to appointment of Talbot as Professor of Municipal Engineering, a chair that embraced sanitary engineering as well.[105]

The course in mining engineering existed mainly on paper until 1886, despite Gregory's efforts to establish a department of mining and metallurgy. Economic interests connected with the extractive industry in Illinois, which was particularly important as a coal producer, also exerted considerable pressure to have the University train students for mining operations. In the 1870's the school spent sizable sums to import apparatus illustrating mines, machinery for handling ores, and metallurgical furnaces. But the site of the University did not favor mining, and the projected program faltered. The few students who registered in the Department took the

[103] *13th Report* (1887), 156.
[104] Scott, *Alumni Record* (1906), 51, 105; Lincoln Bush Folder, Alumni Morgue; Albert F. Robinson to Arthur N. Talbot, Oct. 22, 1882, Talbot Papers.
[105] *15th Report* (1890), 148.

basic civil engineering curriculum and attended lectures on mining topics given by Robinson or Peabody. Yet when Gregory combined the Department of Mining Engineering with the Department of Civil Engineering in 1880, the few future miners objected.

In the fall of 1885, after mining interests in the state renewed their demands, Peabody appointed Theodore B. Comstock to the chair in mining engineering. He had graduated from Pennsylvania State with a B.A. in 1868 and from Cornell with a B.S. two years later. After occupying the chair in geology at Cornell until 1879, he had superintended a mine in Colorado before reporting to Urbana at the outset of 1886.[106] Comstock devised a well-planned curriculum similar in the first two years to that in civil engineering, except for more chemistry. The third year featured geology, mining engineering, assaying and metallurgy, and the fourth emphasized technical work along with courses required of all seniors — mental science, constitutional history, and political economy. Within its means the University liberally supplied equipment, and Comstock fitted up a laboratory in the basement of the Chemistry Building. Although Illinois was the thirteenth institution to establish work in mining, students avoided the Department. A total of 9 had enrolled between 1881 and 1886, and 17 in the years Comstock remained at Urbana. His reports to Peabody, which mingle generous flattery with warnings against any action that might cause him to leave, offer insight into the man's character. Comstock simply failed to return in 1889 after summer vacation, and later complained to a student about Peabody's treatment of him.[107]

Peabody thought the right man could invigorate the Department, and in August, 1891, shortly after the Regent resigned, the Board appointed Walter J. Baldwin to the chair at $1,600, the lowest salary paid any full professor. Baldwin wanted Illinois to specialize in a course in coal-mining, but Acting Regent Burrill lacked enthusiasm for this proposal. Baldwin resigned early in 1893, having concluded that the location and surroundings of the University precluded large development of mining education. Authorities sold the mining engineering machinery, but 16 years later the

[106] *Illinois Senate Journal* (1883), 271, 880; Superintendent of Public Instruction, *Fifteenth Biennial Report,* 7; *13th Report* (1887), 53.
[107] *13th Report* (1887), 157-60; *14th Report* (1889), 154-57; Superintendent of Public Instruction, *Nineteenth Biennial Report,* 7.

coal-mining interests of Illinois and a new Dean of the College combined to re-establish the Department.[108]

The University contributed significantly to the remarkable development of architecture which occurred throughout the country in the late nineteenth century. Architecture had reached its nadir in America after the Civil War. The Greek Revival tradition passed away about 1860, leaving in its place only a romantic eclecticism. The French Mansard Roof and the Victorian Gothic styles, particularly the latter, influenced the carpenter-builders and the few professional architects at work. But a mélange of other "styles" helped make the era one of bad taste, as exemplified in Chicago's Crosby Opera House, completed in 1865 and described as "an Italo-Byzantine French Venetian structure with Norman windows."[109]

In the next decade, however, Americans began working out the promise of better days. The Romanesque Revival, inspired by Henry Hobson Richardson, became the vogue after 1877, the year Richardson finished his greatest work, Trinity Church in Boston. This robust style conquered a number of cities including Chicago, and during the last half of the Romanesque period Chicago enjoyed a brief architectural supremacy. Among the individuals involved in building skyscrapers there in the 1880's were Dankmar Adler, Louis Sullivan, William LeBaron Jenney, Daniel H. Burnham, and John W. Root. Designed mainly in the Romanesque and Renaissance styles, these early skeleton cages of iron and steel presented complex problems of mechanical, electrical, and sanitary engineering. But just as local architects gained distinction for their city, the official adoption of the Classic style for the World's Columbian Exposition held in Chicago in 1893 inaugurated a new era in American architecture. New York, having never succumbed to the Romanesque, now seized the leadership in architectural fashion and gave Classic eclecticism a new popularity.[110]

[108] 15th Report (1890), 149; 16th Report (1892), 20, 53, 112, 136, 205, 240; 17th Report (1894), 78, 97, 213.
[109] Hugh Morrison, Louis Sullivan, Prophet of Modern Architecture (New York, 1935), 54.
[110] Thomas E. Tallmadge, The Story of Architecture in America (New York, 1927), chs. vi-ix. My remarks on architectural developments in this volume have benefited from a critical reading by Professor Alan K. Laing of the University of Illinois.

The gradual improvement in standards of architectural excellence which accompanied the evolution of style in the late nineteenth century rested upon a vast increase in the number of educated architects. Some took their training at the École des Beaux-Arts in Paris, and a diminishing number did so in American architects' offices. But many graduated from the schools of architecture in this country. Ricker trained a large proportion of the latter at Illinois, one of three architectural schools in the nation until 1881, when Columbia established a fourth, and the only one in the region until Armour Institute of Technology opened in 1893. Enrollments at Illinois averaged 22 a year from the fall of 1881 to the spring of 1887, and 66 a year from 1887 until June, 1892. The freshman class alone totaled 100 in 1891-92. During that decade eight new schools of architecture opened in the United States, and in 1896 Illinois enrolled 25 per cent of the 273 regular students who attended American architectural schools. Many came from great distances to study with Ricker at Urbana.[111]

Ricker moved with the times, as indicated both by his personal eclecticism and the evolution of his Department's curriculum. He drew mainly on the Second Empire style in designing the Chemistry Laboratory (1878, later Harker Hall), and the Natural History Building (1893). The French Mansard Roof influence was strong in the Drill Hall (1890, later the Gymnasium Annex), and the Romanesque dominated the Library (1897, later Altgeld Hall). James M. White and students in the Department of Architecture helped with the latter.

In the course of study Ricker tried to combine both construction and design, but from the outset emphasized the need to ground students thoroughly in the principles of scientific construction and to fit them for office work. Criticized for giving his students too much engineering and too little art, Ricker acknowledged the justice of the charge. But at the same time he always insisted that correct taste and the power of designing formed the keystone in the educa-

---

[111] *Ibid.,* 235-36; F. H. Bosworth, Jr., and Roy Childs Jones, *A Study of Architectural Schools* (New York, 1932), 3; Superintendent of Public Instruction, *Nineteenth Biennial Report,* 7; Turpin C. Bannister, "Pioneering in Architectural Education," *Journal of the American Institute of Architects,* XX (Aug., 1953), 77; *16th Report* (1892), 235.

tion of the architect, and gave considerable effort to instruction which sought to further these goals. The main courses for this purpose were History of Architecture, Aesthetics of Architecture, and Architectural Designing. Since there were no suitable works in English for the former two, Ricker translated and adapted French and German texts. He used Rudolph Redtenbacher's *Tektonik,* translated as *The Architectonic of Modern Architecture* (1884), to teach aesthetics, the foundation of good design. Only two terms were given to Architectural Designing, although Ricker termed it the most important study in the entire program.

Despite his desire to improve taste, Ricker allowed the emphasis to be on technical studies. These included architectural drawing; shop practice; graphical statics; elements of wood, stone, brick, and metal construction; elements of sanitary construction; estimates, agreements, and specifications; and heating and ventilation. Pressure from students led in 1885-86 to introduction of a course in Architectural Perspective. Ricker found his pupils unable to take proper notes on lectures and there were few texts available. He therefore published his own lectures and texts, often adapted or translated from foreign works, by the blueprint method. During 1884-85 his assistant Stratton reproduced about 30,000 pages by this cheap means.[112]

Ricker's alertness to the needs of the profession, and particularly the Chicago area, led to important changes in architecture in the early 1890's. The University dropped the one-year Builder's Course after June, 1892, and introduced a new Architectural Engineering curriculum. The latter evolved naturally out of the experience which convinced Ricker that few students were competent in both design and engineering and in response to Chicago's need for men trained to erect steel-frame buildings.[113] The spurt in architectural enrollments after 1887 paralleled the boom in skyscrapers, and Ricker included their designers among the nonresident engineering lecturers he brought to the campus at this time. Jenney and

[112] *13th Report* (1887), 146-53; *14th Report* (1889), 143-49; "Faculty Record," II, Sept. 19, 1884.
[113] Nathan C. Ricker, "The Story of a Life" (typewritten MS. autobiography, Urbana, 1922), 31-32.

William Sooy Smith talked on tall-building construction, and Dankmar Adler, during an 1892 visit to speak on the design of auditoriums, confirmed Ricker's belief that the University could support a program in Architectural Engineering. The catalogue of 1891-92 announced such a course "for those students preferring the mathematical and structural side of architecture to its artistic side, and for those who wish to acquire a thorough knowledge of iron and steel construction as it is now executed in architectural structure."[114] The offering was the first of its type in the United States. Subsequently the regular course added more work in design at the expense of mathematics, mechanics, and resistance of materials.

Students trained in both programs became successful architects, joining the ranks of those sent out before the 1890's. The first crop from the late 1870's included Joseph C. Llewellyn, a Chicago architect; Clarence H. Blackall of Boston; Samuel A. Bullard of Springfield, who also served for years on the University's Board of Trustees; and Mary L. Page (class of 1878), perhaps the first woman to complete an architectural course. In the 1880's Ricker trained Arthur Peabody, who became Supervising Architect of the University of Wisconsin, and Henry Bacon, who studied at Urbana from 1885 until 1888 without graduating. Bacon designed many monuments which housed statues executed by Augustus Saint-Gaudens or Daniel Chester French, and gained lasting recognition as the architect of the Lincoln Memorial in the nation's capital. Among Ricker's students in the 1890's were James M. White, who remained at Urbana in the Department of Architecture and later took charge of physical development of the campus; Albert C. Phelps, who joined the Cornell architecture faculty; Alfred Fellheimer, a New York architect and authority on the planning of railroad stations; and William L. Steele, William E. Drummond, and Walter Burley Griffin, members of the Chicago school of architects that included Louis Sullivan and Frank Lloyd Wright.[115] In 1912 Griffin won an international competition for the design of Canberra, the Australian capital city.

[114] *Catalogue, 1891-92*, 80. On the nonresident lecturers, see *ibid.*, 8; *Catalogue, 1892-93*, 10; and *16th Report* (1892), 234.
[115] See Mark L. Peisch, *The Chicago School of Architecture: Early Followers of Sullivan and Wright*, Columbia University Studies in Art History and Archaeology, No. 5 (New York, 1964).

Imperceptibly and without design, liberal arts lost ground within the University during the early 1880's. Peabody's continued refutation of the stale charge that the University emphasized literary at the expense of technical studies probably contributed to the result. Otherwise, the only significant change in the College of Literature and Science in the early years of his regency restricted the students' freedom in choosing their studies. For years the catalogues had given scope to Gregory's desire for the greatest possible latitude by saying in connection with the Literature and Science programs, "The large liberty allowed in the selection of the special studies of his course will permit the student to give such direction to his education as will fit him fully for any chosen sphere or pursuit."[116] The catalogue of 1882-83 silently omitted that statement. The new policy imposed prescription within the field of choice.

In the School of Ancient Languages and Literature, the smaller division within the College, Professor Crawford and an assistant, usually a woman who doubled as preceptress, handled the instruction. The required course here included six terms of Latin, three of Greek, three more of Latin or French, three more of Greek or German, and ancient history. In teaching, Crawford used the classical languages to instill a critical use of English rather than merely for the mental discipline they afforded. But the number enrolled in the School averaged only 10.5 a year between 1881 and 1891. Some pupils left Urbana to finish their classical educations in the East, and in 1886 Crawford confessed disappointment that authorities had done nothing to inform the public of the University's strength in ancient languages. His duties as Librarian and Professor of History offered him other outlets, however, and in 1886 Nathaniel Butler, Jr., took the chair of Latin. Butler's emphasis on the value of Latin in instilling mental discipline marked him as a conservative pedagogue.[117]

The School of English and Modern Languages, which enrolled an average of 98 students a year during the decade after 1881, exhibited deference to the past by "affording a training equivalent

[116] This statement appeared in the form quoted at the time the College of Literature and Science first arose. See the *Catalogue, 1871-72*, 47.
[117] Superintendent of Public Instruction, *Nineteenth Biennial Report,* 7; *13th Report* (1887), 173; *14th Report* (1889), 175-77.

to the ordinary studies of the classical languages."[118] Moreover, its curriculum permitted a choice between Latin and English in the first two terms of work. Normally, however, students started by surveying the entire field of British and American authors from the mid-sixteenth century to the present and ended the first year with a term of rhetoric. As sophomores they studied the English classics, and as seniors took Anglo-Saxon, Old English, and philology. Joseph C. Pickard taught these subjects. The School also required one year of French and two of German, which Snyder taught. He and an assistant, normally a young woman, instructed all the classes in French and German. In addition to serving as Dean, Snyder handled about six classes and 200 students daily.

The curriculum of both schools in the College required mathematics and science. The three courses in the former were trigonometry, conic sections and geometry, and a term of either advanced geometry or calculus, depending on which the faculty thought the students could handle. The seven mandatory courses in science included one each in physiology or biology, zoology or botany, astronomy, chemistry, physics, and geometry, and a second in either chemistry or physics.

Four other subjects were common not only to the curricula in Literature and Science but to practically every program within the University. History was one. Students in Literature and Science and in the School of Natural History took five required courses — in the junior year, ancient, medieval, and modern history, and in the senior year, history of civilization and constitutional history. Those in other programs took one of the latter, normally constitutional history, which emphasized British and touched on American developments. Crawford inherited responsibility for these courses, and did so well that Peabody appointed him Professor of History in 1881 along with his other duties. Crawford's approach to the teaching of history placed him far ahead of Gregory and of most history professors throughout the nation, where there were about 20 full-time teachers of professorial rank by 1885. He spared his students the drudgery of learning dates and facts by heart from a text, but re-

[118] *Catalogue, 1884-85,* 76; Superintendent of Public Instruction, *Nineteenth Biennial Report,* 7.

quired library reading for most lessons, regarding "the habit of looking up topics in various authors as valuable as the information thus
gained." By comparison, Henry Pratt Judson taught history at the
University of Minnesota from 1885 to 1891 by textbook and recitation and required outside reading only in connection with the
writing of one paper. More vital, Crawford tried to connect events
philosophically, which led him to show how cause and effect worked
in the lives of nations as of individuals, and that history is one continuous whole. He emphasized social and cultural history before
these approaches became familiar, and moved beyond political and
military matters to stress the manners, customs, and religion of peo-
ples. He assigned frequent papers on such topics as the relation of
the useful and fine arts, of education, and of religion to civilization.[119]

Yet none of Crawford's pupils is known to have become a professor or writer of history, and Illinois was relegated to the statistical
tables in Herbert B. Adams' *The Study of History in American Colleges and Universities* (1887). The Johns Hopkins professor devoted a chapter each to describing historical studies at Harvard,
Yale, Michigan, Cornell, and his own institution; and also mentioned Wisconsin, Columbia, Rutgers, Syracuse, and Pennsylvania
in a chapter on American history. The tables, however, show that
Crawford took a more advanced attitude toward the teaching of
history than the professors in most institutions.[120]

Mental science, logic, and political economy, courses of the type
traditionally taught to all seniors before the Civil War, retained a
strong grip at Illinois through the 1880's. Peabody assumed responsibility for them, less because of any special competence than
because custom assigned the duty to the Regent. His views in these
areas were probably more conservative than Gregory's, but what he
actually offered his classes is not a matter of record. At any rate
he proved much less successful than his predecessor. *Cecil's Book
of Natural History,* the anti-Peabody publication anonymously is-

[119] Joseph J. Mathews, "The Study of History in the South," *Journal of Southern
History,* XXXI (Feb., 1965), 4; *13th Report* (1887), 171 (the source of the
quotation); Henry Johnson, *The Other Side of Main Street* (New York, 1943),
56-57.
[120] Herbert B. Adams, *The Study of History in American Colleges and Universities,* U.S. Bureau of Education, Circular of Information No. 2, 1887 (Washington, 1887); *13th Report* (1887), 171-72; *14th Report* (1889), 172.

sued in 1883, charged him with knowing little or nothing about mental science, logic, and political economy. Nearly all seniors, it asserted, were sorry to have wasted time under Peabody's tutelage. He probably continued to teach these courses after 1883, but a discreet silence about the whole matter makes it impossible to be certain.[121]

Peabody first awoke in 1886 to the serious imbalance between the technical and literary sides of the University. Science, he said, had been the Isaac, and literature the Ishmael of the household. Despite assertions to the contrary, the institution had cherished agriculture and the mechanic arts. It supported colleges devoted to those studies with lands, laboratories, museums, workshops, apparatus, and machinery, and merely permitted the College of Literature and Science to live. The result was an obvious tendency toward weakness in the latter College. Peabody did not intend to rob Isaac to pay Ishmael, for he believed science must always have the leading place in the University. But he insisted on fostering literature and science, believing liberal education an essential balance to technical education and desiring to arrest the flight of Illinois youths to study the liberal arts in other states.[122]

In 1886 his major proposal for improvement called for raising the admissions requirements. He wanted applicants to pass an examination in Caesar, Cicero, and Vergil *before* matriculating in the College, and not to make up Latin *after* entering. This reform would equalize as nearly as possible the admissions standards for the technical and literary colleges. Although the change promised to irritate students and high schools, Peabody believed the University could best aid the latter by refusing to accept their poorly prepared graduates. His stand probably proved as unpopular then as it would now, but Peabody never lacked courage. The Board authorized the proposal to take effect in September, 1887, and perhaps significantly the drive to oust Peabody began about that time.[123]

Introduction of a rhetoric and elocution requirement for all students in the University also reflected the desire to upgrade the

[121] [Going], *Cecil's Book of Natural History*, 3. The "Faculty Record," II, Sept. 19, 1884, shows that mental science was being offered at that time.
[122] *13th Report* (1887), 84, 139-40.
[123] *Ibid.*, 84.

quality of work. Experience with a succession of elocution teachers supported by fees of student participants had led to dissatisfaction. By 1885 Peabody believed the failure to provide all pupils training in the arts of effective writing and speaking constituted the greatest deficiency in the University, and the graduates of the technical schools were particularly poor in this regard. The literary societies reached only about a third of the students and were as likely to foster as to correct errors and mannerisms. He therefore proposed the establishment of a chair and a required course. In place of stage rant and "the cheap and common tricks that bring down the house," Peabody wanted pupils taught to write clear and intelligible English and to speak in an upright and manly way. To distribute the onus of imposing new requirements, Peabody told the Trustees it might aid him and prevent any question from arising if they would formally voice the wish which many had privately expressed that all students take part in the work.[124] He appointed James H. Brownlee of Southern Normal University at Carbondale, who assumed direction of a Department of Rhetoric and Elocution at the beginning of 1886. Brownlee taught all students theme-writing in the first two years and oratory in the last two, and each senior presented an original oration at chapel exercises. For the first time in many years the University won the Intercollegiate Oratorical Contest in 1887.

Peabody's reform remained largely forensic until the second Morrill Act permitted expansion and stimulated reorganization of the College during the academic year 1890-91. The two schools now divided into four courses. The School of Ancient Languages and Literature gave way to Ancient Languages and to Latin and Science. The former enabled pupils to study both Latin and Greek, and the University established a chair in Greek which Charles M. Moss of Illinois Wesleyan came to fill. The latter permitted those enrolled to avoid Greek and concentrate on Latin, which Herbert J. Barton of the high school at Illinois State Normal took over. The School of English and Modern Languages split into courses in English and Science and in Philosophy and Pedagogy. The former perpetuated the curriculum of its predecessor, but required two years of French as well as two of German. Misael R. Paradis, a

---

[124] *Illini,* March 16, 1881; *13th Report* (1887), 46, 85, 140.

native of Montreal, Canada, and a Presbyterian clergyman, became Professor of French.[125]

The latter represented the most significant new departure. From its opening the University had avowedly aimed at training teachers for higher institutions, especially ones that emphasized industrial education, and had included philosophy of education in the mental philosophy course required of all seniors. But it also held itself aloof from preparing teachers for the place they were most urgently wanted — the secondary schools. The rapid expansion of the public schools in Illinois in the late nineteenth century created a need for more than 4,000 new teachers yearly — a need which the teacher-training schools at Carbondale, Normal, and Chicago simply could not meet. As a result the vast mass of schoolteachers received little formal training and were unequipped for their duties. Many graduates of the University naturally entered teaching — 20 per cent of all alumni, reported Peabody in 1885.[126] But the University did nothing about the practical side of their preparation, a supreme irony for an institution which was founded to improve the lot of the common man and had taken a utilitarian cast from the day of its opening.

Several forces at work from 1886 to 1890 led the University into shouldering an obligation to train teachers for the schools. The general background was the new educational philosophies associated with German theorists like Froebel and Herbart and a bit later with the American scientific psychologists William James, G. Stanley Hall, and John Dewey. A more immediate pressure came from the Illinois State Teachers' Association, whose annual meeting in December, 1885, asked the University to establish a chair in pedagogy and pledged the Association's cooperation in securing the necessary legislation. Peabody defended the University against an implicit charge of negligence by saying that everyone had recognized the course in English and Modern Languages as a teachers' course. But he and the Board cordially received the request, and included $2,000 for the position in their next appeal to the legislature. The

[125] *Catalogue, 1890-91,* 59-68.
[126] Selim H. Peabody, "The University of Illinois" (MS. of 1885 address to the Illinois State Teachers' Association), 24. However, this figure probably exaggerated. On another occasion Peabody reported 11 per cent. See Superintendent of Public Instruction, *Eighteenth Biennial Report,* 95.

University's ability to handle science facilitated expansion in this direction. The ISTA had probably turned to Urbana rather than the normal schools because the University could train teachers in this area of rapid growth in school curricula. Peabody urged the importance of science as a foundation for teaching in his effort to invigorate the College of Literature and Science in 1886. Moreover, the University's capacity in this field differed so greatly from that of the normal schools that there could be no unfriendly competition between them. But the General Assembly's failure to furnish funds delayed action until 1890.[127]

At that time the University established a course in Philosophy and Pedagogy designed especially for those who intended to enter the teaching profession. Its first two years of studies followed the other courses in Literature and Science, and the last two included ten terms of technical work. These were in educational psychology, science of instruction, logic, special methods, mental science, school supervision, history of education, philosophy of education, and two philosophy courses. The second Morrill Act enabled Peabody to meet the request of the Teachers' Association, and he appointed Charles DeGarmo, who had studied in Germany and returned to Normal, as Professor of Psychology in December, 1890. DeGarmo took up his duties at the beginning of 1891, and probably devised the new program carried in the catalogue for 1890-91, which the Faculty approved on March 4, 1891. He also laid plans to offer courses in sociology and in the principles of science, and left a distinctly favorable impression on students before resigning the following September to become President of Swarthmore College.[128]

It should be unmistakably clear from the preceding remarks that Peabody contributed considerably to the academic advancement of the University. He took no place among the leaders of the

---

[127] *13th Report* (1887), 97, 139-40; *14th Report* (1889), 40.
[128] *Catalogue, 1890-91,* 65-68; *16th Report* (1892), 20-21, 37; "Faculty Record," III, 53. DeGarmo's service at the University from January to June, 1891, coincided with the severe disturbances which led to Peabody's forced resignation. During this period the Faculty devoted considerable time and effort to coping with student rebels and imposing demerits, and probably the negative impressions which DeGarmo gained from this experience made him particularly receptive to an outside offer. See pp. 319-25 below.

movement to develop university ideals in the United States, for he did not emphasize graduate training or research. He did try, however, to obtain a first-rate faculty, and professors both conducted important research and trained scholarly investigators at Urbana during his administration. Moreover, he strove to raise academic standards and to bring order out of the confusion introduced by the elective system. Perhaps most men called to the regency would have done the former, for the times were ripe in the 1880's to enable the state universities to move to higher levels of performance than had been possible earlier. Yet not everyone would have attempted the latter, for the general drift in higher education favored freedom of choice for the student. His educational philosophy led Peabody to resist this trend, and he may also have believed that elective freedom often thrust a cruel burden on students totally unprepared to handle it. No doubt many youths shared the experience of Ralph D. Lewis, a country boy who entered the University with enthusiastic anticipation just before Peabody's new prescription became effective. Lewis had no definite idea of what he wanted to take or any advice to guide him. Having studied Greek for hours each night in the attic of his country home before reaching Urbana, he started in classics. Then he switched to horticulture, and ended with civil engineering. Lewis performed excellently by the usual standards, but 30 years after graduating he bitterly criticized a system which had allowed him to inflict a hodgepodge upon himself.[129]

Peabody's academic policy, despite its failure to emphasize graduate studies, held promise for the future. Eventually the colleges and universities of the nation followed a course similar to his by requiring students to "major" and "minor," or to seek both concentration and distribution in their studies. Although some dissatisfaction with Peabody arose over his new policy of prescription, the main source of opposition to him sprang from his insistence that the academic life of the University must be central. This view led Peabody to oppose extracurricular activities that pressed for a new place on the campus at the close of the century. Perhaps most of all, Peabody's personal style, a blend of formalism and authoritarianism, counted heavily against him.

[129] Ralph D. Lewis to Ira O. Baker, Cleveland, Dec. 20, 1913, Edmund J. James Papers.

CHAPTER EIGHT

The Conquests of Earnest Effort

PEABODY'S ADMINISTRATION COINCIDED with a particularly stormy era in American higher education, and turbulence marked the emergence of an unmistakably modern type of collegiate life. The conflict which disrupted many campuses for over a decade after 1880 sprang from the tension between two ideas concerning the primary purpose of a college. The traditional conception regarded it as a center for intellectual discipline and moral training. A newer conception considered it a school of general experience in which formal study was at most one among many competing interests. Finding academic ideals incapable of effectively enlisting their imaginations, students spent their best efforts on a round of undergraduate activities. The extracurriculum therefore acquired unprecedented importance in these years, and it developed new social and athletic emphases. The world which students created for themselves apart from the formal and compulsory side of college life threatened the intellectual integrity of higher education. As President Woodrow Wilson of Princeton later observed, the side shows became so diverting that they swallowed up the circus, "and those who perform in the main tent must often whistle for their audiences, discouraged and humiliated."[1]

The problems generated by this transition became acute during the years of Peabody's tenure at Illinois, and especially in those institutions where the faculty and the students became polarized around two distinctive educational ideals — the ideal of discipline and the ideal of freedom.[2] Most faculties, however much they might differ over the relative worth of general intellectual discipline as opposed to professional preparation, thought the college was a place for study. They opposed the new stress on extracurricular activities while offering no substitute for it. They failed to arouse enthusiasm for scholarship and frequently perpetuated the disciplinary rules which minutely governed student life. The students had changed with the times. Most of them were not preparing for the learned professions, and many entered college with no definite aims. College years, they thought, were intended for enjoyment as much as for study, and they demanded freedom to devise a mode of campus life which suited their personal needs.

Hence the professors and their pupils became antagonists. The turmoil became widespread and often boiled down to grim and open warfare between the president and the student body. Battles of this type were common in the 1880's and 1890's. Dartmouth, Bowdoin, Purdue, Union College, the University of Missouri, and Amherst were among the colleges disrupted. Disaffected young men rebelled through boycotts, strikes, and demonstrations. Often they appealed over the heads of local authorities to college governing boards and legislative assemblies, and sometimes members of these bodies conspired with campus rebels. Frequently the most promising students

[1] Woodrow Wilson, "What Is a College For?" *Scribner's,* XLVI (Nov., 1909), 576.
[2] On the two ideals, see Henry S. Pritchett, "The College of Discipline and the College of Freedom," *Atlantic Monthly,* CII (Nov., 1908), 604.

led the agitation. At Amherst the mastermind behind the student rebellion against President Merrill E. Gates in the 1890's was Harlan Fiske Stone, a future Chief Justice of the United States.[3]

One of the sharpest controversies occurred at the University of Illinois, where the Regent symbolized everything embodied in the older ideal of discipline. Peabody considered college chiefly a place for intellectual training and moral enlightenment, and even before Wilson he feared the encroachment of the side shows upon the main tent. Student clubs and activities were hard to control, and Peabody strongly believed in closely regulating student life. For him docility among pupils was a virtue, and he cherished what was technically called a "quiet term." But the students at Urbana represented the new ideal of freedom, and rightly or wrongly they were more in tune with the spirit of the times than was the Regent. No less earnest than their predecessors, they nevertheless channeled their enormous energy into less academically oriented pursuits. Inevitably they met resistance, and the resulting conflict both agitated Peabody's administration and led finally to his ouster.

The style of college life which originated in the late nineteenth century has profoundly shaped higher education in the twentieth, and this reason alone makes it vital to understand why events followed the course they did. But it is harder to account for than to describe the life outside the classroom in the decade or so after 1880. Naturally, no single cause can adequately explain what occurred, and even to attribute the outcome to the interaction of several forces may oversimplify. Nevertheless, three influences prevailed in the new pattern of undergraduate activities at Urbana and in the conflict which roiled the University of Illinois. Briefly they are environment, imitation, and hostility toward the administration.

The environment fostered boredom, and neither the local community nor the college authorities provided adequate means for fighting this monster. The towns of Champaign and Urbana possessed over 10,000 souls by 1890, and their opera houses featured more entertainments — lectures and concerts — than had been

[3] Claude Moore Fuess, *Amherst: The Story of a New England College* (Boston, 1935), 253-54.

available when the University opened. Nevertheless the two inland towns offered little escape from academic routine. Probably the student rebellions of the period occurred more readily in colleges located in rural areas, as was the University, than in cities. At any rate, the monotony of life on the prairie forced youths to create their own diversions.

The officials of the University confined their efforts to the formal and compulsory side of student life, and assumed no responsibility for using the remaining time, the bulk of a student's waking hours, to educate or otherwise occupy their charges. The faculty and the students occupied two different worlds. The traditions of impersonality and even hostility bequeathed by the old-time college governed in this area, and not the relative smallness of the academic community. Taft was an unusual professor in that he invited pupils into his home, but he departed in 1882. As Regent, Peabody occasionally held a reception for the senior or junior class. Faculty members generally failed to attend chapel or literary society programs, and they had practically no interest in college sports until the 1890's.

Nor did the authorities furnish students the opportunity for a common life beyond the classrooms, chapel, and military drill. A rule closed all University buildings at 6 P.M. each school day, thus preventing individuals from spending evenings and weekends in either the laboratory or library.[4] The library, however, opened from 2 to 5 P.M. each Saturday. Moreover, there was no life in college halls at Urbana after 1881. Opposition to the residential housing philosophy weighed most heavily in American higher education in the late nineteenth century as a result of the combined influence of the German universities, which only imparted instruction and otherwise left pupils entirely to their own devices; the financial limitations of the state universities; and an earlier history of unfortunate experience with the dormitory system in the United States. A few individuals were still occupying the Old Dormitory when Peabody became Regent, although a tornado had demolished its western wing during the previous spring. But the place had a bad reputation because the University had seriously erred in allowing men to live

4 "Faculty Record," II, Dec. 9, 1881.

there under insufficient guardianship. Peabody knew the problem, for shortly after he took office the Faculty expelled a sophomore for taking a woman of ill repute to the dormitory. (It also ordered him to leave town immediately in order to prevent the matter from being made public.)[5] The following spring a chance discovery revealed an ignited powder train leading to combustibles in the basement of the building. Peabody labeled the dormitory "a constant menace to good morals," and the Board ordered its destruction in the summer of 1881. Despite these difficulties, however, the residential philosophy exerted such a strong influence that in 1886 the Trustees formed a five-man committee including Peabody to make plans for a ladies' hall and boardinghouse and a men's dormitory, each to accommodate at least a hundred students. But nothing came of this effort.[6]

Consequently students made their own arrangements for room and board. Some lived with their families or in private homes in Champaign or Urbana, and others in rooming houses that sprang up around the campus. Few dined in any meaningful sense of that term; instead, they fed themselves at lunchrooms, at an expense to health, or in one of the numerous boarding clubs that arose to meet the need. Merrill's, one of the most popular, boasted 35 members. The University's failure to provide a residence hall or commons helped produce a very thin social atmosphere, and the fragmentation of the student body into roominghouses and boarding clubs aggravated the boredom. A student poet described the craving for excitement in order to relieve the monotony of continued study, and an account of college life which included class fights among the social activities of the students went on to ask, "What else was there for us to do?"[7]

To provide an answer, students sought to create their own social atmosphere. They turned to organizations of various types, literary and dramatic ventures, social affairs, class activities, and sports. Success here resulted partly from intensity, for the young

[5] *Ibid.,* Dec. 8, 1880.
[6] *11th Report* (1882), 183, 189; *13th Report* (1887), 21; *14th Report* (1889), 22, 44.
[7] *Sophograph* (1890), 10; Charles Albert Kiler, *On the Banks of the Boneyard* ([Urbana], 1942), 30.

men and women still believed they could shape their destinies by hard work. The class of 1881 expressed that conviction in its motto, "Earnest Effort Conquers," and Class Orator Willis A. Mansfield used the motto at Class Day. "Earnest effort, energy, will," said Mansfield, "is the power which moves the world and shapes its destiny." Regarding genius as one of the sceptered gods of the past, Mansfield concluded, " 'Earnest Effort' sits upon its throne, its crown, success; its sceptre, power; and at its feet the world must bow."[8] Adherence to this tenet persisted throughout the decade, although students increasingly conquered new realms of college life rather than of college studies. But students tried to balance the competing claims as they debated the primary purpose of college. Should a student try to store his mind with facts, acquire social polish, or have a few years of grand good times? Always the answer came that the ability to work, the attainment of power to use the mental faculties for some worthy end, constituted the real aim of education.[9] But practice increasingly belied profession.

Imitation also goaded the student body into trying to develop the full round of undergraduate activities found in other colleges. The Gregorians had already imported many of these, but they had carefully borrowed only wholesome customs and eschewed childish or noxious ones. The students continued to live in a competitive world, and they thought it better to be dead than out of collegiate fashion. Of what worth was a degree from Illinois if the world marked the University down as a place for academic grinds? Thus the students had to imitate the pattern of college life which was gaining hold throughout the nation. Unlike their predecessors, they copied such questionable practices as ritualized violence. But Greek-letter fraternities and athletics enlisted their strongest feelings.

Hostility toward the administration probably oversimplifies the many disparate elements which combined in a third influence that shaped college life and the conflict at the University in the 1880's. This feeling takes us into the realm of social psychology, and it is hazardous to push the evidence too far. Yet there can be no doubt

[8] *Illini*, June 8, 1881.
[9] *Sophographs* afford the best illustration of this theme. See especially the issues of 1885, pp. 25-27; and 1889, p. 54.

that students became fed up with conditions in the University. Their ideal of discipline clashed with the ideal of discipline held on high. They disliked curricular prescription and found several teachers inadequate. They objected to their treatment as high school pupils, to the strict rules and the black marks imposed for violations, and to the fact that they lived under the authority of a group with which they had little acquaintance or sympathy and which governed them without their consent. Peabody became the main focus of their hostility, and it is not unfair to say that some of the spontaneous and ritualized violence was directed at him. But generalized expressions of discontent proved insufficient, and ultimately students seized an opportunity to throw him out.

Peabody knew that deep student unrest existed when he assumed the regency, and he initiated reforms which restored order within three years. The discipline and government of the campus constituted a central problem when the headship of the University changed. Peabody had no use for Gregory's liberal views on the subject. He considered American students immature for self-government, and maintained that universities needed discipline as long as students who were unprepared to accept the responsibilities of manhood attended them.[10] This attitude seemed justified by the difficulties which the College Government then confronted. But the students had supported the system by a vote of 212 to 61 in the spring of 1880, and Peabody tried conscientiously to make the best of the inheritance.[11]

A reform in 1880 restored considerable power over internal discipline to the Faculty. An attack on the Government's legality had brought from the Attorney General a ruling that the system was legal but could not fine students. The Board then removed doubts about the basis for the plan by formally approving the Faculty's authorization of it, except for the provision allowing for imposition and collection of fines.[12] The Government therefore became purely

[10] Selim H. Peabody, "The American University," MS. of Anniversary Day address, March, 1882, pp. 12-14, 20.
[11] *Illini,* Jan., 1880.
[12] Gregory to James K. Edsall, Jan. 22 [Jan. 2], 1880, "Regents' Letterbook, 1879-1894"; *10th Report* (1881), 222, 230.

a voluntary association. Some students chose to abide by the decision of their fellows. The Marshal apprehended wrongdoers and brought them before the College Court, where attorneys and judges found the trial proceedings enormously interesting. They took their duties seriously — in one saloon case an attorney summoned 62 witnesses — and adopted "Greenleaf on Evidence" and "Chitty on Pleadings" as reference works. The Court could refer any pending case to the Faculty. Students again complained about performing the disciplinary work of the Faculty, and now added that they lacked any revenue to operate. Late in 1880 the Board authorized $25 a year in lieu of fines to support the work.

The reform gave the Faculty both original and appellate jurisdiction over all students. This tribunal tried offenders who did not care to go before their peers, and it could call up for its own consideration any case before the College Court. Decisions of the latter acquired new respect when the Faculty sustained and even increased its penalties. But the Faculty itself punished many students for visiting billiard halls or saloons, usually suspending the former for the remainder of the term and the latter for the remainder of the college year. They announced these judgments in chapel.

Although the Government was not totally ineffective after 1880, it aggravated rather than reduced tension. It embittered relations between teachers and their pupils because many of the latter considered it a system of espionage. The feeling of opposition grew even among law-abiding persons. Perhaps more important, the system became a bone of contention among students, dividing them into Government and anti-Government factions. It appears that the two lower classes and the *Illini* usually comprised the former, while the two upper classes and the secret fraternities made up the latter. The elections for Government offices early in 1881 were unusually tumultuous. Many campaigned aggressively for candidates not on the regular ticket who had been chosen with a view to breaking up the mechanism.[13]

In December, 1881, Peabody initiated a reform of discipline which undermined the College Government. Gaining authorization from the Faculty to codify all the existing University laws, he pub-

[13] *Illini,* Sept., 1880; Feb. 24, 1883; *Sophograph* (1882), 45.

lished his handiwork the following year in a small pamphlet entitled *Rules for the Government of Students in the Illinois Industrial University*. This compilation contained a significant new provision of which there is no record of either Faculty or Board authorization. Peabody had inserted a matriculation pledge, a familiar disciplinary device of an older era. The *Rules* required every applicant for admission to file a written "promise that during my connection [with the University] I will perform all duties with fidelity, will yield loyal and instant obedience to all lawful authority, and at all times will strive to maintain a gentlemanly, or lady like, demeanor, in public and in private, always mindful of my own good name and of the fair fame of the University which I seek to join."[14]

A week after the *Rules* appeared the General Assembly adopted resolutions which indicted the Faculty for lack of confidence in the students and returned to that body the powers of government entrusted to the pupils. Peabody viewed this "flurry of passion" as an organized attack on the Government, and decreed that the system must be constitutionally abrogated if at all. In March, 1882, the General Assembly, acting with less than the 50 students needed for a quorum, retaliated against the administration by naming two women — Dora A. Andrus and Fronia R. Cole — for President. Miss Andrus' victory made her the first woman to head the College Government, but under the circumstances the triumph must have tasted bittersweet. In the fall of 1882 the campus newspaper defied anyone "to mention a single particular in which this Government has done good during the last year." The *Illini* observed that the plan was "as dead as an Egyptian mummy." But the funeral rites had yet to be held.[15]

The animus against the College Government produced by continual class and factional rivalries, to be described below, was the final straw, and under the load the Government expired in 1883. At a vote taken late in May, 77 students favored continuing the scheme, 110 opposed it, and about 120 were too indifferent to cast

[14] "Faculty Record," II, Dec. 9, 1881; the *Rules* were published in Champaign, 1882. The quotation is at p. 4.
[15] "Secretary's Book, College Government [1881-1883]," 10, 21, 45; Selim H. Peabody, "An Educational Experiment," National Educational Association, *Journal of Proceedings and Addresses, 1889* (Topeka, 1889), 544; *11th Report* (1882), 221; *Illini*, Nov. 25, 1882 (the source of the quotations).

a ballot. The Faculty therefore resumed all authority previously committed to the College Government, whose functions ceased at the end of the college year. The noble experiment had failed, and Peabody rightly believed that its elimination removed a seriously disturbing element within the University. But the replacement he sponsored created even greater trouble.[16]

Rowdyism suddenly assumed significant proportions at the University, and the fact that this occurred just as students became disillusioned with Gregory and Peabody may indicate that aggression and violence met a psychological need. In March, 1881, the student press was still boasting that the University had not copied silly and harmful traditions from older colleges. In fact, however, they had begun to do so during the troubled times of Gregory's exit and Peabody's arrival. In October, 1879, the tree planted by some seniors was uprooted within a day, and in the winter and spring terms of 1881 students manifested a spirit of restiveness. They put a buggy on the peak of the Old Dormitory and gave cremation exercises a vogue. In March, for example, a hundred students and a band paraded through town with Wood's "Co-ordinate Geometry" and then burned the book and buried its ashes under an inscribed marker in front of University Hall. These rites, popular in the age of compulsory courses and texts, revealed attitudes toward Peabody's new regime. The natural savagery of college youths also found release in tearing up stiles, fences, and boardwalks. And someone removed the stairs leading to the second story of the old Mechanical Building one evening while students were in rooms on that floor.[17]

Class spirit had been running high before 1880, but now it turned into conflict which bordered on dangerous warfare, although the students considered it good sport. The main rivalries set the two upper and two lower classes against each other. The juniors and seniors initiated what became a continuing battle when some seniors planted a class tree early in 1881. Juniors immediately tarred and feathered the tree, and somehow the Faculty got the names of five students involved. On February 22 the professorial tribunal dismissed the case against Comma N. Boyd and James G. Wadsworth

[16] "Faculty Record," June 1, 1883; *12th Report* (1885), 233.
[17] *Illini*, March 2, 1881; Nov., 1879; March 30, April 27, 1881.

as not proved, and found the other three — S. W. Colton, Herbert Turner, and Arthur M. Bridge — guilty in varying degrees.[18] Two days after the convicted trio had read in chapel a paper acknowledging their wrong and apologizing to the Faculty and the senior class, the five members of the TAR Society published a new edition of the *Vindicator*. This pedestrian four-page sheet denounced seniors as "a brainless set of petty tyrants" and harshly condemned individual members of the class. It also attacked the College Government, whose presidency Wadsworth had just turned over to Bridge in January, 1881. At this time Marshal Charles G. Armstrong, a sophomore, was apprehending wrongdoers so zealously as to elicit threats of reprisal. The *Vindicator* charged "Contemptible Goldarned" Armstrong with lying to convict innocent men and with having many a good drink with the seniors. "Government or anti-Government?" asked the *Vindicator*. "That is the question. Whether 'tis better in the university to spy the actions and foot-steps of one another, or to let the faculty do their duty as 'twas assigned them."[19]

Five seniors then prepared to retaliate in print, and a party of juniors rushed the *Illini* office to prevent the work. When a constable and Professor Burrill appeared at the disturbance, Wadsworth argued that it was improper to use the equipment of a press belonging to the faculty and students for the intended purpose. Burrill agreed, and the seniors therefore printed their *Vindicator* privately. This chaste two-page organ quoted Professor Snyder as saying the earlier *Vindicator* had contained "the least wit and the most dirt of any publication that was ever issued here."[20] But the tradition of privately issued defamatory publications had taken firm root by 1881, and Snyder had not yet seen the worst.

Seniors planted another tree at the northwest corner of University Hall later that spring. Richard E. Dorsey and Henry L. McCune set out one evening to uproot it, and were surprised by some seniors hiding out with shotguns in the branches of evergreens nearby. The Faculty suspended Dorsey and McCune indefinitely,

[18] "Faculty Record," II, Feb. 22, 1881. The "Faculty Record" erroneously names W. E. Bridge rather than Arthur M. Bridge. The two men were brothers.
[19] *Vindicator*, Feb. 24, 1881.
[20] *Ibid.*, March 5, 1881. Copies of both issues are in the Arthur N. Talbot Papers.

but before it had done so some students who were determined to get the tree had organized a raiding party. Each member went armed with a shotgun to guard the expedition's hatchet-bearer, and the defending seniors fired on the aggressors. Friends extracted over 100 pieces of birdshot from the person of one victim. These "heroic" deeds rather than co-ordinate geometry furnished the real substance of college life.[21]

The revival of fraternities further aggravated the situation. Peabody had been a fraternity man, and upon taking office he did not warn against secret societies. This omission was taken as a green light. A few men may have reorganized Delta Tau Delta in 1880 (Francis M. McKay and John H. Morse, both 1881 graduates, claimed membership), but Sigma Chi became the leading fraternity during Peabody's administration. The friendship which led to its establishment had been formed at the Interstate Oratorical Association meeting at Oberlin in 1880, but before the Illinois petition for a chapter was acted upon by the parent body the tree imbroglio had intervened. Since both of the warring factions contained Sigma Chi petitioners, the parent chapter sent an emissary to settle the rival claims for recognition. He favored the underclassmen, and the seven charter members of Sigma Chi at Urbana included Arthur M. Bridge, Richard E. Dorsey, Henry L. McCune, and James G. Wadsworth. Following a fancy banquet, formal installation of the chapter took place in the early hours of May 31, 1881. Members wore their badges on the campus that spring, and they believed that in conversations with Peabody he had countenanced their organization.[22]

The future for fraternities at Illinois looked bright. These were the years when the movement was gaining its greatest strength nationally, and none could deny the obvious advantages in terms of housing, boarding, and sociability which Greek-letter clubs might offer students at Urbana. In the autumn the membership of Sigma

[21] "Faculty Record," II, June 4, 6, 1881; *Illini,* June 8, 1881; Kiler, *On the Banks of the Boneyard,* 28-30.
[22] *Illini,* Dec. 1, 1880; Kiler, *On the Banks of the Boneyard,* 10; Franklin W. Scott, ed., *The Alumni Record of the University of Illinois* (Urbana, 1906), *passim* for the years involved; Joseph C. Nate, *The History of the Sigma Chi Fraternity, 1855-1930* (4 vols., n.p., 1925-31), II, 173-76.

Chi rose to 16, and the men rented a hall in a Champaign business building. Other students were in touch with Beta Theta Pi and Phi Gamma Delta, and hopes were running high.

But at Illinois as throughout the country the opposition still remained strong. Gregory had indoctrinated the Board on the subject, its members still recalled the strife created by the Delts, and President Emory Cobb especially disliked fraternities. Peabody, reporting the organization of Sigma Chi to the Trustees, called attention to Gregory's and the Board's adverse findings of 1876. In effect he recommended suppression and the Board now took formal action in line with its earlier advisory resolution. On September 14 it termed the existence of fraternities "unwise, and detrimental to the best interests of the institution," and directed the Regent to secure their abandonment.[23] Peabody notified the Sigma Chi's to disband, but took no further action until he learned that students were trying to vitalize the fraternity chapters.

Then he imposed an antifraternity pledge whose form he borrowed from Princeton, where President McCosh had employed it in 1875 to conquer a serious evil. Early in December the Faculty ordered that after January 1, 1882, no student be admitted to any class until he had deposited a signed oath promising that while at the University he would not join or be connected with any college secret society. In addition, no student was to receive an honorable discharge or a certificate or diploma of graduation unless he stated upon his honor that he had had nothing to do with these organizations as a member or otherwise while in college.[24] Peabody had probably learned enough about the local Sigma Chi's to warrant changing his mind, and he also took courage from President Emerson E. White of Purdue. In the fall of 1891 an Indiana circuit court upheld White in his long battle against Sigma Chi.[25]

Dissatisfaction with the oath became acute, and Sigma Chi's severely criticized Peabody for his change of attitude. Students petitioned the Board to rescind the pledge, and when it refused in March, 1882, angry fraternity men tried to kill off the College Government. Sigma Chi's in the TAR Society made the Government a

[23] *11th Report* (1882), 192.
[24] "Faculty Record," Dec. 2, 1881.
[25] Nate, *History of Sigma Chi,* II, 179-80.

main target in the *Vindicator,* and in 1883 they threw their weight against the perishing system. Plans to petition every meeting of the Trustees led that body to refuse even to consider such appeals. Hence a determined band combined with fraternity interests throughout the state to carry their case to Springfield. They found a precedent in Indiana, where in 1882 the Supreme Court had reversed the lower court. Although it held invalid the rule of the Purdue Trustees which made membership in a Greek-letter fraternity a disqualification for admission, the Court declared that the governing body possessed the power to prohibit any connection between social fraternities and the University. President White tried to evade the consequences of the decision, with the result that fraternity men carried the case to the legislature, which repudiated his policies in 1883. Now Sigma Chi's and other fraternity men in Illinois inaugurated a campaign in Springfield to change the Board and to secure legislative action.[26]

Students harbored many grievances by the spring of 1883, and they vented their hostilities dramatically. At Class Day exercises on June 4 Elisha B. Durfee and Henry P. Little chose to shock the authorities with presentations which a local newspaper described as obscene lectures with illustrations. The Faculty expelled both seniors for insulting the sense and decency of the audience and disgracing the University.[27] Early on graduation day a scurrilous pamphlet entitled *Cecil's Book of Natural History; About the Great Ones of '83* appeared around the two towns and on the campus. This anonymous parody of Peabody's volumes on science for children attacked the Government, certain professors, and Peabody himself in vicious text and crude woodcuts. Word quickly reached Peabody that Judson F. Going was implicated. A senior and 25 years old, Going was a prominent student and had recently been a senator in the Government.[28]

[26] *Ibid.,* 180-82; Edward C. Elliott and M. M. Chambers, *The Colleges and the Courts: Judicial Decisions Regarding Institutions of Higher Education in the United States* (New York, 1936), 13-14; William Murray Hepburn and Louis Martin Sears, *Purdue University: Fifty Years of Progress* (Indianapolis, 1925), 66-67, 72-73.
[27] "Faculty Record," II, June 5, 1883; Champaign County *Herald,* June 13, 1883. Ten years later the Faculty authorized the granting of a degree to Little. See "Faculty Record," III, 206.
[28] A copy is in the Alumni Class Files.

He castigated this system for its espionage character. Playing upon the initials of recent Government officers, *Cecil's Book* sketched acidulous portraits of Fred D. ("Faculty Dog") Pierce, John T. ("Judas Telltale") Kenower, and Henry P. ("Hypocritical Pusilanimous" [*sic*]) Little. Going termed McCune, who had re-entered the University and edited the *Illini* during 1882-83, a "mongrel whelp." Although once ousted, "his piteous whines touched the sympathetic gizzard of the ring-master who offered to train him for exhibition."[29]

Going used even stronger language to denounce four faculty members who had completed their first year at Urbana in June, 1883 — E. B. Morse in Classics, young Cecil H. Peabody, Benjamin C. Jillson, and William McMurtrie. The burden of the charge against them was academic incompetence. "A State University is no place for a dead beat to attempt to learn a profession at the expense of her students."[30] But disagreeable personal qualities also received mention. Going viewed the appointment of a "gruntling hog" and "putrid carcass" as a curse resting on Peabody, and in a bad poem said it was better to let Selim go, to let his memory rot, than to let the fair school go down beneath a scheming plot. This first published expression of a desire to remove the Regent, however misguided, aimed seriously at academic improvement.

Cecil's Book singled out Peabody himself as its main target. "I, Shameless Hypocrite Peabody, was born on April 1st [fools day] 1829," began the text, and the "autobiography" went on to describe the slips Peabody had made since taking office. His Anniversary Day address in 1882 had been disastrous, and his teaching had proved that he knew little about mental science, logic, and political economy, thus making four-fifths of his students sorry to have wasted their senior year at Urbana.[31] The pamphlet caricatured his children as the simian offspring of a wondrous project

---

[29] [Going], *Cecil's Book of Natural History*, 3.
[30] *Ibid.*, 11.
[31] *Ibid.*, 2. Two contemporary accounts give force to some of the charges. On Peabody's Anniversary Day address in 1882, see the *Illini*, March 18, 1882. On student discontent, see the Champaign County *Gazette,* Feb. 23, 1881, which says there had been talk among seniors in regard to leaving the University and graduating at Ann Arbor.

> . . . planned by S. H. P.,
> To make old Darwin's theory
> As plain as A.B.C.[32]

When Peabody learned of the pamphlet he hastily assembled the Faculty before commencement. Going confessed his responsibility and the professors struck his name from the graduation list. At a special meeting the next day, June 7, the Faculty failed to uncover sufficient evidence to convict two of four students implicated, and the other two did not appear. Going was one of these. He sent word that he considered his own case judged and had nothing to report about his fellow students. Having made other plans, he thought it best to carry them out.

These plans prompted Going to appeal to higher authority. He went to a member of the Board to whom he defended *Cecil's Book* "as one of great benefit to the University and its students."[33] Probably he discussed Peabody's shortcomings and asked for his removal. When the Faculty met in September it found no evidence of Going's contrition for issuing what the authorities called "a scurrilous, indecent, and blasphemous publication."[34] It reaffirmed its earlier action and recommended withholding Going's commission in the State Militia. But Going then carried his case to both Governor John M. Hamilton and the Board. The Governor upheld the Faculty, although at one point the Faculty instructed Peabody to write to Hamilton and stiffen his resolution. The Board directed the Faculty to restudy its decision, but in 1885 that body reaffirmed its earlier rulings.[35]

Peabody survived the turbulence which rose to a peak in the spring of 1883, and he restored to the campus a condition of relative peace. Perhaps the antagonists decided to live and let live, but the new situation is also attributable to the fact that Peabody increased his control over the various agencies of student life. He "solved" the

[32] [Going], *Cecil's Book of Natural History*, 9.
[33] "Faculty Record," II, Sept. 14, 1883 (an excellent summary of the episode to this date).
[34] *Ibid.*
[35] *Ibid.*, March 14, 21, April 4, 1884; April 3, 10, 1885; Peabody to Hamilton, Sept. 25, 1883, April 4, 1884, "Regents' Letterbook, 1879-1894."

continuing problem of internal discipline by establishing a demerit system to replace student self-government. Under the new scheme individual teachers could award up to ten demerits for any infraction of good order; the collective Faculty could impose as many as an offense warranted. A total of 200 demerits brought dismissal from the University, but a student could remove 30 black marks by going an entire term without receiving any. The Faculty adopted the plan after due deliberation in May, 1884, but the decision seems not to have been made public until early the next year. The *Illini* only indirectly criticized the controls by praising the lack of rigid discipline at Amherst and Harvard, but the students probably registered their real feelings in a satirical broadside labeled "Rules for the Illinois Industrial Training and Reform School." Nevertheless, starting in the fall of 1883 the discipline was the best it had been since 1878. And that situation lasted about four years.[36]

The campus newspaper contributed to an atmosphere favorable to "loyalty, order, and studious habits."[37] During the first two years of Peabody's administration the editorship of the self-supporting *Illini* became increasingly prestigious. A committee of the Student Senate managed the enterprise, but the two main literary societies actually dominated the choice of editor. In September, 1880, Charles H. Dennis, a Philomathean, took that post. He converted a monthly semi-literary journal into a semi-monthly *newspaper* which was book size and usually ran 20 pages an issue. It carried advertisements and reported events in other colleges, but emphasized campus and alumni news. Dennis entertained hopes of vitalizing the organ by speaking freely upon matters relating to the students and the University. "We must have our say," asserted the *Illini*, "and on the side which we think is right. To stir up idle and useless tumult is surely not the office of a college paper, but to express

---

[36] "Faculty Record," II, March 28, April 18, May 2, 1884; *Additional Regulations for the Government of Students of the Illinois Industrial University, Adopted Between March 10, 1882, and February 10, 1885* (n.p., n.d.); *Illini*, March 2, 1885; Champaign County *Gazette*, Feb. 25, 1885. A copy of the broadside is in "Student Broadsides," Student Organization Alphabetical File.
[37] The phrase represents Peabody's ideal, and he enjoyed reporting this condition of affairs to the Board. See, for example, *11th Report* (1882), 221.

the truth and the whole truth is its right and duty."[38] Noble words! But the *Illini* failed to manifest a critical spirit, and perhaps the basic reason was a failure to realize that controversy is the lifeblood of a university. Dennis expressed pleasure that the University had no political club, which he considered a "useless element of discord among college students."[39] Both he and his immediate successor, George W. Bullard, an Adelphic and a mouthpiece of the administration, devoted the publication to safe and familiar themes. Small wonder that the *Illini* had fewer student than nonstudent subscribers, and that most of the latter were alumni. And small wonder that anonymous editors issued scurrilous publications which offered the best vehicle for free (if strong and often indecent) expression.

But the very idea of an independent student newspaper caused apprehension in official circles. The Faculty therefore brought the *Illini* under its control in the autumn of 1882. It declared that the equipment in the printing office was University property, and announced that students could use it only under prescribed regulations and supervision. The student Senate's nominees for editor and business manager had to receive Faculty confirmation before they could discharge their duties. Most significantly, the Faculty held the editor responsible for everything printed in the *Illini* except advertisements, and specifically decreed, "He may not permit the insertion of any article reflecting upon the character of any student or officer of the University, nor upon the rules or the managment thereof."[40]

This reform brought protest from students and alumni. An *Illini* editorial argued that the equipment had been purchased with money put up and solicited by students. Some alumni offered to buy out the state's interest in the equipment, but the governing body ruled that the Board would hold in trust all property purchased for printing a newspaper, whatever the source.

The expiration of the College Government necessitated new arrangements in order to give students some liberty within a framework of authority. Peabody undoubtedly took the initiative for rules which the Faculty promulgated on October 26, 1883. These vested

[38] *Illini*, Oct. 20, 1880. Dennis went on to a newspaper career and rose to the editorship of the Chicago *Daily News* from 1925 to 1934.
[39] *Illini*, Oct. 20, 1880.
[40] "Faculty Record," II, Sept. 22, 1882.

student control of the campus newspaper in an Illini Board, composed of 13 student members elected by their various classes. No more than one person from each class could belong to the same literary society. The Illini Board was to have supervision over the newspaper, but none of its regulations became effective until approved by the Regent. Each May the Illini Board was to nominate an editor and business manager, and if approved by the Faculty they had charge of the paper during the ensuing college year. As before, the rules held the editor responsible for the contents and prohibited negative criticism. The Faculty reserved a right to remove the editor and business manager whenever the interests of the University warranted.[41]

Some students complained about these provisions, and the nature of their protest is most revealing. Samuel W. Parr, editor of the *Illini* at the time, represented a committee of the literary societies in proposing changes which aimed at obtaining more power on the Illini Board for the upper at the expense of the lower classes and for literary societies at the expense of "independents." The Faculty met the group most of the way, reducing the representation of the freshman and sophomore classes on an 11-member Illini Board and establishing a system of cumulative voting. This enabled students to give one candidate as many votes as the number of representatives to be elected from his class. A senior, for example, could cast four ballots for one person. This scheme facilitated control of the editorship by the literary societies, and Parr expressed his satisfaction.[42] Content with the crumbs of power, the students readily surrendered the loaf of principle — the right to engage in free and responsible criticism. No one revealed any awareness that open discussion of issues served a vital educational function and thus constituted perhaps the most important justification for the existence of a college newspaper.

As a result the *Illini* was mainly a "house organ" during Peabody's administration. The literary societies obtained the editorship during all but two of these years, and incumbents of that position generally became cheerleaders for the administration. They hailed

[41] *Ibid.,* Oct. 26, 1883.
[42] *Ibid.,* Dec. 7, 14, 17, 1883; *Illini,* Dec. 10, 1883; Jan. 28, 1884; *12th Report* (1885), 219.

the victory of temperance forces in local elections, backed Peabody's ban on fraternities, defended the University against hostile criticisms, and urged everyone — trustees, faculty members, and students — to promote the good name of the institution throughout the state. One editor even warned his fellow students not to walk on the grass. He was Thomas Arkle Clark, who invested his professional life at the University. Clark's immediate successor, Clarence A. Shamel, was perhaps the least docile. He gently questioned the advisability of the Faculty's censorship of Tolstoy's "Kreutzer Sonata," but kept the *Illini,* a semi-official publication sent to high schools for advertising purposes, free of controversial matter during the crisis of 1891 when he was leading the anti-Peabody agitation.[43]

Most editors dispensed platitudes which all too faithfully reflected the spirit of the University. They urged class loyalty and school spirit, endorsed coeducation, and advised students to use the Sabbath properly. They stressed the advantages of participation in a literary society until late in the decade, when they gave increasing emphasis to athletics.

The *Illini* faithfully reflected the fear of political heterodoxy which prevailed within the University, and it almost completely avoided partisan matters. Only two editors took an interest in the subject in these years, and both served during presidential campaigns. In 1884 John E. Wright wanted the student press to take a straight Republican line, hardly a controversial stand in light of the party allegiance of the area. Four years later Nathan A. Weston urged discussion of political issues while insisting that the *Illini* remain independent.

Like their class fights, the students' involvement with politics should be considered mainly as a social activity. True, these young men and women showed a keener interest in contemporary problems than had their predecessors. The content of their essays and orations testifies to this concern, as does the formation in 1883 of a Society of Political Education, a study group designed to supplement course work.[44] But they still regarded live partisan politics with suspicion and turned to it primarily for fun. Like Halloween,

[43] *Illini,* Dec. 9, 1889; Nov. 22, 1890.
[44] "Faculty Record," II, Feb. 16, 1883; *Illini,* Feb. 24, 1883.

darkness in excited political times afforded a pretext for manufacturing local sensations. The boys' participation in election meetings in the campaign of 1884 brought much local criticism. When students held a "funeral" for Carter Harrison, the Democratic Mayor of Chicago who lost a gubernatorial bid to Richard J. Oglesby, Champaign police broke up the demonstration. They arrested and brought to trial two students, and many others joined in presenting gold-headed canes to two Champaign gentlemen who sided with the demonstrators.[45] These affairs aroused apprehension. Authorities feared that student partisanship would compromise the institution, and Peabody therefore pointed out to pupils the vital necessity of political neutrality so far as the University as a whole was concerned. Officials also feared the risk to life and limb from turbulent rallies, a realistic consideration at a time when one student vividly recalled seeing a man killed during a political demonstration. Probably both reasons account for the Board's ruling of December 9, 1890, that University buildings and grounds were not to be used for political purposes.[46] There was little danger that political partisanship would subvert the search for truth at Illinois, and much danger that avoidance of political discussion would deprive students of an essential part of their education. In all likelihood this far-reaching decision adversely influenced the University as an *intellectual* community while at the same time benefiting it *institutionally*.

One important new publication first appeared in this decade — the *Sophograph* in 1882. Both class spirit and a desire for more ways of relieving monotony induced the sophomores to issue the magazine. An annual, it contained both essays and comments on the college year, and affords an excellent view of the student mind. Some issues, notably those of 1882 and 1890, are particularly valuable in illuminating conflicts among the students and friction between the students and their teachers. But the language is often guarded because the Faculty closely supervised each edition. Before the decade ended the *Sophograph* had taken on many features of a yearbook, which it later became.

[45] *Sophograph* (1885), 44; Champaign *Times,* Nov. 25, 1884; *Illini,* Nov. 3, 17, Dec. 1, 1884.
[46] Champaign County *Gazette,* Oct. 3, 1888; *16th Report* (1892), 47.

The Greek question did not vanish immediately after the anti-fraternity ban became effective at the beginning of the year 1882. The pledge disclosed that previously unknown societies were flourishing. The prospects of those without charters were shattered, but the Sigma Chi's continued a *sub rosa* existence with a handful of men in college aided by a few resident alumni who never surrendered their charter. An organization known as the Ten Tautological Tautogs facilitated their purpose. It had been founded as a burlesque on college secret societies and its membership was secret. Its yearly meetings, called "bivalves" and unknown to outsiders until after the event, were the occasion for a good dinner and the cup that cheers. In light of the antifraternity ruling, some Tautogs jokingly asked Peabody whether this organization would come under the ban, and in the same spirit he told them that it applied only to *real* secret societies. But since the Tautogs who returned to the campus in 1882 were also Sigma Chi's, the burlesque secret society became a means of perpetuating the real secret society. Upon leaving college the Tautogs were made regular members of Sigma Chi. They stilled their consciences as best they could by Jesuitical construction of Peabody's statement.[47]

The fraternity interests who carried their case to Springfield in 1883 hoped for much, since both the new Governor, John M. Hamilton, and the new Speaker of the House, Lorin C. Collins, were Sigma Chi's. The net positive gain at this time was a more considerate attitude in previously hostile quarters. But the Sigma Chi's had won a victory at Purdue in 1883 and then completed a centralization of their national fraternity government by 1884. These achievements prompted some students and the Grand Council of Sigma Chi to ask the Board late in 1885 to abolish the pledge system. Grand Tribune Walter L. Fisher of Chicago, later Secretary of the Interior under President Taft, presented a circular for the Council stating eight reasons for admitting fraternities. The document included a bold bid for controlling discipline on the campus. The Council asserted that Sigma Chi had centralized its power in a tribunal which was prepared to settle disputes between its members

[47] William A. Heath, "The Mythology of Illinois," *The Illinois*, III (May, 1912), 413-14.

and college authorities. A special committee of the Board rejected this aggressive proposal with some asperity the following March. It said that the ban on fraternities had originally aimed at improving discipline within the University, and had actually achieved that end. The institution therefore did not need a remedy for a non-existent disease. It was intolerable even to consider allowing an outside authority, a secret society loyal to its own interests, to arbitrate differences on the campus. In addition, Fisher said that a chapter of Sigma Chi had continued a desultory existence at Urbana. The circular insinuated that the University authorities might as well repeal the obnoxious rule since alumni and officials of Sigma Chi would help students violate it anyway. Worst of all, the Council threatened to use its influence with the General Assembly to defeat the University's appropriation unless the pledge were abolished.[48]

The Board naturally rejected the petition. Faced with this disfavor, the active members, the alumni, and national officials decided to wait for a better day. During the winter of 1885-86 the Sigma Chi chapter at Urbana became inactive. In these years the *Illini* expressed strong opposition to fraternities, primarily on the grounds that they were antidemocratic. But fraternity interests throughout the state did not surrender. A group of alumni continued their effort to change the method of selecting the Board. They also considered Peabody the architect of their misfortunes, and the Greek issue furnished one justification for the systematic attempt to remove him.[49]

The dam erected against secret organizations diverted student interests into other channels. Of the various agencies of collegiate life, the three literary societies enjoyed the greatest prominence at Illinois. They remained strong at Urbana longer than on many campuses because the authorities ruled out their main competition. In many ways, however, the literary societies were surrogates for social fraternities. Only a minority of the student body belonged, about a third of the total, but most of the seniors.[50] The men's

[48] *Illini,* Dec. 14, 1885; *13th Report* (1887), 75-77, 81-82; Nate, *History of Sigma Chi,* II, 183-84.
[49] *Illini,* April 5, 1886; Peabody to Jonathan B. Turner, Sept. 26, 1891, Carl Stephens Papers; Kiler, *On the Banks of the Boneyard,* 11.
[50] *Illini,* Jan. 19, Feb. 4, 1881; June 8, 1882.

organizations, the Adelphics and Philomatheans, at times engaged in sharp and even bitter rivalry. This became especially keen in the spring of 1882, when the competition was for members and student offices, especially control of the *Illini*. But perhaps fraternity factionalism accentuated the difficulty. In a contest for the upper hand in the Inter-Society Oratorical Association in the spring of 1882, the heads of the two hostile factions were both Adelphics. But Judson F. Going was a Phi Delta Phi, and James G. Wadsworth a Sigma Chi.[51] Significantly, the contest between the Adelphics and Philos abated after the fraternities were banned.

During the time of troubles from 1880 to 1883 the "lits" were at low tide. Peabody manifested his attitude at the very opening of his administration. The promptness with which he cut off the supply of illuminating gas to the club rooms at 10 P.M., the hour appointed by the rule, had never been surpassed.[52] Probably his fear of secret student societies led him to prevent the literary groups from continuing into the small hours. In these years students themselves complained about lack of interest and lowered standards in the traditional exercises. Attendance at weekly meetings lagged, few competed for oratorical honors, speakers prepared inadequately, and much of the talk was empty. And yet audiences praised performances indiscriminately.

Criticisms all but vanished about the time peace returned to the campus in 1883, and the literary societies resumed their traditional role of nourishing intellectual interests outside the classroom. Ideally, a weekly program aimed at helping each individual member to think and speak effectively rather than at pleasing an audience. Wit had a place, but the general tone was serious. Music was interspersed among declamations, poems, essays, orations, and debates. The latter enjoyed great prestige because of the conviction that debate developed mental agility and the capacity to speak extemporaneously, which was considered vital to later success.[53]

Both the campus and local newspapers gave more attention to literary society activities than to sports. They reported weekly programs, which afford a good clue to shifting intellectual interests.

[51] *Ibid.*, April 15, May 13, Nov. 4, 1882; "Faculty Record," II, May 10, 1882.
[52] *Illini*, Sept., Nov. 3, Dec. 1, 1880.
[53] *Ibid.*, Oct. 17, 1881; April 15, 1882; Oct. 4, 1886.

Students still debated such jejune issues as whether woman has had greater influence on society than money. Many of their topics indicate a bias toward literary as opposed to scientific culture. They debated, for example, the resolution that the pursuit of literature is more ennobling than the pursuit of science, and the resolution that scientific discoveries are tending toward materialism. But in 1885 the editor of the *Illini* decried the increasing emphasis on scientific subjects.[54] In addition, the interest in contemporary problems was growing. Students gave attention to prohibition, the protective tariff, the limitation of immigration, popular election of the President, abolition of Mormonism, and American control over the Isthmus of Panama. Probably there was considerably less anti-Catholicism in these efforts than in the 1870's.[55] But the literary societies rarely gave campus issues a formal place on their programs.[56]

The weekly forensic training prepared members for the big oratorical meetings held on the campus and throughout the state. In addition to the declamation contests of the various societies, the Inter-Society Oratorical Association sponsored an annual competition. But the high point of the year was the Intercollegiate Oratorical Contest held each October on the campus of a different college. An enormous enthusiasm attended these affairs. They combined forensic and athletic contests, but baseball remained subordinate to oratory until the 1890's. The Faculty granted students leave of absence to attend, and 50 to 60, including about a dozen women, usually made the trips. Hosts of others saw them off at the railroad station in the early hours, and eagerly awaited news of oratorical and baseball victories. The group that went to Galesburg in 1880 wore the University colors, silver on a cardinal background, which the students had adopted late the previous year.[57] At that meeting delegates from participating schools elected James G. Wadsworth of the University to head the Intercollegiate Oratorical Association.

[54] Champaign County *Gazette,* March 16, May 11, 1881; Nov. 19, 1884; *Illini,* May 25, 1885.
[55] Champaign County *Gazette, passim;* J. V. E. Schaefer, "The American Common School System," an address delivered March 27, 1891, glorified the common schools and attacked Roman Catholicism. A copy is in the Talbot Papers.
[56] In March, 1885, the Adelphics and Philos debated the recently established demerit system. Champaign County *Gazette,* Feb. 25, 1885; *Illini,* March 2, 1885.
[57] *Illini,* Nov., 1879; "Faculty Record," II, *passim; Sophograph* (1884), 44.

Students valued these gatherings for many reasons, including the fact that they offset the college's geographical isolation. But Peabody viewed them with concern, and in 1883 tried to induce the students to withdraw from the state competition. He offered to establish two cash prizes in oratory in return for disengaging. Students rejected the proposition.[58]

The literary societies also amused themselves with such fare as skits, mock trials — at one Philomathean entertainment, Thomas A. Clark had to answer charges of breach of promise[59] — and musical selections. They worked up their own programs for public performance and sponsored lectures, humorists, and concert artists in order to fill their treasuries and enrich the local cultural climate. These undertakings were financial risks, since local townspeople turned out only for well-known figures and the literary society enmities of the early 1880's prevented each men's group from attending the programs of its rival. After the bitterness subsided about 1883, however, the men's literary societies joined the Alethenai in appointing a committee to take charge of a University lecture and entertainment series.[60]

At Urbana the literary societies were gaining rather than losing strength at a late date. One reason was the official opposition to social fraternities and collegiate sports, the main competitors of the "lits." Another was the increase in enrollments in the late 1880's. And of course the societies met both intellectual and social needs. Many therefore contended that the Adelphic and the Philomathean organizations, each of which could nicely handle about 50 members, were inadequate for a largely male student body of 400. (The Alethenai always constituted a special case, and it had never been a power in student affairs. Nor did the talk of forming a coeducational literary society bear fruit.) Early in 1891 the Faculty approved a petition for a new organization, and 26 members formed the Academy.[61] Viewed in national collegiate perspective, the formation at this time of a new literary society manifested a regressive campus.

[58] *Illini,* Jan. 13, Nov. 26, 1883; *Sophograph* (1884), 45.
[59] Champaign County *Gazette,* Oct. 30, 1889.
[60] *Illini,* Nov. 11, 1882; Oct. 1, 1883.
[61] *Ibid.,* Nov. 25, 1889; Feb. 5, 21, 1890; "Faculty Record," III, 42, 45, 50.

In addition to these traditional organizations, a number of specialized societies occupied a significant place in student life. They had begun to appear during Gregory's administration and mushroomed after 1880, recruiting members from the entire University and thus cutting across lines drawn by the college classes and the literary societies. Although the Scientific Association disbanded in the 1880's, there were such groups as the Telegrapher's Society, the Macaulay Society, the Temperance Association, the Senatorial Association, the Society of Political Education, and the Chess Club. Among the aggregations formed along scientific or professional lines were the Chemical Society, the Agricultural Club, the Architectural Association, the Blackstonian Association (a group of prospective law students), the Society of Mechanical Engineers, the Society of Civil Engineers, and the Natural History Society. Both students and faculty members belonged to the latter, whose members observed things in nature and made systematic reports on their observations. Both Burrill and Forbes occasionally presented weighty scientific papers to the circle. The Civil Engineers periodically published the better papers read to its members. Students needed authorization from the Faculty both to establish these associations and to publish a journal or magazine.[62]

Students organized their own religious societies, and many tried to promote evangelical Christianity and a spiritual atmosphere on the campus. But much of the religious program was part of the formal and compulsory side of college life, and chapel increasingly engendered opposition. In fact, the foundations of nonsectarian Christianity within the University were weakening during Peabody's administration, but the process was so gradual that few appreciated the significance of what was occurring.

The governing body officially removed prayer and the reading of scripture from the Board's order of business in June, 1880, apparently considering continuance of these exercises inappropriate.[63] Their choice of a scientist to replace a clergyman as head of the University alarmed a public which was still worrying about Darwin

[62] "Faculty Record," II, *passim; Sophograph* (1887), 30-31.
[63] *10th Report* (1881), 244.

and the Higher Criticism. A visiting preacher voiced the common suspicion in announcing after a sermon to students, "I tell you, I have given this godless University a good shaking to-day."[64] The need to cultivate a reputation for piety helps explain the heavily religious content and imagery of Peabody's public addresses. Yet Peabody was determined to preserve the old collegiate religion. He had been active in church work before assuming the regency, and while in that position he ordinarily worshiped with Presbyterians in Champaign. In addition, he believed that religious exercises were a necessary part of the culture and education offered by higher institutions of learning. In his opinion the desire to free colleges and universities from all sectarian influences did not require the exclusion of Christianity, for Christianity was no sect.[65]

In place of the required Sunday afternoon worship, Peabody established a monthly series of sermons by prominent clergymen of various denominations at which attendance was voluntary. He probably borrowed the idea of a denominational pulpit from Cornell, which pioneered along these lines in 1875. Private individuals supplied the funds for the discourses, which numbered ten in an academic year. Attendance was usually good, and students found the annual series attractive. In one three-year period exactly half of the sermon titles — such as "Thinking," "Real Power," and "Industrial Progress and the Extension of Life" — contained no specific religious references.[66] In all likelihood this nonsectarian venture promoted a vague belief in a hazy religion. At the same time Peabody was giving unmistakably Christian baccalaureate sermons each year.

Most students were at least conventionally religious. Campus publications frequently said that the question of Christianity was one which should deeply concern every young man and woman.[67] The literary societies sometimes opened with prayer and sponsored

[64] Katherine Peabody Girling, *Selim Hobart Peabody, a Biography* (Urbana, 1923), 156.
[65] See the brief notes on a discussion of "The Place of Religion in Higher Education" reported in National Educational Association, *Journal of Proceedings and Addresses, 1888* (Topeka, 1888), 437.
[66] *12th Report* (1885), 53; *Catalogue, 1884-85,* 86.
[67] An excellent example is the essay, "Important Elements in College Life," *Sophograph* (1885), 27. See also *Illini,* Dec. 17, 1888.

lectures by such noted clergymen as Henry Ward Beecher and T. DeWitt Talmage, whose humor and cheerful common sense were greatly appreciated. A number of the more earnest students came together in the Christian associations. The YMCA grew in strength and gained a companion in 1884 with establishment of the YWCA.[68] The Faculty encouraged these organizations, which included some of the ablest students, and Professor Burrill took the most active interest in their work. In line with a national trend, the Christian associations shifted from Bible study to public evangelism. This was the decade in which American collegians concluded that they could carry Christ to the entire world before their generation died, and the organizational expression of this venture, the Student Volunteer Movement, had its greatest success in Midwestern coeducational institutions. But the University of Illinois was no center of this achievement.

At Urbana the Christian associations worked with local churches, studied foreign missions, held religious services on Sunday mornings and Wednesday evenings, and proposed carrying on the University discourses when they were discontinued in 1889. They found the battle against liquor especially challenging. This struggle rose to a climax in the spring of 1881 with municipal elections in both towns on the question of outlawing saloons. The dry forces imported a number of speakers, including Frances Willard and the celebrated John B. Gough. The literary societies sponsored the latter and made money on the lecture. When the vote outlawed saloons in Champaign and Urbana — the victory was not permanent — George W. Bullard, editor of the *Illini* and a prominent Y leader, praised the outcome for removing from students the terrible possibility of becoming addicted to strong drink while in college. The student Marshal suddenly had little to occupy him.[69]

A neo-puritanical moral code which drew strength from the prevailing evangelical Protestantism and the rural environment continued to blanket the campus, and some students began to find it suffocating. The Faculty prohibited smoking in University buildings (although the *Illini* briefly advertised cigarettes),[70] and the

[68] "Faculty Record," II, June 6, 1884.
[69] *Ibid.*, III, 16, 18; *Illini*, Jan. 19, Feb. 2, March 2, April 13, 27, 1881.
[70] "Faculty Record," II, Dec. 9, 1881.

weight of local sentiment opposed not only smoking and drinking but also card-playing and dancing, particularly on University property. Some young men and women resented paying hostage to these attitudes. Knowing that an inaugural ball had been held at the Capitol, for example, they charged hypocrisy when Peabody forbade dancing in University buildings on the ground that the state forbade it.

Liberal religion gained a foothold at Urbana during this decade. In 1881 a student address on Paine, Voltaire, and Ingersoll attracted a large audience. Seven years later the newly formed Unitarian Society sponsored a series of lectures. But few students or faculty members abandoned the more orthodox denominations for either Unitarianism or unbelief. Probably the small denominational colleges produced a more intense skepticism than did the state universities at the time.[71]

But the students did become increasingly opposed to compulsory chapel. This inherited program posed a problem which admitted of no easy solution. It was still the rule in American higher education. The University of Wisconsin had pioneered among state institutions in making attendance voluntary in 1868. Harvard took the lead among private colleges and in 1886 abolished a chapel requirement which had stood for a quarter of a millennium. The Harvard chaplain at the time was Francis Greenwood Peabody, a relative of the Regent. In nearly all other schools of higher learning, however, the traditional religious rite remained in force. And the Illinois Peabody set himself against the many influences which were undermining its foundations.[72]

Students found the daily assemblies monotonous and boring. Men still had to form in military ranks and be checked off before the march into the ceremony. Peabody tried to make the specifically religious component brief, and yet it caused grumbling. Critics maintained that a phonograph could have said the Lord's Prayer

[71] *Illini*, March 16, 1881; Feb. 20, 1888; John Bascom, "Atheism in Colleges," *North American Review*, CXXXII (Jan., 1881), 36.
[72] Merle Curti and Vernon Carstensen, *The University of Wisconsin: A History, 1848-1925* (2 vols., Madison, 1949), I, 409; Hugh Hawkins, "Charles W. Eliot, University Reform, and Religious Faith in America, 1869-1909," *Journal of American History*, LI (Sept., 1964), 191-213.

more effectively than did the Regent.[73] Even the secular part of the programs met opposition. The novelty of every senior giving a chapel oration, introduced in 1887, soon wore thin. Occasionally an older speaker informed or entertained, but too often an authority lectured on discipline. And students continually objected to the fact that faculty members rarely observed the duty they imposed on their pupils.

Despite the steady rumbling, no one anticipated the direct assault on the system launched by Foster North in 1885. A senior in the School of Natural History, North had entered the University from Kewanee in the autumn of 1879, a green and bashful youth with a poor command of language.[74] Later he dropped out for two years to recoup his finances and his health. A diligent student with a satisfactory record of scholarship and conduct, North was within a few weeks of graduation when he precipitated a crisis. Unknown to others, he was the agnostic son of an agnostic father and had progressively become irritated with chapel. Finally reaching the point where he "used to mentally dam — yes, god dam — old Peabody and his damned old prayers," North quietly absented himself.[75] He had not attended during most of the spring term when the Faculty called upon him to comply with the rules. When he refused it concluded: "If he claims conscientious scruples against attendance at chapel he may be excused; if not, he will be suspended."[76] North refused to sign a form stating that attendance at worship was repugnant to his religious convictions and in violation of his rights of conscience. He took the position that he had no religious convictions to which chapel could be repugnant. Never openly admitting his agnosticism, he refused to ask a favor for himself which was not accorded to others. He also asserted that the Faculty had no right to impose a requirement which conflicted with the religious freedom guaranteed by the state Constitution. On April 30, 1885, Peabody suspended North indefinitely.[77]

[73] The point is tellingly made, among other places, in *Doc's Compulsory Entertainment, or Junior Juggernaut* [Urbana, 1887?].
[74] The best evidence on North himself is in Foster North, *The Struggle for Religious Liberty in the University of Illinois* (Los Angeles, 1942).
[75] *Ibid.*, 30.
[76] "Faculty Record," II, April 17, 1885.
[77] Peabody to North, April 30, 1885, "Regents' Letterbook, 1879-1894"; North, *Struggle,* 10; *13th Report* (1887), 63, 67-68, 70.

North petitioned the Trustees for relief in June. But the Board rejected a motion to award a degree when North finished his work. Only George A. Follansbee of Chicago and John T. Pearman of Champaign supported the plea. In September a committee headed by the Board's President, Sylvester M. Millard, recommended that North's petition be referred to the Attorney General for an opinion on the constitutional question raised. Follansbee, a Unitarian with a Harvard law degree, objected in a minority report which combined a powerful appeal for North's constitutional rights as a citizen with a recognition of practical realities. He contended that the religious exercises at chapel were acts of worship. Since the Illinois Constitution declared that "No person shall be required to attend or support any ministry or place of worship against his consent," any rule was objectionable which deprived an individual of the benefit of a public institution like the University because he failed to consent to attend worship. One could no more be deprived of a right to public instruction by such a rule than he could be legally deprived of liberty or property for failure to attend public worship. North asked no favor but demanded a reserved constitutional right, said the Chicago lawyer, and a willingness to excuse him for conscience did not obviate the constitutional objection.[78]

But Follansbee also urged that the constitutional issue had nothing to do with the wisdom of the right to abstain. He thought that students should receive religious instruction during their formative period, and in arguing for retention of chapel and its beneficial influence he frankly based his position on expediency. To reassure parents who wanted chapel and at the same time to discourage student defectors who might bring about its demise, Follansbee argued that if chapel were kept most students would conform and those who refused could win exemption by pleading conscience.

Except for Dr. Pearman, Follansbee's colleagues rejected this temporizing approach and adopted Peabody's single-minded report, which approached the issue from a totally different perspective. The Regent regarded University attendance as a privilege and stressed North's insubordination. All students were obligated to conform to the rules. Since no overt act had been required of North, who

[78] *Ibid.*, 43, 62. Follansbee's report is at pp. 63-64.

could have secured an excuse as a matter of right, the system safe-guarded his conscience. Stripped of disguises, therefore, North's real purpose was to overthrow chapel and "coerce the consciences of all the God-fearing and Christian" officers and students of the University. "That the people of the State of Illinois ever dreamed," declared Peabody, "that, as the outcome of a misinterpreted consti-tutional provision, Christianity, the God of Heaven and Earth, and the Bible as His written word could be ruled out of its State Uni-versity, so that it should be unlawful to read the Scriptures, or to pray to Him, within its walls, is a conclusion too monstrous to be entertained."[79] The Board approved and forwarded these com-ments to Attorney General George Hunt, who adopted Peabody's reasoning and concluded that none of North's constitutional rights had been violated. Governor Oglesby made one of his rare Board appearances at the meeting which approved Hunt's opinion on December 8, 1885. On the following day the Trustees dramatized their position by carefully recessing in order to attend chapel.[80]

North failed to rally any support, but the victory over him proved to be Pyrrhic. The *Illini* defended compulsory chapel as valuable in assembling students for general purposes.[81] This attitude suggested that North's irreligious belief went deeper than his class-mates' religious belief. Although serious chapel disorder soon fol-lowed North's suspension, it is difficult to isolate the religious component of this protest. Many students probably regarded the religious ceremonial as a hollow formality, the tribute a state uni-versity owed to public expectations, a piece of hypocrisy to be endured.

But North could not accept the situation, and he seems to have formed at this time the obsession with righting accounts which dom-inated the remainder of his life. Rather than an honest agnostic, North was actually an intolerant dogmatist whose creed was a super-ficial and pessimistic naturalism. He viewed faith as a species of dishonesty and "a barnacle upon the ship of intellectual progress, J. Christ to the contrary notwithstanding," and imputed to his op-ponents worship of an "infant-roasting" god.[82] Failing in 1889 to

[79] *Ibid.*, 66-69. The quotation is at p. 69.
[80] *Ibid.*, 72.
[81] *Illini,* May 11, 1885; Jan. 25, 1886.
[82] North, *Struggle,* 30.

gain readmittance by appeals to the Regent, the Board of Trustees, and the Supreme Court, North made a second plea to the Supreme Court for a writ of mandamus. In March, 1891, this tribunal unanimously sustained the Faculty and the Board. The Court declined to issue a writ presented to settle mere abstract rights unless it was brought in the name of the people or unless the petitioner showed a substantial interest, which North allegedly had not done. Justice Jacob W. Wilkins followed the Peabody-Hunt thesis and found nothing unlawful in the rule compelling chapel. The Bill of Rights was designed to protect citizens, not students who voluntarily placed themselves in the government of others. Conscience was the only right North had been deprived of, held Wilkins, and North had expressly said this was interfered with in no way. North was only using the Constitution as a shield for insubordination and attempting to furnish others an excuse for disobedience.[83]

Peabody lost his office at the University shortly after this Supreme Court decision. Immediately after the Board decided to let him go, he requested the Trustees to print and publicly distribute a statement of the North case including the Supreme Court's opinion, with a view to "its beneficial influence on the good fame of the University." Although denominational suspicions of the Urbana institution were abating at the time,[84] in Peabody's view "Nothing could so surely set at rest certain slanderous accusations which have so

[83] *Foster North v. Board of Trustees of the University of Illinois* (137 Ill. 296). Trustee William L. Abbott (class of 1884) was instrumental in having the Board vote North the B.S. degree (as of 1885) in 1914. After receiving his diploma at a Champaign commencement, where a Roman Catholic priest read the scripture and prayed, North returned it with the charge that one could still not obtain a degree at Illinois without being subjected to religious worship. Viewing himself as robbed of his rights, he then initiated a long discussion on religious freedom in correspondence with Presidents James, Kinley, and Willard and in the public press. Abbott, a successful engineer, lost patience and called North a "nut" who was a failure because he coddled his hobby. North, a California masseur, replied that one had to endure the *odium theologicum* in order to defend a constitutional right not to worship, and took comfort in support in his battle from Catholics and Jews if not from Protestants. (North, *Struggle,* 20-48.) The Supreme Court of Illinois found prayer and Bible-reading in public schools unconstitutional in 1910 (245 Ill. 344). North claimed that this decision vindicated him, but it had nothing to do with compulsory worship in the University. The Court's decision in his case seems never to have been reversed, but of course the ending of the chapel requirement removed any need to do so.
[84] See the *Northwestern Christian Advocate,* Jan. 30, 1884; and the Champaign County *Gazette,* Oct. 23, 1889.

constantly been flung at the University, as a circulation of this document."[85] Accordingly, authorities published a pamphlet entitled
Foster North vs. Board of Trustees, University of Illinois, with the
revealing subtitle *The Bible in the University of Illinois.* Largely a
collection of documents, this propaganda vehicle omitted all reference to the minority report written by Follansbee. Truth was a royal
quality, the chapel motto declared, but the sovereign people of Illinois were not to be trusted with all of it. Ironically, Peabody's triumph over North soon became hollow with elimination of the
chapel requirement.

Earnest effort conquered in cultural, social, class, and athletic
realms as well as in the various student societies. Dramatic and
musical activities became popular, supplementing the Glee Club
and the University Band which had appeared earlier as handmaid-
ens to the chapel and the military organization. Early in 1881 a
University group put on the opera "Maud Muller" in a Champaign
theater, and a year later students were attending the "Cantata of
Esther." Some of these were civic ventures, for Champaign and
Urbana were offering a richer cultural life than they had a decade
previously. Choral unions, orchestral groups, and the like were
being formed throughout the decade. These provided students their
own entertainment and enriched their education in areas where the
formal program offered little.[86]

Students also exerted deliberate effort to create class and college spirit, which they considered to be necessary for the full enjoyment of undergraduate life. Shortly after college class lines
emerged in the mid-1870's, the symbols of these distinctions made
their appearance. The seniors imported from Eastern colleges the
custom of wearing black plug hats as their mark and privilege, the
juniors followed suit by adopting white plugs and carrying canes,
and the sophomores donned mortarboards. Class badges, pins, and
rings took their place alongside such emerging traditions as the
Seniors' Class Day, the Junior Exhibition, the *Sophograph,* and the

[85] *16th Report* (1892), 99.
[86] *Sophograph* (1882), 11; Champaign County *Gazette,* Feb. 9, 1881; *Illini,*
May 25, 1881; Feb. 24, 1882.

Freshman Sociable.[87] Meanwhile, the student body was clamoring for manifestations of school spirit. The quest for badges and colors to symbolize the whole University led, as noted, to adoption of silver and cardinal in 1879. Instead of singing songs borrowed from other colleges, students wanted their own songs so they could express "our patriotism for our own institution." *The American College Song Book,* published in the early 1880's, included a number of songs written by men from the University.[88] The rise of intercollegiate athletics necessitated a college yell, and in 1888 students adopted this little gem: "Rah Hoo Rah, Zip Boom Ah, Hip Zoo, Rah Zoo, Jimmy blow your Bazoo, Ipsidi Iki, U of I, Champaign."[89] These customs should not be dismissed as harmless juvenile antics. They represented a search for the unity which had been a hallmark of life in the old-time college, and a strong pride in alma mater.

Social activities acquired unprecedented favor as the gap widened between college studies and college life. In addition to picnics, nutting parties, sleigh rides and the like, various college organizations and classes sponsored gatherings during the year in the rooms of the literary societies and the Christian associations. On occasion the latter held such an affair in a local church. The Faculty laid down rules which restricted the number of open meetings the literary societies could conduct each year, and they combined to offer a Union Sociable. These occasions took place in their adjoining rooms in University Hall and highlighted the year for an inner coterie, although "independents" found them less attractive. Early in the decade music, dancing, and other forms of sociability constituted the program, but later, opposition to dancing and card-playing in society halls developed.[90] Now many members also found these evenings stuffy.[91]

During the 1880's the student organizations transferred much of their social activity from the campus to local hostelries and opera houses. Commercial establishments offered escape from a measure

[87] *Sophograph* (1882), 13, 19; Champaign County *Gazette,* Dec. 1, 1880; Feb. 16, 1881.
[88] *Illini,* Jan., 1879 (the source of the quotation); Oct. 20, 1880; Dec. 9, 1889.
[89] *Ibid.,* April 23, 1888.
[90] *Ibid.,* Oct., 1880.
[91] Champaign County *Gazette,* Jan. 14, 1885.

of Faculty control and better opportunity than University buildings for cards, dancing, smoking, and drinking. Banquets and dances constituted the big social events. Seniors had organized a dancing club in 1878 only to meet resistance from Gregory, but his departure stimulated a revival of the activity. The University Battalion sponsored a Military Hop and promised to make it an annual event, a Valentine Ball was held, and for a time the literary societies danced in their own halls. But the main initiative came from a number of student clubs formed especially for the purpose, such as the XLCR. These groups conducted series of dances, perhaps at the Columbian Hotel in Urbana or the Griggs House in Champaign. Students later tried to have more dances held on the campus, but Peabody told them in chapel that dancing would hurt the University's reputation.[92]

In theory student participation in exhibitions and public exercises furthered intellectual goals. The literary societies and each of the college classes were conducting exhibitions by the end of Gregory's administration. But in 1882 a Faculty ruling terminated the freshman and sophomore exhibitions, and those of the upper two classes became all-important during Peabody's regime.[93] Commencement afforded seniors an opportunity to display musical talent and express ripened thought, both on Class Day and at graduation exercises. The custom of having only students speak at Commencement prevailed throughout these years. For the Junior Exhibition, which the Faculty allowed to be held during the winter term, elaborate preparations went into a variety of instrumental and vocal selections, a class song and history, a poem, recitation, and a few orations. An oratorical prize established by Roland R. Conklin, a graduate of the class of 1880 who was doing well in life, enlivened the competition. Nicely printed programs accompanied the Junior Exhibition. Anniversary exercises continued to be held, and occasionally the Junior Exhibition took place in the afternoon, followed by a round of other activities in the evening. When March 11 fell on a Sunday in 1888, the University's twentieth anniversary, the

[92] *Ibid.*, Jan. 19, Feb. 9, March 2, 7, 1881, and *passim; Illini,* March 25, 1889.
[93] "Faculty Record," II, Dec. 9, 1881.

ceremony was observed the following Tuesday out of deference to the Sabbath.[94]

In practice, however, the exhibitions provided rowdies an excellent opportunity to create disturbances. Perhaps excessive class spirit accounts for most of this difficulty, although the influence of monotony and the antagonism which students cherished toward Peabody must also be considered. At any rate, the violence intensified as the opposition to Peabody deepened. Conditions were not good in 1885. An *Illini* editorial in March of that year rejoiced that cane rushes, hazing, prize fighting and the like, so common to many colleges, had no place at the University. But in that same edition of the newspaper a student asked why the timid Faculty had failed to punish persons known to have disturbed various public meetings. He wondered if things had reached the point where "a few sneaking rascals are able to trample on all order within these walls and run matters to suit themselves?"[95]

Conditions soon worsened, as Charles A. Kiler's account of the thrill afforded by the Freshman Sociable in 1888 and its sequel vividly illustrates. The freshmen secretly planned a banquet and dance to be held at the Columbian Hotel. Word leaked out and sophomores prepared to disrupt the event. Several of them waylaid Kiler, the toastmaster, as he set out to pick up his date. Kiler gained the door of her house just as Dick Chester and Jerry Bouton rounded the corner "with murder in their eyes." Kiler tells of running a gauntlet of "eye water" (benzyl bromide) and attempted physical assault all the way from Champaign via streetcar to Urbana, with two Urbana ladies returning from a church dinner in Champaign brandishing butcher knives to repel the sophomores. At the door of the Columbian Hotel one freshman had a peck of flour poured over his head.

The freshmen retaliated by publishing a bogus *Sophograph,* and a year later, as sophomores, they offered to help protect the

[94] Champaign County *Gazette,* Nov. 13, 1889; "Faculty Record," II, Nov. 18, 1887; Clarence A. Shamel Diary, entry of March 13, 1888, Charles H. Shamel Papers. The Faculty had for the first time omitted holding anniversary exercises in 1886 because of the disturbances at them the previous year. See *Illini,* March 30, 1885; "Faculty Record," II, Jan. 29, 1886.
[95] *Illini,* March 30, 1885; see also June 10, 1885; and *Sophograph* (1886), 49.

freshmen from the depradations of the juniors —"the worst bunch of goons that ever attended Illinois — that wild and wooly bunch in '91."[96] The freshmen secretly arranged to hold their sociable in Danville, but the juniors managed to ruin the dance by filling the hall with stink water and dousing the lights. So the sophomores set out to ruin the Junior Exhibition by appointing committees to kidnap the participants and lock them up in horse stalls at the fairgrounds, then near the University. Kiler's party set out to seize the class orator, who escaped by jumping from the second story of his rooming house and later bit an assailant. The roughness which accompanied another attempted kidnapping threw a streetcar from the tracks; ten people were hurt and a woman's leg broken. In desperation the sophomores then went to the chapel to disrupt the program which they had failed to prevent. Tying small glass vials of "eye water" to their heels, they joined the audience and spoiled the festivities by releasing the acrid fumes.[97]

Along with social fraternities, athletics became a prominent feature of American college life in the late nineteenth century. One authority has said that the year 1880 marks the dividing line in this development. It separates the old era of informal college sports from the new era of big-time intercollegiate athletics.[98] In its early years the University had moved in step with the national evolution. A period of simple beginnings culminated in the autumn of 1879 when the baseball team from Urbana entered its first intercollegiate contest. Peabody entered office the next year, and in the ensuing decade the University lagged behind rival institutions in the athletic order of march.

During these years young men and women became sports enthusiasts for many reasons. Individual as opposed to team activities provided an enjoyable escape from routine while also promoting health. Since tennis, golf, and boating had not been introduced at Illinois, gymnastics remained popular. Although the gymnasium movement was a holdover from an earlier period in college ath-

[96] Kiler, *On the Banks of the Boneyard,* 35.
[97] *Ibid.,* 31-41; *Sophograph* (1890), 36-40; Champaign County *Gazette,* Dec. 11, 18, 1889.
[98] Howard J. Savage *et al., American College Athletics* (New York, 1929), 21.

letics, the University had done little by 1880 to develop suitable facilities. Students complained that the University possessed the poorest gymnasium in the state. Although their promptings led Peabody to obtain small sums for apparatus and repairs, students assumed the main responsibility for the gym.[99] They hired instructors from their own ranks and raised funds by giving gymnastics exhibitions and charging fees. But the Faculty refused to allow students complete control. In 1885 it established a managing committee which included the Professor of Military Science and three students from the Athletic Association.[100]

Despite the gym's popularity, competitive team sports offered greater appeal. They provided as much exercise, considerably more fun, and an excellent means of forging class and college spirit. Baseball remained the king of college sports at the time, and the most important student teams were those organized by each class and the University nine. The competition between the class teams enabled the Baseball Association to pick the best players for the University ball club. It played home games with civic clubs like the Covington Blues from Indiana, but the important encounters were those with other colleges held in connection with the Intercollegiate Oratorical Contest each October. At Galesburg in 1880 the University team defeated Knox College in the overture to the oratory, and a few days later the losers sent a purse of $15 to the Urbana boys to help defray expenses. "This," said a Champaign newspaper, "is doing the handsome thing."[101]

At Knox College the team from the University had taken the field in motley garb, and school pride required uniforms. The Baseball Association therefore sponsored a drive to raise funds for the purpose. Various student groups put on exhibitions and entertainments, and splendid new outfits arrived in May, in time for the trek to Jacksonville, where the club met Illinois College at the Interstate Oratorical Association contest which attracted schools from six states. The University won what passed as the state championship at the October intercollegiate games in 1883 and 1886. Students celebrated all victories by gathering around a big bonfire and then

[99] *Illini,* Nov. 11, 25, 1882; *12th Report* (1885), 208; *13th Report* (1887), 30.
[100] "Faculty Record," II, Jan. 30, 1885.
[101] Champaign County *Gazette,* Oct. 20, 1880.

parading over to Champaign, upsetting wagons and privies in their enthusiasm.

Football aroused little enthusiasm for several years, although in the 1870's students had introduced what they called football and played it on Thanksgiving Day in 1878. Probably their game was in reality soccer, for the modern version of football was only in the process of developing at the time. Urbana backers of "football" put up goal posts on the campus in the fall of 1881, but the sport attracted few followers the next year.[102] One report says that Peabody revived the dormant football club in 1882 with a few encouraging words, but probably most of the officials and students considered this activity too rough. In the 1880's football justified President Eliot's epithet "brutal," and it made little headway in this decade.[103]

Students were providing the chief impetus for athletics, and to do so in the face of lack of support from the Faculty required organization. The baseball and football associations, formed by students, carried the load for a time. These two groups combined in the Athletic Association, which won Faculty approval on April 20, 1883. Leaders of the agency immediately sponsored the first successful Field Day, an Eastern collegiate custom which had been moving westward. Most students viewed the May event at the Champaign County Fairgrounds as a joyous holiday from classes, but the AA regarded the track, field, and baseball competition as a training program for athletes. The AA also assumed major responsibility for management of the gym.

Meanwhile, the University joined the State Baseball Association, which developed as an offshoot of the Illinois Intercollegiate Oratorical Association. Athletics ranked behind oratory at the annual state contests in the 1880's, but the call for a separate organization for sports had arisen soon after the state forensic contests started. Urbana students were eager to promote intercollegiate athletics, citing as one advantage their advertising value to the University. Late in 1882 the Faculty gave the Baseball Association permission to affiliate with the SBA.[104] In the fall of 1887 a constitu-

[102] Illini, Dec., 1878; Oct., 1880; William A. Heath, "History of Athletics," MS. in the Stephens Papers; Savage et al., American College Athletics, 20.
[103] Illini, Oct. 28, Nov. 11, 1882; Savage et al., American College Athletics, 22.
[104] Illini, Oct. 14, 1882.

tion for the Illinois Intercollegiate Athletic Association was drafted. Its purpose was to conduct football and baseball contests among members, the colleges in the Illinois Intercollegiate Oratorical Association which wished to join. Urbana students pressed the Faculty for permission to affiliate, but on June 1, 1888, it refused. Besides evidencing coolness toward intercollegiate sport, the Faculty probably objected to vesting control in an off-campus body. In the fall of 1889, however, a Faculty committee headed by Peabody authorized University representation in the IIAA on the understanding that two minor changes would be made in its constitution.[105]

While students laid the foundations for the new athletic era at Illinois, they had to convince themselves that they were doing the right thing. As late as 1888 student writers were rejoicing that the athletics craze sweeping over other institutions had not hit Urbana. They insisted that the proper work of college youth was intellectual, and that "mental and moral claims" ranked "higher, nobler, and holier, than any which the body has upon us."[106] Nevertheless they found a way to have their cake and eat it too by arguing that college sports contributed to health and mental growth. Campus publications explained that the leading scholars at Harvard and Yale were also athletes.[107]

Throughout the 1880's the Faculty discouraged the growth of college athletics but made few formal pronouncements on the subject. For example, the professors banned the playing of baseball near University Hall in May, 1881, and two years later refused to allow Field Day to take place on the campus. In response to a petition from some baseball players (including George Huff), the Faculty ruled in 1888 that students could not be excused from University classes for sports. A year later in rejecting the request of women students for a calisthenics program, the Faculty declared that such training could hardly be considered " 'necessary' to the highest culture."[108] Peabody took the lead here, and Burrill alone

[105] *Ibid.*, May 21, 1888; "Faculty Record," II, June 1, 1888; III, 2 (Sept. 20, 1889).
[106] *Illini*, Feb. 6, 1888.
[107] *Ibid.*, Nov. 14, 1887; *Sophograph* (1887), 27-28; (1888), 32, 37.
[108] "Faculty Record," II, April 13, 1888; *15th Report* (1890), 77 (the source of the quotation).

stands out from his colleagues. As Acting Regent in 1889 he told the Trustees that Illinois lagged behind other schools in physical culture and that robust health was an essential prerequisite for the best scholarship. For the first time, moreover, he made the gymnasium available for use on Saturdays.[109]

However, Peabody launched a new era in the fall of 1890 by meeting the pressure at least part way. He acknowledged the existence of a great desire for gymnastic exercises and sports, and confessed that the University had neglected these matters and left their management to students. Now Peabody wanted to follow the example of such schools as Amherst and Cornell, hire a professor of physical culture, and make physical training compulsory for all men. In December he used $1,000 of the funds made available by the second Morrill Act to hire Mauritz Schmidt, a graduate of the Normal Turner Gymnasium in Milwaukee, as Instructor of Gymnastics. In April, 1891, the Faculty accepted managerial responsibility by appointing a Committee on Athletics consisting of three professors.[110]

But Peabody did nothing to encourage outdoor team sports; students themselves took the initiative, and they made football an intercollegiate sport. Scott Williams entered the Preparatory School in 1889, having played football at Illinois State Normal University. Despite local opposition to the "brutal Indian game" he aroused sufficient interest to form a team in 1890, and the boys won permission to play Illinois Wesleyan at the annual state Intercollegiate Oratorical and Athletic Contest that fall. The tyros from Urbana lost by a score of 16 to 0, but shortly thereafter the team accepted a challenge which the President of Purdue issued in a chapel address. Although the best athletes on the campus still despised the lowly new sport, they punished themselves in the name of school spirit by enlisting for the encounter. Scott Williams, a freshman, coached the Illini, which a superior Purdue eleven flattened by 62 to 0. But the University players learned fast, and nearly 300 persons watched

[109] *15th Report* (1890), 115.
[110] *16th Report* (1892), 21-22, 38-39; "Faculty Record," III, 72 (April 20, 1891). The Committee consisted of Professors Rolfe, Talbot, and Barton.

them beat Illinois Wesleyan by 12 to 6 in their first home football game on Thanksgiving Day.[111]

The Athletic Association, to which all male students could belong, built a sports field at the north end of the campus where the original building had stood. The Board authorized the project, appropriated $350 to grade the grounds, and laid down rules. These forbade gambling, limited participating college teams to two professional players each, and entrusted supervision to the AA, which could charge admission. To raise the $1,200 needed to prepare a track and baseball diamond, build a grandstand with 300 seats, and erect a fence, the AA solicited subscriptions and gave entertainments. Early in 1891 the group successfully sponsored a show in the Walker Opera House in Champaign, and then students got excused from class to take their acts on the road, to neighboring towns and as far away as Purdue. The Athletic Park, later Illini Field, opened for Field Day in May, 1891.[112] Certainly sports united the student body in a common interest and provided opportunity for splendid displays of college solidarity.

About 1887 conditions within the University began to change rather suddenly. There arose a new era of disorder in which disaffected parties focused their wrath on Peabody. The reasons for this development are both numerous and complex, but in all likelihood the explanation lies in the fact that dissatisfaction with Peabody's policies and person simply reached a critical point. He represented college studies as opposed to college life. In 1886 Peabody had insisted on raising certain admissions requirements, and in that same year the Board had rejected the demand of the Grand Council of Sigma Chi that the University admit fraternities. These events, along with the negative attitude toward athletics for which Peabody was known, freshly demonstrated what many considered the Peabody blight.

---

[111] *Illini*, Nov. 22, Dec. 6, 1890; Carol Francis Pullen, "A History of Intercollegiate Football at the University of Illinois" (unpublished master's thesis, University of Illinois, 1957), 6-8.

[112] *16th Report* (1892), 39, 48, 67, 69-71, 88; "Faculty Record," III, 72; Champaign County *Gazette*, April 22, May 12, 1891; *Illini*, May 16, 1891.

In addition, Peabody symbolized the detested disciplinary regime. Students lived under strict rules and found compulsory chapel and military drill especially irksome. The demerit system proved offensive. "It seems inconsistent in this age and country," said the *Sophograph* edited by James Steele, "to educate young men and women in republican sentiments and at the same time attempt to govern them by a set of laws in the making of which they have no voice at all; laws which are executed by a body of men with whom they have little acquaintance and few tastes or sympathies in common."[113]

And perhaps most important, students disliked Peabody's style. They found him cold and aloof, and distrusted the man. In 1882, for example, the *Illini* had credited him with fairness and good intentions in handling a dispute within the Inter-Society Oratorical Association, but had also observed that students misunderstood and misconstrued his motives because he had conferred privately with the disputants and failed to give the student body his views on the matter.[114] In later years students took sly digs at the Regent in print, but the suspicions suddenly deepened. "The indescribable mixture of hate and despondency that lurks in the student's eye as he asks for his note from the regent is a subject for psychological research," wrote a reporter early in 1887.[115]

Doc's Compulsory Entertainment, or Junior Juggernaut, an anonymous parody of class and literary society souvenir programs which probably appeared in the spring of 1887, revealed the serious rift between students and faculty. The versified text lampooned

> 'profs' in various classes
> Well known to all the student world
> As Selim's choicest asses.

But the authors singled out Peabody for special ridicule, and the pamphlet gained power primarily from its biting caricature of Peabody as a ventriloquist with puppet professors on his lap. Horace Taylor, who graduated in 1887 and became an artist on the staff of Chicago and New York newspapers, probably drew the cartoon, showing an obvious debt to Thomas Nast. The only special point

[113] *Sophograph* (1890), 50.
[114] *Illini,* May 13, 1882.
[115] Champaign County *Gazette,* Jan. 12, 1887.

the publication made was that Peabody's $4,000 salary might be better spent.[116]

In the autumn flagrant violation of rules began to mark the growing discontent. Chapel and military drill constituted the main source of trouble. To maintain order the Faculty devoted considerable time to hearing cases and awarding demerits, 25, 50, 75, and even 100 at a time. The tension abated between October, 1889, and May, 1890, when Peabody was in Europe on official leave for what had been diagnosed as "nervous indigestion." When he returned a faculty member suggested that the University Band play "Hell to the Chief" at a reception to mark his arrival. But some culprits who stole the mouthpieces and slides from the band instruments prevented any music, and students turned the whole ceremony into a very frosty affair. Shortly thereafter they defied Peabody when he refused to allow a commencement banquet and ball in the new Drill Hall, and when he put in an unexpected appearance at the dance a "welcoming committee" turned a hose on him.[117]

By late 1890 a crisis was inevitable, and a disruption in the military class precipitated the train of events which led to Peabody's ouster. In January, 1891, the Faculty ruled that William G. Miller, a junior and a captain, could not continue his military studies and had to revert to the rank of private because his academic average had fallen well below the 85 required of those in the military course.[118] A conflict ensued in which Miller's fellow officers from the junior and senior classes petitioned the Faculty for his reinstatement on February 2. Their grounds included the assertion that the University owed it to the military students not to make conditions so difficult as to prevent a sufficient number of them from performing both their military duties and regular academic work.[119] But the

[116] A copy of the eight-page pamphlet bearing no publication date is in the Alumni Class Files, 1888.
[117] Champaign County *Gazette,* Dec. 18, 1889; *15th Report* (1890), 111, 126-27; Girling, *Peabody,* 180-81; Kiler, *On the Banks of the Boneyard,* 43-44; "Faculty Record," III, 29. It should nevertheless be noted that Thomas A. Clark said in the spring of 1888, "The most perfect harmony has existed between the students and faculty" during the academic year. *Sophograph* (1888), 59.
[118] "Faculty Record," III, 51, 52, 54. After re-examination in one course, Miller's average came to 75.3 without his military grade of 80, which made his total average 76.5.
[119] "Military Disturbance Report, 1891," Peabody Papers; also printed in *15th Report* (1890), 83.

Faculty informed the petitioners in writing on the morning of February 3 that it would be unwise to modify the rule for Miller.[120]

On that same morning most of the officers immediately abdicated their commands and submitted resignations in order to force Miller's reinstatement. When Peabody went into the halls where students were forming for chapel he met complete confusion. Instructors managed to get the students into chapel, but Peabody went there and met a tempest of hoots and hisses. The Faculty decided to suspend chapel and military drill temporarily, and meanwhile it began lengthy talks with the military students, all but one of whom had by now resigned.[121] After the Regent told them that the Faculty would not treat with rebels, the military students withdrew a document in which they had asserted that their resignations were final. Now they tried to secure Miller's reinstatement for the remainder of the term. But on February 9 Peabody announced that "no compromises or conditions will be accepted," and gave his adversaries until 3 P.M. the next day to file a written withdrawal of their resignations.[122] In the meantime he brought pressure to bear upon the parents of the students involved. As a result all the offenders except James Steele and George L. Pasfield withdrew their resignations. On February 10 the Faculty suspended Steele and Pasfield for the remainder of the academic year and ordered them to leave the University.[123]

This decision afforded a good opportunity to an anti-Peabody ring headed by Clarence A. Shamel, a senior and editor of the *Illini;* his brother Charles H. Shamel, who had graduated in 1890 and stayed on for advanced study; and Charles A. Kiler, a junior. They instigated a protest meeting on February 11 at the Champaign Opera House to appeal from the Faculty to the Board of Trustees. Nearly 400 students, about four-fifths of the student body, and some townspeople attended the orderly gathering which chose Charles H. Shamel chairman and resolved that Peabody had exerted the power given him by the Faculty in a harsh, unjust, and arbitrary manner

---

[120] "Faculty Record," III, 55.
[121] *Ibid.;* Champaign County *Gazette,* Feb. 4, 1891; [Bogus] *Illini,* Feb. 21, [1891].
[122] "Faculty Record," III, 56.
[123] *Ibid.,* 57; *Illini,* Feb. 21, 1891 (both the bogus and regular editions).

in applying a dormant rule to remove Miller. A majority of those present signed a petition asking the governing body to restore Steele and Pasfield. Copies went to each trustee, and Richard P. Morgan and Francis M. McKay replied sympathetically.[124]

The campus activists also effected an alliance with alumni in Chicago. Robert E. Orr, an 1882 graduate influential there, told the students to obey the authorities and leave the initiative to the Chicago club of alumni. He said that they had set out in September, 1884, to remove Peabody from the University, and "you can all rest assured that it will be done by the end of the college year."[125] Orr urged the young men to go to George R. Shawhan, a stubborn trustee who lived in Urbana, and tell him that a wholesale exodus of students would occur if Peabody remained.

Not content to wait, some students published a bogus *Illini* on February 21. The authors consciously recalled the role of their predecessors in forcing Gregory's resignation, and expressed the hope that Peabody would imitate Gregory and not have to be fired. His basic fault lay in giving a first-class state a third-class university, and two main reasons justified the conclusion. Peabody's character and relations with students constituted one grievance. Critics charged that Peabody had become increasingly astringent during the past five years. He arrogantly sought only his own glorification and had reduced some of his subordinates to sycophants or spies while driving away others. Peabody's educational policies furnished grounds for a second criticism. A prescribed curriculum and the harsh enforcement of rigid disciplinary rules suited an old-time college rather than a modern university. Restrictions on personal liberty were shameful and had been abandoned by all institutions of importance. Yet Peabody had warned *Illini* editors not to publish political articles, had inspired untruthful stories in local newspapers during the recent military revolt, and had resorted to the low trickery of a Chicago politician in his continued warfare against athletics. "It is conceded everywhere," said the bogus *Illini,* "that a college is not alone known

[124] Champaign County *Gazette,* Feb. 18, 1891; *Illini,* March 21, 1891; Morgan to Kiler *et al.,* Feb. 16, 1891; McKay to Messrs. Shamel and others, Feb. 18, 1891, Charles H. Shamel Papers.
[125] Orr to Charles H. Shamel, Feb. 19, March 27, 31, 1891, Charles H. Shamel Papers.

by its course of study but also by its athletics."[126] Peabody's incumbency in an office for which he was unfit accounted for the low attendance and rank of the University, and he owed it to the students, the faculty, and the people of Illinois to resign.

These charges probably stimulated the disobedience and rowdiness which became prevalent. Many men refused to attend military drill after it was resumed, and some attended chapel in order to wire the Bible shut or cut the webbing from under the Regent's chair. A Color Rush between the freshman and sophomore classes turned into a serious Donnybrook, and the Faculty, interpreting the roughhouse as a manifestation of rebellion, suspended 11 ringleaders. Newspapers printed the rumor that over a hundred additional participants would be "fixed," and that many students were planning to transfer to the University of Michigan. On the night of April 11 some students broke into the Military Hall and stole the swords, rifles, and small arms. The turmoil caused an unprecedented rash of failures at the end of the spring term, and students attributed the cause to the retaliation of the Faculty. That body was spending inordinate effort in awarding demerits.[127]

In the midst of this confusion the Board met in Urbana on March 10 and 11 for its annual meeting. Members agreed upon a motion offered by Alexander McLean and Morgan to review the Faculty's handling of the military upheaval. The Board spent one entire day on the case, hearing from a committee of students which included Charles H. Shamel and Kiler, and from Peabody, Burrill, and the deans. Meanwhile, two students were examining official records of academic grades in order to prove the central point at issue: whether the rule on scholarship had been fairly applied to Miller. Student spokesmen contended that Peabody had acted arbitrarily because the rule had been dormant, and alleged that he had admitted this fact. Peabody replied that the records since 1880

[126] [Bogus] *Illini,* Feb. 21, [1891]. The paper was widely distributed, but few copies survived. If the regular *Illini* editor, Clarence A. Shamel, got out this imitation, he threw dust in the readers' eyes by criticizing Clarence Shamel and the regular *Illini* for being on the "sucker" side, which meant allying with the Faculty and Peabody.

[127] Champaign County *Gazette,* March 4, 11, 1891; Champaign County *Herald,* March 11, 1891; *Illini,* March 7, April 4, 1891; *16th Report* (1892), 97; "Faculty Record," III, 61, 65, 69, and *passim* for the period January-June, 1891.

demonstrated that the rule applied to Miller had been a living and not a dead one. He showed that a number of students had been required to make up course standings before being allowed to proceed in their military studies. Moreover, in those cases where the Faculty had used its discretion, the students' grades in their regular subjects had been notably high. On another issue Peabody's foes charged that Steele and Pasfield had offered to resign in any form that might meet Faculty approval. Peabody disagreed, and he denied the charge that the Faculty had entrusted settlement of the matter to him. Peabody's conduct on the specific issues in question was at every point defensible, and that of the students was not. He concluded by asking the significant question, "Where does the discipline of the University lie? Who is responsible for its enforcement?"[128]

The Board answered these pertinent queries by a pusillanimous bit of expediency which was unfair to everyone concerned. On the one hand, the Faculty had acted in good faith and enforced the rules with reasonable uniformity and impartiality. On the other hand, the military students had not generally known or understood the rules. The governing body therefore recommended that the two suspended students be "restored to duty" at the end of the term and that a Trustees' committee revise the rules and regulations for the government of students. The rules were then to be printed in large type and conspicuously posted! Obediently, the Faculty then voted to readmit Steele and Pasfield on March 30. The committee of students and all the class presidents applauded the decision of the Board.[129]

The Trustees should have backed Peabody or fired him; under the circumstances he should have resigned. But he was 62 and apparently hoped to ride out the storm. Hence the campaign of liberation continued. The Trustees met in Chicago on April 10 and received a pro-Peabody statement signed by 57 alumni. But they did nothing about the regency, although McKay had already written

---

[128] Peabody, "Special Report upon the Action of the Faculty of the University of Illinois upon Military Affairs," MS. in the Peabody Papers; also printed in *16th Report* (1892), 81-87 (the quotation is at p. 87). See also pp. 71, 73, 74, and the *Illini*, March 21, 1891. Nelson W. Graham first took his seat as a member of the Board at the March 11 session.
[129] *16th Report* (1892), 80-81; "Faculty Record," III, 65; Champaign County *Gazette*, March 18, 1891; *Illini*, March 21, 1891.

to Cambridge seeking a new head. The anti-Peabody forces held the advantage, including strategic positions in newspaper offices. The pack included Edward W. Pickard, '88, who worked in the city editor's room at the Chicago *Evening Post,* and James Steele, editor of telegraphic news at the Chicago *Herald.* "Tell Kendal," Steele wrote Charles H. Shamel on June 3, "if he will send dispatches [from Champaign] mingled with gall and bitterness from now until the trustees meet I will see that they get in . . . I can intensify anything that comes."[130] Clarence A. Shamel went to stimulate his cohorts in Chicago, where, in addition to attending church twice on Sunday, he called on the college newspapermen and McKay, who asked him back a second time. McKay was "red hot against his majesty and says there is no doubt he will not be reelected in June."[131]

The denouement came in Urbana during commencement week. In his baccalaureate sermon Peabody noted that since conscience was often an inadequate guide, a government of laws had to be enforced. The next evening at the Senior Reception the printed program tastelessly attacked individual faculty members as well as Peabody. The Order of Dance included many numbers ridiculing Peabody, such as "Dock's Last Chicago Can Can," "S.H.P.'s Only Hope (Resign)," and the "Grand Out-Going March."[132]

The Trustees met late the following afternoon, June 9, and Emory Cobb, the senior member, nominated Peabody for election to another term. A tie resulted. Supporting Peabody were Cobb; Lafayette Funk, President of the State Agricultural Society; Alexander McLean; Henry Raab, State Superintendent of Public Instruction; and Shawhan. Opposing were Samuel A. Bullard, President of the Board; John H. Bryant; Nelson W. Graham; McKay; and Morgan. Peabody then gave his regular report, and before commencement exercises the next morning submitted his resigna-

[130] Steele to Charles H. Shamel, June 3, 1891; see also Pickard to Friend Shamel, March 2, 1891, both in Charles H. Shamel Papers; *16th Report* (1892), 87.
[131] Clarence A. Shamel to Charles H. Shamel, May 25, 1891, Charles H. Shamel Papers.
[132] "Programme of Dance, Annual Senior Ball, Class of '91, Monday, June 8, 1891," Charles H. Shamel Papers.

tion.[133] The Board made it effective September 1. At the annual meeting of the Chicago club the Peabody pack "rejoiced openly . . . over the game brought down."[134]

Peabody's reputation has long suffered. Both he and his antagonists contributed to this result by analyzing the events of his departure too narrowly. Peabody himself thought he was the victim of injustice, attributing his downfall to systematic opposition which began at the time of his antifraternity stand and gained power with the law making trustees elective.[135] His opponents held him mainly responsible for the institution's failure to become a first-class state university quickly. But a larger perspective shows that both views oversimplify and puts Peabody in more favorable light.

The disruption at the University of Illinois arose inescapably from the clash between the ideal of discipline and the ideal of freedom. Peabody represented the former, and deserves considerable credit for his achievement. He possessed a clearly formulated philosophy of education and maintained that a college existed primarily for mental training and moral influence. His views enabled him both to introduce more order and higher standards than Gregory had bequeathed, and to develop a type of undergraduate curriculum which gained currency in the twentieth century. And fully as significant, his philosophy led Peabody to insist that the side shows of college life remain subordinate to college studies. But Peabody committed a fatal error: in attempting to preserve valid principles he ran the University like a disciplinary citadel.

The students refused to give primary loyalty to a curriculum which was becoming more rigid. They assumed responsibility for rounding out their education and enriching their experience beyond the classroom because the University failed to do so. Only part of this informal life endangered intellectual purposes, and Peabody had begun to bow to the pressure for it before 1891. If he opposed fraternities, for example, he attempted to build dormitories. If he

[133] *16th Report* (1892), 89, 108. Peabody asked the Board to make his March statement on the military crisis part of its official minutes.
[134] Robert E. Orr to Charles H. Shamel, June 12, 16, 1891, Charles H. Shamel Papers.
[135] Peabody to Jonathan B. Turner, Sept. 26, 1891, Stephens Papers.

distrusted intercollegiate sports, he acknowledged the Faculty's need to accept and control college athletics. But Peabody yielded to student pressure belatedly, and in any case his style weighed heavily against him. Earnest effort had already conquered many new realms, and now earnest effort conquered Peabody himself. Repeated and widespread manifestations of student discontent forced action by the Board, and after Peabody's forced resignation Orr warned Charles H. Shamel that authorities laid much of the trouble at the latter's feet because "you're the man that killed 'Cock Robin.' "[136]

Neither Peabody nor his antagonists were either wholly right or wholly wrong. The vital legacy of their struggle for the University and for higher education in general was the profound question, could college life be kept subordinate to college studies and could the ideals of freedom and of discipline be creatively reconciled?

[136] Robert E. Orr to Charles H. Shamel, June 16, 1891, Charles H. Shamel Papers.

CHAPTER NINE

Toward a Modern University

THE TIMES WERE RIPE in 1891 for elevating the University, and Peabody's departure freed the Board of Trustees to initiate a major tranformation. This effort required a new chief executive, but the governing body spent years in finding a man suitable for the position. Three reasons account for their difficulty. First, the Trustees were unanimous in their ambition to create at Urbana one of the outstanding universities in the country. Thus they wanted a leader who could set the University on the road to greatness. This necessitated someone with a national reputation, a man whose name would immediately shed luster on the aspiring institution. Available candidates who fit the bill were few in number. Second, the Board was not united on the critical issue — the type of greatness desired for the University. However, several members, probably a majority, thought the scientific and technical departments were strong enough to take care of themselves, and sought to emphasize the "cultural" side in the appointment of a president.[1] Third, the Trustees originally set their sights for a prominent scholar, preferably someone in a discipline related to the liberal arts. But gradually they moved to the new view that an administrator was best fitted to head the institution.

The long and frustrating search actually began the day Peabody submitted his resignation. The Trustees immediately took matters into their own hands, setting up a five-man committee with no faculty representatives, headed by Francis M. McKay and Nelson W. Graham.[2] The former, in fact, had already laid the groundwork for the exploration now launched by the new group. In April McKay had sought names from President Eliot and John Fiske, the famous historian who lived in Cambridge and moved in the Harvard orbit. McKay even asked Fiske if he himself would consider a proposition, adding that they expected to pay from $6,000 to $10,000 for the right man.[3] Fortunately Fiske declined, offering as reasons the doubt that he possessed the requisite executive ability (surely an accurate appraisal, for he could not even manage his personal finances successfully), the fact that the $10,000 salary mentioned was much less than he was already earning by literary labor, and that having always lived within the smell of salt water he was getting too old to leave it. McKay also urged Herbert B. Adams, a professor of history at Johns Hopkins, to consider the vacancy.[4]

The selection committee ignored the many who applied directly

[1] Thomas J. Burrill to Dr. Stockbridge, March 3, 1894, Andrew S. Draper Letterbooks.
[2] The members were the three school administrators on the Committee of Instruction, Francis M. McKay, Henry Raab, and George R. Shawhan, along with Emory Cobb and Nelson W. Graham. *16th Report* (1892), 109.
[3] McKay to Charles W. Eliot, April 4, May 25, 1891, Harvard University Archives; McKay to John Fiske, April 5, 1891, Henry E. Huntington Library and Art Gallery.
[4] Fiske to McKay, Cambridge, July 10, 1891, Henry E. Huntington Library and Art Gallery; Milton Berman, *John Fiske: The Evolution of a Popularizer* (Cambridge, Mass., 1961); McKay to Adams, July 22, 1891, Johns Hopkins University Library.

and rejected others after careful consideration. These included Horatio S. White, Dean of the Faculty at Cornell, and Andrew S. Draper, a lawyer and Republican politician who in 1892 had just failed of re-election as New York State Superintendent of Public Instruction after six years in office. Burrill considered Draper the man for the job, and the Faculty recommended him in a resolution to the Board. But the Trustees ignored the advice, fearing to elect someone who was not college-bred and too much a politician.[5]

The committee met refusals from two prominent men of different types to whom they offered the headship. On an interviewing trip to the East in the spring of 1892, McKay and Graham waylaid Woodrow Wilson at his Princeton classroom door and told him they had come to look him over for the vacancy. A young professor who had already won a name by publishing articles and two important books on politics, Wilson found the visitors very intelligent and impressive. Equally impressed, McKay later informed Wilson that he and Graham would recommend him at a salary of $6,000 provided he indicated at the earliest practicable moment his readiness to accept. McKay added that with proper management the school could soon be made "one of the first state universities in the land."[6]

Mrs. Wilson favored the move, and Wilson's first impulse strongly inclined him to accept. He was prepared to believe that the University of Illinois had, potentially, a great future, although it was less well-advanced than other state institutions. But on reflection he wondered whether the job would keep him from original scholarly work. He knew of the difficulties faced by presidents forced to extract grants from legislatures and manage political boards of trustees, and concluded "that what we are considering is, not the general question of *a* college presidency, but the special question of *this* college presidency."[7] In many ways, nevertheless,

[5] *Cultivator and Country Gentleman,* LVII (1892), 206; Burrill to James Hall, on the back of the letter from Hall (of Albany, N.Y.) to Burrill, March 5, 1892, Burrill Correspondence, 1892, 1894; "Faculty Record," III, 125; James E. Armstrong to Draper, Feb. 26, 1894, Andrew S. Draper Personal Letters; James E. Armstrong to Franklin W. Scott, Nov. 12, 1918, Carl Stephens Papers.
[6] McKay to Wilson, New York, April 30, 1892, Woodrow Wilson Papers, Library of Congress.
[7] Wilson to Ellen Axson Wilson, May 9, 1892, quoted in Ray Stannard Baker, *Woodrow Wilson, Life and Letters: Princeton, 1890-1910* (Garden City, N.Y., 1927), 22.

the fact that the University had to depend so largely upon the legislature for its means of support and growth attracted Wilson, for it aroused "the latent politician" within him.[8] But ultimately he declined, insisting that his only ground was an unwillingness to subordinate his literary plans to executive duties.

Washington Gladden was among the candidates who visited Urbana on invitation. A Congregational minister from Columbus, Ohio, Gladden had won national attention for books and sermons which were in the vanguard of the Social Gospel movement. At commencement exercises in 1892 he gave an address on "The True Socialism," and subsequently the Board authorized its committee to offer Gladden the headship at a salary not to exceed $6,000. Gladden also declined, giving only this explanation in his *Recollections:* "I visited Champaign and looked over the field, but concluded that I would rather remain in Ohio."[9]

The Trustees had nothing to show by the summer of 1892, and nearly two years of still further effort produced no result. Though embarrassed by the failure, the Board felt it more important to find the right man than to hasten the selection. In the spring of 1894, however, the original committee yielded to a new one headed by James E. Armstrong. Although several professors were being considered at the time, Armstrong concluded that the office required organizational and executive ability. He wanted a man who could attract to the University legislative and public support. The spotlight then again focused on Draper, whose political and administrative talents now looked attractive. Armstrong, Graham, and Burrill visited him in Cleveland, where he was Superintendent of Schools, and invited him to meet the Trustees in Chicago. After an interview on April 13 the governing board unanimously offered him the job. Draper set his price high — a $7,000 salary and a free house — and accepted on May 10. He took office on August 1, and the next day the Trustees changed the title of the University's executive from Regent to President.[10]

[8] Wilson to McKay, Princeton, May 12, 1892, Woodrow Wilson Collection, Princeton University Library.

[9] Washington Gladden, *Recollections* (Boston, 1909), 414; see also *16th Report* (1892), 251.

[10] T[homas] J. B[urrill], "In Quest of a President," *The 1903 Illio* [Urbana, 1903], 37-38; Armstrong to Franklin W. Scott, Nov. 12, 1918, Stephens Papers; *17th Report* (1894), 241, 269.

While the Trustees spent three years looking for Peabody's successor, Thomas Jonathan Burrill was at the helm. Burrill, in fact, presented good claims to the office in his own right, although he said that he greatly preferred his own Department to the presidency. At the same time he admitted that the Board had never offered him the job by unanimous action, and thought no man could afford to accept it otherwise. Public speculation about the reasons for not selecting Burrill placed him in a delicate position.[11] Probably one reason was the Board's interest in obtaining an outsider, and in addition the desperate desire for a "big" name with proven executive capacity counted against the local faculty member. Yet the Board seriously underestimated him. The members could not have known the tremendous ability of Burrill. For over two decades both Gregory and Peabody as well as the Trustees had drawn heavily on his good reputation with students and faculty members to ease them out of difficult situations. Burrill had not only honored these calls but also gave his superiors the utmost in loyal support. Unfortunately, everything about the man made him seem an upholder of the status quo, and the Board was looking for reform. In all likelihood no one suspected how much Burrill disagreed with the old order of things. And yet as soon as he assumed power he initiated changes which inaugurated a new era. Burrill deserves the main credit for laying the foundations of a distinctly modern type of university at Urbana, and it is quite possible that the Board erred in selecting Draper rather than Burrill.

The transformation of the University under Burrill began with his reorganization of the internal government. The Board of Trustees had long complicated problems by not confining itself to the formulation of policy. Burrill knew in intimate detail the evils which resulted when the Trustees dictated appointments, meddled with the curriculum, or heard appeals from disgruntled students. In his strongest statement he said one guiding principle should be proclaimed without hesitancy: "that the internal educational and disciplinary affairs must be vested in the faculty without appeal and only under the most general rules and regulations."[12] The Trustees'

[11] Burrill to Dr. Stockbridge, March 3, 1894, Draper Letterbooks; *16th Report* (1892), 112; B. F. J., in *Cultivator and County Gentleman*, LVII (1892), 206.
[12] Thomas J. Burrill, *Our University: An Address Delivered Before the University Assembly of the University of Illinois* [Bloomington, 1894], 11-12.

highest responsibility rested in their selecting proper administrative officials, and once chosen these must exercise full authority at their own discretion. But rather than lecture members of the governing body on the proper conduct of their office, he attempted to check the Board by erecting a countervailing power.

Burrill placed a premium on the role of the Faculty in the life of the University. As a collective body the professors had never exerted much power before 1891. Although in theory the entire Faculty had controlled the discipline and studies subject to the general direction of the Board, in practice the regents had imposed their will on the institution and remained in power as long as they pleased the Trustees. Now, however, Burrill called upon the Faculty to assume an active share in the government of the school. He took the advanced position which the first Americans had tried to carry along with them from European universities: "Professors are sometimes spoken of as working for the college. They are the college."[13]

At the opening of the academic year in 1891 Burrill prompted reorganization of the Faculty. That body established a new committee structure designed to give the professors more weight in affairs and to free the Regent and the collective Faculty from numerous details. Nine standing committees were now to deal with University Extension, Preparatory Schools, Advertisement and Publications, Military Affairs, Athletics, Public Exercises, Students' Welfare, the Library, and the Museum. Members of each committee were to be elected by the Faculty upon nomination by the Executive Committee. This latter agency included the Regent, the Vice-President (Shattuck succeeded Burrill in that office in September, 1892), and the deans of the colleges. Since the Executive Committee was empowered to act for the Faculty whenever necessity required, it gradually became a potent body, and developed later into the Council of Administration. A new set of Faculty bylaws adopted a year later and approved by the Board provided for election by the general Faculty of the dean of each college.[14]

In addition, Burrill recognized the need to enhance the dignity,

[13] President Paul Ansel Chadbourne in his inaugural address at Williams College, 1873, as quoted in Richard Hofstadter and Walter P. Metzger, *The Development of Academic Freedom in the United States* (New York, 1955), 274.
[14] "Faculty Record," III, 94-95 (Oct. 5, 1891); 147-51 (Sept. 12, 1892).

economic welfare, and security of the professors. He thought faculty members needed the greatest possible liberty within their own departments, and a feeling of appreciation. The highest type of service came from men who loved their work and whose interest in it exceeded that of an employee. Hence in June, 1892, Burrill condemned the rule which made the term of faculty duty the whole year and required professors to secure leave of absence for vacations. He said the rule was in spirit unmitigably bad and had created antagonism rather than loyalty to the University. The Board immediately rescinded it, but deferred action on Burrill's recommendation that it adopt a policy of sabbatical leaves. In the spring of 1894, however, the Trustees granted Professor Snyder a leave of absence for the next academic year at half pay, and his was the first sabbatical. Since he had already submitted his resignation, his leave was as much a terminal leave and a reward for lengthy service as it was a sabbatical.[15]

In 1891 the University was paying its faculty lower salaries than most Midwestern universities and it lacked both a classification scheme for ranks and provision for salary increases. Two-thirds of the entire staff consisted of full professors, most of whom received $2,000 a year, the others less. About that time Minnesota was paying $2,400, Michigan and Wisconsin $3,000, and the new University of Chicago fixed the salary of head professors at $6,000 to $7,000. At Urbana the remainder of the faculty consisted of one assistant professor and about equal numbers of instructors and assistants, whose pay ranged from $500 to $1,600 yearly.[16] Burrill's main effort to correct the deficiencies came in the spring of 1893. He proposed the following classification of ranks and maximum salaries: professors, $2,500; associate professors, $2,000; assistant professors, $1,600; instructors, $1,200; and assistants, $1,000. Special pay raises and promotion would result from merit. Burrill suggested that assistants and instructors be engaged for ten months (the academic year). Individuals in the three professorial ranks were initially to

[15] *16th Report* (1892), 230, 239; Burrill, *Our University*, 12. For the old rule, see *10th Report* (1881), 245. See also *17th Report* (1894), 229.
[16] *16th Report* (1892), 101; Richard J. Storr, *Harper's University, the Beginnings: A History of the University of Chicago* (Chicago, 1966), 74; Merle Curti and Vernon Carstensen, *The University of Wisconsin: A History, 1848-1925* (2 vols., Madison, 1949), I, 593-94n.

be appointed for one year, and "permanently engaged during the pleasure of the trustees" if they proved satisfactory during the probationary year.[17]

At the same time Burrill recommended that building lots near the University be leased to professors at nominal rates. Many desired to live in that area but hesitated to invest in houses because of the uncertainty of tenure and the difficulty of selling if they took another job. When an individual departed, the University should accept the buildings at a fair valuation. Burrill thought this plan, which Cornell had long tried with excellent results, would advance the welfare of the University.

At a later date such a proposal would have been called socialistic, but Burrill met no criticism for his progressive idea, although the Trustees did not endorse it. After lengthy study they adopted most of his other recommendations. The Board established the five proposed faculty ranks and authorized regular annual pay increases until the maximum sums were reached. These they set about midway between the existing levels and the figures suggested by Burrill. Deans could earn $2,500, professors $2,250. At the same time the Board expressly stated that no promotion or pay increase for length of service could be made except by specific vote of the Trustees, and that body vested in itself the annual election of the deans of the colleges.[18]

The concepts of academic tenure and academic freedom as understood today were not clearly formulated in the late nineteenth century. Burrill, however, argued that the type of professor desired should in effect if not in form have a life appointment. He tried to realize this ideal in several ways. The existing low salaries enabled him to advance his point, for he contended that reasonable assurance of stability of tenure partially offset the disadvantage.[19] In 1893 he urged the scheme which in effect offered permanent positions to the three professorial ranks after a one-year probationary period. But how permanent was permanent? Upon what conditions and by what methods could a professor be discharged? These questions had not troubled the University when Gregory forced out Manly Miles

[17] *17th Report* (1894), 103-4.
[18] *Ibid.*, 120, 236-37.
[19] Burrill, *Our University,* 12; *16th Report* (1892), 230.

in 1876 or when Peabody dismissed Don Carlos Taft in 1882. But Burrill held a progressive view on academic freedom, and the Board dismayed him when it fired Professor James D. Crawford in 1893.

The immediate issue involved Crawford's private life, although little is known about the details. Crawford had joined the faculty in 1873. Late in 1887 his wife succumbed after an illness of three months, and about that time he acquired a reputation as a philanderer. A student publication which was probably issued in 1887 called Crawford a "Don Juan." In June, 1891, the printed program of the senior class ball listed "Crawford's Dance for Hugging Other Men's Wives" on the Order of Dance and "Try to determine which man's wife Crawford goes to see most" as an "Intermission Topic."[20] In referring to the matter in August, 1893, Burrill mentioned Crawford's relations with another woman and outside influences which had embittered both their lives during the previous three years.

But the larger issue involved academic freedom. The Executive Committee of the Board had made up its mind during the summer to discharge Crawford. Burrill informed Napoleon B. Morrison, a coal company president from Odin, Illinois, who sat on the Committee, that if Crawford "is guilty of conduct unbecoming a true gentleman, — to say nothing more, — the Board must not hesitate to condemn him." Yet he insisted that Crawford (and the woman in question, if she chose to appear) be given a hearing before judgment. Quite apart from the fairness due Crawford, Burrill was even more concerned for the effect the failure to grant a hearing might have upon the University. "The greatest calamity that could befall an institution of this kind," he warned Morrison, "is a serious breach between the Trustees and the Faculty." While no one criticized the good intentions of the Trustees or mistrusted their desire to treat the case justly, there was a very strong undercurrent of feeling that a principle was on trial of more consequence than an individual's conduct.[21]

Although Burrill wanted the case to go to the entire Board, the

[20] *Doc's Compulsory Entertainment, or Junior Juggernaut* [Urbana, 1887?], 6; "Programme of Dance, Annual Senior Ball, Class of '91, Monday, June 8, 1891," Charles H. Shamel Papers.
[21] Burrill to Morrison, August, 1893, "Regents' Letterbook, 1879-1894." Only part of this copy of Burrill's five-page letter can be made out, and with extreme difficulty, because the ink has badly faded. Both quotations are from the letter.

Trustees granted no hearing. The Executive Committee curtly notified Crawford that the Committee "deems it inadvisable to continue
your services as professor in that institution. Your salary will be paid
until the 1st of September next." At the meeting of the Board on
September 12 the Committee reported that it had examined certain
matters concerning Crawford and after thoroughly satisfying itself
had informed him of his discharge. The Board approved the action,
and later denied Crawford's claim to be paid his regular salary for
September. The junior and senior classes met on September 20 and
passed a resolution which praised Crawford for his abilities and service to the University, expressed "sincere regret at his removal," and
assured him of sympathy, respect, and unshaken confidence in his
integrity. According to the *Illini* the Faculty passed similar resolutions, but the "Faculty Record" does not mention any such matter.
The students did not criticize the Board for violating academic
freedom and tenure, and in all likelihood both the Faculty and
the students understood these considerations little better than the
Trustees.[22]

The importance of courting public favor and wringing money
from Springfield remained as acute as ever after 1891. Although the
University enjoyed a good reputation in engineering and scientific
circles, it probably commanded little more favor with the general
public than it had a decade or two earlier. In 1891 the Homer
Enterprise declared that three colleges in the state ranked higher
than the University. About that time Governor Joseph W. Fifer
infuriated students by referring to their institution as Champaign
University, and President William R. Harper annoyed them by locating the school at Bloomington.[23]

[22] *17th Report* (1894), 178, 205; *Illini,* Sept. 27, 1893. Crawford later lived
in destitution in Redlands, California, in an $800 house built out of contributions
from the alumni. When a pension of $30 a month from a fund raised by the
alumni dried up, former students asked Governor Frank O. Lowden and President Edmund J. James to help Crawford. On October 20, 1917, the Board
granted Crawford a retirement allowance of $30 a month until further notice.
See Franklin W. Scott to President James, Sept. 11, 1916, James General Correspondence, Box 133; Mrs. P. T. Spence to Governor Lowden, Feb. 19, 1917,
James General Correspondence, Box 125; and the Crawford File, James General
Correspondence, Box 150.
[23] *Illini,* Oct. 17, Nov. 16, 1891; Feb. 29, 1892.

The Committee on Advertisement and Publications established in 1891 secured the adoption of a plan for publicizing the institution. Some of the familiar policies remained in use. The University disseminated descriptive circulars and lithographs and furnished information to newspaper correspondents. But on top of this the Committee proposed to make known its willingness to use the facilities of the University's technical departments to perform services for the public. The scheme was not entirely novel. University chemists were already gratuitously examining the potability of municipal water supplies, even though Peabody had discouraged the practice. Now, however, the plan was to volunteer services in return for public favor. Rather naively, the Committee also urged faculty members to write for professional journals and to attend professional meetings. It recommended that the University bear some of the expenses for such of this participation as benefited the institution alone.[24]

Students remained perhaps the most active propagandists. The Committee urged them to write for their home papers using information supplied by the press bureau, and Burrill enlisted them in a campaign to flood the state with descriptions of their *educational* experience at Urbana. But intercollegiate athletics became far more important as a means for advertising the University, and Burrill acknowledged their value for this purpose.[25]

The opening of the refounded University of Chicago in 1892 probably stimulated a desire to make the state University better known, although the two schools entered into no immediate rivalry. The *Illini* expressed the belief that the University of Illinois would be affected but little, although hopefully for the good, by the establishment of "another great institution" so close.[26] In June Nathaniel Butler resigned a full professorship of English at Urbana to accept an associate professorship at Chicago, but Michigan and Wisconsin rather than Chicago prompted the Board when it ingenuously resolved early in 1893 "that the University should be placed on a par

[24] The Committee included Professors Morrow, Talbot, Palmer, and Brownlee. Its recommendations are in the *16th Report* (1892), 164-65.
[25] *Illini*, Oct. 17, 1891; *17th Report* (1894), 59, 156.
[26] *Illini*, Feb. 15, 1892.

with the best of the other state universities."[27] The Trustees asked the hearty cooperation of the alumni in this effort, and announced an intention to ask the General Assembly for ample means to realize the goal.

The election of John P. Altgeld as Governor in November, 1892, most vitally affected the University's relations with the state. The first Chicagoan to become chief executive and the first Democrat in that office since the founding of the University, Altgeld assumed genuine interest in the institution. Both personal and political reasons account for his concern. Altgeld had grown up in poverty and without formal schooling and was ardently Jeffersonian in politics. His intensely democratic feelings led him to oppose endowed universities as aristocratic and to believe that public higher education would do much for both individuals and the state. He had considered the University's needs for more buildings, more teachers, more students, more carrying of liberal learning to all the people, and more money. In addition, Altgeld doubtless saw a political opportunity in the situation. The Board had been Republican since the founding of the University, and Altgeld complained about the lack of support and bad management which Republicans had given the institution. But now for the first time the Board contained a majority of very able Democrats. In 1890 John H. Bryant, Nelson W. Graham, and Richard P. Morgan won election, and in 1892 James E. Armstrong, Napoleon B. Morrison, and Isaac S. Raymond. Thus six out of nine trustees were Democrats during Altgeld's first two years in office. He knew his party could get credit for advancing the welfare of the University.[28]

The manner in which Altgeld eased the University's appropriation through the legislature in 1893 was his first great service to the institution. Late in 1892 the Board had decided to ask for $551,000 for the next biennium, a figure that greatly exceeded anything previously granted. In 1891 the General Assembly had made available $134,200, including $70,000 for the Natural History Building. The Board could easily justify the enlarged request

[27] *17th Report* (1894), 76; see also "Faculty Record," III, 164.
[28] *The Mind and Spirit of John Peter Altgeld*, ed. Henry M. Christman (Urbana, 1960), 1-13 (Editor's Preface); Andrew S. Draper, "Governor Altgeld and the University of Illinois," *Alumni Quarterly*, VII (April, 1913), 77-82.

because of the rapidly expanding student body and the desire to improve the University's comparative standing. It therefore sought $120,000 for the general operating fund, a threefold increase over the sum given for that purpose in the previous biennium. It also requested $375,000 for buildings. At the time the campus badly lacked sufficient space for most academic purposes, and Burrill pleaded for buildings devoted to agriculture, engineering, a library, a museum, a preparatory school, a women's gymnasium, and an auditorium. Upon recommendation of the Executive Committee, the Faculty decided to ask for engineering, library, and museum buildings. All were absolutely necessary. Ricker drew up plans, and in June, 1892, the Board voted that a library and engineering building be erected as soon as practicable. The Faculty restated the need for all three, and the Board included them in its request.[29]

There was much uncertainty in Urbana as to what the Democrats in Springfield would do. Burrill wished that the people of Illinois could be made to understand the high cost of running a first-class university. He tried to enlist alumni and former students to help in the legislative campaign, and informed correspondents of the discrepancy between the University of Illinois' expenditure and that of Cornell and of the University of Chicago. Cornell, with five times the annual income of Illinois, was asking for $150,000 a year for current expenses compared to the $60,000 requested by Illinois.[30]

A heated hearing before the Senate Committee on Appropriations dashed all hopes. Legislators with fixed opinions cut out the amounts proposed for new buildings and reduced the operating fund to the old figure. The Committee recommended an appropriation of $96,500 rather than the $551,000 asked. Officials from the University knew nothing about Altgeld's attitude, but they easily secured an interview and laid their case before him. He spoke with the chairman of the Committee, and the Committee met again. Now it proved cordial rather than hostile, and agreed to appropriate $160,000 for an engineering building and $120,000 for instruc-

[29] "Faculty Record," III, 120, 166; *16th Report* (1892), 254-56; *17th Report* (1894), 73.
[30] See, for example, Burrill to William H. Hinrichsen [?], [Dec. 30, 1892]; Burrill to Henry M. Dunlap, Jan. 25, 1893, both in "Regents' Letterbook, 1879-1894."

tional expenses. Altgeld had gained $240,000 for the University overnight by telling the Committee that he would sponsor an addition to the tax rate in order to provide liberal support for Urbana. With the sums granted for other purposes, the total appropriation for the biennium came to $295,000. The increased appropriation for the University was the most important advance of the whole legislative session.[31]

Altgeld also manifested his interest by visiting the campus and often addressing the students. He first spoke at commencement in 1893, when he had already endeared himself for his stand toward the University and its appropriation. A tumultuous cheer arose when Burrill introduced the Governor, whose remarks breathed a strongly democratic spirit. His theme, the question of what to do for a living, enabled him to praise practical builders. His assault on most wielders of authority as moral cowards reflected the crisis in his own mind a short time before he pardoned three men convicted as participants in the 1886 Haymarket Riot. Altgeld also observed that life was a struggle which required perserverance, aggression, and hard labor to win success. He revealed his prejudice against the aristocratic universities of the East and congratulated students on attending a state university. Altgeld made a deep impression.[32]

Altgeld attended several meetings of the Board and interested himself in efforts to publicize the University. On one occasion he secured adoption of a proposal to use $1,000 to prepare a statement of the special advantages of the University to be signed by the President of the governing body and sent to all male teachers in the state. He also urged the speedy completion of the engineering building. Trustee Morrison, a member of the comittee to locate the structure, declared that on the ground originally proposed the building would not be observed either from the Illinois Central Railroad or from Champaign and Urbana. Morrison noted that the University would thereby "lose the benefit of imposing architecture for advertising purposes," and recommended high ground for the site.[33]

---

[31] Thomas J. Burrill, "Governor Altgeld's Methods," *Alumni Quarterly,* VII (April, 1913), 83-84; Ray Ginger, *Altgeld's America: The Lincoln Ideal* VERSUS *Changing Realities* (New York, 1958), 75.

[32] *Illini,* May 8 [June 8], 1893.

[33] *17th Report* (1894), 120, 182 (the source of the quotation), 265.

The biggest single promotional effort in these years was the University's participation in the World's Columbian Exposition at Chicago in the summer of 1893. For over two years the Faculty made careful preparations, revealing the institution's character by planning to make its emphasis as follows: College of Engineering, 5,000 square feet of space at a cost of $5,350; College of Natural Science, 3,350 and $3,050; College of Agriculture and Agricultural Experiment Station, 2,000 and $2,000; Art Department, 600 and $600; College of Literature and Science, 300 and $600.[34] Although many private American colleges and universities arranged educational exhibits at Chicago, only nine state universities did so, and of these Michigan and Illinois alone made a serious effort.[35] The University of Illinois could not vie with many older institutions in such respects as showing portraits of presidents and famous authors from among its former students, but its nine carloads of apparatus for instruction, students' laboratory and shop work, natural science collections, and photographs in the Illinois State Building afforded thousands of citizens their first impression of the type of education available at their state University. Burrill asserted that the University's display was the largest and most varied showing among the exhibits made by all the American and foreign educational institutions at the Columbian Exposition, and he was sure that participation was worth in public recognition the considerable expense involved.[36]

A new academic era opened as Burrill led in developing a narrow collegiate institution into a broad university. The process began in the fall of 1891,[37] and the reasons for the transformation were numerous. Perhaps most basic, the nation had come of age since the founding of the University, and Burrill knew that the land-

[34] *16th Report* (1892), 157-61.
[35] Richard Waterman, Jr., "Educational Exhibits at the Columbian Exposition," *Educational Review*, VII (Feb., 1894), 129-40; Selim H. Peabody, "The Educational Exhibit at the Columbian Exposition," National Educational Association, *Journal of Proceedings and Addresses, 1892* (New York, 1893), 583-90.
[36] Burrill, *Our University*, 1; *17th Report* (1894), 197; Superintendent of Public Instruction of the State of Illinois, *Twentieth Biennial Report* (Springfield, 1894), 12.
[37] For evidence that students immediately sensed the big change, see James Steele to Charles H. Shamel, Oct. 10, 1891, Shamel Papers.

grant institutions had to minister to the scientific, technical, and social needs of urban and industrial America.[38]

The reforms for which he deserves chief credit rested upon an improved financial basis resulting from the Morrill Act of 1890 and larger state appropriations. Moreover, a steady growth in enrollment brought new opportunity. The student body shot from 509 in the academic year ending June, 1891, to 718 three years later, and during the 1890's no state university in America experienced such a rapid advance as Illinois. (Since the Preparatory School annually averaged 175 pupils in these years, enrollment in the University proper did not pass 500 until 1893-94 — a full quarter-century after the institution had opened.) Some attributed the dramatic increase to athletics and a new college spirit ushered in by Peabody's removal, but in fact it was part of a rising national tide which began in the late 1880's as higher education became more vital to individual and social welfare. Yet Illinois commanded no place on the list of 26 universities and colleges in the United States which had an enrollment of a thousand or more students by the spring of 1894.[39]

Moreover, authorities worked hard to attract high school students. In 1891 the Faculty's Committee on Preparatory Schools obtained approval for sending a catalogue to each graduate and an illustrated circular to every student on the list of accredited schools. More important, the Committee later improved the accreditation system so as to allow the University to add both private schools and public high schools beyond Illinois to its approved roster. The number of accredited schools rose from 60 in the academic year ending June, 1891, to 113 two years later. But the Board rejected a proposal to send a circular to every high school student in Illinois.[40]

Burrill, thinking the University would be better off without its preparatory department, wanted Champaign and Urbana to estab-

[38] On this point see Earle D. Ross, *Democracy's College: The Land-Grant Movement in the Formative Stage* (Ames, Iowa, 1942), 181-82.

[39] Superintendent of Public Instruction of the State of Illinois, *Twenty-first Biennial Report* (Springfield, 1896), 146; Burrill, *Our University*, 5; Austen Kennedy DeBlois, *The Pioneer School: A History of Shurtleff College, the Oldest Institution in the West* (Chicago, 1900), 278; *Illini*, March 29, 1894. The list included the following universities: California, Cornell, Iowa, Kentucky, Michigan, Minnesota, Nebraska, Northwestern, Washington (St. Louis), and Wisconsin; and Illinois Wesleyan College.

[40] "Faculty Record," III, 103, 136-37, 163-64; *17th Report* (1894), 27, 219.

lish a union high school with special courses for those planning on entering the University. But the two towns were unwilling, and the Preparatory School gained a new lease on life. The University extended its curriculum to two years and in 1893 brought in Edward G. Howe as its Principal.[41]

Within the University proper, enrichment and liberalization of the curriculum figured most prominently in the innovations. The catalogue listed 175 courses of instruction in 1891-92, including important new work for which Peabody had laid foundations in three areas of engineering — electrical, municipal and sanitary, and architectural — and in philosophy, psychology, pedagogy, and physical culture. Burrill added few entirely new fields of study, but reinvigorated several older ones — notably English, history, political economy, mathematics, and Romance languages — and expanded the offerings in others, chiefly engineering and science. In 1893-94 the catalogue listed 252 courses, an increase of 45 per cent in two years which came mainly in advanced classes.[42]

The number and quality of the faculty increased in order to keep pace. The instructional corps rose from 46 to 64 in the years under review, not counting the staffs of the State Laboratory of Natural History and of the Agricultural Experiment Station. Burrill viewed the quality of instruction given as the critical element in an institution of learning, and valued teaching power over teaching facilities — buildings, libraries, and laboratories. The Board's Committee of Instruction, consisting of school administrators, joined Burrill in the search for professors trained at leading American universities and armed with Ph.D.'s. McKay actively sought names of candidates for vacant positions, and informed Herbert B. Adams of Johns Hopkins that the University would like a man with European training for its chair of Psychology and Pedagogy.[43]

Though no formal vote had been take on the subject, Burrill told the Trustees during his first year in office, "I believe it is unanimously thought by members of the Faculty that the courses of study

[41] *16th Report* (1892), 198, 261-62; *Illini,* April 11, 1892; *17th Report* (1894), 128.
[42] Superintendent of Public Instruction, *Twentieth Biennial Report,* 5-6.
[43] *Ibid.,* 5; McKay to Adams, Oct. 7, 1891, May 29, 1893, Johns Hopkins University Library.

can be much improved by the introduction of the elective system, instead of the rigidly prescribed list of studies."[44] Under the former an Illinois undergraduate could obtain either a degree by completing an authorized course of study or a full certificate by completing 36 studies (term courses) of his own selection. Peabody had considered the route to full certificates a detriment to good discipline and sound scholarship, and in 1889 the governing board approved his recommendation to cut off graduation by certificate after 1891. Under Peabody a degree candidate had free choice between 13 different four-year courses, each made up of 36 or more subjects. To graduate, a person had to complete the entire course as offered.[45]

Under Burrill the Faculty restored to students the utmost freedom of choice of study. It rejected the former system except in respect to the technical courses in the College of Engineering. In the other colleges — Agriculture, Science, and Literature (the latter two received these new names in the spring of 1892) — the reform which was progressively realized over two years harmonized the desires of students with the demands of sound educational practice. In brief it operated as follows. The University required 40 term credits — a term credit was five classes a week for one term — for graduation. A student could select his own studies from the lists of required and elective courses for each college which were printed in the catalogue. In principle the University specified the minimum of required work, although the amount varied. For example, the College of Agriculture required 24 and the College of Literature 11 credits in 1891-92, and two years later 16 and 9 respectively. A student chose the remainder of his work from three lists of electives. The principles behind the rules governing the choice from these separate lists gave even the beginning student elective freedom, obligated everyone to choose two courses (majors) in the field of intended study and pursue them consecutively for at least two years, to choose three courses (minors) from a larger list of cognate studies, and either to take more work in a familiar study or to branch out into a new one by electing additional credits from any of the three lists.

[44] *16th Report* (1892), 203-4.
[45] *13th Report* (1887), 91-92; *15th Report* (1890), 14-15, 51-53; Superintendent of Public Instruction, *Twentieth Biennial Report*, 6.

The system produced an almost infinite variety of courses, and guided the student to a progressively more comprehensive treatment of his field. The new arrangement enabled seniors to specialize in laboratory or seminar work. Burrill considered the elective system the greatest advance made during his administration. Any losses resulting from sliding into easy courses of instruction were, he thought, more than offset by gains in general enthusiasm for study. The reform made teaching and study more pleasant, and brought Illinois into line with modern university ideas.[46]

Since the people of Illinois still felt little need for agricultural education or research, the College of Agriculture continued its steady march toward oblivion. In 1892-93 seven students enrolled in the regular courses of the College. The following year the number fell to three — one senior and two freshmen.[47] Recognizing the futility of pushing the four-year program, Morrow emphasized the briefer offerings the College sponsored. The two-year Junior Course in Agriculture was the more promising of these, but it attracted only five students in 1892-93 and three the next year. Ironically, the Free Short Course which was held at Urbana during the winter term secured the largest following. The University widely advertised the lectures on practical topics by members of the faculty and visitors, and admitted 18-year-olds without examination. Twenty-three young men who possessed no interest in the science or principles of agriculture attended in 1892-93, and 25 the year thereafter.[48]

Thus Morrow relied on agricultural exhibits, the farm press, and attendance at meetings to preach the gospel of improved husbandry. He supervised the University's exhibit at the Columbian Exposition, and tried unsuccessfully to prompt the land-grant colleges into making a collective exhibit there. Although several members of the Urbana faculty addressed groups of farmers throughout the state, Morrow carried the main load. In one year he gave 26

[46] Superintendent of Public Instruction, *Twentieth Biennial Report*, 6.
[47] In addition, six special students registered in Agriculture in 1892-93, and one graduate student and one special student in the following year. *17th Report* (1894), 15-16.
[48] *Ibid.;* Illinois State Department of Agriculture, *Transactions for 1891,* o.s., XXIX (Springfield, 1892), 226-28; *Transactions for 1893,* o.s., XXX (Springfield, 1894), 35-39.

out of 70 lectures taken to the hustings, mostly at farmers' institutes. Morrow found the administration of these gatherings unsatisfactory. The legislature appropriated $50 to each county to support such work, but many held no institute and those which did would improve with central supervision. He suggested that the University resume control over the institutes, and try to attract younger audiences.[49]

Morrow also inaugurated short schools designed for special agricultural interests in different parts of the state. This plan envisioned a school for dairymen in the north of Illinois, one for general agriculturists in the center, and one for horticulturists in the south. By this means Morrow hoped to combine the farmers' institutes with conventions sponsored by the dairy, agricultural, and horticultural societies and with the university extension movement. The schools were to supplement rather than supplant the institutes. The first of them took place at Dixon and at Mount Vernon in late 1893 and early 1894 respectively. At the former three agricultural experts from the University gave 20 lectures in a four-day meeting. A good-sized audience but few young people turned out.[50]

None of these efforts offset the deep discouragement of the Board with the sad plight of the College of Agriculture. All but possibly two members regretted spending money in trying to teach a handful of boys practical farming. The discontent became acute during the academic year which opened in the fall of 1893, and Trustee Napoleon B. Morrison led an attack which resulted in the dismissal of Morrow.

Morrison found in Morrow a vulnerable target. He was a poor practical farmer and destitute of mechanical skill. He had allowed the University farms to fall into very bad physical condition, and in 1893 asked the Board for changes with respect to their management. Morrison headed the Farm Committee of the Trustees, and gladly obliged. The Committee rented the Stock Farm to a reliable farmer and sold off much of the stock. Moreover, it turned over operation of the Experimental Farm to the Agricultural Experiment Station.

[49] *17th Report* (1894), 223, 227; *Illinois Laws* (1891), 14-15.
[50] Illinois State Department of Agriculture, *Transactions for 1893,* 38; *17th Report* (1894), 23, 171, 194, 200, 223.

These changes relieved Morrow of farm supervision, and the Farm Committee announced that "divorcing the University from the active duties of farming, will contribute to the welfare and prosperity of the University and the professor of agriculture."[51]

The immediate issues which precipitated a crisis arose in the spring of 1894 and involved research. Morrison belittled the results of the Agricultural Experiment Station, which Morrow directed and on whose Board of Direction Morrison sat, and criticized the failure to establish a dairy school. The University of Wisconsin had already moved into this area, and the Illinois State Dairymen's Association had recently passed a resolution recommending establishment of a dairy school at Urbana. In March a question arose within the Board of Direction of the Experiment Station over whether to sell off steers kept for feeding experiments and purchase cows for dairy tests. On Morrison's motion, all the members of both the stock and the dairy committees of the Board of Direction except Morrow were appointed to institute the change. Morrow, who had just been re-named to direct the Station, interpreted the action as a lack of confidence in him and submitted his resignation in order to place the matter before the Board of Trustees.[52]

In March the Board postponed consideration of the issue until June. At the same time, however, it appointed a committee which included Morrow to reconstruct the agricultural courses of instruction. Members were authorized to visit other institutions to gather ideas.[53] Meanwhile, on April 13 the Board invited Draper to accept the presidency of the University. Someone, perhaps Morrison, got Draper's ear, for he demanded Morrow's resignation as a condition of acceptance.[54] A good deal of public support rallied behind Morrow before the governing body officially dealt with his resignation on August 1. Morrow's backers made an effort to retain him as pro-

[51] Eugene Davenport to A. S. Alexander, Woodland, Mich., Oct. 25, 1933, copy in author's possession; *17th Report* (1894), 82, 170-71, 204-5 (the source of the quotation).

[52] *17th Report* (1894), 223, 225, 226, 228, 240; *Breeder's Gazette,* March 21, 1894; Burrill to Jonathan Periam (editor of the *Prairie Farmer*), March 24, 1894, Draper Letterbooks.

[53] *17th Report* (1894), 237.

[54] James E. Armstrong to Draper, Englewood, Ill., April 27, 1894, Draper Personal Letters.

fessor of agriculture if not as agriculturist to the Experiment Station, but this proved impossible. Official records show that the Trustees went into executive session and accepted the resignation; a farm journal reported the vote was four to three.

Morrow's unfortunate lot had been to preside over the College of Agriculture during the dark period when its difficulties derived from general and ineradicable causes. He used his considerable powers of persuasion to promote the welfare of the whole University, and to keep alive faith in agricultural education. But these talents had not been enough. Farm journals protested his dismissal, and his successor accurately evaluated his contribution by calling Morrow the "John the Baptist" of agricultural education at Illinois.[55]

The College of Engineering faithfully mirrored the demand for technical training in modern society. About 60 per cent of the entire student body registered for engineering programs in the early 1890's, and their course preferences reflected the changes at work in contemporary America. Mining engineering never caught on at Urbana, and the University dropped it altogether. Muncipal and sanitary engineering attracted only five students by 1893-94, but it was a growing field. In these years mechanical and civil engineering were both losing ground, the former dropping from 53 to 48 students in the period studied, and the latter from 75 to 73. Architecture grew at a slower rate than the newer field of architectural engineering (from 75 to 81 as compared with 11 to 13), but electrical engineering mushroomed more rapidly than any course of instruction in the entire University. Its annual registration in the four years to 1893-94 was 1, 29, 58, and 84 respectively. By 1894 it enrolled more students than any other single program.[56]

The pressure of numbers strained the existing facilities and resources, and led to an aggressive search, frequently stimulated by the petitions of engineering students, for more space, more money, and more instructors. The one building for which the legislature appropriated funds in 1893 was Engineering Hall. A number of junior men augmented the faculty in Engineering, which constituted

[55] *Prairie Farmer*, April 7, 1894, 2; *17th Report* (1894), 265; *Breeder's Gazette*, Aug. 8, 1894.
[56] *17th Report* (1894), 15-16.

nearly a third of the total instructional corps within the University. A few of these stand out, including two recent graduates of the College, James M. White (1890) in architecture, and John H. Powell (1891) in general engineering drawing. Dean Ricker, noting the difficulty of obtaining the services of competent graduates after they had been away from the University for a few years, wanted Powell promoted to assistant professor.

But it is doubtful that the few senior appointments infused great strength. In mechanical engineering Charles W. Scribner, a Princeton alumnus and a successful professor at Iowa State, spent only the year 1892-93 at Urbana. Reinvigoration of that Department awaited the arrival in 1893 of Lester P. Breckinridge. The departure of Samuel W. Stratton represented a great loss. Two men in physics and one in electrical engineering replaced him. The ranking member of the trio was Daniel S. Shea, who held two degrees from Harvard, had served in the New Hampshire legislature, and went directly to Urbana after taking his Ph.D. at the University of Berlin. He remained less than four years, and resigned for a position with the Catholic University of America, where he later became Dean of the Faculty of Science.

Science was steadily increasing its influence in late nineteenth-century America, and the universities were a main institutional center of this development. Peabody had upgraded the quality of science instruction and secured an appropriation for a new science building during his administration, but many felt that his effort to maintain parity between scientific and humanistic education inhibited science. When Peabody resigned they reorganized the College of Science at the same time that they devised a new elective system. These innovations facilitated much greater specialization in science.

In place of the two separate schools (Chemistry and Natural History), the studies in the College were arranged into four groups — the natural, physical, and mathematical sciences, and philosophical subjects. Each group existed for educational rather than administrative purposes, and in all but one case required the cooperative efforts of different departments. The chemical group included

Professors Palmer and Parr and embraced all the work offered by the Department of Chemistry. Here a student could choose courses designed to train pharmacists and practical chemists as well as teachers of chemistry and research chemists. But the number of interested persons fell off, from 43 in chemistry in 1892-93 to 37 the following year, when there were also seven in pharmacy.[57]

The natural science group moved into the new Natural Science Building in the fall of 1892. In the main address at the dedication of that structure President David Starr Jordan of Stanford appropriately heralded the growing importance of science in the American college curriculum, and especially the elective system and the introduction of advanced work in science.[58] Burrill, Forbes, and Rolfe presided over the departments of Botany, Zoology, and Geology respectively, and taught in addition to those subjects biology, entomology, physiology, mineralogy, and anthropology, a new course of instruction. Fifty-four students registered in the group in 1892-93, and 62 the following year, about a third of whom were women. Probably many of these were preparing themselves to teach science in the high schools.[59]

The mathematical group of studies included the entire offering of University courses in pure mathematics, physics, and astronomy. The emphasis on mathematics represented a distinct improvement over former years. The instruction comprised three different lines designed to meet as many different purposes. Students from various colleges could take programs which continued for either two terms, two years, or longer. To graduate as a bachelor in mathematics, one had to complete required studies in that subject as well as those from a list of electives in either astronomy or physics. In 1893 Edgar J. Townshend joined the faculty as an assistant professor of mathematics. In 1900 he took a Ph.D. at the University of Göttingen and spent a long career at Illinois, where he became Dean of the College of Science in 1906.

[57] The sources which document the reforms in this College and in the others are both too scattered and too numerous to cite, but the best statement of the end result described above is in the *Catalogue, 1893-94,* 47-65. See also *17th Report* (1894), 15-16.

[58] *Illini,* Nov. 29, 1892.

[59] *17th Report* (1894), 15-16.

The philosophical group included "those sciences which deal both with man as an individual, in the mental and moral spheres, especially as these are connected with his physical being, and also with man in society."[60] This peculiar combination and its location in the College of Science represents a stage in the evolution of thought and in the organization of academic disciplines in higher education. The key to the grouping is in mental science, an older branch of philosophy which had long been branching into psychology and pedagogy. The branches of study embraced by the philosophical group were psychology, pedagogy, economics, and philosophy, and each developed into a separate department. These disciplines also formed part of the College of Literature, and the faculty members charged with responsibility in the various areas will be discussed in that connection.

Women's rights advocates made a spirited bid to improve the status of women in the University during Burrill's tenure. The movement originated as part of the reaction against Peabody, who had killed off the School of Domestic Science and educated women on equal terms with men. Charles H. Shamel and Katherine L. Kennard, both of the class of 1890, sparked the agitation during the summer of 1891. Revival of the School of Domestic Science formed one of their goals. Shamel convinced his co-worker that "the Peabody blight" had brought about its extinction, and she drummed up and presented to the Board petitions, papers, and letters favoring its revival. For example, she prompted the Peoria Woman's Club to send to the Trustees a petition bearing 250 signatures, and wrote on the subject for a farm publication.[61] Making the University a "Co-educating as well as a Co-educational institution" constituted a second goal.[62] Petitioners beseeched the governing board in the name of Reason, Truth, and Justice to appoint women to the faculty and to make them full professors.

This crusade, which gained strength and took on added dimen-

[60] *Catalogue, 1893-94,* 62.
[61] Kennard to Charles H. Shamel, Aug. 25, Sept. 15, Oct. 15, 1891; Clarence A. Shamel to Charles H. Shamel, Dec. 13, 1891, Charles H. Shamel Papers; *16th Report* (1892), 205, 218.
[62] *16th Report* (1892), 150-51.

sions during 1892, reflected the attitude toward the higher education of women which John M. Gregory and his wife had popularized at Illinois. In essence they viewed education in household management and in aesthetic subjects as the special province of women. Gregorians, especially the women students of the late 1870's, provided the main drive behind the movement. In the spring of 1892 the Alumni Association recalled the unique contribution of Mrs. Gregory from 1874 to 1880 and went on to ask the Board to name "a representative woman" to the faculty. At the same time the Alumnae Association urged that instruction in domestic science form a part of the education open to women, that the departments of art and music be expanded and made more permanent, and that "social culture in its highest forms should be a part of the training of college women."[63] To realize these purposes the Alumnae Association recommended the erection of buildings with special laboratories for investigations in household science, sanitation, and aesthetics, and with a variety of other rooms designed to improve the condition and facilitate the scholarly attainments of women at the University. The Faculty also aided this pro-Gregory movement. At its request, the Board authorized the conferring of an M.S. degree upon Louisa Allen Gregory at commencement in June, 1892.[64]

The Trustees unanimously favored appointment of a woman to the faculty, but justifiably rebuffed the demand that they name a full professor in domestic science. Kate Kennard suggested three names for the position, but even she was not sure that any of them met the standard of perfection demanded.[65] In June the Board established an assistant professorship in English literature and agreed to fill it with a woman. Katharine Merrill, a graduate of Kansas State and of Bryn Mawr who had just completed a master's degree at the Harvard Annex (Radcliffe), got the appointment. She arrived in the autumn and served as Preceptress in addition to teaching.

[63] *Ibid.*, 218-19.
[64] "Faculty Record," III, 143; *16th Report* (1892), 229, 237.
[65] *16th Report* (1892), 218; Samuel A. Bullard to Charles H. Shamel, Aug. 31, 1891; Kennard to Charles H. Shamel, April 3, 20, 1892, Shamel Papers. The persons recommended were Celia Parker Wooley of Chicago, Rose Colby of Peoria and Normal, and Sarah Raymond of Bloomington.

Nevertheless, the pressure to do more for women continued. With Kate Kennard as Recording Secretary, the Alumnae Association again urged appointment of a representative woman as *full* professor and insisted that the appropriation needed for a women's dormitory could not be delayed until the legislative session of 1895. In addition, nearly 70 women students used the argument that the University had done much for the men but nothing for the girls as a plea for the erection of a dormitory or cottage for women near the campus, which was inconveniently located between the two towns. The Trustees said their financial situation made action impossible, and suggested that private entrepreneurs in Champaign and Urbana might undertake such a building.[66]

The general desire to aid women students persisted, and in place of Peabody's type of equality the prevailing opinion now favored offering women education different from that given to men. Burrill asked Professor Merrill to investigate the possibility of establishing a department for women, and her report revived the philosophy behind the "Learning and Labor" motto. Miss Merrill valued both manual and intellectual training for women, and suggested that domestic or sanitary science was uniquely suited for this purpose. It covered all the questions relating health to morals, and included the science of nutrition, which the University alumnae stressed. After studying similar programs at M.I.T., Pratt Institute of Brooklyn, and the University of Chicago, Miss Merrill included nutrition and other essentials in her proposed domestic science curriculum.

She also urged a program in physical culture as a means of improving the personal appearance of the women and refining their manner and dress. She thought that conditions of living were particularly hard on girls at Urbana, and yet no regular classroom instructor could properly tell them to improve their appearance. But a gymnasium teacher had the right and duty to do so, and undoubtedly she herself had undertaken the job in her capacity as temporary gym instructor. Now she recommended a compulsory program of gymnastic exercises for all women students and employment of a woman to teach physical culture in the broadest sense.

[66] *17th Report* (1894), 18, 51-52, 72.

The establishment of a Department of Physical Culture for Women followed, and Anita M. Kellogg arrived in September, 1893, to teach that subject and oral rhetoric.[67]

Although the University remained a men's school — about 17 per cent of the students belonged to the second sex — a minority persisted in its determination to do better for the girls. A movement to put a woman on the governing board led both political parties to run women candidates in 1894. The Republicans put up Lucy Flower and the Democrats Julia Holmes Smith. Mrs. Flower, a professional Chicago altruist, garnered more votes than any other candidate and took her seat as the first woman trustee.[68] But unfortunately the philosophy behind the demand to improve the condition of women at the University reflected the attitude of Gregory rather than of Peabody. It led to an emphasis on subjects considered especially appropriate for women, and to construction of a Women's Building, a female ghetto in a male University.

Illinois in 1891 unquestionably had the resources to make its institution at Urbana a cultural capital of the Midwest. And yet the College of Literature was a severe and inexcusable disappointment. Indeed, its condition might fairly be called shameful. The three technical colleges, and especially Engineering, overshadowed their companion. They got the bulk of the money from a practical-minded and tightfisted legislature, and they attracted the students. In 1891-92 the former enrolled 411 students compared to 120 in the latter, and in the fall of 1892 the technical colleges rose to 431 students while the liberal arts college fell to 111. But what should have been even more humiliating was the fact that in 1891-92 the College of Literature, Science, and Arts at the University of Michigan attracted 193 Illinois students compared to the 120 in the College of Literature at Urbana. And surely other youths fled their native state to take their liberal arts education in a variety of places other than Illinois.[69]

[67] *Ibid.*, 79-81, 246.
[68] J. David Hoeveler, Jr., "Lucy Flower: Professional Altruist," unpublished course paper written for the author and submitted for publication.
[69] Superintendent of Public Instruction of the State of Illinois, *Nineteenth Biennial Report* (Springfield, 1892), 6; *Illini*, April 25, 1892.

In this sense especially the commonwealth of Illinois remained laggard in higher education as it had been throughout the nineteenth century. To account adequately for this situation is not easy, but it has already been shown how the leadership of the state had always failed to advance beyond a strictly utilitarian approach to higher education. The political leadership was little if any worse than the educational leadership. Jonathan B. Turner had, especially in the clinches, taken a low utilitarian view of higher education,[70] and Gregory had tried to convince the people that the richest learning would pay in a cornfield or in a carpenter's shop. "Prove that education, in its highest form, will 'pay,' " he had said in his inaugural address, "and you have made for it the market of the world."[71] The trouble with this perilous argument was that no one could prove to Illinois taxpayers that the richest learning "paid." Peabody had refused to take that line.

As a result the University was pouring forth a steady stream of technicians to transform the physical environment and raise the standard of living. In Francis Wayland's terms, they could survey its lands, construct its roads, build and navigate its ships, cultivate its soils, and establish its manufactures.[72] But the University was not pouring forth a similar stream of men and women to deal with the multifarious political and social problems of Illinois and of a maturing industrial nation. Where were the graduates who could as mayors, legislators, and governors elevate and redeem the political life of the state? Where were the graduates who could make life better for immigrants in the Chicago slums and industrial workers in the meat-packing plants or in Pullman's sleeping-car works? Where were the graduates who could construct and insure the support of a system of public education in which freedom of inquiry weighed more heavily than football? And where were the graduates whose literary, historical, and philosophical writings lit beacons for the spirit?

Questions of this type underlay a rising demand for larger development of the College of Literature. Peabody had initiated efforts in this direction, and some members of the Board had empha-

[70] See pp. 44-48 above.
[71] *1st Report* (1868), 182.
[72] See pp. 25-26 above.

sized the "cultural" side of the University in their search for his successor. The trend accelerated rapidly between 1891 and 1894, with enrichment and expansion of the curriculum the major goal. The students in this College were best situated to profit from a varied program of studies because they enjoyed the greatest degree of elective freedom despite the state law of 1873 in regard to the three courses which students could choose.[73] After the dropping of chemistry and physics in 1893-94, the nine term credits required were in history (three), mathematics (two), military (two), and English and oral rhetoric (two). In addition, students had 15 restricted electives and 16 totally free electives.[74]

With slight encouragement the fields of study embraced by the two former schools in the College quickly prospered. Peabody had given classics a boost by establishing separate chairs in Greek and Latin in 1890-91 and calling to them Professors Moss and Barton respectively. As one of his last acts he appointed Thomas A. Clark, who figured prominently in the University's later history, to an instructorship in Latin and English. Enrollments in classics more than doubled between 1891 and 1894 (from 17 to 39), and in the latter year the Faculty undid Peabody's work by reducing the admissions requirement in Latin. But the foundations for Illinois' later eminence in the classics were not laid in this period.[75]

When Nathaniel Butler resigned the chair in English in 1892, the Board divided over the naming of his successor. McLean favored L. M. Castle, a Springfield high school teacher, but his colleagues voted to call a graduate of Columbia University, Daniel K. Dodge. Some unpleasantness ensued, for a few months later Dodge offered and the Board refused his resignation. With the assistance of Katharine Merrill and of Clark, Dodge aimed at developing general culture rather than preparing students for specialized research in the field. His Department devoted nearly equal time to

---

[73] The law does not seem to have weighed heavily, although in June, 1892, the Board appointed a committee to consider what changes, if any, should be made in the requirements in regard to studies made under the 1873 act. *16th Report* (1892), 191, 254.

[74] "Faculty of Literature and Science Record," Jan. 16, 1894; *Catalogue, 1893-94,* 68.

[75] *16th Report* (1892), 14, 109; *17th Report* (1894), 15-16, 221.

English and American literature, and upperclassmen elected literature much more than they did language courses.[76]

The University fortified the work in modern languages by adding a woman assistant professor in German and by establishing in 1893 a Department of Romance Languages. This put the teaching of Spanish and Italian as well as French on a regular basis. James D. Bruner, who later took a doctorate at Johns Hopkins, came to fill the position vacated by Professor Paradis. But English and modern languages were not "hot" fields, and enrollments in the two together fell from 104 students in 1891-92 to 79 in 1893-94.[77]

The most important innovations involved the building or rebuilding of other departments. Several — economics, political science, history, philosophy, psychology, and pedagogy — evolved out of the few studies which had traditionally been required of all seniors at Urbana and in the liberal arts colleges of the early nineteenth century. These fields generated intellectual excitement. Burrill grasped their significance for modern culture, and the competition of other universities spurred the governing board. In 1893, for example, the University of Wisconsin was spending $5,000 beyond its regular library budget for the purchase of books on history and economics alone. The professors Burrill recruited after extensive searches were a new breed of promising young men with fresh Ph.D.'s from leading universities. A few, notably David Kinley, Evarts B. Greene, and Arthur H. Daniels, figured prominently in the University for over a period of four decades.

In the summer of 1893 Kinley joined the staff as an assistant professor in charge of economics, politics, and social science. He had solid academic credentials — an A.B. from both Yale and Johns Hopkins, where he had studied with William Graham Sumner and Richard T. Ely respectively, and a Ph.D. taken under Ely at Wisconsin. Kinley taught several economics courses, sociology, social pathology, and political science, and become a full professor at the

---

[76] Butler had joined the faculty in 1886 to teach Latin and later became Professor of English. See also *16th Report* (1892), 250; *17th Report* (1894), 52; Daniel K. Dodge, "English at the University of Illinois," *Dial*, XVI (May 1, 1894), 261-62.
[77] *17th Report* (1894), 15-16, 128; Superintendent of Public Instruction, *Nineteenth Biennial Report*, 7.

end of a year. Burrill finally selected Greene for the position in history over a large field of candidates in the summer of 1894. Greene had spent his early years in Japan, where his father served as a Congregational missionary, and had completed his Ph.D. in American history under Albert Bushnell Hart at Harvard. He studied at the University of Berlin for a year before going to Urbana.[78]

The School of Philosophy and Pedagogy which Peabody had launched by calling Charles DeGarmo to a chair in psychology now branched into many parts. DeGarmo had established himself as a leading Herbartian in America before joining the Illinois faculty, and there he blazed a trail for a strong Herbartian influence. In DeGarmo's terms, this meant giving scientific precision to instruction and moral training by founding them upon an adequate system of psychology and ethics.[79] DeGarmo's abrupt resignation in the fall of 1891 meant that the courses in philosophy and pedagogy which he probably outlined had no teacher during that academic year. In 1892 the University named William O. Krohn, a Yale Ph.D. who later earned a medical degree, Assistant Professor of Psychology and entrusted him with the program in philosophy and pedagogy. Krohn gave a psychological orientation to eight courses he taught in those two fields, and in addition offered courses in basic, educational, and experimental psychology. In the former he used as a text William James's recently published *Principles of Psychology* (1890). Krohn also established a psychological laboratory, the first of which in the United States had arisen at Johns Hopkins in 1885.[80]

The University founded philosophy and pedagogy as separate fields in the summer of 1893. Daniels, who had taken a divinity degree at Yale and a Ph.D. at Clark, joined the staff and presented a range of courses in philosophy along with two in ethics. Frank M. McMurry, like DeGarmo a Herbartian brought from Illinois State

[78] *17th Report* (1894), 61, 121, 128, 229; see also the Draper Letterbooks.
[79] Charles DeGarmo, *Herbart and the Herbartians* (New York, 1896), 4, 9. DeGarmo had published books based on Herbart in 1889 and 1890. See *ibid.*, 205, 266-67.
[80] *Catalogue, 1892-93*, 117-20; W[illiam] O. K[rohn], "Laboratory Psychology," *Illini*, May 8 [June 8], 1893; "Faculty Record," III, 159.

Normal University, became Professor of Pedagogy. His appointment freed Krohn to devote his attention to the Department of Psychology, where he continued to give one course in educational psychology.[81]

Burrill hoped that with McMurry the University could develop a strong Department of Pedagogy. He asked Henry Raab, State Superintendent of Public Instruction, for guidance in the matter, and in March, 1894, his long efforts to forge a closer tie with the state normal schools bore fruit with the decision to admit their graduates to the pedagogy curriculum as soon as they entered the University. McMurry laid out eight courses, including history of education, philosophy of education, educational administration, a "methods" course, and one in practice teaching. In the spring of 1894 the University established a model school to facilitate the union of theory and practice and provide a research facility in pedagogy.[82]

But Frank McMurry resigned after one year, and Burrill strove hard to replace him with his brother Charles McMurry, another Herbartian of Illinois State Normal whose writings had gained him a great reputation and whom Burrill now considered the better of the two brothers. By this time, however, Draper had accepted the presidency. He favored the appointment of William J. Eckoff, a German-born, doctrinaire Herbartian with Ph.D.'s from both New York and Columbia universities. Eckoff arrived with Draper to head the Department of Pedagogy in the fall of 1894.[83]

In the fields taught by men with doctorates, the College of Literature introduced seminars for undergraduates in 1893-94. Kinley, Daniels, Krohn, and McMurry all offered "seminary" courses which permitted advanced students to examine problems critically and to pursue special investigations.

Another innovation led to incorporation of the School of Art and Design into the College of Literature as a Department.

[81] *17th Report* (1894), 122, 128, 138, 166-67; DeGarmo, *Herbart and the Herbartians,* 123-29, 268.
[82] Burrill to Raab, March 2, 1894, Draper Letterbooks; *16th Report* (1892), 199, 209; *17th Report* (1894), 219, 221, 229.
[83] Burrill to Draper, June 26; Burrill to Francis M. McKay, July 11, 13; Burrill to James E. Armstrong, July 19, 1894, Draper Letterbooks; *17th Report* (1894), 265, 268; DeGarmo, *Herbart and the Herbartians,* 267-68.

Founded in 1877, the School had supplemented the courses of study in other areas, particularly those of a technical nature, and also appealed to women students. But it was a service facility and existed somewhat on sufferance. The School had been temporarily closed in 1879 and reopened because of its demonstrated usefulness to students of agriculture, architecture, engineering, and natural science. Peter Roos, who directed the School, appealed to the Board in 1885 to allow students to graduate in Art and Design under conditions equivalent to those in other University departments. The Trustees referred the matter to the Faculty, and in 1886 a committee consisting of the four deans and Peabody denied the request. It thought a course of study in Art and Design lacked sufficient educational, disciplinary, and cultural value to merit a bachelor's or similar degree, and even insisted that candidates for a full University certificate rather than a degree take only a third of the 36 required credits in Art and Design. This suspicion of the educational value of art fixed the School into position as a service facility, and led Roos to resign in 1890.

Frank W. Frederick, a Boston art school graduate, succeeded him, and for the next three years the School attempted to afford students of various colleges an opportunity to learn the freehand drawing their courses required, and to others a chance to study industrial design or other branches of art. These purposes remained in force when Art and Design became a department in the College of Literature in 1893-94.[84]

The governing board still insisted that music constituted no part of any University course of studies, although Burrill wished to nudge them into including it in the curriculum. Clara Kimball, the teacher of music, hoped that the elevation of standards would permit her to establish a school of music when she returned in 1893 after a year in Germany and Italy. But the most the Board did was to provide vocal and instrumental lessons on a fee basis, and in 1894 Miss Kimball resigned.

However, the Trustees did furnish Dean Snyder funds to invigorate the humanities by sponsoring special courses of lectures.

[84] "Faculty Record," II, Feb. 26, 1886; III, 34-35; *13th Report* (1887), 85, 91-92; *Catalogue, 1893-94,* 70-71.

Among the speakers in the first series in 1892-93 were Denton J. Snider, a leader of the American school of Hegelians in St. Louis; Charles F. Thwing, who spoke on American colleges and American life; and Percy M. Reese, who talked about ancient Rome and the Caesars.

By 1894, then, the College of Literature was pulsating with new life. Probably its changed conditions as much as his health prompted Snyder to resign as Dean at the end of the academic year. Nearly 60, the veteran soldier was not old, but younger warriors trained specifically for the battles of the "seminary" rooms were now essential. David Kinley had already impressed his superiors as unusually able, and he led the rising demand for larger development of the College of Literature. Kinley's appointment as Dean of the College marked a new era and resulted in invigorating that part of the University.

Professional training in law and medicine and organization of a graduate school became hallmarks of the modern American university in the late nineteenth century. If a land-grant institution like Illinois did not pioneer in these developments, it nevertheless felt compelled to follow the lead of universities that did. The demand for a law department, occasionally voiced by students earlier, became more insistent after Peabody resigned. More than 50 students petitioned for its establishment in 1892, and influential members of the legal profession echoed the call. Burrill thought a law school could flourish in a rural environment, and in 1893 the Board asked the General Assembly for $40,000 during the next biennium to get legal training under way. Despite a large number of lawyers in that body, the legislature killed the proposal and another four years passed before a law school opened at Urbana.[85]

The first efforts at medical education were also premature. In this case the initiative came from the College of Physicians and Surgeons, a proprietary medical school in Chicago. Institutions of this type, most of which had no connection with a university, had proliferated wildly in the nineteenth century to meet the demand for

[85] Champaign County *Gazette,* Jan. 28, 1891; *Illini,* Dec. 17, 1891; *16th Report* (1892), 205, 218-19, 253; *17th Report* (1894), 62, 73.

doctors. The entrepreneurs were frequently practitioners of medicine and professors in the schools themselves, and commercial motives often outweighed professional ones. The zeal for profits led to shortened curricula, low requirements, and lectures rather than the more expensive laboratory and clinical methods of teaching. Proprietary medical schools, a product of the national spirit of free enterprise and *laissez-faire,* imperiled the people's health and brought American medical degrees into disrepute. By the end of the century Chicago was notorious for some ten low-grade proprietary medical colleges which were in operation there.[86]

And yet forces were at work as the century ended which assured Chicago's importance as a center of medical education. One of the most prominent was the movement to incorporate the three best regular proprietary schools as medical departments of local universities. Chicago Medical College, the first to merge, became an integral part of Northwestern University in 1891. Rush Medical College affiliated with the University of Chicago in 1898 (and turned over the last of its holdings in 1924). The College of Physicians and Surgeons made its overture to the University of Illinois in 1891, nominally became the medical department of the University in 1897, and permanently united with it in 1913.[87]

Five practitioners had established the College of Physicians and Surgeons in 1881 as a typical proprietary enterprise. The condition of employment of each professor was the purchase of $2,000 worth of stock, which gave the holder a vested property right in his department of instruction. The undertakers avowed improvement of medical education as their aim, but according to William E. Quine, an early faculty member and later Dean, the founders actually sought "to provide teaching positions for ambitious members of the profession who could not find accommodations in the colleges then existing."[88] The venture immediately ran into dissension and debt. The dominant four incorporators expelled the one insurgent among

[86] Henry E. Sigerist, *American Medicine,* tr. Hildegard Nagel (New York, 1934), 132-33; Thomas N. Bonner, *Medicine in Chicago, 1850-1950: A Chapter in the Social and Scientific Development of a City* (Madison, 1957), 44-45.
[87] Bonner, *Medicine in Chicago,* 62, 108-9, 111, 116.
[88] William E. Quine, "History of the College of Physicians and Surgeons of Chicago," *Plexus,* XVII (July 20, 1911), 256.

them in order to maintain their control, but brought in his friend Quine to a vacancy on the governing board. By 1891 the College stood on the brink of bankruptcy with a deficit of $30,000.

At this point the College began a reorganization movement directed by Quine and Bayard Holmes, a homeopathist and a pioneer in introducing laboratory instruction in Chicago. They initiated reforms which greatly improved the medical education offered by the school during the ensuing decade.[89] At the outset, during the depths of the crisis, the College announced that it would consider a union with the University of Illinois upon mutually satisfactory terms. Holmes, brought in as Secretary and Educational Director in July, 1891, outlined to the Trustees at a meeting in Champaign in December a means by which the University and the College could affiliate. He proposed a partnership by which the College would become the medical department of the University. One University trustee would immediately take a seat vacated for the purpose on the Board of Direction of the College. The University would teach some of the courses in the medical school in Chicago in return for stock representing the value of its instructional costs. The Trustees' representation on the Board of Direction would increase as its stockholdings increased, and eventually the University would own the College.[90]

The day of the commercial medical school was fast ending, and a scheme for allowing a public institution to buy out a sinking if refurbished ship presented endless complications. But the Executive Committee of the Trustees visited Chicago and reported favorably on the College. They knew that other universities were merging with proprietary medical schools, and agreed that colleges of medicine did best in large cities. The College, one of the three best in Chicago and getting better, was willing to sell.

Nevertheless, legal questions troubled the Executive Committee. Members asked the Attorney General of Illinois for an opinion, and he said that the Trustees had no authority to enter the University into partnership with a private corporation. He also invited the

[89] *Ibid.*, 258; Bayard Holmes, "Medical Education in Chicago in 1882 and After," *Medical Life,* XXIX (Jan., 1922), 32-33, 36-41.
[90] *16th Report* (1892), 171-72, 196.

Board to consider whether medical education fell within the studies allowed by the law of 1873.[91] There the matter stood for some time. After taking office Governor Altgeld initiated discussion of affiliation with Quine, but did not at the time favor proceeding. However, at Draper's inauguration Altgeld reopened the issue, and a few days later the President of the Board invited a proposition from the College.[92] The negotiations which ensued brought the College of Physicians and Surgeons and the University into even closer relations, but that long and tortuous story cannot be told here.

Establishment of a Graduate School by name in 1892 came more easily, partly because Burrill built on foundations laid much earlier. But the question of dating the origins of graduate study at Urbana is tricky. The first college graduate to continue his studies at the University, Robert R. Warder of Clevis, Ohio, entered in the spring term of 1869 to study analytical chemistry. The University listed Warder as a "resident graduate," a familiar term from the pre–Civil War era of American higher education.[93] Between 1869 and 1892 some fourscore of resident graduates studied at the University.[94]

A majority pursued almost exclusively undergraduate work, and for several reasons. Some studied fields other than those in which they had labored during their first four years; others found it necessary when the University began awarding degrees in 1878 to complete requirements for a degree rather than a certificate. In the years through 1879 the University listed 36 resident graduates of this type, of whom 11 were women.

A minority of resident graduates took advanced study for a master's degree. The old-time college had customarily given the master's degree "in course" to any graduate with an A.B. who blamelessly followed a liberal calling for three years. But in the 1870's the best Eastern colleges demanded earned master's degrees, and Illinois followed suit. At Urbana the reform came during the

[91] *Ibid.,* 221-22.

[92] Quine, "History of the College of Physicians and Surgeons," 259.

[93] *2nd Report* (1869), 69; *Catalogue, [1869],* 25; Richard J. Storr, *The Beginnings of Graduate Education in America* (Chicago, 1953), 1.

[94] My conclusions rest mainly on the published data in the *Reports* of the Board of Trustees and the *Catalogues* from 1869 to 1894, the "Faculty Record," and the Permanent Record (of students) in the Registrar's Office.

changeover from certificates to degrees. On June 1, 1877, the Faculty agreed to require one year of postgraduate study or two years of professional study and an acceptable thesis for a master's degree. Later that year delegates from state universities at the conference on degrees sponsored by Illinois at Columbus, Ohio, concluded that henceforth no master's degree should be awarded "in course." Early in 1878 the Faculty at Urbana announced that it would give master's and equivalent degrees only to those who had successfully completed a year of prescribed study and presented an acceptable thesis, or after a term of successful practice with a thesis.[95]

Under these provisions the University conferred its first degrees in June, 1878. At that time it bestowed both the B.S. and master's degrees upon six members of the faculty. Ricker received an M. Arch., Rolfe and Scovell, M.S.'s; Fernando Parsons, the instructor of commercial subjects, an M.L.; Ira O. Baker of Civil Engineering and Alexander C. Schwartz, an assistant, C.E.'s.[96] In 1879 the University granted the first earned master's degrees for successful completion of a year of advanced study. Emma E. Page, who had studied mainly domestic science in her fifth year, won an M.L. in the School of English and Modern Languages, and Henry S. Reynolds an M.S. in the School of Natural History.[97]

The earned degrees awarded in 1879 preceded by a few months the completion of plans for systematic graduate training. The various colleges worked on this problem during the year, but most of them finished devising their programs in the fall. The general principles agreed upon called for a year of advanced work along the lines of the bachelor's degree, with emphasis upon original research and presentation of a thesis (later set at not less than 2,000 words). The College of Literature and Science required three terms in each of three areas — philosophy, history, and social science; language and philology; mathematics or science — and a thesis. The other colleges specified a year of technical studies in advance of what the University currently taught in those areas. Students were not to attend regular classes but to follow a program adapted to their indi-

[95] "Faculty Record," I, 232, 245-46.
[96] 9th Report (1878), 93-94.
[97] 10th Report (1881), 179; Emma E. Page File, Permanent Record, Registrar's Office; "Faculty of Literature and Science Record," May 26, 1879.

vidual needs under a professor's supervision, but they could select additional studies from the regular University curriculum. Another route was open to graduates of the College of Literature and Science and the College of Engineering. Those who engaged in appropriate professional work for at least three years after receiving a bachelor's degree and presented a satisfactory thesis could claim a second degree. But the others had to follow prescribed programs, and in 1880 the general Faculty ruled that it must approve these before candidates for master's degrees commenced them.[98]

At least 42 different resident graduates, including 15 women, studied at the University from 1880 through 1891. Seven remained longer than one year, some of whom were staff assistants. But a majority consisted of "artificial" graduates; only 11 "genuine" graduates carried to completion a prescribed course of advanced study. These varied considerably. Lorado Taft, for example, entered his fifth year with excess undergraduate credits and got a master's degree in 1880 for two history and three geology courses (the latter taught by his father). Jerome Sondericker, an assistant, studied nine courses in civil engineering and mathematics, and it took him three years to earn his C.E. degree. Mrs. Myrtle E. Sparks received an M.A. in ancient languages for a program of reading in original and secondary works on Greek and Roman literature, philosophy, and art. Most resident graduates who completed their courses went into high school or college teaching, but some entered professional practice as engineers or experiment station experts. (Meanwhile, several Illinois undergraduates had gone on to further education in other American institutions and in Germany.)

Burrill was convinced that graduate work at Illinois was totally inadequate when he assumed office. The University had to keep pace with other institutions, including Chicago, Clark, and Stanford, new universities which were all emphasizing advanced study. But more important, Burrill considered research, the special province of the graduate school, essential to a university. He thought it stimulated undergraduates by insuring lively teaching. An instructor who

[98] "Faculty Record," II, Nov. 14, 21, 28, Dec. 5, 1879; June 4, 1880; Dec. 9, 1881; "Faculty of Literature and Science Record," March 31, Dec. 5, 1879; "Record Book of the College of Natural Science," Nov. 17, 1879.

only retailed the facts of others gradually grew cold, but an active researcher propagated fire in the classroom. And research was the only basis for scholarship and for public recognition. The University might as well sell out at once as to make no marked addition to the world's store of knowledge.[99]

A productive research scientist himself, Burrill could authoritatively say that Illinois had subordinated teaching to research "in a very marked degree," and especially in Engineering.[100] Despite good intentions, the members of the Board were unqualified to deal with this problem. In the words of Burrill, for whom gentle reproof was harsh criticism, "they are wanting in the kind of knowledge that will best insure them against errors and best enable them to guide affairs in the best possible way."[101] Burrill himself therefore sparked the organization of the Graduate School. His key proposal, made in the spring of 1892, called for the establishment of four fellowships at $400 each for graduate students. The holders could pursue advanced study and assist in instruction in return for their stipend. Their teaching would free the professors from routine duties for personal research. Several universities were already granting graduate fellowships, and the Board accepted the plan. The catalogue issued before June announced the Graduate School by name.

It quickly expanded and acquired better organization. With pressure from the Alumni Association, the Trustees in March, 1894, authorized the Faculty to announce that Illinois would award the degrees of doctor of philosophy and doctor of science. The Faculty set the requirement at three years of advanced work, the last one or first two of which were to be spent in residence. The candidate had to demonstrate power of independent research and of original thought, and submit (in 50 printed copies) a thesis which made a contribution to knowledge. In 1894 an Administrative Committee (identical to the Executive Committee) assumed direction of the Graduate School.

Under these arrangements it changed character but began to

[99] *16th Report* (1892), 204.
[100] Burrill to R. H. Thurston, Nov. 23, 1893, "Regents' Letterbook, 1879-1894."
[101] *Ibid.* Burrill also suggested to Thurston, who made the address at the laying of the cornerstone for Engineering Hall, that he include in his remarks a word concerning research in a university.

flourish. The University now distinguished between two types of students in the School. Resident graduates were students working for a second bachelor's degree in fields other than those in which they had earned their first degree. They had to earn at least nine additional term credits in the second course and present a thesis. Graduate students were those who registered as candidates for master's or doctor's degrees. The flow of students moved in the latter direction. Nine resident graduates had enrolled in 1891-92, but the next year there were five of them and four graduate students, including the first two fellowship holders — Alice May Barber in natural science and Herman S. Piatt in classics. The next year there were 12 resident graduates and ten graduate students. Except for Warder, the resident graduates from 1869 to 1893 had taken their undergraduate work at the University, but in 1893 the first of the students with bachelor's degrees from other schools entered Illinois to pursue advanced study. Harvard, Ohio State, and Colorado State sent the first three.[102] Thirteen persons applied in 1893 for the four fellowships, which rose to six the following year. By 1894, then, a promising foundation had been erected, but only a foundation. Another decade passed before the Graduate School became an important actuality.

Besides regular academic programs, both the summer school and university extension became vital agencies of American higher education in the late nineteenth century. Illinois provided no leadership for either movement. The Faculty had decided against undertaking a summer session in 1879, and probably with good reason.[103] But the University had not fallen too far behind other institutions by the early 1890's, and at that time it began trying to catch up.

The first summer session would probably have been held in 1892 except for the Columbian Exposition. Authorities expressed support for the venture, and felt that demand among schoolteachers warranted the program. But professorial involvement with the Exposition necessitated postponement, and the University inaugurated its

<hr>

[102] Janet Propper, "The Development of Graduate Education at the University of Illinois, 1868-1908" (unpublished seminar paper written for the author), 21.
[103] "Faculty Record," I, 288-89.

A class in the School of Art and Design in the 1880's.

The Chemistry Laboratory about 1890.

The library in University Hall about 1890.

Metal-working shop about 1890.

Thomas J. Burrill about 1888. Appointed to the faculty in April, 1868, Burrill served as Acting Regent from 1891 to 1894.

An annual picnic sponsored by the Natural History Society, perhaps at White Heath in May, 1891. Stephen A. Forbes is at the center in the last row wearing a derby; Thomas J. Burrill is just to the left of the tent wearing a straw hat.

Dean George E. Morrow, the "John the Baptist" of agricultural education at the University from 1878 to 1894.

Stephen A. Forbes.

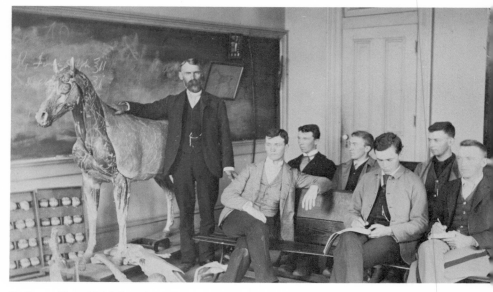

Professor Donald McIntosh instructs a veterinary medicine class about 1890, using one of the celebrated papier-mâché horses of Dr. Auzoux.

Charles A. Kiler, a student activist in the class of 1892.

Professor James D. Crawford, whom the Board of Trustees peremptorily dismissed in 1893 after 20 years of service.

Food chemistry class about 1890.

University of Illinois Band, 1892.

The Museum of Natural History about 1890.

The Art Gallery about 1892.

Edward Snyder and students.

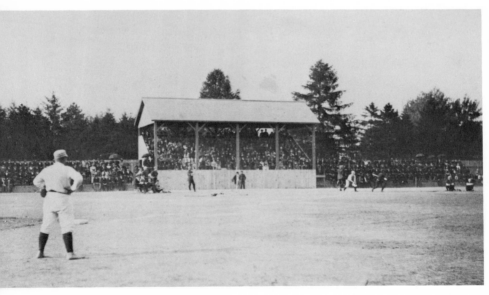

A baseball game in the Athletic Park (later Illinois Field). The man at first base is probably George Huff.

summer school with a four-week session in 1894.[104] It included general subjects and pedagogy and aimed mainly at public-school teachers. Students could earn regular credit where the work equaled that of a full term, and also remove conditions. The Faculty proposed offering 20 courses, but the Board eliminated half. Those actually taught were botany, chemistry, English, history, mathematics, physical culture, physiology, psychology, political economy, and zoology. Classes in mathematics, chemistry, and pedagogy drew the largest followings from the 38 registrants, of whom 25 were public-school teachers and 8 regular University students. Frank McMurry was slated as Director, but his resignation in June, 1894, left David Kinley in charge. The first session operated at a deficit, but continuation of the summer school was never in doubt.[105]

Meanwhile, university extension was spreading like a prairie fire, and Illinois caught and fanned the flame. The idea of disseminating education to all the people through a wide variety of agencies had figured significantly in the pre–Civil War movement to reform higher education. But agriculturists had written their will into the Morrill Act, and the early land-grant institutions had stressed agricultural extension alone. In the late nineteenth century, however, a new type of extension developed, stimulated by the success of university extension in Britain. Men connected with the Chautauqua Literary and Scientific organization drew up in 1886 the Chautauqua University Extension plan. They proposed cooperation with universities and with such agencies as public libraries, labor unions, and YMCA's in order to carry learning to a large audience.[106]

The extension movement mushroomed. Over two dozen states and territories undertook some form of the work by 1891. Their efforts were chiefly agricultural and faded quickly, except in two centers. At Philadelphia the American Society for the Extension of University Teaching arose in 1890 for the purpose of making every college and university in the country a center of extension. Edmund

---

[104] *Ibid.*, III, 117; *Illini,* March 12, 1892.
[105] "Faculty Record," III, 219, 221; *17th Report* (1894), 198, 234-35, 271-73; *Catalogue, 1893-94,* 82-84.
[106] Herbert B. Adams, "University Extension and Its Leaders," *Review of Reviews,* III (July, 1891), 602, 604.

J. James, the son of a Methodist circuit rider and an ardent apostle of educational evangelism, became its Head. He had a weighty advisory committee which included the presidents of Cornell, Stanford, Wisconsin, Michigan, and the new University of Chicago — William R. Harper. A Baptist scholar of the Old Testament, Harper created at Chicago another center of extension. He established University Extension as one of three basic divisions in the new institution and appointed Nathaniel Butler, formerly of the Urbana faculty, its Director. (Harper also brought James, who served as President of the University of Illinois from 1904 to 1920, to Chicago as Dean of the College of Teachers.) For many at Chicago, Extension was "the secular counterpart of evangelism."[107]

The University of Illinois, desiring public acceptance, could not ignore the challenge. Fittingly, the Methodist Burrill led willing colleagues into the ripening field. The Faculty Committee on University Extension, consisting of Forbes, Ricker, and Moss, arranged an experimental extension program for citizens of Champaign and Urbana during the winter of 1892. Nathaniel Butler gave the first lecture of a series on English language and literature in the chapel on January 19. Forbes offered a series on biology, Stratton one on electricity, and Crawford another on English constitutional history. The audiences numbered about 300, and each person received a printed syllabus which outlined the main points of the subject and furnished references for reading. Often a brief quiz preceded the formal lectures.[108]

Meanwhile, the University had affiliated with the University Extension Society for Chicago and the Northwest. Tentatively formed in May, 1891, at a meeting which Peabody and DeGarmo attended upon invitation, the Extension Society took better form the following November when representatives from Illinois, Northwestern, Lake Forest, Chicago, Wisconsin, Beloit College, Indiana, and Wabash College gathered in the city of Chicago. The delegates established a central bureau to match invitations and speakers, and agreed to insure each institution the largest autonomy in its own

---

[107] *Ibid.*, 606-7; Louis E. Reber, *University Extension in the United States* (Washington, 1914), 5-6; Storr, *Harper's University,* 196 (the source of the quotation).
[108] "Faculty Record," III, 100, 109; *16th Report* (1892), 156, 176, 198; *Illini,* Feb.-April, 1892, *passim.*

extension efforts. Between February and June, 1892, professors from Urbana gave 12 lecture courses in various parts of the state. Butler, gifted with the happy facility of pleasing while instructing, was most in demand. A course consisted of six lectures, usually held on successive Friday or Saturday evenings, since the Illinois instructors, unlike the Extension faculty at Chicago, added this work to their regular classroom teaching. The Society's bureau distributed materials for the courses, but the Illinois Faculty insisted on doing its own examining and establishing the conditions upon which it would issue certificates and officially record a student's attainments. Nearly a thousand persons attended the courses sponsored by the University in the academic year ending in June, 1892.[109]

This auspicious beginning encouraged authorities to announce some 20 University Extension Lecture Courses taught by 15 members of the faculty for the academic year 1892-93. The subjects covered most of the areas included in the regular curriculum, and the courses aimed at duplicating the University work insofar as practicable. As of December the only series in progress was one by Professor Frederick at Streator in the history of art. As Burrill pondered the advisibility of taking more active promotional measures, he recommended severing all ties with the reorganized Society of the Northwest for University Extension. The Society was now asking member institutions for annual dues, and in addition the Urbana Faculty thought the University should possess complete autonomy in respect to its extension work in Illinois.

By the autumn of 1893 Extension was not yielding the rich harvest anticipated. Although circulars announced the availability of 12 courses for the coming year, several indicators point to lack of public response. Perhaps economics explains part of the difficulty. The Board appropriated little for the work, and each course of six lectures cost a local community $90 and expenses. But perhaps the University itself undermined Extension by fostering big-time athletics. Many citizens would pay to see a football game quicker than to hear lectures on "Philosophy Among the Greeks," or even "Applications of Chemical Investigations to Practical Agriculture."[110]

[109] "Faculty Record," III, 76, 117, 122-24; 16th Report (1892), 156, 176, 227.
[110] Superintendent of Public Instruction, Nineteenth Biennial Report, 10; "Faculty Record," III, 168; 17th Report (1894), 21, 51, 59; Illini, Oct. 25, 1893.

"Libraries are gauges of intellectual development," observed the *Illini* in 1891, and judged by that standard and the state's relative prosperity, Illinois was shamefully backward.[111] The library of the University had made a promising beginning under Gregory, but its rate of growth in books slowed considerably after 1880. In that year the institution boasted 12,550 volumes, a decade later about 19,000, and in 1894 roughly 26,000.[112] This rate of growth approximated the national average for libraries of higher educational institutions (a doubling every 15 years), and yet Illinois fell well behind the state universities with which it desired parity. The reason was the state's refusal to provide money for books. The legislature appropriated $1,500 a year for the purpose from 1887 to 1889, but it reduced the sum to $1,000 a year from 1889 through 1893.

A good library was indispensable in a modern university, and when Burrill assumed command in 1891 he acted at once to establish one. He immediately asked the Board to assign $4,000 from the U.S. fund to buy books for the state University, half of it in 1891 and half the next year. In December the Trustees appropriated $2,000 from the money supplied by the second Morill Act for this purpose.[113]

Improvement of the library received high priority in the request prepared a year later for the biennial appropriation from Springfield in 1893. Although the Trustees and the Faculty agreed in considering library and engineering buildings absolutely essential, the legislature deleted the $125,000 desired for the former, and even Altgeld did not restore the item. It was 1897 before the University acquired a library building. To support his plea for a doubling of the number of books within a few years, Burrill compared Illinois with other universities for the benefit of the Trustees. At the time Illinois had over 21,000 volumes, while Cornell possessed 110,000, Michigan 83,000, Minnesota 28,000, Wisconsin 26,000, and Iowa 22,000. Nebraska pressed Illinois with 20,000, but it was opening

[111] *Illini,* Oct. 17, 1891. It should be noted, however, that the article praised the Library of Natural History housed at the University and owned by the state of Illinois as "without doubt, the best in its line west of the Alleghany mountains."
[112] Superintendent of Public Instruction of the State of Illinois, *Thirteenth Biennial Report* (Springfield, 1881), 187; *15th Report* (1890), 186; *18th Report* (1896), 22.
[113] *16th Report* (1892), 137, 152.

a new library building in 1894. The Trustees agreed in 1892 to ask the state to provide $5,000 a year for all library purposes. Since Cornell was spending $15,800 a year for the purchase of books alone, Michigan $7,500, and Wisconsin $4,000 for general books plus $5,000 for works on history and economics, the figure was not large. The General Assembly granted a lump sum for current expenses, and the Board's Finance Committee earmarked $5,000 for the library. Four-fifths was spent on book purchases. These special efforts, including the use of federal grants, only kept the University from falling further behind by 1894.[114]

Burrill also put the library under a Director with sole responsibility for its operation. Crawford had headed the library and taught history, and his dismissal provided an opportunity to make better arrangements. While Professor Moss temporarily held the position, Burrill made an extensive search for a man who could give the facility professional care. In 1894 he appointed Percy F. Bicknell, an assistant librarian at the Franklin Institute Library in Philadelphia, to the job.[115]

Peabody's departure opened the way for important changes in the handling of students, and the most important brought an end to parternalism and harsh discipline. The two trustees and four deans appointed in June, 1891, to revise the rules governing students secured the adoption of their report by the Board the following December. The authors perpetuated most of the former regulations, but they abolished the loyalty oath, substituting in its stead a simple statement that reason as well as loyalty bound students to observe laws which were necessary to the organization and operation of the school. More important, they did away with the demerit system, putting in its place a warning system. The new plan made it the duty of faculty members to admonish students for delinquencies and when necessary to report them to the Regent and put them on warning. A sufficient number of warnings made a wrongdoer liable to suspension or expulsion by the Faculty. It appears that the clumsy scheme, which gave authorities the

---

[114] *17th Report* (1894), 61, 73, 139, 250.
[115] Lucile E. Wilcox, "History of the University of Illinois Library, 1868-1897" (unpublished master's thesis, University of Illinois, 1931), 61.

power needed to deal with serious misdeeds, was the best they could devise.[116]

The reform proved beneficial. The students now confronted the opportunity to justify the trust confided in them, and the Faculty no longer had to devote a considerable part of its collective attention to punishing student malefactors. Yet the students could not easily conquer the habit of creating disorder, and ritualized class conflict especially bred trouble. The reputation for toughness fostered by some students led others to fear leaving their rooms after dark in 1891, and as late as 1893 the Freshman Sociable discredited the institution. Upperclassmen threw bottles of chemicals into the waiting room and the railroad cars as the freshmen and their dates entrained under the protection of the Champaign police for their party at Bloomington. A day later the Color Rush perpetuated the feud between freshmen and sophomores, and furnished newspapers throughout the state the type of sensational account which they delighted in reporting.[117]

No evidence suggests that the Faculty employed the warning system during these years, but the debacle of late 1893 led to special action. The Faculty placed all authorized class assemblies and other student meetings held on University premises under its own supervision and protection and strictly forbade interference with them or disorderly conduct in the vicinity. At the same time the Faculty reminded students of their duty always to obey the laws which governed the conduct of citizens generally. The Faculty rejected the idea that it should enforce the civil law with respect to students, but it accepted responsibility for taking cognizance of all their public acts which might morally or socially injure any student or bring just criticism upon the University.[118]

Meanwhile, however, other changes had also improved the atmosphere. The revision of rules reduced the compulsory military obligation. Ever since 1881, when seniors were excused from compulsory drill following the rebellion against Gregory, the University had maintained the requirement for all other male students. Now

[116] *Rules for the Government of Students* (Urbana, 1892), 3; *16th Report* (1892), 192-93, 254; *17th Report* (1894), 38-39.
[117] *Illini,* Nov. 2, 1891; Nov. 29, 1893; March 7, 1894.
[118] "Faculty Record," III, 229-30; *17th Report* (1894), 196-97.

authorities excused juniors also (while still insisting that federal and state laws made military instruction a duty rather than a matter of choice for either students or the University). The revised code required every male pupil to study military tactics once a week for two terms, and every male student except those excused for physical disability or other sufficient cause to take military drill twice a week for six terms. They were expected to complete these obligations during their freshman and sophomore years.[119]

The reduced requirement met general satisfaction and eliminated a chief source of disciplinary trouble. But the reform also undermined the advanced program. The special inducements — military scholarships for all commissioned student officers and a chance for a commission in the State Militia upon graduation — did not attract upperclassmen. In the winter term of 1893 all the juniors enrolled in the military course withdrew because of the burden of their regular studies. Thus student resistance shattered the idea, born during the Civil War and its aftermath, of creating a miniature West Point at Urbana.[120]

The demise of compulsory chapel, which collapsed at Urbana like the one-hoss shay, also created a better atmosphere. As soon as Burrill grasped the reins he induced the Faculty to terminate the military formation for entering and leaving chapel, a constant source of misdeeds.[121] Without announcing the fact, authorities stopped checking attendance at chapel shortly thereafter, although the University continued to hold a chapel exercise. Members of the Board attended the ceremony as late as May, 1893, and Burrill thought regular student attendance was among the best in the nation.[122] But in the fall of 1893 laboratories, shops, and drawing rooms were excluded from the rule requiring all University rooms to close during the assembly period, and in March, 1894, the Faculty resolved

---

[119] *11th Report* (1882), 173-74; *16th Report* (1892), 149-50, 177, 193-94; "Faculty Record," III, 93-94.
[120] *Illini,* Oct. 6, 1891; *17th Report* (1894), 110-17, 246-47; Burrill to Capt. D. H. Brush, Feb. 5, 1894, "Regents' Letterbook, 1879-1894." It is worth noting that in 1892 the University of Illinois Battalion ranked fourth in the nation in the number of cadets, after Arkansas, Ohio Wesleyan, and Ohio State.
[121] "Faculty Record," III, 85, 87-88; *Illini,* Oct. 6, 1891.
[122] Burrill to A. Bowen, Oct. 14, 1892, "Regents' Letterbook, 1879-1894"; Burrill to Draper, June 26, 1894, Draper Letterbooks.

to discontinue the exercise after June.[123] In recommending this policy to the Trustees, Burrill explained that it would permit better use of time for academic purposes in an increasingly large and complex institution. "Other reasons" also lay behind the suggestion, but Burrill never elaborated on this vague phrase. He admitted privately that most students would not miss the rite, and Draper later wrote that chapel came to an end because it had become irrelevant — "really a bore to everybody."[124] On this pathetic note the University abandoned the ancient practice, and a decline in religious fervor facilitated public acceptance of the act.

Some familiar features of student life responded to general developments more than to the liberal administration of Burrill. The Christian associations gained a new opportunity for service as religion lost its official hold in the University. Bible study, the Student Volunteer Movement, and prohibition remained central concerns, but John R. Mott, the YMCA leader, met no response when he visited Urbana and suggested a revival. In 1892, however, the Christian associations launched a campaign to raise $25,000 and put up their own building. They quickly secured pledges of over $11,000 from within the University and from alumni, but not one cent from residents of Champaign and Urbana.[125]

The projected building raised an important question about the legal status of religion in the University. Burrill hoped that the University might lease land to such helpful organizations, but Judge Joseph O. Cunningham, a former trustee, gave it as his opinion that the Board could not use University property for this purpose. "It cannot be claimed," he said, "that the propagation of any religion or any form of the Christian religion is among the purposes for which the institution was created, though good morals may be inculcated and enforced by its officials."[126] Cunningham asserted that the Christian associations were nonsectarian as to the evangelical churches, "yet as to Hebrews, Catholics, Mohammedans, Par-

---

[123] "Faculty Record," III, 209, 238.
[124] *17th Report* (1894), 217-18; Burrill to Draper, June 26, 1894; Draper to B. F. Peadro, March 10, 1902, Draper Letterbooks.
[125] Burrill, *Our University*, 6-7; *16th Report* (1892), 200, 228; *Illini*, May 22, 1892.
[126] Cunningham to Burrill, Nov. 12, 1892 [1893], Burrill Correspondence, 1892, 1894; see also Burrill to Cunningham, Nov. 24, 1893, "Regents' Letterbook, 1879-1894."

sees, and Universalists, are sectarian."[127] Specifically Protestant activities long enjoyed unofficial encouragement, but a new sensitivity
to this favoritism was dawning, as Nelson W. Graham, President of
the Board, revealed in asking, "Are we not making the Y.M.C.A.
rather too prominent in the University?" He thought that fitting
up a room in which the Y held daily Protestant services looked that
way, and reminded Draper that "we are the State Institution for
the whole people Jews, Catholics, Agnostics or whatnot."[128]

Control of the campus newspaper remained a cooperative
student-faculty undertaking. The man chosen as editor-in-chief of
the *Illini* occupied an important office. The Faculty acknowledged
his role in agreeing to remit his fees, but failed to go along with a
proposal to allow academic credit for the job in the College of Literature.[129] The *Illini* retained its familiar character until 1893 under the successive direction of Charles A. Kiler and William J.
Graham. They issued a magazine-size semi-monthly divided into
several departments, and prided themselves on printing and binding
the newspaper in their own print shop, unlike other college newspapers which employed professionals.

Knowing they had much to learn by closer relations with neighboring institutions, *Illini* representatives helped form the Western
College Press Association at Chicago in May, 1891. Its objectives
were to facilitate an exchange of ideas, to promote fraternalism
among college editors, and "to come to the defense of any college
paper that is being imposed upon."[130] Representatives from Illinois
— Kiler, Frank D. Arms, and Professor Crawford — met with editors and business managers of the newspapers at Northwestern,
Michigan, Wisconsin, and eight Midwestern colleges at the Association meeting in Chicago in 1892. Ideas gained here and the
practice of other institutions induced the editor, William C. Tackett,
to launch the *Illini* as a weekly newspaper in September, 1893. If
for no other reason, he argued, Illinois had to make the change to
keep pace with the best universities.[131]

[127] *17th Report* (1894), 202.
[128] Graham to Draper, Feb. 15, 1895, Draper Letterbooks.
[129] "Faculty Record," III, 135, 224, 225-26.
[130] *Illini*, March 28, 1892; Charles Albert Kiler, *On the Banks of the Boneyard*
([Urbana], 1942), 23.
[131] *Illini*, Sept. 20, 1893.

The *Illini* became livelier and *au courant* in these years. Editors fulsomely praised the great changes occurring at the University, and urged students to concern themselves with political issues even if they did not follow their own advice. The most significant change was in the coverage of athletics. The *Illini* reported college sports in copious and loving detail, and insisted that athletics had done wonders for the institution.

In the spring of 1892 the freshman class decided with Faculty urging to forego production of a *Sophograph* during the next year. They thought that an additional bit of maturity would insure better efforts by contributors, and in 1894 brought out the first Junior Annual, a photographic and literary record of college life which later took the name of the *Illio*.

The literary societies finally lost their central importance at Illinois when Greek-letter fraternities and big-time athletics arrived, but a shift in intellectual interests also undermined these outposts of gentility. Public address no longer constituted the nation's dominant rhetorical tradition, and a more technically oriented society refused to treat literature as the handmaid of all knowledge. Thus literary interests fell to a low plane within the University. In the academic year which opened in September, 1892, the societies had to dispense with their usual declamation and oratorical contests for lack of participants, and the six judges at the annual Inter-Society Oratorical Contest in 1893 outnumbered the five contestants. Seniors now emancipated themselves from the chapel and commencement orations which they had formerly valued, and celebration of Anniversary Day, an elocutionary indulgence, fell into eclipse.[132] However, a quickened interest in contemporary issues offset the diminished concern for formal forensics. An *Illini* editorial urged University debaters to engage other Midwestern teams in political topics, and students revived the dormant Blackstonian Society in order to debate the live questions of the day. At one meeting members resolved in the negative the question, "Resolved, That the attitude of the white people of the United States toward the colored people is unjustifiable."[133]

[132] *Ibid.,* Nov. 15, 1892; May 23, Nov. 1, 1893; "Faculty Record," III, 117, 162, 178, 185.
[133] *Illini,* Feb. 15, 1892; Feb. 7, 1894 (the source of the quotation).

In 1891 the Adelphics and Philomatheans became important entrepreneurs of culture when they established at an expense of $1,250 a "lecture course" consisting of dramatic readings, lectures, and concerts by such organizations as the Boston Symphony and the New York Philharmonic. But students provided much of their own entertainment, and musical groups enjoyed great popularity in the 1890's. These included military and concert bands, a choir, glee club, male quartet, orchestra, and a mandolin, banjo, and guitar club. Nearly all of these groups gave concerts in the local and neighboring communities, and in 1893 the consolidated Glee, Mandolin, and Banjo Club made a week's tour of central Illinois. Burrill encouraged such trips as beneficial to members and to the welfare of the University.

Peabody's departure enabled the side shows to swallow up the circus. The Trustees lifted the "iron-clad" pledge against Greek-letter fraternities in September, 1891, at their first meeting after Peabody departed, and the new rules governing students which were adopted in December made way for the arrival of the Greeks.[134] Fraternities enjoyed excellent prospects at Illinois, for despite their disadvantages — and some thought these considerable — they could fill a real void in the social life at Urbana and insure their own success by ministering to the great need for board and room. Students lost no time. Thirty-five of them jumped the gun and formed a chapter of Kappa Sigma in October, but Sigma Chi was the first to receive official approval on December 14. Robert Lackey, a Purdue football star invited to Illinois as the first football coach, took the job mainly in order to organize a Kappa Sigma chapter. He recruited George Huff, a star athlete, and Frank D. Arms, an athletic organizer, as charter members, and early in 1892 the Faculty gave its formal blessing to Kappa Sigma. In the fall Phi Kappa Sigma and the first sorority, Alpha Chi Omega, arose, the latter out of the Alethenai Literary Society. Five local fraternities appeared by early 1893, and in elaborate ceremonies a year later two of these became the Urbana chapters of Phi Delta Theta and Delta Tau Delta.[135]

[134] *16th Report* (1892), 151, 193, 195.
[135] Champaign County *Gazette,* Oct. 21, 1891; "Faculty Record," III, 98, 109-10, and *passim; Illini,* Nov. 15, 1892; March 14, 1893; Feb. 15, April 19, 1894; and *passim.* See also Stewart S. Howe, "The Early Fraternity History at the University of Illinois," *Banta's Greek Exchange,* XVI (Oct., 1928), 300, 302-3.

Official sympathy and favorable environmental factors made the University a prime field of opportunity for national Greek-letter organizations.

The earliest fraternities assumed immediate social leadership of the campus and demonstrated an affinity for athletics and women. In March, 1892, the Sigma Chi's held a reception at No. 7 Main Street, their rented club rooms, for members of the governing board and the faculty, and in April they entertained Ann Arbor visitors when Michigan played Illinois in baseball. In the fall the Kappa Sig's arranged to have the election returns brought to members and their ladies in the club's rooms. Meanwhile, both groups were giving parties on weekday evenings at which mixed couples enjoyed cards, refreshments, and dancing until the small hours. The *Illini* described the Phi Delta Theta installation ceremony, at which dancing continued until 3 A.M., as one of the most brilliant society events of the season. Sumptuous fare became common at student festivities in the 1890's, and the menu for the Delta Tau Delta inaugural banquet at the Columbian Hotel, which is typical of the period, was as follows:[136]

Blue Points

Cold Turkey   Cold Ham

Fillet of Veal   Fresh Peas

Deviled Crabs

Sweet Breads, a la Delta

Salted Almonds

Chicken Sandwiches   Salmon Salad

Preserved Tomato Tarts

Vanilla Ice Cream

Angel Food   Nut Cake

Coffee

That meal was far removed from the beans and mush which Gregorians had eaten in the Old Dorm.

Athletics surged forward under Burrill's blessing. Unlike Peabody, he thought intercollegiate games did not seriously divert students' attention from academic work, and even praised them for improving the attitude of students and for publicizing the University.[137] Several faculty members began to burn incense at the altar

---

[136] *Illini,* March 12, April 11, April 25, May 22, Nov. 15, 1892; April 19, 1894.
[137] *16th Report* (1892), 156.

of the new god, and the public suddenly discovered the existence of the University through its athletic teams.

The University now left behind the state athletic league to seek a bigger one. The annual contest of the Illinois Intercollegiate Oratorical and Athletic Association, held at Monmouth in October, 1891, climaxed the old order. Oratory had become the tail on the athletic kite at these meetings. Baseball, track and field events (added in 1889), and football (included in 1891) dominated the three-day affair. At Monmouth the contingent of over 80 students from Urbana showed boorish disinterest in the oratory. The University had already won the state athletic championship two years running, and its athletes cared only for another victory and permanent possession of the silver cup. Knox and Monmouth jealously united to defeat the Illini, who were ahead in points when authorities called the games on account of student gambling.[138]

After Monmouth the student-managed Athletic Association worked to form a new league comprising the more important Midwestern institutions. Illinois invited these schools to send athletes to Urbana on May 13, 1892, for the Western Intercollegiate Field Day. The home team easily won the meet, and in the evening representatives from Northwestern, Lake Forest, Washington University (St. Louis), the College of Christian Brothers (St. Louis), Rose Polytechnic Institute, Iowa College (Grinnell), and Illinois College met in the Adelphic Literary Society rooms and organized the Western Intercollegiate Athletic Association, the precursor of the Intercollegiate Conference of Faculty Representatives and thus of the Big Ten. Delegates elected Frank D. Arms of Illinois the first President.[139] In October the University won 107 out of a possible 131 points at the contest of the state oratorical and athletic league. This sports victory gave Illinois the state athletic championship four times in a row, and to the mutual satisfaction of everyone the University thereupon withdrew from the Illinois Intercollegiate Athletic Association.[140]

The University began to enjoy phenomenal success as it moved into the big collegiate arena. Baseball and football got the lion's

[138] *Illini,* Oct. 16, 1891; Kiler, *On the Banks of the Boneyard,* 16-19.
[139] Kiler, *On the Banks of the Boneyard,* 21-22; *Illini,* May 22, 1893.
[140] *Illini,* Oct. 13, 1892.

share of the attention. In 1892 the varsity played its first big intercollegiate baseball game with Michigan on April 20, when a crowd
of 500 watched Ann Arbor trounce Illinois 18 to 0. That year students arranged six additional games in the Western College League,
which Northwestern, Lake Forest, and Beloit invited them to join,
and one with Illinois Wesleyan. The next year the team played a
22-game schedule, with George Huff as captain and R. F. Caruthers
of St. Louis as coach. It met colleges in five games, universities in
eight, and civic and athletic club teams in nine, winning 14 and
losing 8 encounters. The climax of the year came in June when the
team went on the road for nine days, playing at Ann Arbor, Detroit,
London (Ontario), Cleveland, and Oberlin. During the summer
the Illini nine played Vanderbilt, Wisconsin, and Virginia in the
World's Fair Intercollegiate Baseball Series at Chicago. The following year the club made a northern swing which took it in May
to Chicago, Ann Arbor, London and Norwalk (Ontario), and
Oberlin. Authorities were not blind to the advertising value of these
adventures.[141]

After Illinois belatedly adopted intercollegiate football in the
autumn of 1890, that game rapidly dethroned baseball as the leading college sport. Players who had disliked the game in 1890 took
it up enthusiastically a year later. Robert Lackey, the former Purdue halfback whom the students had engaged, was the coach. Occasionally he played with the team, for the rules were very loose and
the use of "ringers" commonplace. The University eleven acquired
a reputation for roughness, but they won all seven of their games
with Illinois colleges.

In 1892 University officials finally hired a football coach.
Since Eastern football was the best in the nation, they selected
Edward K. Hall, fresh from Dartmouth, where he had been captain
of the football team and an excellent scholar. He took the job at a
salary of $1,000, half that paid full professors.[142] Sixty aspirants,
more than 10 per cent of all the men enrolled, turned out for the
team, and Hall developed a small squad for which Frank Arms

---

[141] Donald L. Wolf, "A History of Intercollegiate Baseball at the University of
Illinois" (unpublished master's thesis, University of Illinois, 1958), 17-22, 126.
[142] Howard Roberts, *The Big Nine: The Story of Football in the Western Conference* (New York, 1948), 64; *16th Report* (1892), 250.

arranged 14 games, some with colleges and athletic clubs, and others with leading Midwestern universities. The team's most remarkable demonstration of prowess was a Western trip of six games played in eight days at St. Louis, Omaha, Lincoln, Baldwin and Lawrence (Kansas), and Kansas City. Eleven players, six substitutes, and three press correspondents made the journey. The Illini won four and lost two games, and drew an audience of a thousand at Lawrence. An enthusiastic crowd gathered at the Big Four depot to welcome the athletes home, and at a victory banquet in the Carter House the next night Professor Krohn, a research-minded scholar who published books, acted as toastmaster. Two Chicago newspapers published special write-ups of the team.[143]

Football had obviously arrived, pulling the University along with it. Many reasons account for its sudden popularity, but it is hard to escape the conclusion that its triumph over baseball derived largely from that fact that it was more brutal. Serious injuries were frequent in the days before protective equipment and rules, and it appears that Americans manifested an atavistic interest in the gladiatorial aspects of gridiron combat. The age of spectator sports was dawning, and people took their violence vicariously.

Modern intercollegiate athletics profoundly and in some ways beneficially influenced the institution. First, they put the University on the map as no previous promotional program had done. Contemporaries erred in attributing the sudden spurt in enrollments to sports, but rightly said that athletics advertised the University before the public and compelled neighboring institutions to respect Illinois. "We are now classed with the greatest of Western colleges by everyone," asserted an *Illini* editorial in 1893, and candor forced the writer to add that "the athletic association has done more toward making this institution great and respected than all the other departments of the University combined."[144] Second, athletics improved relations between the students and the faculty. Barton, Crawford, Krohn, Rolfe, and several younger instructors joined Burrill in

[143] The *Illini* devoted a supplement to the trip on Oct. 31, 1892; see also the *Illini,* Nov. 15, Dec. 13, 1892, and Carol Francis Pullen, "A History of Intercollegiate Football at the University of Illinois" (unpublished master's thesis, University of Illinois, 1957), 10-12, 90.

[144] *Illini,* May 8 [June 8], 1893.

sanctioning the irresistible demand for intercollegiate games. And in cheering the varsity from the sidelines they removed a big source of internal conflict. Third, the rise of big-time sports probably reduced the incidence of student-created disorders, although athletics were only one of several factors producing a healthy change. Sports channeled student energies into a new form of ritualized conflict.

Nevertheless, athletics exerted a seriously harmful influence. The crux of the case against them is that they diverted the University from its central mission as a place of scholarship, a center of free inquiry, a beacon of light in a world that badly needed illumination. Contemporaries glimpsed the dangers, but they allayed their innermost fears that athletics led to intellectual deterioration by insisting that sports actually improved scholarship. In 1894 the *Illini* reported that the academic average of the football players was better during the season than at other times, and Professor Barton gained a measure of local fame for a chapel sermon on the text (Proverbs 20:29), "The glory of young men is their strength," in which he urged the Athletic Association to fill and permeate the University with the spirit of rational athletics so that everyone would appreciate the close connection between sports and scholarship. And contemporaries stilled their apprehensions by assuring themselves that football could not possibly degenerate into a professional sport.[145] To be sure, athletics gained quick publicity for the status-conscious University, but in doing so created cultural conditions which made it harder for the institution to fulfill its proper role. By 1894 one could safely predict that the high schools of the state would emulate the University and emphasize athletics, and that public expectations would force future governing boards and presidents to demonstrate a healthy interest in sports.

Although Burrill valued athletics for clearing the bad atmosphere under Peabody, he also devised new means of improving internal conditions which emphasized the intellectual purposes of the University and contributed to the social development of students. The *Illini* contended that the antagonism which had always characterized relations between students and professors arose because they had no social contact,[146] and Burrill probably realized

---

[145] *Ibid.*, Nov. 29, 1892; March 14, 1893; March 15, 1894.
[146] *Ibid.*, Nov. 22, 1893.

that athletics alone could never fill the gap. He may also have consciously tried to find ways of offsetting the awesome rage for intercollegiate sports. At any rate, he created two organizations designed to bring students and faculty closer together. Late in 1893 he organized the University Assembly, which consisted entirely of faculty members, graduate students, and seniors. Others could attend by ticket the meetings held twice each term at which representatives from different departments presented papers. Morrow presided over the first Assembly on January 24, 1894, at which Professors Kellogg and McMurry spoke and Burrill gave the address later published as *Our University*.[147]

An equally auspicious new beginning was the Student's Assembly, established early in 1894. It embraced the remainder of the student body, and divided them into small sections each in charge of a faculty member who was to learn as much as possible about the "character, worth, health, and environment" of each individual entrusted to his care.[148] The Student's Assembly was an advisory system and a good deal more, and it is worth noting that the emergence of the modern university led to a conscious attempt to do for students what had not previously been done.

During his administration Burrill acceded to rather than resisted the welling demand for extensive changes in college life. He destroyed lingering vestiges of the old collegiate regime by abolishing the loyalty oath, the demerit system, and compulsory chapel; welcomed secret social fraternities as well as big-time intercollegiate athletics; and devised new means for improving student-faculty relations. These steps met approval and restored peace to the campus. They gave rise by 1894 to a pattern of student life whose main outlines have changed little in subsequent years.

In like manner Burrill tried to reconstruct the whole University so as to direct it into the mainstream of national life. He facilitated specialization by enlarging the curriculum and restoring the elective system, invigorated the liberal arts, and made important beginnings in professional education. These measures, which laid the foundations of a modern university, brought Illinois abreast of the

---

[147] "Faculty Record," III, 216-17; *Illini*, Jan. 24, 1894.
[148] "Faculty Record," III, 226-27.

leading American centers of higher education. Burrill also gave the Faculty a significant voice in formulation of educational policy, and tried to realize that part of academic freedom which is today called procedural due process. In the two latter respects he was probably in advance of most of his contemporaries.

He accomplished much in a short time, and it would appear that the Trustees arrested a promising presidential career when they finally selected Draper. But firm judgments about Burrill as an administrator are hazardous. It is hard to determine what he really believed as opposed to what he thought various situations required. Apparently he saw potential conflicts between college studies and college life, for example, but bowed to the inevitable and accepted, even encouraged, the latter. As of 1894 his wisdom in the matter was left for time to determine. Moreover, how can one reconcile Burrill's conduct before 1891 with his actions during the next three years? As Regent he initiated policies which were often totally at variance with those he had loyally supported and promoted as Gregory's and Peabody's chief lieutenant. Perhaps changed conditions account for some of the difference. And perhaps the loyalty he gave his superiors and the University, which a man of deep convictions cannot lightly have offered, reflected a determination to make the institution succeed which characterized many of its early members. This quality is entitled to our sincerest admiration, but it is also worth noting that such loyalty can easily become incompatible with the basic purpose which a university exists to serve.

Epilogue

THE UNIVERSITY OF ILLINOIS in its first quarter-century was neither the lengthened shadow of any one man nor the embodiment of any single idea. It was rather the product of several men and ideas which worked a vast reconstruction of American life and thought during the nineteenth century. The institution owed its establishment to forces which gathered momentum in the 1840's. Important among these was the land-grant movement in higher education which culminated in the Morrill Act.

This measure established a vital connection between the national government and higher education. The principle of federal aid for this purpose was not in itself new, but the distribution of such an immense patrimony to the states so invigorated the precedent as to provide a fresh start. Since that time the formula for distributing federal funds has changed and the amounts bestowed have greatly increased, but the link between Washington and the academic community remains firm. It has proved a determining factor in the nation's rise to world scientific and technological supremacy.

The College Land Grant Act prompted many new educational ventures and provided the immediate stimulus behind the founding of a university at Champaign-Urbana. It gave a technological and utilitarian character to the nation's higher education without foreclosing other types of development. Leaders of the industrial education movement had stressed the need for agricultural and mechanical education for the working classes. They cherished science mainly for its practical benefits but failed to appreciate the full importance of theoretical knowledge. Distrusting experts, they harbored a Jacksonian faith in the common man's capacity to develop science. Moreover, they insisted on equality of educational opportunity in order to avoid emerging class distinctions. Yet they provided no solution for many fundamental problems attendant upon the reconstruction of higher education. Nor did the congressional debate over the Morrill Act illuminate these questions. That measure called for emphasis on the branches of learning related to agriculture and the mechanic arts without excluding other scientific and classical studies. The Organic Act which established Illinois Industrial University in 1867 offered no further guidance as to what knowledge was of most worth.

This ambiguous mandate permitted a struggle between competing conceptions of higher education to dominate the early history of the University. Theoretically the governing board, which enjoyed ultimate legal authority, possessed the greatest capacity to determine policy. But the Board as such gave little positive direction. Most of its members lacked special competence in educational matters, they shared no single opinion, and they inevitably surrendered the initiative to the regents. Only a few trustees left a distinctive impress on educational policy. Matthias L. Dunlap stands out for his obstructionism, while Willard C. Flagg's proposals for agricultural experimentation led to fruitful programs. Although the Board did serve the useful purpose of keeping the University in touch with public opinion throughout the state, much of its effort was negative. It served as a brake rather than an accelerator.

The regents occupied the most strategic position in the early life of the University, and Gregory enjoyed the unique privilege of writing on a clean slate. He steered a middle course, trying to combine the best of the old education with the best of the new. He kept faith with the past in perpetuating those features of it which he deemed most worthy. Accordingly, he assigned higher education a moral purpose and developed the University as a nonsectarian Christian institution. In addition, he attempted to make seven traditional liberal arts subjects in the Department of General Science and Literature the core of the University's regular curriculum. The studies of all other departments were to provide a parallel curriculum.

The "regular and parallel" curriculum was not new — it dated from the 1820's — but it furnished an excellent device for Gregory. In addition to respecting the past he was alert to the forces which were effecting social change in his own age. Both science and youth's demand for freedom ranked high among these. Gregory considered it essential to base practical studies upon the underlying sciences, and to grant students elective freedom. He optimistically believed that his regular and parallel curricula would enable students to unite theory with practice, or "Learning and Labor." If not the most advanced, his curricular ideas were nevertheless far removed from the prescribed classical-mathematical course of study of the traditional college.

Yet Gregory's moderate program alienated radicals on the governing body and in the General Assembly. Convinced that the Regent had betrayed the industrial education movement, they enacted a law which effected a more utilitarian emphasis throughout the University. Later, when the example of Germany prompted Gregory to call for emphasis on research, the Trustees ignored his request. These opposing forces prevented the University from developing primarily as a trade school or as a true university. Yet Gregory's administration at Urbana ended on an ironical note. The failure of his vaunted program in self-government demonstrated the inherent difficulty in resolving this perennial problem. Student discipline was the rock on which his career at Illinois finally foundered.

Peabody was even less concerned than Gregory with education for utility. He took his stand on the principles of the Yale Report, and insofar as possible restored the essential outlines of the past. Feeling no need to imitate German universities, the second Regent subordinated research to teaching. Although Peabody reinstituted the prescribed curriculum within each chosen area of studies, he nevertheless improved the sciences and introduced other new subjects at Illinois. He early recognized the dangers inherent in the growing divergence between scientific and humanistic education, and insisted that every graduate obtain a basic competence in both. His strengthening of the College of Literature and Science facilitated this goal in an institution where technological studies enjoyed the upper hand.

In Peabody's view a college existed primarily for intellectual and moral enlightenment rather than for social and athletic purposes. But these preferences complicated his task, for he held office at the critical period when the side shows of college life first began to swallow up the circus. Unfortunately, Peabody defended the ideals he valued most by employing the repressive techniques of the old collegiate regime. In doing so he gave Illinois the character of a disciplinary barracks and left the impression that scholarly ideals could not co-exist with fraternities and athletics. He also aroused the fierce opposition of students and alumni, whose concerted campaign for a new regime made them important architects of the University.

Burrill quietly opened the windows and let in fresh air. He enlarged the curriculum and restored the elective system, thus facilitating specialization by students and research by the faculty. He abandoned outmoded and unpopular aspects of the older pattern of college life, and presided over the introduction of the full round of extracurricular activities which characterize modern American universities. These reforms met wide public acceptance and put Illinois on the same highway as the leading private and state universities, although it marched at the rear of the procession.

The slow pace of development in the first quarter-century is noteworthy. A basic reason is that much of the "new" education offered at Urbana differed too little from the old education available elsewhere. Gregory bears some accountability for this; Peabody considerably more. But conditions beyond the control of either man were even more responsible. The liberal arts college had long been the characteristic form of American higher education, and it still possessed a remarkable capacity to shape the emerging university. Residents of the state often found little difference between Urbana and the private denominational colleges. The agricultural community was particularly disappointed. Before the University could materially aid farmers, a body of agricultural science had to be created, and this did not occur until about the 1890's. Meanwhile, however, the University had made important contributions in agriculture, architecture, botany, domestic science, mechanical engineering, entomology, and zoology. But despite pioneering in specific areas of research or education the University as a whole was not a pioneer. The nation did not look to it for leadership as it did to Johns Hopkins University.

The attitude of the state government also shares responsibility for the slow progress. Illinois had been notably conspicuous in failing to found a state university (as opposed to a normal school) before the Civil War, and the General Assembly remained very parsimonious in dealing with the institution after it opened. Peabody once complained that every neighboring state except Kentucky furnished more money for higher education than Illinois. Yet by 1894 new levels of state support appeared possible. Governor Altgeld took far more interest in the University than had his Republican predecessors, a higher proportion of youths were now going to college, and intercollegiate football was making the public aware of the school. By 1894 the practical success of the University was assured.

But many problems of higher education still provided a challenge, and Illinois had an obligation to help solve them. The government of higher education, for example, left much to be desired. The students had always exerted a decisive influence in shaping the University, and obviously they would continue to do so in one way or another. It behooved the authorities to give the students some official responsibility for making decisions about matters of importance to them, but progress along these lines came late. Meanwhile, a pressing issue of academic government arose at another level — among the Trustees, President, and Faculty. When it first opened Illinois had understandably adopted the prevailing American system under which the Board entrusted management of the institution to a President who was responsible only to lay trustees rather than to the Faculty. This situation deprived professors as well as students of an effective voice in determining academic policy, an ironic situation for a country which prided itself on its democracy. Burrill was the first executive to encourage the growth of a countervailing power in the Faculty at Urbana, and a struggle erupted when the autocratic Draper replaced him. A long battle afforded Illinois a splendid opportunity to contribute to the solution of an issue given new urgency as universities came to occupy an increasingly critical role in society.

In addition there remained the challenge of finding an adequate set of goals by which to guide the progress of the institution. For it was clear that the ideals which had given central unity of purpose to American higher education down to the late nineteenth century were no longer adequate for a modern university. The authorities at Urbana apparently felt little need to search for a philosophy of education which would restore lost unity. But their attempt to vitalize the liberal arts at Urbana reflects indirect concern with the larger issue. The University had already trained hosts of scientists and technicians who had contributed significantly to the elevation of material welfare in America and beyond, and its record to date made clear that the University would contribute further to the advancement of science and technology, both of which were still in their infancy. But there was at least some awareness that such an emphasis was insufficient for a true university. Illinois needed to do far more in the liberal arts than its boldest leaders had yet envisioned, and in a variety of academic disciplines as yet unnamed, in order to exert a comparable influence on the spiritual welfare of the nation.

Bibliography

PRIMARY SOURCES

This book rests mainly on unpublished and published primary sources, and unless otherwise indicated the former are all located in the University of Illinois Archives. All things considered, the collection of original materials bearing on this period of the institution's history is remarkably rich and varied. Yet there are almost no papers which show the inner workings of the Board of Trustees and its committees or the manner in which individual members of the governing body exercised their office. And little of the official correspondence of the regents survived. Albert Lee, an assistant in President Draper's office, said that Draper had all the previous correspondence destroyed with the exception of a single letterbook which somehow escaped. (Professor Clarence W. Alvord to President David Kinley, June 15, 1920, Kinley Papers, 1920-21, Box Sa-Sty, Semi-Centennial History File.)

[393]

UNIVERSITY RECORDS AND PERSONAL PAPERS

Additonal Regulations for the Government of Students of the Illinois Industrial University, Adopted Between March 10, 1882, and February 10, 1885. n.p., n.d.

Alumni Class Files, 1873-97.

These contain memorabilia of class day, commencement, literary society and dance programs, invitations for student events, student government campaign tickets, and prize-winning orations.

Alumni Morgue.

A large file of folders with photographs and various types of information on deceased alumni, former students, faculty members, and trustees.

Board of Trustees of the University of Illinois, published *Reports*, 1868-94.

These official minutes are a key to the formulation of academic and administrative policy, and contain reports by the regents and much additional information. Although extremely valuable in themselves, these bare official bones must be fleshed out with other materials.

"Board of Trustees Proceedings," 1867-97.

These are the manuscripts of the published reports cited in the previous entry. I consulted them only where problems arose with the printed official version.

Thomas J. Burrill Correspondence, 1892, 1894.

Contains some of Burrill's correspondence as Acting Regent.

Thomas J. Burrill Papers, 1863-64, 1875, 1877-78.

These include a boyhood reminiscence, a journal, and professional and personal papers.

Catalogue of the Art Gallery, Illinois Industrial University: Comprising a Brief Description of Each Cast and Picture with an Introductory Notice of the Various Schools of Art. Champaign, 1876.

Although the catalogue fleetingly mentions the fine arts in America, it demonstrates that Gregory almost entirely identified art and culture with Europe.

Circular and Catalogue of the Officers and Students of the University of Illinois. Champaign, 1867-94.

These academic annals, whose title varies slightly over the years, are an important key to intellectual history.

"W. G. Curtiss Scrapbook, 1878-1882."

A valuable collection of student memorabilia.

"Andrew S. Draper Letterbooks," 1894-1904. 34 vols.

General correspondence, of which only the first volume comes within my present purview.

Andrew S. Draper Personal Letters, 1894-1904.

>A selected collection of papers arranged by topics, some of which are useful.

Matthias L. Dunlap Papers, *ca.* 1850-70.

>Dunlap preserved many of his "Rural" articles in the Chicago *Tribune* in scrapbooks.

"Faculty of Literature and Science Record," 1878-1909.

>Mainly the chaff routinely ground out at faculty meetings in the College.

"Faculty Record," 1868-1901.

>Discovered in the attic of the Administration Building well after I began my research, these three manuscript volumes are indispensable to my study.

John M. Gregory Papers, 1838-98.

>These contain important private and official correspondence; manuscripts of lectures, sermons, articles, and addresses; copies of publications; lecture notes, the Scrapbooks, and other papers; but not the diary that Gregory kept for years.

"I.I.U. Senate Journal," 1877-83.

>Valuable in showing the operations of the Student Senate and its management of the *Illini*.

Natural History Survey, Chief's Correspondence, 1871-1909.

>A vast collection of the correspondence of Stephen A. Forbes, barely touched in the research for this book.

Selim H. Peabody Papers.

>The manuscripts, mainly holograph, of Peabody's baccalaureate sermons and other addresses constitute the bulk of this collection.

Permanent Record, Registrar's Office.

>These materials are especially valuable in showing individual academic programs, and related papers often furnish additional biographical data on students.

Burt E. Powell Papers.

>The papers which Powell gathered in the preparation of his volume on the establishment of Illinois Industrial University. They contain documents which illuminate the movement for industrial education in Illinois.

"Publications Scrapbook, 1868-1890."

>A record of the Regent's office which includes materials used to publicize the University and to articulate it with the high schools.

"Record Book of the College of Natural Science," 1878-1905.

>A manuscript record of Faculty meetings.

"Regents' Letterbook, 1879-1894."

>Contains outgoing correspondence of Regents Gregory, Peabody,

and Burrill. Mostly routine, but a few items are extremely important. Presumably this is the letterbook which escaped Draper's despoliation.

Rules for the Government of Students. Champaign, 1882; Champaign, 1892.

"Secretary's Record, College Government, 1870-1881."

This and the following item illustrate the workings of the important but unsuccessful experiment in student government.

"Secretary's Book, College Government, [1881-1883]."

Charles H. Shamel Papers, 1874-1949.

The collection embraces an autobiography, diary, correspondence, and other papers, as well as the diary of Clarence A. Shamel. The material sheds important light on the role of students in the forced resignation of Peabody.

Carl Stephens Papers, 1912-51.

This collection includes important source materials and correspondence which Carl Stephens, former Director of the Alumni Association, assembled in doing research on a history of the University which he completed but never published.

Arthur N. Talbot Papers, 1877-1915.

As a student Talbot preserved materials relating to college life, and his collection contains the only known copies of important student publications and other items relating to the military rebellion against Gregory.

Andrew D. White Papers.

Some 16 letters from Gregory to White during the period 1860-84 are in the Collection of Regional History and University Archives of the John M. Olin Research Library at Cornell University. Copies of some of these are in the Gregory Papers, but they are not completely legible.

NEWSPAPERS AND PERIODICALS

Some of the items that follow were used systematically for the entire period covered by this book or for the entire period of the life of the publication that is relevant to this volume; others were used selectively.

American Association for the Advancement of Science, *Proceedings.* Washington and elsewhere.

American Journal of Education. Hartford.

Contains valuable articles on the quest for a national university which put the land-grant movement in context.

Army and Navy Journal. Washington.

Breeder's Gazette. Chicago.

Champaign County *Gazette*.
> Studied intensively for the academic years 1880-81, 1884-85, autumn of 1889, winter and spring of 1891, and selectively for other years. Extremely valuable.

Champaign County *Herald*.

Champaign *Times*.

Chicago *Inter-Ocean*.

Chicago *Standard*.
> A Baptist newspaper for which Gregory often wrote. It often befriended the University.

Chicago *Tribune*.
> Powerful and perverse with respect to the University, the *Tribune* nevertheless offers good information on the rise of the institution. It carried the attacks on Gregory written by Trustee Matthias L. Dunlap under the pseudonym of "Rural."

Culivator and Country Gentleman. Albany and Philadelphia.
> Considerable comment on agriculture at the University of Illinois is found here.

Harvard Graduates' Magazine, Cambridge, Mass.

Illini.
> The student newspaper is indispensable in studying the University, and it illuminates much in the official *Reports* of the Trustees and the *Catalogues* that would otherwise be obscure.

Illinois Farmer. Springfield, 1856-64.
> Matthias L. Dunlap replaced Simeon Francis as editor in 1860, and the paper is negatively valuable in showing that Jonathan B. Turner and the hope of an agricultural college in Illinois did not completely dominate the attention of farmers in the state.

Illinois State Agricultural Society, *Transactions*. Springfield.
> Both this and the following item demonstrate the efforts of organized agricultural and horticultural groups in the state to establish a state university and to make the institution serve their purposes.

Illinois State Horticultural Society, *Transactions*. Various places.

Illinois State Journal. Springfield.

Illinois Teacher. Peoria.

National Educational Association, *Journal of Proceedings and Addresses*. Published at the place of the annual meeting. Earlier titles differed.
> These volumes reveal the problems that educational leaders of the late nineteenth century considered significant, and provide important perspective on developments at Champaign-Urbana.

Northwestern Christian Advocate. Chicago.
> A Methodist publication which mirrors the shifting attitudes

toward the University of one of the strongest religious denominations in the state.

Prairie Farmer. Chicago.

This journal, the strongest farm paper in the state, is indispensable to an understanding of the land-grant movement in Illinois and the formative stage of the University.

Society for the Promotion of Collegiate and Theological Education at the West, *Annual Reports.* New York and Boston.

Sophograph.

This annual publication of the sophomore class sheds valuable light on aspects of student life.

Student.

Predecessor of the *Illini.*

STATE AND FEDERAL GOVERNMENT DOCUMENTS

Congressional Globe.

Debates and Proceedings of the Constitutional Convention of the State of Illinois, Convened at the City of Springfield, Tuesday, December 13, 1869. Springfield, 1870.

Department of Public Instruction, City of Chicago, *Fourteenth Annual Report of the Board of Education for the Year Ending July 3, 1868.* Chicago, 1868.

Illinois House Journal.

Illinois Laws.

Illinois Private Laws.

Illinois Revised Statutes.

Illinois Senate Journal.

Illinois State Department of Agriculture, *Transactions.* Springfield.

Journal of the Constitutional Convention of the State of Illinois. Springfield, 1870.

Report of the Commissioner of Patents for the Year 1851, Part II: Agriculture. 33 Cong., 1 Sess. Senate Exec. Doc. No. 118. Washington, 1852.

Part of the Turner plan for an industrial university is printed here.

"Report of Joint Select Committee to Visit Champaign County," *Illinois Reports* (1865), I, 319-20.

Reports to the General Assembly of Illinois (Illinois Reports).

These volumes include several reports made to different sessions of the General Assembly which relate to the University, especially in the period to 1880.

"State Militia Commission Records 1861-1875," Vol. A, Adjutant General's Records, Illinois State Archives, Springfield.

"[State Militia] Commission Records 1875-1879 [1880]," Vol. 20, Adjutant General's Records, Illinois State Archives, Springfield.

Superintendent of Public Instruction of the State of Illinois, *Biennial Reports*. Springfield.

These volumes contain valuable data, reports, and articles on education in Illinois. Often the reports submitted by the regents of the University include material not found in the official *Reports* printed by the Board of Trustees.

Superintendent of Public Instruction of the State of Michigan, *Twenty-third Annual Report*. Lansing, 1860.

[U.S. Department of Agriculture], *Proceedings of the National Agricultural Convention, Held at Washington, D.C. February 15-17, 1872*. 42 Cong., 2 Sess., Senate Misc. Doc. No. 164. Washington, 1872.

[U.S.] Department of Agriculture, *Proceedings of a Convention of Agriculturists, Held in the Department of Agriculture, January 10th to 18th, 1882*. Washington, 1882.

[U.S.] Department of Agriculture, *Proceedings of a Convention of Agriculturists Held at the Department of Agriculture, January 23-29, 1883 (Second Convention)*. Washington, 1883.

[U.S.] Department of Agriculture, *Proceedings of a Convention of Delegates from Agricultural Colleges and Experiment Stations Held at the Department of Agriculture, July 8 and 9, 1885*. Washington, 1885.

U. S. Statutes at Large.

WRITINGS BY FACULTY AND TRUSTEES

Burrill, Thomas J., "Aggressive Parasitism of Fungi," Illinois State Horticultural Society, *Transactions for 1873*, n.s., VII (Chicago, 1874), 217-21.

———, "Anthrax of Fruit Trees; or The So-Called Fire Blight of Pear, and Twig Blight of Apple, Trees," American Association for the Advancement of Science, *Proceedings*, XXIX (Salem, Mass., 1881), 583-97.

———, "The Bacteria: An Account of Their Nature and Effects, Together with a Systematic Description of the Species," *11th Report* (1882), 93-157.

———, "Blight of Pear and Apple Trees," *10th Report* (1881), 62-84.

———, "Governor Altgeld's Methods," *Alumni Quarterly*, VII (April, 1913), 83-84.

Provides good information to show how Altgeld eased the appropriation for the University through the legislature in 1893.

———, "In Quest of a President," *The 1903 Illio* [Urbana, 1903], 37-38.

An excellent statement about the three-year search for a president which led to the selection of Andrew S. Draper in 1894.

———, "New Species of Micrococcus (Bacteria)," *American Naturalist,* XVII (March, 1883), 319-21.

———, *Our University: An Address Delivered Before the University Assembly of the University of Illinois.* [Bloomington, 1894].

A general statement of Burrill's plans for development, and particularly valuable for its strong insistence that the Board leave the internal management of the University to the Faculty.

[———], "A Page of University History." James Faculty Correspondence.

A valuable statement of the attempt to translate the Morrill Act into reality at Illinois under Gregory in the early years.

———, "Pear Blight," Illinois State Horticultural Society, *Transactions for 1877,* n.s., XI (Chicago, 1878), 114-16.

Draper, Andrew S., "Governor Altgeld and the University of Illinois," *Alumni Quarterly,* VII (April, 1913), 77-82.

Flagg, Willard C., "The Farmers' Movement in the Western States," *Journal of Social Science,* VI (July, 1874), 100-115.

[———], *The Illinois School of Agriculture.* [Alton, 1864].

This publication, perhaps a separate pamphlet or part of a periodical, shows one of the many ideas about the type of agricultural college that should be established in Illinois with the proceeds of the Morrill Act.

Forbes, Stephen A., "History of the Former State Natural History Societies of Illinois, *Science,* n.s., XXVI (Dec. 27, 1907), 892-98.

———, "War as an Education," *The Illinois,* III (Oct., 1911), 3-10.

Gregory, John M., "Agricultural Facts and Theories," *2nd Report* (1869), 123-28.

———, "The American Newspaper and American Education," *Journal of Social Science,* XII (Dec., 1880), 61-68.

———, "College Secret Societies," *Present Age,* I (March 16, 1882), 163-65.

———, "Dr. Nott," *Michigan Teacher,* I (May, 1866), 155-62.

[———], "Dr. Wayland as a Teacher," *Michigan Teacher,* I (March, 1866), 73-76.

———, "An Experiment in College Government," *International Review,* X (June, 1881), 510-18.

———, *The Hand-Book of History and Chronology.* Chicago, 1867.

———, "Military Drill in Colleges," *Illini,* June, 1879.

———, "Physical Training in College," *Present Age,* III (Feb. 21, 1884).

An unpaginated copy of this article is in the Gregory Papers, but I have been unable to find any library which possesses this number of *Present Age,* and therefore do not have the inclusive page numbers.

————, *The Right and Duty of Christianity to Educate. Inaugural Address [as] President of Kalamazoo College, September 20, 1864.* Kalamazoo, 1865.

————, *The Seven Laws of Teaching.* Boston, 1886.

————, "The Study of History," *Illinois Teacher,* XIV (June, 1868), 194-95; (Aug., 1868), 268-71.

————, "Syllabus of Lectures on Mental Science, to Senior Class of Ill. Ind'l. University." Gregory Papers.

————, and Osborn R. Keith, "Report on the Paris International Exposition of 1878," *Reports to the General Assembly of Illinois at Its Thirty-first Regular Session Convened January 8, 1879,* IV, Sec. H. Springfield, 1879.

Gregory, Louisa C. Allen, "The School of Domestic Science of the Illinois Industrial University," U.S. Bureau of Education, *Industrial Education in the United States: A Special Report* (Washington, 1883), 279-85.

K[rohn], W[illiam] O., "Laboratory Psychology," *Illini,* May 8 [June 8], 1893.

Miles, Manly, " 'Ensilage' of Fodder: Preserving Green Feed by Burial," *Cultivator and Country Gentleman,* XLI (1876), 627-28.

————, *Silos, Ensilage and Silage.* New York, 1889.

Morrow, George E., "Agricultural Education," *Illini,* Feb., 1877.

————, "Report of the Agricultural Department," *University of Illinois Bulletin No. 2* ([Urbana], 1886), 21-24.

Parr, Samuel W., "Historical Sketch of the Chemistry Department," *University of Illinois Bulletin No. 25,* XIII (Urbana, [1916]), 16-29.

Peabody, Selim H., "The Duty of the State Towards Its University," *12th Report* (1885), 57-72.

————, "The Educational Exhibit at the Columbian Exposition," National Educational Association, *Journal of Proceedings and Addresses, 1892* (New York, 1893), 583-90.

————, "An Educational Experiment," National Educational Association, *Journal of Proceedings and Addresses, 1889* (Topeka, 1889), 539-46.

[————, Chairman], Report of the Committee on Higher Education, "The Elective System in Colleges," National Educational Association, *Journal of Proceedings and Addresses, 1888* (Topeka, 1888), 268-75.

————, "Illinois, Its Present and Future Greatness," *12th Report* (1885), 73-85.

[————, Chairman], Report of the Committee on Technological Education, "Pedagogical Value of the School Workshop," National Educational Association, *Journal of Proceedings and Addresses, 1886* (Salem, Mass., 1887), 305-17.

————, "Special Report upon the Action of the Faculty of the University of Illinois upon Military Affairs," *16th Report* (1892), 81-87.

————, "The Value of Tool-Instruction as Related to the Active Pursuits in Which Pupils May Subsequently Engage," National Educational Association, *Journal of Proceedings and Addresses, 1889* (Topeka, 1889), 98-103.

————, "What Work Is Legitimate to the Institutions Founded on the Congressional Act of 1862," *11th Report* (1882), 55-63.

Ricker, Nathan C., "Letter to the Editor," *American Architect and Builder,* I (Oct. 21, 1876), 343.

WRITINGS ABOUT FACULTY AND TRUSTEES

Abbott, William L., "The Grave of John Milton Gregory," *Alumni Quarterly,* VIII (July, 1914), 166-69.

Baker, Ira O., "Nathan Clifford Ricker, '72," *Alumni Quarterly,* VI (April, 1912), 97-101.

Barrett, J. T., "Thomas Jonathan Burrill (1839-1916)," *Phytopathology,* VIII (Jan., 1918), 1-4.

Beardsley, Henry M., "Dr. Gregory and the Students at Illinois," *Alumni Quarterly,* VIII (July, 1914), 162-65.
Valuable in showing Gregory's influence on students in the early 1870's.

Brown, F. C., "Samuel Wesley Stratton, 1861-1931," *Science,* LXXIV (Oct. 30, 1913), 428-31.

Bullard, Samuel A., "Alexander McLean, Trustee," *Alumni Quarterly,* II (Jan., 1908), 1-8.

Burrill, Thomas J., "Boyhood Biography, a Personal Sketch," typewritten MS. Burrill Papers.

————, "Makers of the University: Selim Hobart Peabody," *Alumni Quarterly,* IV (July, 1910), 203-13.

————, "Melville Amasa Scovell, '75," *Alumni Quarterly,* VI (Oct., 1912), 289-91.

[————], "Memorial Address on George E. Morrow," [April 8, 1900]. Burrill Papers.

Clark, Thomas Arkle, "Edward Snyder — a College Memory," *Alumni Quarterly,* I (April, 1907), 61-68.

Davenport, Eugene, "Dr. Thomas Jonathan Burrill Memorial Address," Illinois State Horticultural Society, *Transactions for 1916,* n.s., L (n.p., 1917), 67-97.

————, "George Espy Morrow," in L. H. Bailey, ed., *Cyclopedia of American Agriculture,* IV. New York, 1909.

————, "A Tribute to 'The Grand Old Man,' Thomas Jonathan Burrill," *Illinois Agriculturist,* XX (May, 1916), 712-13.

Credits Burrill as the real father of the College of Agriculture at the University of Illinois.

————, "What One Life Has Seen," MS. autobiography. See the Appendix: "Notable People I Have Known and Seen." Davenport Papers.

Dodge, Daniel K., "Edward Snyder," *Alumni Quarterly,* IX (July, 1915), 171-74.

Catches mainly the personal side.

Sixty Years a Builder: The Autobiography of Henry Ericsson. Chicago, 1942.

This book discusses John M. Van Osdel, a Chicago builder-architect and an original member of the Board of Trustees.

Forbes, Stephen A., "The Life and Work of Professor George E. Morrow," a paper read at a memorial service at the University Chapel, April 8, 1900. Agriculture Dean's Office.

An excellent evaluation.

[————], "Stephen A. Forbes," *Scientific Monthly,* XXX (May, 1930), 475-76.

This autobiographical sketch from a letter written by Forbes in 1923 contains some details not found in other accounts.

————, "Thomas Jonathan Burrill," *Alumni Quarterly and Fortnightly Notes,* I (July 15, 1916), 409-17.

Another excellent evaluation.

Haven, E. O., "Rev. John M. Gregory, LL.D.," *Michigan Teacher,* I (June, 1866), 195-97.

Hottes, Charles F., "Personal Recollections of Dr. Thomas J. Burrill and the Bacteriology of His Time," typewritten MS. Stephens Papers.

Howard, L. O., *Biographical Memoir of Stephen Alfred Forbes, 1844-1930.* National Academy of Sciences Biographical Memoirs, XV. Washington, 1932.

James, Edmund J., "The President's Tribute to Thomas Jonathan Burrill," *Alumni Quarterly and Fortnightly Notes,* I (May 1, 1916), 336-37.

Memorial of the Funeral Services for Stephen Alfred Forbes. [Urbana, 1930].

Contains several different tributes, including a biographical account by Earnest Browning Forbes, the son of Stephen.

Moss, Charles M., "Makers of the University: Thomas Jonathan Burrill," *Alumni Quarterly*, II (Oct., 1908), 134-231.

Ricker, Nathan C., "The Story of a Life," typewritten MS. autobiography. Urbana, 1922.

"Sagamores of the Illini: Samuel Wesley Stratton, '84," *Alumni Quarterly*, IX (April, 1915), 75-78.

"Sketch of Manly Miles," *Appleton's Popular Science Monthly*, LIV (April, 1899), 834-41.

The best evaluation of Miles. Also printed in Michigan State Board of Agriculture, *Annual Report*, XXXVIII (1899), 422-28.

Smith, Erwin F., "In Memoriam Thomas J. Burrill," *Journal of Bacteriology*, I (May, 1916), 269-71.

Ward, Henry B., "Stephen Alfred Forbes, a Tribute," *Science*, LXXI (April 11, 1930), 378-81.

WRITINGS ON UNIVERSITY LIFE AND EVENTS

[Bogus] *Illini*, Feb. 21, [1891].

Brown, R. L., "John M. Gregory — an Appreciation." A. G. Allen Research File, 1898-1920.

Burr, E. M., ed., *Class History of the Class of 1878*. [Urbana], 1911.

Doc's Compulsory Entertainment, or Junior Juggernaut. [Urbana, 1887?].

An indication of student dissatisfaction with Peabody, and particularly valuable for Horace Taylor's powerful caricature of Peabody.

F., J. [James Faulkner?], "Brief History of Societies," *Illini*, Jan., 1875. Deals with literary societies.

Gladden, Washington, *Recollections*. Boston, 1909.

[Going, Judson F.], *Cecil's Book of Natural History: About the Great Ones of '83*. [Urbana, 1883].

A crude and malicious attack by an author who considered taste irrelevant when substantial issues were at stake.

H., B., "Our Military Department," *Illini*, Feb., 1879.

Harden, E. E., "History of the Scientific Association," *Illini*, June, 1879.

Harwood, S. Dix, "The *Student* and the *Daily Illini*." Stephens Papers.

Hayes, C. I., "Early History and Reminiscences of the Adelphic Society." *Illini*, June, 1879.

Heath, William A., "History of Athletics." Stephens Papers.

———, "The Mythology of Illinois," *The Illinois*, III (May, 1912), 411-17.

An account of the origins of fraternities.

Howe, Stewart, "Early Days of Illinois Fraternities," *Illinois Alumni News,* VI (April, 1928), 292.

"Important Elements in College Life," *Sophograph* (1885), 25-27.

Jeffers, Charles P., "Athletics at the University, 1869-1874." Stephens Papers.

[————], "The Retrospect of Seventy-Four," a class history in the form of a typewritten poem. Alumni Association, Class of 1874 (University Archives).

Jordan, David Starr. *The Days of a Man.* 2 vols. New York, 1922.

Kiler, Charles Albert, *On the Banks of the Boneyard.* [Urbana], 1942.
    A memoir which casts important light on the nature of student life in the last years of Peabody's administration.

"The New Chemical Laboratory of the University of Illinois," *Metallurgical and Chemical Engineering,* XIV (April 15, 1916), 421-24.
    Includes a history of the Department of Chemistry.

North, Foster, *The Struggle for Religious Liberty in the University of Illinois.* Los Angeles, 1942.
    Invaluable for biographical details on North.

Foster North vs. Board of Trustees, University of Illinois: The Bible in the University of Illinois. Urbana, 1891.
    The pamphlet on the Foster North case which Peabody asked to have printed and distributed.

Pierce, John L., and Henry M. Beardsley, "History of the Illini," *Illini,* March 10, 1883.

Potter, Frances A., "Those Early Days," *Alumni Quarterly and Fortnightly Notes,* I (Oct. 15, 1915), 23-28.

"Programme of Dance, Annual Senior Ball, Class of '91, Monday, June 8, 1891." Charles H. Shamel Papers.

Raymond, Isaac S., "The Beginning," *Alumni Quarterly,* VI (July, 1912), 193-96.
    An inaccurate reminiscence on the literary societies by a former student.

Reporter.

"Sagamores of the Illini: Henry Mahan Beardsley," *Alumni Quarterly,* VIII (July, 1914), 192-95.

"Sagamores of the Illini: Roland Ray Conklin," *Alumni Quarterly,* VIII (Oct., 1914), 273-75.

Schaefer, J. V. E., "The American Common School System." Talbot Papers.

[State Universities and Colleges], *Proceedings of the Conference of the Presidents and Other Delegates of the State Universities and State Colleges, Held at Columbus, Ohio, December 27 and 28, 1877.* U.S. Bureau of Education, Circular of Information No. 2, 1879, Appendix B. Washington, 1879.

"Student Broadsides." Student Organization Alphabetical File.

Vindicator, Feb. 24, 1880; Feb. 24, March 5, 1881.

Whittlesey, Joseph H., "Circular to Presidents, Members of the Faculty, and Trustees of Colleges of the United States," May 20, 1867. Gregory Papers.

Wilson, Henry, "Report of the General Secretary of the Board of Directors University of Illinois Young Men's Christian Association," April 10, 1929. Kinley Papers.

WRITINGS RELATING TO EARLY EDUCATIONAL REFORM

Adams, Charles Francis, Jr., *A College Fetich: An Address Delivered Before the Harvard Chapter of the Fraternity of the Phi Beta Kappa, in Sanders Theater, Cambridge, June 28, 1883.* Boston, 1883.

A slashing attack on the reverence for dead languages and on the superficial learning imparted at Harvard in the 1850's.

"Address of Professor A. D. Bache," American Association for the Advancement of Science, *Proceedings,* VI (Washington, 1852), xli-lx.

The address as President of the AAAS in which Bache marked out the plan of the scientific Lazzaroni for a national university and an academy of science.

Bache, Alexander Dallas, "A National University," *American Journal of Education,* I (May, 1856), 477-79.

Barnard, Frederick A. P., *Letters on College Government and the Evils Inseparable from the American College System in Its Present Form.* New York, 1855.

An excellent analysis of the failure in the United States of the disciplinary and dormitory systems borrowed from England.

Autobiography of Peter Cartwright, ed. Charles L. Wallis. New York, 1956.

Eliot, Charles W., "The New Education: Its Organization," *Atlantic Monthly,* XXIII (Feb., 1869), 203-20; (March, 1869), 358-67.

The Complete Works of Ralph Waldo Emerson, I. 12 vols. New York, 1883-1906.

Emerson on Education: Selections, ed. Howard Mumford Jones. Classics in Education No. 26. New York, 1966.

The book includes a thoughtful Introduction to this neglected subject.

Gould, Benjamin Apthorp, Jr., "An American University," *American Journal of Education,* II (Sept., 1856), 265-93.

"Industrial Universities: Resolutions of the General Assembly of Illinois Relative to the Establishment of Industrial Universities, and for the Encouragement of Practical and General Education Among the People." 33 Cong., 1 Sess., House Misc. Doc. No. 31. Washington, 1854.

The Works of Philip Lindsley, D.D., ed. LeRoy J. Halsey. 3 vols. Philadelphia, 1866.

[Marsh, James], *Exposition of the System of Instruction and Discipline Pursued in the University of Vermont.* n.p., n.d.

> Here Marsh describes reforms at Vermont in the late 1820's which influenced Wayland and thus indirectly influenced Gregory.

"Memorial of Alden Partridge," 26 Cong., 2 Sess., House Exec. Doc. No. 69, II, 4-5. Washington, 1841.

"Memorial of the Industrial Convention of the State of Illinois," *Illinois Reports* (1853).

"Memorial of J. S. Skinner," 30 Cong., 1 Sess., Senate Misc. Doc. No. 120. Washington, 1848.

"Original Papers in Relation to a Course of Liberal Education," *American Journal of Science and Arts,* XV (Jan., 1829), 297-351.

> The Yale Report.

Peirce, Benjamin, *Working Plan for the Foundation of a University.* Cambridge, Mass., 1856.

Rafinesque, Constantine Samuel, *Celestial Wonders and Philosophy, or The Structure of the Visible Heavens with Hints on Their Celestial Religion, and Theory of Futurity.* Philadelphia, 1838.

State of New York, Messages from the Governor, IV (1843-1856), ed. Charles Z. Lincoln. Albany, 1909.

Sturtevant, Julian M., *An Autobiography,* ed. J. M. Sturtevant, Jr. New York, 1896.

Tappan, Henry P., *University Education.* New York, 1851.

Ticknor, George, *Remarks on Changes Lately Proposed or Adopted, in Harvard University.* n.p., 1825.

Papers and Correspondence of Jonathan Baldwin Turner, 1831-1910. Illinois Historical Survey, University of Illinois.

> The collection comprises originals and copies of letters and papers which touch on the full range of Turner's interests, including educational reform.

Turner, Jonathan B., *Industrial Universities for the People, Published in Compliance with Resolutions of the Chicago and Springfield Conventions. And Under the Industrial League of Illinois.* Jacksonville, 1853.

> Ironically, the University of Illinois has no copy of this pamphlet published in compliance with resolutions of conventions of the Industrial League.

————, *Industrial University Education.* Chicago, 1864.
> Turner wrote this pamphlet at the request of U.S. Commissioner of Agriculture Isaac Newton, who found it too radical and refused to print it.

————, "The Millenium [*sic*] of Labor," Illinois State Agricultural Society, *Transactions,* I (Springfield, 1855), 55-61.

————, *A Plan for an Industrial University for the State of Illinois, Submitted to the Farmers' Convention at Granville, Held November 18, 1851.* n.p., 1851.

Wayland, Francis, *The Education Demanded by the People of the United States.* Boston, 1855.

————, *Report to the Corporation of Brown University, on Changes in the System of Collegiate Education, Read March 28, 1850.* Providence, 1850.

————, *Thoughts on the Present Collegiate System in the United States.* Boston, 1842.

White, Andrew D., *Autobiography.* 2 vols. New York, 1907.

SECONDARY SOURCES

UNPUBLISHED MANUSCRIPTS AND DISSERTATIONS

All of the theses and dissertations listed below are in the libraries of the institutions at which they were written. The papers written for the author are in his personal possession. The other materials are located as indicated or are in the University of Illinois Archives.

Baker, Ira O., and Everett E. King, "A History of the College of Engineering of the University of Illinois, 1868-1945," mimeograph MS. 2 vols. Urbana, [1947].
> A compendious reference work begun in 1920.

Barber, William J., Jr., "George Huff: A Short Biography." Master's thesis, University of Illinois, 1951.

Bayles, Frederick P., "Dr. Henry J. Detmers, His Life History in Germany and in the United States." MS. in the possession of Mrs. R. F. Huehner, Pound Ridge, N.Y.

Brown, Donald R., "The Educational Contributions of Jonathan Baldwin Turner." Master's thesis, University of Illinois, 1954.

Dunlap, Henry M., "A History of the Illinois Industrial University." 2 vols. [Urbana, 1937].
> This is a legislative history written by a graduate in the class of 1875 who long represented the local district in the General Assembly. The first volume is largely concerned with the period through the early 1890's.

Dupree, A. Hunter, "The Morrill Act and Science." MS. in the author's possession.

Hoeveler, J. David, Jr., "Lucy Flower: Professional Altruist." Course paper written for the author and submitted for publication.

————, "Philosophy at the University of Illinois, 1868-1880." Seminar paper written for the author.

Kersey, Harry A., "John Milton Gregory as a Midwestern Educator: 1852-1880." Doctoral dissertation, University of Illinois, 1965.

McGrath, Earl James, "The Evolution of Administrative Offices in Institutions of Higher Education in the United States from 1860 to 1933." Doctoral dissertation, University of Chicago, 1936.

Propper, Janet, "The Development of Graduate Education at the University of Illinois, 1868-1908." Seminar paper written for the author.

Pullen, Carol Francis, "A History of Intercollegiate Football at the University of Illinois." Master's thesis, University of Illinois, 1957.

Stephens, Carl, MS. history of the University of Illinois.

Stephens, University Historian from 1943 to 1950, completed a history of the University in 1947 but never published it. I sampled the manuscript at the beginning of my research.

Stillman, Rachel, "The Problems Faced by the University of Illinois in Acquiring a Medical School." Seminar paper written for the author.

Tucker, Timothy, "University of Illinois Trustees' Elections: A Yardstick. " Course paper written for the author.

Turner, Fred H., "The Illinois Industrial University." 2 vols. Doctoral dissertation, University of Illinois, 1931.

Wagner, Robert L., "The Economic Thought of John Milton Gregory." Course paper written for the author.

Wilcox, Lucile E., "History of the University of Illinois Library, 1868-1897." Master's thesis, University of Illinois, 1931.

Wilson, Robert A., "A History of the Administration of Intercollegiate Athletics at the University of Illinois." Master's thesis, University of Illinois, 1948.

The work is mainly a series of biographical sketches of coaches.

Wolf, Donald L., "A History of Intercollegiate Baseball at the University of Illinois." Master's thesis, University of Illinois, 1958.

BOOKS

Adams, Herbert B., *The Study of History in American Colleges and Universities*. U.S. Bureau of Education, Circular of Information No. 2, 1887. Washington, 1887.

The Mind and Spirit of John Peter Altgeld: Selected Writings and Addresses, ed. Henry M. Christman. Urbana, 1960.

Bailyn, Bernard, *Education in the Forming of American Society: Needs and Opportunities for Study.* Chapel Hill, 1960.
This essay corrects earlier, mistaken notions as to whether the colonial colleges were state or private (denominational) institutions by showing the nature of their relationship to the sources of public support.

Baker, Ray Stannard, *Woodrow Wilson, Life and Letters: Princeton, 1890-1910.* Garden City, N.Y., 1927.

Bardolph, Richard, *Agricultural Literature and the Early Illinois Farmer.* Urbana, 1948.

Bateman, Newton, and Paul Selby, *An Historical Encyclopedia of Illinois.* 2 vols. Chicago, 1905.
Contains helpful information, and some good illustrations of experiment farms and University buildings.

Bates, Ralph S., *Scientific Societies in the United States.* New York, 1945.

Beal, W. J., *History of the Michigan Agricultural College.* East Lansing, 1915.

Belting, Natalia M., *The Beginnings: Champaign in the 1850's and 1860's.* [Champaign], 1960.

Bennett, Charles Alpheus, *History of Manual and Industrial Education up to 1870.* Peoria, 1926.
———, *History of Manual and Industrial Education, 1870-1917.* Peoria, 1937.

Berman, Milton, *John Fiske: The Evolution of a Popularizer.* Cambridge, Mass., 1961.

Bevier, Isabel, *Home Economics in Education.* Philadelphia, 1924.

Bishop, Morris, *A History of Cornell.* Ithaca, 1962.

Blackmar, Frank W., *The History of Federal and State Aid to Higher Education in the United States.* U.S. Bureau of Education, Circular of Information No. 1, 1890. Washington, 1890.

Bogart, Ernest L., and Charles M. Thompson, *The Industrial State, 1870-1893.* The Centennial History of Illinois, IV. Chicago, 1922.

Bonner, Thomas N., *Medicine in Chicago, 1850-1950: A Chapter in the Social and Scientific Development of a City.* Madison, 1957.
Well done, and helpful.

Bosworth, F. H., Jr., and Roy Childs Jones, *A Study of Architectural Schools.* New York, 1932.

Brink, McDonough & Co., *History of Champaign County, Illinois.* Philadelphia, 1878.

Bronson, Walter C., *The History of Brown University, 1864-1914*. Providence, 1914.

Brown, S. W., *The Secularization of American Education*. Teacher's College, Columbia University, Contributions to Education No. 49. New York, 1912.

Brubacher, John S., and S. Willis Rudy, *Higher Education in Transition*. New York, 1958.

A general but useful survey of the subject.

Butts, R. Freeman, *The College Charts Its Course: Historical Conceptions and Current Proposals*. New York, 1939.

A broad-gauged and valuable history of the curriculum in American higher education which is written from a "progressive" bias that makes some of the interpretations suspect.

————, and Lawrence A. Cremin, *A History of Education in American Culture*. New York, 1953.

Carriel, Mary Turner, *The Life of Jonathan Baldwin Turner*. n.p., 1911; 2nd ed., Urbana, 1961.

Turner's daughter wrote a loving biography which is helpful on some details, but the work should be used with the greatest caution. What Turner really needs is a good critical biography which shows the full range of the man and does not exploit him for partisan purposes. The revised edition of this book served no useful scholarly purpose.

Chittenden, Russell H., *History of the Sheffield Scientific School of Yale University, 1846-1922*. 2 vols. New Haven, 1928.

Coates, Charles Penney, *History of the Manual Training School of Washington University*. U.S. Bureau of Education, Bulletin No. 3, 1923. Washington, 1923.

Cole, Arthur C., *The Era of the Civil War, 1848-1870*. The Centennial History of Illinois, III. Chicago, 1922.

Cook, John Williston, *Educational History of Illinois*. Chicago, 1912.

Coulson, Thomas, *Joseph Henry: His Life and Work*. Princeton, 1950.

Cremin, Lawrence A., *The Transformation of the School: Progressivism in American Education, 1876-1957*. New York, 1961.

An excellent work, and especially helpful in putting the development of instruction in shop practice at Illinois in context.

Curoe, Philip R. V., *Educational Attitudes and Policies of Organized Labor in the United States*. New York, 1926.

Curti, Merle, and Vernon Carstensen, *The University of Wisconsin: A History, 1848-1925*. 2 vols. Madison, 1949.

[Cutting, George Rugg], *Student Life at Amherst College: Its Organizations, Their Membership and History*. Amherst, 1871.

Of special use in showing the influence of the literary societies in a New England college.

DeBlois, Austen Kennedy, *The Pioneer School: A History of Shurtleff College, the Oldest Institution in the West*. Chicago, 1900.
Helpful in depicting life in a denominational college in Illinois. The author, President of Shurtleff from 1894 to 1899, says that the state University first became a competitor to Shurtleff in the 1890's.

DeGarmo, Charles, *Herbart and the Herbartians*. New York, 1896.

Demaree, Albert Lowther, *The American Agricultural Press, 1819-1860*. Columbia University Studies in the History of Agriculture, No. 8. New York, 1941.

Drake, William E., *The American School in Transition*. Englewood Cliffs, N.J., 1955.

Dupree, A. Hunter, *Science in the Federal Government: A History of Policies and Activities to 1940*. Cambridge, Mass., 1957.
An excellent work and invaluable in understanding the development of science, which often complemented and often conflicted with the land-grant movement leading to the Morrill Act.

Eddy, Edward D., Jr., *Colleges for Our Land and Time: The Land-Grant Idea in American Education*. New York, 1956.

Eells, Walter Crosby, *Baccalaureate Degrees Conferred by American Colleges in the 17th and 18th Centuries*. Washington, 1958.

Eliot, Charles W., *Educational Reform*. New York, 1909.
Contains Eliot's inaugural address as President of Harvard College.

Elliott, Edward C., and M. M. Chambers, comps., *Charters and Basic Laws of Selected American Universities and Colleges*. New York, 1934.

—— and ——, *The Colleges and the Courts: Judicial Decisions Regarding Institutions of Higher Education in the United States*. New York, 1936.

Fay, Jay Wharton, *American Psychology Before William James*. New Brunswick, 1939.

Ferrier, William Warren, *Origin and Development of the University of California*. Berkeley, 1930.

Fleming, Donald, *William H. Welch and the Rise of Modern Medicine*. Boston, 1954.

Fox, Dixon Ryan, *Union College: An Unfinished History*. Schenectady, n.d.
The book describes Union College during Gregory's days there as a student.

Fuess, Claude Moore, *Amherst: The Story of a New England College*. Boston, 1935.

Fulton, John, *Memoirs of Frederick A. P. Barnard*. New York, 1896.
Apart from its general value in showing the progressive liberali-

zation of Barnard's educational ideas, the book mentions the influence of the Illinois experiment in student government upon Barnard, who tried to introduce it in the early 1880's at Columbia College in New York City.

Gabriel, Ralph Henry, *Religion and Learning at Yale: The Church of Christ in the College and University, 1757-1957*. New Haven, 1958.

Gates, Paul W., *The Wisconsin Pine Lands of Cornell University: A Study in Land Policy and Absentee Ownership*. Ithaca, 1943. This book touches on Illinois' disposition of the land grant provided by the first Morrill Act and illuminates the whole subject.

Ginger, Ray, *Altgeld's America: The Lincoln Ideal* VERSUS *Changing Realities*. New York, 1958.

Girling, Katherine Peabody, *Selim Hobart Peabody, a Biography*. Urbana, 1923. A somewhat defensive but restrained and helpful account by a daughter.

Goode, George Brown, ed., *The Smithsonian Institution, 1846-1896: The History of Its First Half Century*. Washington, 1897.

Goodsell, Charles True, and Willis Frederick Dunbar, *Centennial History of Kalamazoo College*. Kalamazoo, 1933.

Gregory, Allene, *John Milton Gregory: A Biography*. Chicago, 1923. An admiring account by a daughter of Gregory and his second wife. Its greatest value is in extensive quotations from diaries kept by Gregory which have not been located.

Gregory, Grant, *Ancestors and Descendants of Henry Gregory*. Provincetown, Mass., 1938. The author was a son of John M. Gregory, and the book is a useful reference.

[Halliday, Samuel D., comp.], *History of the Agricultural College Land Grant of July 2, 1862*. Ithaca, 1890.

Hamilton, John, *History of Farmers' Institutes in the United States*. U.S. Department of Agriculture, Office of Experiment Stations, Bulletin No. 174. Washington, 1906.

Hansen, Allen Oscar, *Liberalism and American Education in the Eighteenth Century*. New York, 1926.

Hawkins, Hugh, *Pioneer: A History of the Johns Hopkins University, 1874-1889*. Ithaca, 1960. An excellent example of a type of scholarship which will go far in redeeming the study of higher education in America.

Healey, Robert M., *Jefferson on Religion in Public Education*. New Haven, 1962. An important corrective to the many partisan and erroneous views on the subject.

Henderson, Joseph Lindsey, *Admission to College by Certificate*. New York, 1912.

Hepburn, William Murray, and Louis Martin Sears, *Purdue University: Fifty Years of Progress*. Indianapolis, 1925.
The subtitle is not really a clue to this prosaic work.

Hofstadter, Richard, and C. DeWitt Hardy, *The Development and Scope of Higher Education in the United States*. New York, 1952.
This book includes a treatment of professional education.

————, and Walter P. Metzger, *The Development of Academic Freedom in the United States*. New York, 1955.
Excellent in its range and interpretations.

Honeywell, Roy J., *The Educational Work of Thomas Jefferson*. Cambridge, Mass., 1931.
An important and basic study, now somewhat dated.

James, Edmund J., *The Origin of the Land Grant Act of 1862 (the So-Called Morrill Act) and Some Account of Its Author, Jonathan B. Turner*. University of Illinois Studies, IV, No. 1. Urbana, 1910.
An example of special pleading in which the facts are made to fit the thesis.

Johnson, Henry, *The Other Side of Main Street*. New York, 1943.

Jordan, David Starr, *The Trend of the American University*. Stanford, 1929.

Kirkpatrick, John E., *Academic Organization and Control*. Yellow Springs, Ohio, 1931.
The Introduction has a good summary of the historical development of control of American institutions of higher education by lay, nonresident boards of trustees. The author strongly opposed this system of governing American colleges and universities, and his personal bias obtrudes.

Knight, George W., *History and Management of Land Grants for Education in the Northwest Territory*. Papers of the American Historical Association, I, No. 3. New York, 1885.

Knoblauch, H. C., E. M. Law, W. P. Meyer, *et al.*, *State Agricultural Experiment Stations: A History of Research Policy and Procedure*. U.S. Department of Agriculture, Misc. Pub. No. 904. Washington, 1962.

Kuhn, Madison, *Michigan State: The First Hundred Years, 1855-1955*. East Lansing, 1955.

Lewis, Lloyd, *John S. Wright, Prophet of the Prairies*. Chicago, 1941.

Lewis, R. W. B., *The American Adam: Innocence, Tragedy, and Tradition in the Nineteenth Century*. Chicago, 1955.

Lurie, Edward, *Louis Agassiz, a Life in Science*. Chicago, 1960.

Magoun, George F., *Asa Turner: A Home Missionary Patriarch*. Boston, 1889.
> The volume is valuable for understanding Jonathan B. Turner's early family life and the secular and religious history of Illinois in the 1830's.

Marshall, Helen E., *Grandest of Enterprises, Illinois State Normal University, 1857-1957*. Normal, 1956.

Marx, Leo, *The Machine in the Garden: Technology and the Pastoral Idea in America*. New York, 1964.

Matthiessen, F. O., *American Renaissance: Art and Expression in the Age of Emerson and Whitman*. New York, 1941.

Miller, Perry, *The Life of the Mind in America: From the Revolution to the Civil War*. New York, 1965.

Morgan, William H., *Student Religion During Fifty Years: Programs and Policies of the Intercollegiate Y.M.C.A.* New York, 1935.

Morison, Samuel Eliot, *Three Centuries of Harvard, 1636-1936*. Cambridge, Mass., 1936.

Morrison, Hugh, *Louis Sullivan, Prophet of Modern Architecture*. New York, 1935.

Morse, Richard C., *History of the North American Young Men's Christian Associations*. New York, 1922.

Moulton, Forest Ray, ed., *Liebig and After Liebig: A Century of Progress in Agricultural Chemistry*. Washington, 1942.

Nate, Joseph C., *The History of the Sigma Chi Fraternity, 1855-1930*. 4 vols. n.p., 1925-31.

Nevins, Allan, *Illinois*. New York, 1917.
> The only general history of the University heretofore in print, this brief account covers the first half-century of development. It reads well but was of little use. Its focus is narrow, its interpretations often questionable or untenable, and I found too many errors to feel confidence in putting my trust in the book's facts.

————, *The State Universities and Democracy*. Urbana, 1962.
> A short and useful statement.

Newcomer, Mabel, *A Century of Higher Education for American Women*. New York, 1959.

Odgers, Merle M., *Alexander Dallas Bache: Scientist and Educator, 1806-1867*. Philadelphia, 1947.
> A tidy and competent book whose usefulness is limited by the lack of documentation and very brief bibliography.

Osborn, Herbert, *Fragments of Entomological History, Including Some Personal Recollections of Men and Events*. Columbus, 1937.
> This book gives a brief history of entomology in the United

States and includes in its biographical data information on
Stephen A. Forbes.

Paine, A. E., *The Granger Movement in Illinois*. University of Illinois
Studies, I, No. 8. Urbana, 1904.

Parker, William Belmont, *The Life and Public Service of Justin Smith
Morrill*. Boston, 1924.

Patton, Cornelius Howard, and Walter Taylor Field, *Eight O'Clock
Chapel: A Study of New England College Life in the Eighties*.
Boston, 1927.
Valuable in showing the tensions in American higher education
in the 1880's.

Pease, Theodore Calvin, *The Frontier State, 1818-1848*. The Centennial History of Illinois, II. Chicago, 1922.

————, *The Story of Illinois*. 3rd ed., rev. by Marguerite Jenison Pease.
Chicago, 1965.

Peisch, Mark L., *The Chicago School of Architecture: Early Followers
of Sullivan and Wright*. Columbia University Studies in Art
History and Archaeology, No. 5. New York, 1964.
A study of architectural events centering around Chicago from
1893 to 1914 which treats Ricker and many architectural graduates of the University of Illinois. There are many small errors
in details relating to the University, and I cannot follow all of
the author's interpretations.

Periam, Jonathan, *The Groundswell: A History of the Origin, Aims,
and Progress of the Farmers' Movement*. St. Louis, 1874.

Perry, Charles M., *Henry Philip Tappan: Philosopher and University
President*. Ann Arbor, 1933.
The book not only describes Tappan as an educational reformer
but also shows conditions in Michigan higher education during
Gregory's residence there.

Pierson, George W., *Yale College: An Educational History, 1871-1921*.
New Haven, 1952.

Potter, David, *Debating in the Colonial Chartered Colleges, an Historical Survey, 1642 to 1900*. Teachers College, Columbia University, Contributions to Education No. 899. New York, 1944.

Powell, Burt E., *Semi-Centennial History of the University of Illinois, I:
The Movement for Industrial Education and the Establishment
of the University, 1840-1870*. Urbana, 1918.
A diffuse and undigested volume which is essentially a detailed
history of the land-grant education movement in Illinois. The
Appendix contains many valuable documents.

Prescott, Samuel C., *When M.I.T. was "Boston Tech," 1861-1916*.
Cambridge, Mass., 1954.

Rammelkamp, Charles Henry, *Illinois College: A Centennial History,
1829-1929*. [New Haven], 1928.

Raymond, Andrew V., *Union University: Its History, Influence, Characteristics and Equipment.* 3 vols. New York, 1907.
More a compilation than a history, but the first volume includes a history of Eliphalet Nott's regime at Union.

Reber, Louis E., *University Extension in the United States.* Washington, 1914.

Richardson, James D., ed., *A Compilation of the Messages and Papers of the Presidents, 1789-1897,* V. 10 vols. Washington, 1896-99.

Ricketts, Palmer C., *History of Rensselaer Polytechnic Institute, 1824-1914.* 3rd ed. New York, 1914.

Roberts, Howard, *The Big Nine: The Story of Football in the Western Conference.* New York, 1948.

Rogers, Walter P., *Andrew D. White and the Modern University.* Ithaca, 1942.
A somewhat thin book which evaluates White as a leader of American higher education in the late nineteeth century.

Ross, Earle D., *Democracy's College: The Land-Grant Movement in the Formative Stage.* Ames, Iowa, 1942.
A meticulous study which covers the period down to 1890.

Rudolph, Frederick, *The American College and University: A History.* New York, 1962.
The most recent general survey of the subject, the book is well done, contains an excellent bibliography, and was enormously helpful.

Rusk, Robert R., *The Doctrines of the Great Educators.* Rev. ed. London, 1955.
A short, solid account.

Savage, Howard J., et al., *American College Athletics.* New York, 1929.
A classic study.

Schmidt, George Paul, *The Liberal Arts College: A Chapter in American Cultural History.* New Brunswick, 1957.

——, *The Old Time College President.* New York, 1930.
The authoritative treatment of the subject.

Scott, Franklin W., ed., *The Alumni Record of the University of Illinois.* Urbana, 1906.
A useful reference on individual students, trustees, and faculty members.

——, ed., *Newspapers and Periodicals of Illinois, 1814-1879.* Collections of the Illinois State Historical Library, VI. n.p., 1910.

——, ed., *The Semi-Centennial Alumni Record of the University of Illinois.* [Urbana], 1918.

Sheldon, Henry Davidson, *The History and Pedagogy of Amercian Student Societies.* New York, 1901.

Sigerist, Henry E., *American Medicine,* tr. Hildegard Nagel. New York, 1934.

Slater, C. P., *History of the Land Grant Endowment of the University of Illinois.* Urbana, 1940.

Smallwood, William Martin, *Natural History and the American Mind.* New York, 1941.

Smith, Erwin F., *Bacteria in Relation to Plant Diseases,* II. 3 vols. Washington, 1905-14.

Smith, Henry Nash, *Virgin Land: The American West as Symbol and Myth.* Cambridge, Mass., 1950.

Snow, Louis Franklin, *The College Curriculum in the United States.* New York, 1907.

Storr, Richard J., *The Beginnings of Graduate Education in America.* Chicago, 1953.

    A careful examination of the subject in the period down to the emergence of the modern American university.

———, *Harper's University, the Beginnings: A History of the University of Chicago.* Chicago, 1966.

    An excellently researched and well-written study.

Taft, Ada Bartlett, *Lorado Taft: Sculptor and Citizen.* Greensboro, N.C., 1946.

Tallmadge, Thomas E., *The Story of Architecture in America.* New York, 1927.

Tewksbury, Donald G., *The Founding of American Colleges and Universities Before the Civil War: With Particular Reference to the Religious Influences Bearing upon the College Movement.* Teachers College, Columbia University, Contributions to Education No. 543. New York, 1932.

Thorpe, Francis Newton, ed., *The Federal and State Constitutions,* II. 7 vols. Washington, 1909.

Torrey, James, *The Remains of the Rev. James Marsh, D.D., Late President, and Professor of Moral and Intellectual Philosophy, in the University of Vermont; with a Memoir of His Life.* Boston, 1843.

True, Alfred Charles, *A History of Agricultural Education in the United States, 1785-1925.* U.S. Department of Agriculture, Misc. Pub. No. 36. Washington, 1929.

———, *A History of Agricultural Experimentation and Research in the United States, 1607-1925.* U.S. Department of Agriculture, Misc. Pub. No. 251. Washington, 1937.

Tyack, David B., *George Ticknor and the Boston Brahmins.* Cambridge, Mass., 1967.

U.S. Bureau of Education, *Historical Sketch of Union College.* Washington, 1876.

U.S. Centennial Commission, *International Exhibition, 1876,* I, VIII.
8 vols. Washington, 1880.
These two volumes contain information on the University and
on Gregory at the Centennial Exposition in Philadelphia.

Van Santvoord, C., and Tayler Lewis, *Memoirs of Eliphalet Nott, D.D.,
LL.D.* New York, 1876.

Veysey, Laurence R., *The Emergence of the American University.* Chicago, 1965.
A leading example of the critical and perceptive studies of
American higher education which are beginning to appear. I
read this work, which treats the period from 1865 to 1910, when
it was still an unpublished doctoral dissertation (University of
California, Berkeley, 1961) with the subtitle: "A Study in the
Relations Between Ideals and Institutions." The work barely
mentions Illinois, since there was no worthy book in print which
the author could consult, but it proved extremely useful for comparative purposes.

Viles, Jonas, *The University of Missouri: A Centennial History, 1839-
1939.* Columbia, Mo., 1939.

Welter, Rush, *Popular Education and Democratic Thought in America.*
New York, 1962.

Wertenbaker, Thomas Jefferson, *Princeton, 1746-1896.* Princeton, 1946.

Willey, Basil, *The Seventeenth Century Background: Studies in the
Thought of the Age in Relation to Poetry and Religion.* London,
1934.

ARTICLES

Adams, Charles Kendall, "Review of *American State Universities,
Their Origin and Progress,* by Andrew Ten Brook," *North
American Review,* CXXI (Oct., 1875), 365-408.

Adams, Herbert B., "University Extension and Its Leaders," *Review of
Reviews,* III (July, 1891), 593-609.

Ahlstrom, Sydney E., "The Scottish Philosophy and American Theology," *Church History,* XXIV (Sept., 1955), 257-72.

Anderson, L. F., "The Manual Labor School Movement," *Educational
Review,* XLVI (Nov., 1913), 369-86.

Atherton, George W., "The Legislative Career of Justin S. Morrill,"
*Proceedings of the Fourteenth Annual Convention of the Asso-
ciation of American Agricultural Colleges and Experiment Stations, 1900,* U.S. Department of Agriculture, Office of Experiment Stations, Bulletin No. 99 (Washington, 1901), 60-72; also
separately printed: Washington, 1901.

Bannister, Turpin C., "Pioneering in Architectural Education," *Journal of the American Institute of Architects,* XX (July, 1953), 3-8; (Aug., 1953), 76-81.

A helpful article, although it contains many errors.

Bascom, John, "Atheism in Colleges," *North American Review,* CXXXII (Jan., 1881), 32-40.

Carrier, Lyman, "The United States Agricultural Society, 1852-1860: Its Relation to the Origin of the United States Department of Agriculture and the Land Grant Colleges," *Agricultural History,* XI (Oct., 1937), 278-88.

"Clark Robinson Griggs and the Location of the University," *Alumni Quarterly and Fortnightly Notes,* I (Oct. 15, 1915), 17-22.

Comey, Arthur M., "Growth of the Colleges of the United States," *Educational Review,* III (Feb., 1892), 120-31.

Cowley, W. H., "European Influences upon American Higher Education," *Educational Record,* XX (April, 1939), 165-90.

A good survey of the subject from colonial times onward.

———, "The Government and Administration of American Higher Education: Whence and Whither?" *Journal of the American Association of Collegiate Registrars,* XXII (July, 1947), 477-91.

This article traces the role of the faculty, alumni, students, and administration since the Civil War.

Cunningham, Joseph O., "The Genesis of Our Campus," *Alumni Quarterly,* IX (Jan., 1915), 18-21.

Curti, Merle, "America at the World Fairs," *American Historical Review,* LV (July, 1950), 833-56.

Davenport, Eugene, "History of Collegiate Education in Agriculture," Society for the Promotion of Agricultural Science, *Proceedings,* XXVIII (Lansing, 1907), 43-53.

Davenport's attempt to demonstrate that Jonathan B. Turner deserves credit for the land-grant college idea.

Dodge, Daniel K., "English at the University of Illinois," *Dial,* XVI (May 1, 1894), 261-62.

Eliot, Charles W., "National University," National Educational Association, *Journal of Proceedings and Addresses, 1873* (Peoria, 1873), 107-20.

Gates, Paul W., "Western Opposition to the Agricultural College Act," *Indiana Magazine of History,* XXXVII (March, 1941), 101-36.

This article contributes significantly to an understanding of economic and sectional influences in the legislative struggle leading to the Morrill Act.

Goode, George Brown, "The Origin of the National Scientific and Educational Institutions of the United States," American Historical Association, *Annual Report, 1889* (Washington, 1890), 53-161.

Hawkins, Hugh, "Charles W. Eliot, University Reform, and Religious Faith in America, 1869-1909," *Journal of American History*, LI (Sept., 1964), 191-213.

Hildner, Ernest G., "Colleges and College Life in Illinois One Hundred Years Ago," Illinois State Historical Society, *Papers in Illinois History and Transactions, 1942* (Springfield, 1944), 19-31.

———, "Higher Education in Transition, 1850-1870," *Journal of the Illinois State Historical Society*, LVI (Spring, 1963), 61-73.

Holmes, Bayard, "Medical Education in Chicago in 1882 and After: VI. An Adventure in Education," *Medical Life*, XXIX (Jan., 1922), 30-41.

Howe, Stewart S., "The Early Fraternity History at the University of Illinois," *Banta's Greek Exchange*, XVI (Oct., 1928), 300-303. Much of this article is taken directly from Heath's account, but there is some additional material on the period after 1891.

James, Edmund J., "The Life and Labors of Jonathan B. Turner," *Journal of the Illinois State Historical Society*, VIII (April, 1915), 7-22.

———, "The Life and Work of Dr. John Milton Gregory," *Alumni Quarterly*, VIII (Oct., 1914), 241-52. James rated his predecessor highly for insisting that the University of Illinois become a true university, and berated the laggardness of Illinois in higher education.

———, "The Origin of the Land Grant Bill," *Nation*, LXXXVII (Dec. 31, 1908), 649.

———, "The Services of Richard Yates to Public Education," *Journal of the Illinois State Historical Society*, V (Jan., 1913), 481-85.

Janvrin, C. E., comp., "The Scientific Writings of Thomas J. Burrill," Illinois State Horticultural Society, *Transactions for 1917*, n.s., LI (Bloomington, [1917]), 195-201.

Kimball, Sydney F., "The Department of Architecture: Development, Condition, Ideals," *Alumni Quarterly*, VII (April, 1913), 87-96.

McCosh, James, "Upper Schools," National Educational Association, *Journal of Proceedings and Addresses, 1873* (Peoria, 1873), 19-35, 43-44.

McGrath, Earl James, "The Control of Higher Education in America," *Educational Record*, XVII (April, 1936), 259-72. This article traces the shifting character in the origins of American trustees from 1860 to 1930, showing the decline of ministers and the rise of businessmen, bankers, and lawyers. McGrath urges the inclusion of more educators on such bodies and makes the test of a governing board's effectiveness its protection of established principles of academic freedom.

Mathews, Joseph J., "The Study of History in the South," *Journal of Southern History,* XXXI (Feb., 1965), 3-20.

Pease, Theodore Calvin, "Stephen Alfred Forbes, 1844-1930," *Journal of the Illinois State Historical Society,* XXIII (Oct., 1930), 543-48.

Pillsbury, William L., "Historical Sketches of the State Normal Universities and the University of Illinois," in Superintendent of Public Instruction of the State of Illinois, *Seventeenth Biennial Report* (Springfield, 1889), lxxvii-cxvi.

———, "The Influence of Government Land Grants for Educational Purposes upon the Educational System of the State," Illinois State Historical Society, *Transactions for 1901,* Illinois State Historical Library Pub. No. 6 (Springfield, 1901), 30-40.

Pritchett, Henry S., "The College of Discipline and the College of Freedom," *Atlantic Monthly,* CII (Nov., 1908), 603-11.

Quine, William E., "History of the College of Physicians and Surgeons of Chicago," *Plexus,* XVII (July 20, 1911), 255-65.

Ranck, Samuel H., "Alumni Representation in College Government," *Education,* XXII (Oct., 1901), 107-13.

Rider, Fremont, "The Growth of the American College and University Libraries — and of Wesleyan's," *About Books,* XI (Sept., 1940), 1-11.

Roelker, William G., "Francis Wayland: A Neglected Pioneer of Higher Education," American Antiquarian Society, *Proceedings,* LIII (April, 1944), 27-98.

Ross, Earle D., "The 'Father' of the Land-Grant College," *Agricultural History,* XII (April, 1938), 151-86.
A model of judicious and critical historical scholarship which examines the role of Jonathan B. Turner and of Justin S. Morrill and concludes that the rival claims made for both men are not fully substantiated. The article properly gives short shrift to the extravagant assertions made for Turner by writers associated with the University of Illinois.

———, "The Land-Grant College: a Democratic Adaptation," *Agricultural History,* XV (Jan., 1914), 26-36.

———, "The Manual Labor Experiment in the Land Grant College," *Mississippi Valley Historical Review,* XXI (March, 1935), 513-28.

———, "Religious Influences in the Development of State Colleges and Universities," *Indiana Magazine of History,* XLVI (Dec., 1950), 343-62.

Rudy, S. Willis, "The 'Revolution' in American Higher Education, 1865-1900," *Harvard Educational Review,* XXI (Summer, 1951), 155-73.

Runkle, John D., "The Manual Element in Education," [Massachusetts]

Board of Education, *Forty-first Annual Report, 1876-1877* (Boston, 1878), 185-218.

Schmidt, George Paul, "Colleges in Ferment," *American Historical Review,* LIX (Oct., 1953), 19-42.
  Schmidt treats the forces at work in the last half of the nineteenth century.

———, "Intellectual Crosscurrents in American Colleges, 1825-1855," *American Historical Review,* XLII (Oct., 1936), 46-67.

Shryock, Richard H., "American Indifference to Basic Science During the Nineteenth Century," *Archives Internationales d'Histoire des Sciences,* V (1948), 50-65.
  The author attributes the indifference to growing specialization (and thus professionalization) of science and to the rise of a democratic society in which people did not see any reason to support pure science because it did not seem to offer any practical value.

Simon, John Y., "The Politics of the Morrill Act," *Agricultural History,* XXXVII (April, 1963), 103-11.

Smith, Annie Tolman, "Progress of Education for Women," *Report of the Secretary of Interior,* 42 Cong., 2 Sess., House Exec. Doc. No. 1 (Washington, 1872), 514-16.

Smith, George W., "The Old Illinois Agricultural College," *Journal of the Illinois State Historical Society,* V (Jan., 1913), 475-80.

Solberg, Winton U., "The Conflict Between Religion and Secularism at the University of Illinois, 1867-1894," *American Quarterly,* XVIII (Summer, 1966), 183-99.

———, "The University of Illinois and the Reform of Discipline in the Modern University, 1868-1891," American Association of University Professors, *Bulletin,* LII (Sept., 1966), 305-14.

———, "The University of Illinois Struggles for Public Recognition, 1867-1894," *Journal of the Illinois State Historical Society,* LIX (Spring, 1966), 5-29.

Stevens, Neil E., "The Centenary of T. J. Burrill," *Scientific Monthly,* XLIX (Sept., 1939), 288-92.

Turner, Fred H., "Misconceptions Concerning the Early History of the University of Illinois," Illinois State Historical Society, *Transactions for 1932,* Illinois State Historical Library Pub. No. 39 (n.p., n.d.), 63-90.

"University Faculty in 1869-1870," *Alumni Quarterly,* VII (Oct., 1913), 266-71.

Waterman, Richard, Jr., "Educational Exhibits at the Columbian Exposition," *Educational Review,* VII (Feb., 1894), 129-40.

Wilson, Woodrow, "What Is a College For?" *Scribner's,* XLVI (Nov., 1909), 570-77.

Index

changes, 129; and degrees, 165; divided, 270; enrollment in, 109, 266

Andrews, C. N.: and Rockford Committee, 66n

Andrus, Dora A.: student body president, 282

Angell, James B.: and election of trustees, 230

Anglo-Saxon: and School of English and Modern Languages, 267

Ann Arbor, Michigan: and baseball tour, 382

Anniversary Day: description of, 198; exercises omitted, 311n; founding of, 194; and literary societies, 198

Anthrax: and R. Koch, 153

Anthropology: offered, 350

Anticlericalism: and chartering of colleges in Illinois, 18

Anti-intellectualism: and "The American Scholar," 28-29; and Jacksonian democracy, 31; and land-grant college movement, 29

Apple blight: T. J. Burrill's experiments on, 138-39

Apprentice training: compared to college course, 141

Appropriations: and J. P. Altgeld, 338-40; and T. J. Burrill, 342; for Drill Hall, 223; drive to increase, 337-38; failure to provide, 115; importance of, 340; increase in, 340; legislative action on, 339-40; for library, 372; for Natural History Building, 224; for State Laboratory of Natural History, 224; for University, 111, 114, 124, 223-24, 339

Architectural Association: formation of, 300

Architectural Designing: and architecture curriculum, 264

Architectural Perspective: course introduced, 264

Architectural planning: and Union College, 87; and University of Illinois, 93

Architecture: and agriculture curriculum, 239; and J. W. Bellangee, 146; after Civil War, 262; and College of Engineering, 148; and Department of Civil Engineering, 145; foundations solid, 166; and J. M. Gregory, 90, 171; growth of, 262-65, 348; and higher education, 145; and mechanical engineering shop practice, 149; and N. C. Ricker, 148; and Russian system, 149; and School of Art and Design, 360; standards improved, 263; first student in, 146; and University, 263, 391. *See also* Engineering, architectural

Architecture, Aesthetics of: and architecture curriculum, 264

Architecture, Department of: and Builder's Course, 149; course content, 149; curriculum, 263-65; early years, 147-48; enrollment, 150, 254, 263; evolution of, 263-66; formation of, 145; graduates of, 150; and nonresident lecturers, 264-65; and practical training, 148-49; N. C. Ricker becomes Head of, 147; shop practice in, 149; and S. W. Stratton, 257; outstanding students in, 265

Architecture, History of: and architecture curriculum, 264; offered, 148

Architecture and Fine Arts, Department of: and College of Engineering, 107

Aristotelianism: and mental philosophy, 8

Arkansas: lacks state university, 6n

Arkansas, University of: number of cadets at, 375n

Armenia: students from, 131

Armour Institute of Technology: establishes architecture school, 263

Arms, Frank D.: and football tour, 382-83; and R. Lackey, 379; and Western College Press Association,

Boston Symphony: and "lecture course," 379

Botanical Garden: and T. J. Burrill, 139

Botany: and agriculture curriculum, 239; and T. J. Burrill, 102, 106, 152, 153, 251; courses in, 153; and S. A. Forbes's writings, 249n; foundations solid, 166; funds for laboratory, 124; and Literature and Science, 267; microscopes introduced, 154; and natural history, 108, 150; and old-time college curriculum, 8; and C. W. Rolfe, 250; and summer school, 369; and University, 391

Botany, Department of: and T. J. Burrill, 350

Bouton, Jerry: and class fights, 311

Bowdoin College: and W. M. Baker, 99; and extracurricular activities, 275; and J. L. Pickard, 85, 157

Boxing: forbidden, 204; and rise of sports, 204

Boyd, Comma N.: and class conflict, 283-84

Brayman, Mason: and Committee on Course of Study and Faculty, 87; and military program, 82; military training plan of, 97; and state funds, 86

Breckinridge, Lester P.: and mechanical engineering, 349

Bribery: charges in location bids, 79-80

Bridge, Arthur M.: and class conflicts, 284; and Sigma Chi, 285

Bridges: and curriculum changes, 129

Bromby Collection: University fails to get, 151

Bross, William (Lieutenant Governor): and C. R. Griggs, 76

Brown, Alexander M.: biography, 120; defends disinterested learning, 82; and J. M Gregory, 120, on Regent's duties, 127

Brown University: land scrip yield of, 94; reverts to old curriculum,

26; H. Tappan on reforms at, 26; and F. Wayland, 25, 27-28

Browning, Orville H. (Senator): and Morrill Act, 57

Brownlee, James H.: appointed, 270; and Committee on Advertisement and Publications, 337n

Bruner, James D.: appointed, 357

Bryant, Jennie C.: appointed, 196; salary arrangements for, 196

Bryant, John H.: elected trustee, 338; opposes S. H. Peabody, 324

Bryn Mawr: and K. Merrill, 352

Buchanan, James (President): veto of and old-time college, 58; vetoes Morrill Act, 56

Buel, Jesse: and state agricultural college movement, 37

Buel Institute: Farmers' Bill opposed by, 72; substitutes university plan, 72; J. B. Turner's address to, 43-44; university organization bill opposed, 72

Builder's Course: adopted from German model, 149; aim of, 149; and Department of Architecture, 149; dropped, 264

Buildings: appropriations asked for, 339; botany laboratory, 124; Chemistry Laboratory, 124, 125, 150, 263; design of and N. C. Ricker, 147; dormitory, 170; Drill Hall, 223, 263; early improvements, 93; Engineering Hall, 348; greenhouse, 124; Library, 263; new main, 114; Mechanical Building and Drill Hall, 107, 114, 143; Natural History Building, 224, 263; Natural Science Building, 350; need for, 339; State Laboratory of Natural History, 224; University Hall, 115; Woman's Building, 354

Bullard, George W.: *Illini* editor, 291; on local temperance victory, 302

Bullard, Samuel A.: advice of, 204; and architecture, 265; and Board of Trustees, criticizes appointments, 231, elected to, 232, nominated for,

to, 39, 242; and federal government, 237; and W. C. Flagg, 72, 87, 237; friends of lose hope for University, 227; and J. M. Gregory, 237; and Hatch Act, 241; and H. Howard's plan, 39; and Illinois State Agricultural Society, 63; and Illinois State Horticultural Society, 63; and Illinois State Teachers' Association, 63; and industrial education movement, 388; and Industrial League, 52; interest in grows, 39; and Knox College, 60-61; leaders avoid discussion of curriculum, 63; and manual labor, 39; J. S. Morrill on, 57-58; and Morrill Act, 54, 55, 57-58, second, 242; and G. E. Morrow, 134, 237, 345-47, 348; movement for, 23-24; and S. H. Peabody, 237; pioneer schools, 37; and *Prairie Farmer,* 46; early problems in, 105, 132-40; and public lands, 47; and E. Pugh, 38; and Republican platform (1860), 56; and research, 237-38; results mixed at Illinois, 241; E. Ruffin's plan, 39; and Sheffield Scientific School, 38; and short courses, 134; and Shurtleff College, 60-61; and J. S. Skinner, 47; students not attracted to, 254; support lacking, 345; and J. B. Turner, 41-42, 43, 50, 73; and United States Congressional Committee on Agriculture, 54n; University course in, 105; and University enabling act, 72, 81; and J. S. Wright, 46; and Yale, 39, 139

Education, aid to. *See* Aid to education

Education, architectural: attitudes toward, 147-48; and Chicago, 148; and Cornell University, 145; in Europe, 147; and J. M. Gregory, 145; improvement in, 263; pioneer work in, 145; and N. C. Ricker, 147-48; and J. M. Van Osdel, 145-46; and W. R. Ware, 145

Education, engineering: advances in, 140-45; at University, 140-45

Education, German: and H. Tappan, 27

Education, history of: and pedagogy, 272, 359

Education, industrial: agitation for, 23, 28; and agricultural changes, 29; agriculturalist influence, 62, 63; aims of, 40, 50; Chicago convention on, 49-50; and Chicago mechanics, 62; and classics, 49; college for supported, 63; convention called, 60; and Decatur convention, 66; and M. L. Dunlap, 95-96, 110; and R. W. Emerson, 29; and W. C. Flagg, 136-37; friends of lose hope for University, 227; and funding plans for in Illinois, 52; and General Assembly, 50, 60-62; and Granville convention, 66; and J. M. Gregory, 85; and higher education, 388; Illinois movement for, 45; and Illinois State Agricultural Society, 50; Illinois struggle for, 60-63; and Industrial League, 50, 52-53; and industrial revolution, 29-30; and J. A. Kennicott, 48; and land grant, 28, 50, 51; and A. Lincoln, 57; location plan for school of, 63; and manual-labor school movement, 28; and Morrill Act, 54, 55, 57-58; and national educational system, 44; and national welfare, 122; and normal schools, 50; organized support for, 62; and *Prairie Farmer,* 46; and public lands, 47; and public schools, 51-52; and religion, 51, 62; rural support for lacking, 46; and sectarian colleges, 48, 60; and J. Shields, 53; and Smithsonian Institution, 44, 50, 53; and Springfield convention, 50; and H. D. Thoreau, 29; and Transcendentalism, 28-29; and J. B. Turner, 23-24, 42-43, 44-45, 46, 50, 55; and J. A. Wight, 46. *See also* Manual-labor school

Education, mechanical: and industrial education movement, 388; and

Gardening, landscape: and agriculture curriculum, 239; and T. J. Burrill, 162; and J. M. Gregory's curriculum, 90; and farmers' short course, 240

Gardiner Lyceum (Maine): first agricultural school, 37; R. Gardiner founds, 37

Gardner, Daniel B.: and agricultural experiments, 137; biography, 119; meddles in Regent's duties, 119-20, 127

Garman, William H.: and S. A. Forbes, 254n

Gates, Merrill E.: student revolt against, 276

General Science and Literature, Department of: becomes College of Literature and Science, 108; courses in, 91; critics of, 108; and curriculum, 389; and J. M. Gregory, 91; early organization, 108-9

Geneva, New York: and J. C. Arthur, 155

Geography, commercial: and J. M. Gregory's curriculum, 90-91

Geometry: advanced, 267; analytical, 258; descriptive, 258; plane, 8; solid, 8

Geological collection, state: and Board of Trustees, 151, 250

Geological surveys: need for, 33

Geologist, state: and Board of Trustees, 151

Geology: and agriculture curriculum, 239, 250; and Bromby Collection, 151; government support for, 33; and J. M. Gregory's curriculum, 90; and Harvard, 32; and B. C. Jillson, 246; and mining engineering, 250-51, 261; and natural history, 251; and old-time college curriculum, 8; progress in, 250; and C. W. Rolfe, 246; and School of Natural History, 108, 150; and specimens, 250; and state collection, 250; and D. C. Taft, 108, 151; teaching of, 151

Geology, Department of: and C. W. Rolfe, 350

Geology and Zoology, Department of: condition of, 245

German: and chemistry curriculum, 243; early class in, 109; course in, 266; and Department of General Science and Literature, 108; faculty added, 357; and general education courses, 98; and School of English and Modern Languages, 270; and E. Snyder, 102, 156, 267

Germany: and agricultural education, 38; and architectural education, 147; and W. F. Bliss, 102; and Builder's Course, 149; and J. M. Gregory, 122; and S. W. Johnson, 39; students in, 366; students from, 131

Gibson, Charles B.: and Alumni Association, 226; and endowment drive, 228

Gilbert, Sir Joseph Henry: and M. Miles, 106, 135

Gilman, Daniel C.: and J. M. Gregory, 90, 121; and modern university, 84; and University of California, 128n; and University of Illinois, 121n

Gladden, Washington: considered for Regent, 330

Glee Club: and student activities, 309, 379

Going, Judson F.: and Alumni Association, 226; attacks Regent and Faculty, 287-89; graduation denied, 289; and oratorical society factions, 297; State Militia commission withheld, 289; and University name change, 227

Golf: introduced, 312; and rise of sports, 204

Goltra, Moore C.: and University lands, 94

Goodrich, Samuel: and children's natural history books, 217

Göttingen, University of: and A. W. Palmer, 250; and E. Pugh, 38; and G. Ticknor, 11; and E. J. Townshend, 350

Gough, John B.: and literary societies, 302

Hamilton, John M. (Governor): and fraternities, 295; and J. Going, 289
Hamilton, Sir William: and J. M. Gregory, 90
Hanover College: and A. M. Brown, 82
Hansen, Harold M.: appointed, 146; fails to return, 147
Hardin, E. E.: leave of absence for, 212; and rebellion over militia commissions, 208
Harker Hall. *See* Chemistry Laboratory
Harper, William R.: annoys students, 336; and extension, 370; and E. J. James, 370
Harris, William Torrey: and A. S. Draper, 221n; and manual training, 221; and Yale Report, 221
Harrison, Benjamin (President): and second Morrill Act, 242
Harrison, Carter: student "funeral" for, 294
Hart, Albert Bushnell: and E. B. Greene, 358
Hart, Charles F.: and S. A. Forbes, 254n
Harvard Advocate: and news reporting, 201
Harvard Annex (Radcliffe): and K. Merrill, 352
Harvard University: and L. Agassiz, 11, 166; and L. C. Allen, 162; athletics at, 315; and W. F. Bliss, 102; Board of Overseers selection, 228; and compulsory chapel, 303; and G. P. Clinton, 252; criticism of, 21; discipline at, 182, 290; electrical engineering at, 257; and Emmanuel College, 3; endowment of, 4; and federal aid to education, 123; and geology and zoology, 32; graduate students to Illinois, 368; and E. B. Greene, 358; history at, 157, 268; Lawrence Scientific School founded, 32; library at, 174; and modern university, 84; and national university, 35-36; and natural history specialization, 151;

and old-time college, 7; and A. W. Palmer, 250; and S. H. Peabody, 223; and physical education, 204-5; and plant pathology, 154; salaries at, 299n; and J. A. Sewall, 152; and D. S. Shea, 349; and A. P. S. Stuart, 102, 150; and G. Ticknor, 11. *See also* Lawrence Scientific School
Hatch, Frederick L.: nominated for Board of Trustees, 229
Hatch Act: and agricultural education, 237, 241; and federal aid to education, 224, 242; and General Assembly, 239; passage of, 137, 238; provisions of, 238-39
Hayes, Samuel S.: and Board of Trustees, 82; and Committee on Course of Study and Faculty, 87
Hayes-Tilden campaign: and student political activities, 190
Haynie, I. N.: and committee on disposition of the land grant, 65
Heating and ventilation: and architecture, 264
Hegelians, American school of: and D. J. Snider, 361
Henry, Joseph: and A. D. Bache, 34-35; and Industrial League, 52n; and scientific professionalism, 30; and the Smithsonian, 34
Herald, Champaign County: on J. M. Gregory's resignation, 212
Herald, Chicago: and J. Steele, 324
Herbart, Johann F.: and pedagogy, 271
Herbartianism: and C. DeGarmo, 358; and W. J. Eckoff, 359; and C. McMurry, 359; and F. McMurry, 358-59
High schools: and athletics, 384; and enrollments, 235; in Illinois, 130; and Michigan accreditation plan, 131; and University accreditation, 130-31
Higher education: administration of, 126-27, 391-92; and agriculture, 36-40; J. P. Altgeld on, 338; and architecture, 145; and athletics, 312;

Mesmerism: and J. B. Turner, 41
Metallurgy: and agricultural experiment report, 136; and mining engineering, 261. *See also* Mining and Metallurgy, Department of
Meteorology: and agricultural experiment report, 136
Methodist Church: and Board of Trustees, 81-82; and faculty appointments, 103; in Illinois, 176; founds McKendree College, 16; and old-time college, 7; and students, 177
Methods courses: and pedagogy, 272, 359
Michigan: charters agricultural college, 39; high school accreditation plan of, 131; and higher education, 166; and regular income for University, 124; and Morrill Act, 56; and state collegiate association, 195; and state university, 6
Michigan, University of: appropriation drive, 337; and baseball, 382; and Columbian Exposition, 341; fees at, 235; history at, 158, 268; and Illinois liberal arts students, 354; library at, 372-73; and G. E. Morrow, 133; pedagogy at, 159; and S. W. Robinson, 107; salaries at, 333; size of, 342n; student transfer to, 322; and H. Tappan, 27; and trustees' election, 228, 230; and J. B. Webb, 259; and Western College Press Association, 377; and YMCA, 180
Michigan Journal of Education: and J. M. Gregory, 88
Michigan State Agricultural College: and farmers' institutes, 140; and J. M. Gregory, 89; and manual labor, 92; and M. Miles, 105-6
Michigan State Board of Education: and J. M. Gregory, 89
Microscopes: and botanical instruction, 154
Microscopy: and T. J. Burrill, 251
Miles, Manly: and agriculture, 133,

135, 136, 137, 138; appointment of, 105, 127, 133; biography, 105-6; and Convention of Friends of Agricultural Education, 136; experiment station plans, 135; experiments of, 137-38; and farmers' institutes, 140; fired, 128; influences on, 135; and G. E. Morrow, 138; and tenure question, 334-35
Military Affairs, Committee on: formed, 332
Military Department: and federal government, 207; and J. M. Gregory's curriculum, 90; influence on campus life, 176; problems in, 207; reformed, 212; revolt in, 207-9; and E. Snyder, 176; tuition free in, 111
Military Hall: students break into, 322
Military science: and curriculum changes, 129; professor of and gym, 313
Military Science, School of: beginnings, 104; offers courses, 159-60
Military tactics: and J. M. Gregory's curriculum, 90; and S. W. Shattuck, 102-3
Military training program: advanced work in, 375; and compulsory drill, 131-32, 159-60, 318, 374-75; early development of, 175-76; legal foundations of, in Morrill Act, 57, in state law, 82; original proposal for, 97; required credits, 356; size of, 375n; student revolts against, under Gregory, 207-13, under Peabody, 319-23
Mill, John Stuart: and J. M. Gregory, 90, 159
Mill tax: Board of Trustees asks for, 124
Millard, Sylvester M.: and F. North controversy, 305; as President of Board of Trustees, 229
Miller, Perry: on J. Bigelow, 30-31
Miller, William G.: academic average of, 319n; and military disruption, 319-23